Young Mandela

Also by David James Smith

Beyond All Reason: The Crime That Shocked the World

All About Jill: The Life and Death of Jill Dando

Supper with the Crippens

One Morning in Sarajevo: 28 June 1914

Young Mandela

David James Smith

Little, Brown and Company
NEW YORK BOSTON LONDON

Little, Brown and Company
Hachette Book Group
237 Park Avenue, New York, NY 10017
www.hachettebookgroup.com

First American Edition: December 2010
First published in Great Britain by Weidenfeld & Nicolson in June 2010

Little, Brown and Company is a division of Hachette Book Group, Inc. The Little, Brown name and logo are trademarks of Hachette Book Group, Inc.

Library of Congress Cataloging-in-Publication Data
Smith, David James.
Young Mandela : the revolutionary years / David James Smith.—1st American ed.
p. cm.
Includes bibliographical references.
ISBN 978-0-316-03548-4
1. Mandela, Nelson, 1918– 2. South Africa—Politics and government—1961–1978. 3. Apartheid—South Africa—History. 4. Anti-apartheid movements—South Africa—History. 5. Political prisoners—South Africa—Biography. 6. Civil rights workers—South Africa—Biography. 7. African National Congress—Biography. I. Title.
DT1949.M35S65 2010
968.06'5092—dc22
[B] 2010031883

10 9 8 7 6 5 4 3 2 1

RRD-IN

Printed in the United States of America

For Petal
and our children
Sitira, Kitty, Orealla, and Mackenzie

Young Mandela

One

SHOSHOLOZA, MANDELA!

Within hours of Nelson Mandela's arrest, on August 5, 1962, a white Jewish comrade, Wolfie Kodesh, was assigned the unenviable duty of breaking the news to Mandela's wife, Winnie. Kodesh was inclined to be overly cautious and excessively conspiratorial. He had spent five months sleeping on the Observatory Golf Club course and in friends' backyards to avoid arrest during the state of emergency after Sharpeville in 1960. Eventually, it occurred to him to rent a "safe apartment" under an assumed name and sleep there more comfortably instead.

Knowing Winnie was under regular, if not constant, surveillance by the South African Police Services Special Branch, Kodesh had prevailed on Esther, a black woman who was in charge of the distribution of food hampers at the Johannesburg offices of the newspaper *New Age,* to walk ahead of him and make the first approach to Mrs. Mandela at a nearby building where she was then working as a child welfare officer.

When Esther gave Kodesh the signal, the all-clear, he slipped into the entrance. Winnie came down to greet him. Kodesh had been out late the night before at meetings and must have looked scruffy, tired. The shock of

Mandela's arrest and the sadness of the task made it difficult for him to speak.

"Is it him?" Winnie asked.

"Yes." Kodesh realized then that he must finish his task quickly and simply said, "He's been caught at Howick. He's being brought up here, I don't know whether by plane or by car, but the police are bringing him up and he will appear today or tomorrow in the magistrates' court. You must prepare for it."

Kodesh recalled that they probably exchanged a few more words, then said goodbye. He could not remember Winnie crying.

Memory can be an unreliable, inconvenient and sometimes contradictory witness to history. Kodesh is no longer around to ask—he gave this account some years ago in a series of unpublished interviews that are stored in an archive in Cape Town—but Winnie herself says that Kodesh had come, not to her place of work, but to her home, at 8115 Orlando West. (Houses in the townships are commonly known by "stand" or plot numbers, not street numbers.)

Kodesh had not known how to express himself, she said; he just looked at her and cried. She said, is he alive?

Yes.

Where did they arrest him?

Howick.

She had known immediately she saw Kodesh what he was about to tell her and feared Mandela must be dead. Her heart was beating so fast it would burst the chest. She couldn't have faced the world if he had been killed and says she would probably have done something stupid herself, something quite desperate.

An attempt to check the differing accounts from other sources revealed that Winnie had given a long series of interviews a quarter of a century ago, as the basis of a published memoir, in which she appeared to support Wolfie's account. She remembered being at work, at the offices of the Child Welfare Society, and was leaving to do fieldwork in Soweto. As she came out of the lift, she bumped into one of her husband's friends: this was Wolfie. "He was white like a ghost, his hair was standing on end. I noticed he hadn't shaved and was wearing a dirty shirt and trousers as if he'd just jumped out of bed; you could see something drastic had happened."

She could not remember how she got home and had only a vague recollection of throwing her files in the back of the car and driving straight back to her home to be comforted by her sister. It was the collapse of a political dream, she told her interviewer, and the end of family life.

"Part of my soul went with him at that time."

Mandela's arrest ended a period of seventeen months during which he had lived on the run, adopting disguises and an assumed identity to evade the police. His continued freedom had been a great embarrassment to the authorities as well as a thrilling adventure to many in the country's black community—who might have been even more excited had they known what he was really up to during those days: plotting a revolution and launching an underground army, Umkhonto we Sizwe—Spear of the Nation. Much of his activity in those months would remain a secret for years to come.

In these early stages after his arrest, the police knew little of Mandela's role in the terrorist campaign that he had himself initiated. Instead, he was first charged with incitement, as a result of his public calls for a strike, a "stay at home," the year before. It was illegal for all black workers in "essential" services—domestic servants included—to withdraw their labor. He would later be charged with the additional offense of leaving the country without a passport.

Wolfie Kodesh was at the Johannesburg magistrates' court for Mandela's appearance on August 15. The imposing 1940s court building on Fox Street was just across the road from the former law offices of Mandela & Tambo at Chancellor House. Mandela had appeared before Johannesburg magistrates many times, representing clients who were commonly summonsed for petty infringements of the apartheid laws.

As a reporter for *New Age*, Kodesh was on the press bench in the well of the court and saw the seats around him filled with Special Branch detectives. There were police everywhere, with spectators overflowing onto the streets outside. A Free Mandela Committee had been hurriedly formed and Free Mandela slogans were appearing as graffiti all around the country. Kodesh could see the police were jumpy.

Just before the hearing was due to start, Winnie appeared with a suitcase, which she took up to a policeman standing in the dock. "Can you take this change of clothing to Mandela?" Sometime later the magistrate came in and took his seat. The hearing began, and the defendant was called for.

"Mandela!"

Kodesh was looking forward to seeing Comrade Nelson—they had formed a close bond during Mandela's months on the run—and hoped to give him a conspiratorial wink.

Kodesh had noticed Mandela many years ago, long before he ever knew him. He had seen this smart, tall, athletic, handsome figure walking down Plein Street in Johannesburg city center, and had stopped to watch only because people were turning to look at Mandela as he passed.

No revolutionary ever went so well dressed as the young Nelson Mandela. Growing up in the eastern Cape, Mandela had gone barefoot in casual or traditional dress, but he had adopted a formal style in his teenage years that became ever smarter as his life progressed. Mandela favored Khan's, the Jewish tailor shop in central Johannesburg, just opposite the entrance to the Rand Club, a private club that was a bastion of white supremacy.

George Bizos—a lifelong friend who had continued to call Mandela "Nel" even when he was president of South Africa (though only after respectfully checking with him first)—had walked into Khan's one day in the 1950s and seen a white tailor on one knee before Mandela's immaculate frame, sizing up his inside leg with a tape measure.

This was an extraordinary spectacle in apartheid South Africa. Bizos could almost see the horror on the faces of the two white customers who entered the shop. Bizos imagined that whilst they would be shocked that

Khan would make a suit for a black man, they would rationalize that he had done it for the money, rather than for any ideological reasons.

Up came Mandela, up the steps into the dock. Kodesh had never seen anything like it. The effect on the court was electrifying. Gone were the suit and tie and the shiny shoes. Mandela was wearing a traditional Thembu tribal costume, known as a *kaross*, made from the skins of jackals. He wore it at an angle across his chest so that one shoulder was bare. He had beads around his neck and around his legs.

Kodesh glanced at all those policemen. They had gone white—well, of course, they were white already, but the color had drained from their faces—and their eyes were out on stalks at this magnificent figure of a man. To Kodesh he looked a wonderful picture of a "Zulu warrior," though in fact Mandela is not Zulu but from the Thembu group of the Xhosa people. Winnie too is Xhosa, from Pondoland, and there she was in the public gallery, wearing a traditional beaded headdress and ankle-length skirt.

The court fell silent. There were no cries. Mandela did not look around but stared straight ahead at the magistrate. Kodesh was often in court and knew the form: the accused comes in, the magistrate nods and the prosecutor starts to speak. But now the magistrate just sat looking at the accused, caught, it seemed to Kodesh, in Mandela's challenging, transfixing glare, like a snake trapped by a mongoose.

According to Winnie, his costume had been her idea and Mandela knew nothing about it until he opened the suitcase and saw the contents. He had simply asked her to bring him something to wear in court. Of course, she said, as soon as he saw the *kaross* and the beads, he understood their meaning. She had deliberately avoided taking the things to the prison and had arrived late at the court to minimize the risk that they would be confiscated.

Winnie was angry: her husband had been arrested and the Boers were still trying to destroy their culture. To the Afrikaners they were kaffirs, Bantus—nothing. "I was fighting because I wanted to say, I am an

African. This is my country, you're not going to oppress me in my own country."

She had worn traditional dress once before to attend the Treason Trial of 1956 as a spectator. They had refused to let her in, saying she was inciting the people. What? By being herself? By being an African? So now she was fixing them up good, letting her husband wear his *kaross* as a protest. She was so proud when he came into court.

The hearing was brief, a simple remand and adjournment. When it ended, the crowd, which consisted of around 200 Africans and Indians, and twenty white men and women, gathered together in the corridor and began raising their thumbs in salute and singing the African National Congress (ANC) anthem, "Nkosi Sikelel' iAfrika"—God Bless Africa. A report in *The Times* of London described how "as the building echoed with lusty singing, magistrates and court staff came out to watch the procession." The crowd marched slowly out onto the street and stopped traffic as it tried to head for an impromptu protest meeting on the steps of Johannesburg City Hall. The police were determined to stop them and eventually persuaded the crowd to disperse without violence.

While Mandela went back to his cell in the Johannesburg Fort, the Free Mandela Committee were busy coming up with a plan to spring him from jail.

At Liliesleaf Farm, the group's underground headquarters up in the rural northern suburb of Rivonia where Mandela himself had stayed for several weeks, the escape committee spent long hours considering fantastic schemes. The white lawyers Joe Slovo and Harold Wolpe, who had access to Mandela as his defense advisers, were both involved, as were the ANC activist Joe Modise and the Indian Congress communist Ahmed Kathrada.

Kathrada remembered, when going with Slovo to see Mandela in jail, that Mandela was preoccupied with what the police might find at Rivonia.

Is it clean?

Before his arrest, he had left at the farm a considerable volume of incriminating papers, including a handwritten diary and many pages of his thoughts on communism and revolution. Now he wanted—and was given—reassurances that the material had been destroyed. In fact, it was all still there, a deliberate choice made by some of his comrades to preserve the Mandela papers for posterity. It was a decision that nearly got Mandela hanged.

Slovo and his colleagues wondered whether they could get a mask made for Mandela to wear, to exchange places with a prisoner going to court for a minor offense. Or perhaps he could switch robes with one of the group of traditionally dressed relatives who were visiting him from his family home in the eastern Cape. Could they bribe a court officer or prison official?

Eventually deciding a jailbreak was too difficult, they focused on springing him from the magistrates' court, where Mandela was left alone in a cell during lunch breaks. Joe Modise, who was well connected across both the criminal and ordinary working communities of the townships, found an African policeman at the court who was willing to leave the cell door unlocked.

Through a second contact, an African interpreter, they obtained and copied into a modeling-clay mold the key from the court's cell area. An engineer made up a key from this and it worked. They found an open, unguarded door leading from the court into a lane used for deliveries. This meant Mandela could be out and back in Rivonia in thirty minutes—but he was fast becoming famous and would be recognized instantly without a disguise. Some facial hair was needed.

As Slovo later described it, "Over dinner at the Delmonica [possibly Delmonico's] restaurant in Commissioner Street, Cecil Williams, a Party member and full-time theatre director, introduces me to a professional wigmaker with radical social attitudes. He agrees to make, free of charge, an Indian-looking wig, moustache and beard for a subject whose identity is never discussed."

A fresh obstacle appeared in the shape of the wigmaker's daunting list of required measurements of Mandela's face and head. He was obviously a perfectionist. Slovo eventually obtained them during a succession of legal consultations with his client. Mandela himself did the measuring, using lengths of white cotton that Slovo taped into a notebook. The hairpiece was duly delivered. When Modise tried it out on the others to test its effectiveness, they didn't recognize him. It was handed on to a tailor, who sewed it into the shoulder padding of one of Mandela's jackets, which was delivered to him at the prison. They were only waiting now for the next hearing at the court.

Meanwhile, a second opportunity had arisen: the possibility of bribing the colonel in charge of the prison. According to Slovo, a fellow attorney first approached him, saying a client who was at the Fort on remand for fraud had asked him to pass on the message that the prison commander wanted to meet Slovo. As it was a highly unusual request, Slovo feared a trap, so he called the colonel from a public phone, only to be invited to his home. The colonel was waiting on his veranda when Slovo arrived. "I will be brief. I take it you people are interested in Mandela?"

The colonel, who was looking for early retirement to a farm, wanted £7,000. Still mistrustful, Slovo and his comrades decided just to wait and see what would happen with the colonel. Kathrada, meanwhile, was sent to Basutoland to pick up the £7,000 bribe, in cash, in case it was needed in a hurry. The trial date was approaching and Mandela might be free soon anyway, walking out the door of the court in a wig.

In the Fort, Mandela had become friendly with an accused defrauder, the Indian businessman Moosa Dinath. They had started talking when Dinath began joining him on his daily exercises—Mandela's lifelong habit of jogging, running on the spot, push-ups and sit-ups. Dinath evidently had the colonel in his palm already, as he had numerous privileges. One night Mandela saw the colonel take Dinath away. The prisoner was released for the night and came back to prison in the morning. "If I hadn't seen it with my own eyes," said Mandela, "I would not have believed it."

There were those who counseled him against any attempt at escape, fearing it would give the authorities an excuse to shoot Mandela. Eventually, Mandela gave Slovo a note saying they should abandon the escape for the time being—it might be easier as well as more of a propaganda coup if he escaped, later, after his conviction. He added the postscript that the note should be destroyed after it had been read, but this document too was kept and later discovered by the police.

Two days before Mandela's trial Joe Slovo was told that Mandela had just been moved—to Pretoria, an hour's drive away, where the case would now be tried. Slovo was confined to Johannesburg, so he could not advise his client at the trial. Instead, Bob Hepple, a less experienced advocate, the South African equivalent of a barrister, was assigned to take his place. Hepple, who was not yet thirty, was both an advocate and a communist activist, like Slovo. Unlike Slovo, he was increasingly uneasy at his dual role and the risks he was being asked to take.

However, Hepple was happy to be Mandela's adviser, and duly went along to the court at the Old Synagogue in Pretoria for the first day's hearing. As he approached the cell he saw his client changing into his African costume. Hepple had not known about this and was a bit shocked by the spectacle. With hindsight he could see he was reacting to it as a white person but he was worried that Mandela was projecting the image of the noble savage, the stereotypical African with his drum and his leopard skin.

Why are you dressing like this? he wondered. Hepple knew of Mandela as a lawyer, a fully urbanized city boy. He'd never seen him in tribal dress and so far as he knew it wasn't the style of the ANC. Hepple's attitude echoed a wider concern among other white comrades, some of them among the ANC-aligned Congress of Democrats, who also disapproved of the traditional dress and complained that it smacked of "tribalism."

As Hepple later learned, during his hours of discussion with Mandela as they sat together during court sittings and adjournments, Mandela was newly keen to embrace a more Africanist image, for both political and personal reasons. The ANC had been wrong-footed and outmaneuvered by a breakaway faction led by Robert Sobukwe, who had formed a new party, the Pan-Africanist Congress, or PAC. It had been the PAC's protest that had provoked the shootings at Sharpeville in March 1960, galvanizing world attention.

Shortly before his arrest Mandela had spent several months touring independent African countries, seeking support for an armed struggle, and himself undergoing military training. He had been dismayed to find that many of the senior figures among the independence movements in black Africa regarded the PAC as the true leaders of the struggle against apartheid in South Africa. They had a low opinion of the ANC's cozy relationship with whites, Indians and communists of any race.

Some leaders seemed to think Mandela was little more than a stooge of the white communists. Mandela had returned from his tour, dressed in fatigues, with a gun and 200 rounds of ammunition on his belt, determined to present a more exclusive, nationalist image to black Africa.

So on October 15, 1962, Mandela marched into the Pretoria court for the first day of the trial, once again in full tribal regalia. The crowd in the courtroom rose at his entrance—a privilege normally reserved for the judge or magistrate, and not normally accorded to the accused. The people had waited more than an hour for the proceedings to start. There were over 200 Africans in the main area of the court, many of them also in traditional dress, while the whites were upstairs in the gallery.

Mandela complained at the sudden switch from Johannesburg and said there was a high-level conspiracy to make it difficult for him to defend his trial. "One of the rights of a black man is to have counsel of his own choosing, and he has the right to approach a court of law to maintain these rights."

An observer from the British embassy later reported that Mandela seemed tense and out of practice as a lawyer, also showing a tendency to stray off into politics, when he would be interrupted by the magistrate.

Mandela asked for a two-week adjournment and was grudgingly granted a week, which, as Viscount Dunrossil of the Foreign Office pointed out, was round one to Mandela and a minor tactical defeat for the government.

As the hearing ended, Mandela turned to the crowd and raised his fist. *Amandla!* They shouted back at him. He again clenched his fist. And again, ignoring calls for silence from court officials, the spectators cried, *Amandla!*

As they walked from the court, they began singing the ANC anthem while the police, using a megaphone, gave the crowd of singers five minutes to disperse.

Outside they were still gathered together and began singing a new praise-song:

Shosholoza, Mandela!

Advance, Mandela!

It seems likely that the authorities had moved the trial to Pretoria precisely to avoid the public displays of support and affection for Mandela that they had seen on a smaller scale in Johannesburg. They clearly regarded the tribal costume as inflammatory. A nervous young warder was dispatched by the Pretoria prison commander, Colonel Jacobs, to take it from him.

When Mandela refused to hand it over, the warder began trembling and was practically begging, saying he would be sacked if he returned without it. The prisoner was sympathetic and told him to tell his commander that this was Mandela speaking, not the warder.

Then the colonel himself appeared and ordered Mandela to hand over his "blanket." Mandela once more refused, telling the colonel he had no jurisdiction over how Mandela dressed in court and adding that he would fight the case to the Supreme Court if they took the *kaross*. The colonel relented, but only with the understanding that Mandela would not wear the animal skin while traveling to and from the court, to prevent its inciting the other prisoners.

So when the trial finally restarted, a week later on October 22, 1962, Mandela again entered the dock as a proud African, fist clenched, turning to the African spectators, who returned the gesture with their own raised fists and their cries of *Amandla*.

Mandela had one more master stroke to play before the hearing proper began. He had drafted an application for the magistrate, Mr. W. A. van Helsdingen, to recuse himself—to withdraw from the case—on the grounds that Mandela could not get a fair trial and was under no legal or moral obligation to obey laws made by a parliament in which he was not represented. Apartheid did not extend the right to vote to black people.

Mr. van Helsdingen and Mandela were old colleagues—the latter having appeared as an attorney before the former a number of times in the past (and Mandela was equally well known to the state prosecutor, Bosch). Ever courteous, Mandela prefaced his speech by observing that he meant no criticism of the magistrate nor of the prosecutor personally. He did not doubt the magistrate's sense of fairness and justice.

"I might also mention that in the course of this application I am frequently going to refer to the white man and to white people. I want at once to make it clear that I am not a racialist and do not support racialism of any kind, because to me racialism is a barbaric thing, whether it comes from a black man or a white man."

The magistrate replied that there was only one court here today, the white man's. "Which court do you want to be tried in?"

Mandela's response was he had been very aware of injustices all his life and there was no equality before the law as far as black people were concerned.

> Why is it that in this courtroom I face a white magistrate, [am] confronted by a white prosecutor and [am] escorted into the dock by a white orderly? Can anybody honestly and seriously suggest that in this type of atmosphere the scales of justice are evenly balanced?
>
> Why is it that no African in the history of this country has ever had the honor of being tried by his own kith and kin, by his own flesh and blood?
>
> I will tell your worship why!

Mandela said that the purpose of the rigid color bar was to enforce the policy of the country. He felt oppressed by the atmosphere of white domination in the courtroom.

> Somehow this atmosphere recalls to mind the inhuman injustice caused to my people outside the courtroom by this same white domination. It reminds me that I am voteless because there is a parliament in this country that is white controlled. I am without land because the white minority has taken a lion's share of my country and forced me to occupy poverty-stricken reserves... We are ravaged by starvation and disease because our country's wealth is not shared by all sections of the population.

It may be a tribute to Mandela's natural authority and decency, even from the dock, that the magistrate did not stop his speech but allowed him to continue even as he made the most overt criticisms of the very system the magistrate was there to represent and uphold.

"I hate racial discrimination most intensely and in all its manifestations. I have fought it all along my life. I fight it now, and will do so until the end of my days. Even although I now happen to be tried by one whose opinion I hold in high esteem, I detest most violently the set-up that surrounds me here.

"It makes me feel that I am a black man in a white man's court."

The magistrate paused only briefly before rejecting Mandela's application so that the case could begin. It did not last more than a few days. The state called numerous witnesses—a sledgehammer to crack a nut, as Mandela was blatantly guilty of the two charges, had no real defense and no intention anyway of mounting a defense. Not that he told the court that, allowing them instead to think he was planning a lengthy rebuttal with an equal number of witnesses.

Mr. Louis Blom-Cooper, then a young lawyer for Amnesty International, had traveled from the UK to attend the trial as an observer. Late on the second day he told Bob Hepple he had seen the magistrate going off for lunch with two Special Branch detectives, one of whom was a state witness, while the other had been assisting with the prosecution. Hepple told Mandela, now you've really got grounds for asking the magistrate to recuse himself. Mandela was oddly reluctant to use the information, saying he was not basing his case on personal corruption but on politics. He finally decided to make the application but did not want to ambush the magistrate, so he asked Hepple to go and warn him privately beforehand what was about to happen. The magistrate went red in the face and spluttered at Hepple that he had not discussed the case with the officers and they were merely escorting him for his protection. The magistrate again refused to step down and the case continued.

The prosecution concluded the following day, after which the court clearly expected a full defense from Mandela. Instead, he said, my lord, I submit I am guilty of no crime. He would not be calling any witnesses. To his side he heard the prosecutor exclaim, Lord! Mandela planned to make another long speech instead.

Mandela described how his youthful imagination had been fired by tales of tribal warriors who lived "in the good old days before the arrival of the white man" and said he would devote his life to the emancipation of his people. "When my sentence is completed I will still be moved, as men are always moved, by their conscience. I will still be moved by my dislike of the race discrimination against my people when I come out from serving my sentence, to take up again, as best I can, the struggle for the removal of those injustices until they are finally abolished once and for all."

There was a crowd of 150 Africans in the court. When the magistrate adjourned to consider sentence, Mandela as he went down shouted *Amandla!* three times and each time the crowd responded, *Ngawethu!* "Power shall be ours!"

According to Hepple, Mandela was always calm and never lost his authority or dignity. He always expected to receive the maximum sentence of three years for inciting the strike and two years for leaving the country illegally. Five years in total was exactly what he got. The magistrate claimed he had no doubt that Mandela was the leader and mastermind of the stay at home campaign and that he had acted in a way calculated to bring about tyranny and destruction. It was clear, he said, that Mandela's main object was to overthrow the government by unlawful and undemocratic means.

The Times of London, in its report of the final day, described Mandela as "a tall man wearing a jackal skin cloak" and said he repeatedly gave the clenched-fist salute of the banned African National Congress.

"There was a demonstration at the conclusion of the hearing, but no violence, as the crowd from inside singing "Nkosi Sikelel' iAfrika" (God Bless Africa) joined those outside. Women danced in the street and chanted. The police linked arms across the street, urging the crowd along, and the demonstration eventually petered out."

Mandela still had the incriminating writings at Rivonia on his mind. Hepple has a vivid memory of being asked by him to pass along a message: "Please tell them to destroy all my papers at Rivonia." Hepple certainly gave the message, he thinks to Joe Slovo. "But obviously it was never carried out."

Early in the morning of the day that Mandela was due to make his closing speech, Hepple had been sitting with Mandela in his cell, updating him on events outside: in New York, where the UN had voted for sanctions against South Africa for the first time, and in Durban and Port Elizabeth, where there had been explosions—acts of sabotage in support of Mandela's case and the UN decision.

As they talked, there was a knock on the cell door. It was Prosecutor Bosch asking for a private word with Mandela, whom he knew.

"Don't be crazy," said Hepple. "You can't speak to him alone."

Mandela said, "Oh no, it's OK, if he wants to see me you just wait outside."

So Hepple stepped out, leaving the defendant and his prosecutor alone—a rare event in any court. When the prosecutor emerged after a few minutes, Hepple could immediately see that he had been crying. It was plain how emotional he was feeling.

Hepple went back into the cell and asked Mandela, "What the hell's going on?"

"You won't believe this but he's just asked me to forgive him."

"Well, I hope you told him to bugger off."

"No, no, I told him I knew he was just doing his job."

In fact, as Mandela later described it, the prosecutor had said that he had not wanted to come to court that day and for the first time in his career he despised what he was doing. It hurt him that he should be asking the court to send Mandela to prison.

The prosecutor had reached out, shaken Mandela's hand and, bizarrely, hoped everything would turn out well for him.

Two

THE DEFINING MOMENT of Nelson Mandela's childhood came not long after he was born, when his father was, as Mandela describes it in his memoir, "deposed" from the position of chief by the local white magistrate, depriving the elder Mandela of his income, wealth and status. The family's resulting "straitened circumstances," forced Mandela's mother to move to another village many miles away, where Mandela lived until his father's death sometime later.

In Mandela's memoir, and in all the biographies written about him both before and since, the story is told of how his father stood up to the white authorities, refusing to obey the summons to appear before the magistrate to answer a petty complaint lodged against him by one of his own "subjects," involving a stray ox. Instead, his father sent the magistrate a message: *Andizi ndisaqula*—"I will not come, I am girding for battle." Mandela emphasizes that such an act of defiance was regarded back then as the height of insolence, but it reflected his father's belief that the magistrate had no legitimate right of authority over him. It was an act of principle, not a fit of pique. He was steeped in the Thembu tradition and customs in which power and patronage were solely in the gift of the Thembu king, traditionally known as the paramount chief.

His father's defiant message prompted the magistrate to charge him with insubordination. "There was no inquiry or investigation; that was reserved for white civil servants. The magistrate simply deposed my father, thus ending the Mandela family chieftainship."

The impression is of a prestigious lineage summarily and unjustly terminated; a chief—Mandela's own father—humiliated; and a family condemned to hardship.

But the message that Mandela takes from the sequence of events—the myth-building, you could call it—is the way in which they helped to shape Mandela's own character, disclosing traits that he believes he inherited, namely his father's "proud rebelliousness" and his "stubborn sense of fairness."

There are no published sources for this version of Mandela's early history and it appears that Mandela, who acknowledges that he was too young to be aware of this episode at the time, must have heard about it. It would have been passed on to him as part of the oral tradition that he repeatedly refers to in accounts of his formative experiences—stories told around a fire by elders, a history not written down but handed down, verbally, from one generation to the next.

As Mandela himself points out, both his father and mother were illiterate, had no formal schooling and never learned to read or write. Though, of course, this did not mean they were ignorant or lacking wisdom; they were simply living out the last days of a rural way of life going back many hundreds of years.

Despite his family's hardships, Mandela went to school. He was the first in his family to do so, and they supported and encouraged his education. For him the conventions of his past were there to maintain or to break. The choice was his—and he was to do both, often, throughout his life, showing respect and disdain for the old values in almost equal measure.

Mandela the traditionalist; Mandela the modernist: you can take your pick or, better still, see him as a forward-looking leader facing up to the subtle challenge of easing a traditional society into the contemporary world.

In passing on the oral history of his father's downfall, he was observing an important custom but also, perhaps inadvertently, exposing its fundamental weakness as a reliable record. Truth and myth can easily become blurred in the memory, either accidentally or purposefully.

Alongside the oral recording of the past was a parallel archive—the obsessive bureaucracy of the empire and its outposts, a world of white civil servants all busily sending each other notes, memos and letters, and keeping detailed minutes of meetings. Everything was kept and so, by chance, just recently, a treasure trove of documents relating to Mandela's past was discovered in the archives at Mthatha (formerly Umtata), the main town in the eastern Cape.

They not only reveal a completely different account of what happened to Mandela's father but also disclose much about the inner workings of the white authorities and their role in relation to the local communities. There is little evidence in those papers of a rebellion, proud or otherwise, by Mandela's father and every indication that he was suspected, and indeed was guilty of, corrupt practice and abuse of his local powers as a headman.

The corruption was modest, maybe, but it continued for some time before he was finally summonsed. Far from defying the magistrate, he actually bowed to his authority and appeared before him at a lengthy hearing, vainly attempting a defense in the face of substantial evidence. He was found guilty and dismissed from his position.

A careful reading of the original interviews that Mandela gave, for his memoir, also indicates that he was already living with his mother in the new village when his father was dismissed. She was not forced to leave by reason of hardship but was merely living in this far-flung place as one of his father's mini-empire of wives. Polygamy was an accepted practice then and Mandela's mother was the third of his father's four spouses.

"Well, you see, the Chief would then marry as many wives as he could afford," Mandela told his ghost-writer, Richard Stengel. "Each wife would have her own separate kraal, and sometimes they would be separated by 20 miles, as my family for example... So they were widely separated and they led different lives, and my father would circulate, you know, from one house to the other."

What is clearly and indisputably true, according to the oral and established history, is that Mandela was closely related to the Thembu royal line. The Thembu had been incorporated into the Xhosa nation some 400 years earlier when they migrated south towards the coast from the Drakensburg mountains. The Xhosa, in turn, were part of the Nguni people who had lived as hunter-gatherers across southern Africa for nearly a thousand years. The northern Nguni comprised the Zulu and Swazi people, and in the South they included the Sotho, Mfengu, Pondo and Thembu tribes.

According to Mandela he, like everyone else among the Xhosa, belonged to a specific clan and his was the Madiba clan. Hence in later years, he has become widely known as Madiba, the name given to him as a mark of respect.

He traces his lineage from the Thembu king Ngubengcuka, a great leader who died in the early nineteenth century. He had several wives and, according to custom, each represented a royal house of different status. The heir would be chosen from the Great House. Then there was the Right-Hand house and lastly the minor, Ixhiba or Left-Hand house, whose sons were supposed to have influence in settling royal disputes.

Mandela's grandfather was the second son of the Left-Hand house of Ngubengcuka so there was no question of the grandfather or any of his descendants acceding to the royal throne. They were merely cast in the role of court counselors or advisers and this, in turn, was the position Mandela would have been raised to fulfill.

The Thembu occupied a sizeable area of the vast region then known as the Transkei, between the Kei River and the border of Natal in the east, stretching down to the Indian Ocean. It was, and still is, an area of inspiring scale and beauty, with rolling green hills and scattered village communities surrounded by grazing cattle.

The traditional homes were round buildings with thatched roofs, known as rondavels, constructed from a mixture of mud, clay and cow dung, often painted on the outside, typically in shades of white, blue or green. Near the rondavel is the kraal, the pen for the animals. The source of water could be some distance away so that, even today, it is not unusual to see someone, invariably a woman, walking seemingly in the middle of nowhere with a heavy, water-filled pot balanced on her head.

Part of the challenge of reconstruction in post-apartheid South Africa is extending development programs—water, electricity, brick-housing—across rural South Africa. Although it looks like a gentle and unchanging way of life in a glorious landscape, for most people it was back then, as it continues to be today, a struggle to survive. From early in the twentieth century many people, mostly men at first, began flocking to the city of Johannesburg in search of prospects. Eventually Mandela too would follow that path.

Nelson Mandela was born on July 18, 1918, in the village of Mvezo, a small community beside the horseshoe turns of the Mbashe River in the district of Mthatha. He was named Rolihlahla by his father, the word meaning "pulling the branch of a tree" or, more colloquially, as Mandela himself has explained, "troublemaker."

The Great Place, the home of the Thembu king, was some forty miles or so away in Mqhekezweni, but this should not be imagined, in Western terms, as a palace of many rooms, fitted with marble floors or shag-pile carpets, and filled with riches. It was simply a larger than usual group of rondavels set beside an ancient tree beneath which the king and his advisers would meet to settle local affairs.

By the time of Mandela's birth, white authority was already firmly imposed throughout South Africa. The lives of the black African people were rigidly administered by the Native Affairs department in Pretoria, filtered down through a system of regional and local magistrates.

The oral tradition, with its stories of the coming of the white man, would fuel Mandela's sense of injustice. In an unpublished autobiography written in 1964 in his familiar looping style at the time of what became known as the Rivonia Trial, he describes, in shorthand, how his

> political interest first aroused when I listened to elders of the tribe in my village as a youth. Elders told of the good old days before the arrival of the white man. Then our people lived peacefully under the democratic rule of their kings and councilors and moved freely all over their country. Then the country was ours.
>
> We occupied the land, the forest and the rivers. We set up and operated our own government. We controlled our own armies and organized our own trade and commerce. The elders would tell us about the liberation [that] was fought by our ancestors in defense of our country, as well as the acts of valor performed by generals and soldiers during those epic days.

In his memoir Mandela identifies one particular elder, Chief Joyi, as a notable raconteur who railed against the white man for turning "brother against brother" among the Xhosa and for telling the Thembu that their "true chief was the great white queen across the ocean and they were her subjects. But the white queen brought nothing but misery and perfidy to the black people; if she was a chief, she was an evil chief." He refers here to Queen Victoria.

Before the *abelungu*—the white man—appeared with fire-breathing weapons, the people had lived alongside each other in peace. The white man had shattered their *ubuntu*, fellowship, and taken the land, which belonged to no one, as you might seize a horse.

Mandela said Chief Joyi's tales had made him feel angry and cheated, as if his own birthright had been stolen, though he later realized that Joyi's history was not always accurate.

When she visited the eastern Cape in the 1980s, Mandela's first biographer, Fatima Meer, met an elderly woman, Ntombizodwa, who had grown up with Mandela. She also remembered sitting with him, listening to Chief Joyi's stories, recalling "Tatu Joyi" evocatively as

> shriveled and bent and so black that he was blue. He used to cough a lot; it would come in a convulsion and then trail off like the whine of a train whistle. He knew the history of the Thembus best of all because he had lived through a great deal of it. It was from him that we learned about King Ngangelizwe.
>
> The years dropped from his body and he danced like a young warrior when he told us about how he fought in the King's impi [his warriors] against the British.

Ironically, it was the Thembu paramount chief Ngangelizwe who asked the British for protection in 1872. He had ill treated his first wife, and, as a result, she fled home to her father, a rival traditional leader. Ngangelizwe went to the British because he feared retribution from his in-laws. In 1875 he caused the death of the same wife's maid, again provoking the rival's anger—and again he asked for protection. His adversary was "prevailed upon" by the British not to attack but Ngangelizwe still wrote seeking to become a British subject, along with his people. In 1882 he sold the government the piece of land on which the regional capital of Umtata was situated, now the home of the regional chief magistrate. In return he received £1,200 sterling. In 1885 the government formally "annexed" Thembuland.

On New Year's Eve 1914, according to the magistrates' archive, the headman at Mvezo, Hlakanyana, was dismissed, apparently for some corrupt practice involving land he had granted to a white man to build a trading station. It appears that the white man, Mather, may have been involved with an African woman, No-Offisi. Both Mather and the headman were charged and reprimanded. No-Offisi was removed from the land she occupied. The two men hired a lawyer who appealed against the actions taken against them.

The lawyer described Hlakanyana as having given thirty-eight years of service, thirteen as a policeman and twenty-five as headman. In spite of his past loyalty, the appeal fell on deaf ears.

A week later the magistrate came from Umtata to Mvezo to attend a village meeting that had been called for the selection of a new headman. Paramount Chief Dalindyebo (the son and heir of Ngangelizwe) was at the meeting along with just eleven others, including the sacked Headman Hlakanyana. They could not—or would not—nominate a successor, the magistrate recorded.

> I then requested Chief Dalindyebo to make a nomination and he recommended his Uncle Henry Mandela as there is no man in this location suitable for the appointment. Henry Mandela will in my opinion make a good headman as he is a strong man and owing to his status should command respect.
>
> I therefore beg to recommend that he be appointed Headman of location No. 15 called Mvezo to take effect from 6 January 1915 and that he should be granted an allowance of £12 per annum.

It appears from this note that Henry Mandela, Nelson's father, was not actually living in Mvezo at the time of his appointment, three years and six months before the birth of his son. He may have been living in Qunu, or elsewhere with another wife.

The elder Mandela's full name was Henry Gadla Mphakanyiswa Mandela; his dates of birth and death are unrecorded, though Mandela says in his memoir that his father died around 1928 when he believes he was in his early seventies. Mandela recalled him as a tall man, as Mandela himself became, but darker skinned than his son. He recollects, for Richard Stengel, seeing a single photograph of his father, which has since been lost.

While Henry Mandela owed his recommendation for the post of headman to the patronage of his nephew, the paramount chief, it was evidently the magistrate who had the final say. It's also worth noting that this was clearly not a matter of pressing concern to the Native Affairs department in Pretoria. It was not until four months later, on April 19, that an under-secretary troubled to reply to the magistrate's note, approving the appointment of Headman Mandela.

When Paramount Chief Dalindyebo died in 1920 his son from the Great House was too young to accede so a regent had to be appointed as stand-in. On the day of the old king's funeral, the chiefs and headmen met and nominated Jongintaba, Dalindyebo's son by a lesser wife, to play the role.

Henry Mandela took the lead in making the decision. They went to Dalindyebo's Great House wife to tell her, perhaps knowing the news would not be well received. The Great House wife was enraged, protesting that Jongintaba's mother was a mere concubine and had never even been properly married to her husband.

The Great House wife wanted the regency for herself. As she later complained to the magistrate, Jongintaba's mother had been forsaken by the old chief and, when she left, her son was helpless. The Great House wife had taken him in and raised him, while he was ignored by his father who refused to give him any status. Eventually Jongintaba became the Great House wife's servant; she gave him his own wife, as well as stock to start his kraal. "But no sooner is his father dead than he reveals an evil trait in his character by rising up against me." The old queen cannot have been too pleased with Henry Mandela for his role in this attempted insurrection.

She demanded a cart be harnessed to take her to the magistrate. The chiefs declined and said she should *zila*—mourn—instead. They eventually allowed her to leave but refused to provide her with the transport she wanted, forcing her to walk all the way to Umtata.

Henry and another chief signed their own letter to the magistrate, which, far from displaying any spirit of rebellion, was full of obsequious praise for the magistrate and the government he represented, begging the government, as if it were a benevolent father, to "maintain his safe-guidance with his children the Thembus through all generations succeeding the late chiefs and to also protect and advise them at all trying times. . ."

After hearing all sides of the argument, the magistrate was sympathetic to the queen's complaint that Jongintaba was little more than a messenger to her and accepted that it was contrary to custom for a minor-house son to become regent. But neither did the magistrate want a queen — a woman! no, thank you — as regent. He asked the chiefs and headmen to think again. They did — and reached the same decision, apparently again led by Henry Mandela.

It looks as though the elder Mandela backed the wrong horse as the magistrate overruled them and appointed another son instead. Meanwhile, Jongintaba had difficulties of his own; the magistrate noted in a postscript in a letter to a colleague in 1920 that Jongintaba was "addicted to drink, heavily in debt and quite recently there was a writ for civil imprisonment out against him."

The too-young son of the Great House queen did eventually take over the role of paramount chief for himself but when he died suddenly of a fever in 1928 the issue of succession arose once again. This time Jongintaba fared better. The magistrate believed he was recently reformed and allowed him to assume the role. "He is forty-two, intelligent and I feel he will fulfill the role satisfactorily."

Alas, in a few months Jongintaba was back in trouble — if he was ever actually out of it.

Meanwhile, complaints about Headman Mandela had first surfaced in 1925 — when Nelson was aged seven — in reports from the local white trader, Wood, that "Headman Gadla" was still "worrying" a local man to move his kraal. In an apparent reference to Headman Mandela, the white trader said, "There is a good deal of dirty work done by headmen at times and natives look to you [the magistrate] for protection. Selling of sites by headmen is quite a common thing to do — so I am told by natives — and a good cow to the headman will often get a kraal shifted. I give you this information in the interest of justice only. I have nothing against Gadla [Mandela]."

On July 9, 1926, an inquiry began into the conduct of "Headman Mandela of Mvezo Location, Umtata." The case against Headman Mandela opened with the testimony of a "native constable," Amos Dinga, who had been sent to investigate allegations that Mandela had unlawfully allotted land next to the Bashee River to local people. Constable Dinga found the land ploughed, with crops growing. One of the men on it said he had paid Mandela 10 shillings for the land. A third man had been given a second piece of land, which he was not entitled to as he did not have two wives. He claimed Mandela had given him the second plot because the first did not produce good crops. He said he had given Mandela a beast—"a black bull calf, white between the legs"—in return for the land.

Three other men who had been occupying unlawful sites had been ordered to leave a year earlier, but were still there, apparently thanks to the favors of Mandela.

Still another man had asked Mandela for a piece of land and been told it was his for £4 15s which he had paid for with four one-pound notes and some silver. No sooner had he gone to possess the land than another man came along, saying he too had purchased the right to that plot from Headman Mandela.

A final witness claimed he also had given a beast to Mandela but not been assigned any land for two years. Only after paying an additional £4 5s had he received the land. He had asked Mandela for his beast back, but Mandela had refused to return it.

The report of the proceedings shows that Mandela cross-examined the witnesses to no great effect and then gave his own defense—with no witnesses—in which he claimed the beasts had been given as dowry—wedding tributes—not as payments for land. He maintained that stories had been fabricated against him because of an earlier dispute when he had brought legal claims against two locals. People were now acting "in spite against me." He said that one of the men who had ploughed the land was a sub-headman who was supposed to be supervising the land because Mandela was in bad health and unable to look after it himself.

The magistrate who heard the case concluded that the charges against

Headman Mandela were well founded and he was recommending that his services be dispensed with. The decision to sack him from his post was ratified by the chief magistrate a few days later. He had served in the post for eleven years.

In his memoir Mandela cites these events from 1926 as taking place when he "was not much more than a newborn child." If that was true it would mean he was born much later than 1918, but since he also had three sisters, with four dates of birth to chart, it seems unlikely that his own could be so far adrift. It is also puzzling, though, that at the age of eight he was oblivious to such a cataclysmic event. Perhaps this is explained by the fact that, as has already been pointed out, he was already living many miles away in the village of Qunu, having been there for some time—perhaps from birth, and was not banished there when his father was "deposed."

In 2008, Mandela's grandson Mandla was installed as chief at the village of Mvezo, in a gesture intended to right a wrong done many years ago to Mandla's great-grandfather, Henry Mandela. His position gave Mandla nominal authority over some 400 families in the area. At the time, he was holding court at a newly built rondavel of village-hall proportions. When asked whether the ongoing threat from HIV was high among his concerns, he said not; the great threat was cholera sourced from the Mbashe River, which was shared by the people and the animals. Many of the people still did not have access to safe running water.

Mandla, who has made his own study of the family history, said that local folklore favored yet another version of events, in which Headman Mandela was deposed after trying to fine a man a cow for making another man's daughter pregnant. When he insulted the magistrate by refusing to appear before him, the magistrate sent in troops and had him forcibly removed.

Mandla was skeptical of the magistrates' records in the archives. "For me a wrong was done and they needed to justify it so they created the paperwork to do it." If that was true, it was an implausibly complicated stitch-up involving numerous documents. According to Mandla—whose information was gleaned from his talks with the old men of Mvezo who had grown up with these stories — Henry Mandela become very bitter at his reduced wealth and status. "It demolished his entire existence."

Already, in his own brief tenure, Mandla has caused some consternation among archivists by razing what remained of the ruins of the rondavel in which his grandfather had been born and rebuilding it on the exact spot, as part of his plans to create a new heritage site. All that survived was an ancient utility stone.

Mandela's mother, Nosekeni Fanny, gave birth to four of her husband's thirteen children. She was of the Right-Hand house, not the most senior but not the most minor either, and she had three rondavels and a kraal at her home in Qunu. Mandela has memories of his childhood there, tending cattle as a herds-boy, and learning to fight, swim, catch fish and use slingshots to knock birds from the sky. He used smooth, sloping rocks as natural slides and spent most of his time out and about with other boys.

"A boy who remained at home tied to his mother's apron strings was regarded as a sissy," he explains in his memoir. Women, he says bluntly, were regarded as second-class citizens.

Even then, as he remembers, it was like a village of women and children, as most of the men were economic migrants, working on distant farms or gone up to the mines on the hills around Johannesburg, known as the reef. The rondavels of his mother's home were never quiet, always busy with visits from friends and relatives. Mandela has no recall of ever being alone.

Though she must have been the dominant parental presence in his formative years, Mandela offers little by way of recollection of his mother, who died in 1968, apparently aged seventy-five. She stayed from time to time with her son in Johannesburg but otherwise lived out her life in Qunu. Mandela's youngest sister, Leabie, remembered that her mother had herself built the rondavels she occupied, the men helping only with the thatched roofs. One was used for cooking, one for sleeping and one for storing grain and other food. There was no furniture in the properties in the European sense; they slept on mats and used their elbows for pillows. The stove was a hole in the ground covered with a grate. The rondavel would fill with smoke when they were cooking as there was no chimney, only a window through which the smoke could escape.

Her mother, along with her children, worked hard planting and harvesting, taking the mealies—the corn—off the cob and then grinding them between two stones either to store or to make bread. Leabie could never remember a time when they did not have to buy mealies to supplement their own, so they were never quite self-sufficient. But they did not have to buy milk as their cows and goats always gave them a good supply.

Unlike her husband, Nosekeni was a devout Christian, and even though the concept of formal education was alien to her, she did not resist when some fellow Methodists said her son was a bright young man and ought to go to school. At the age of about seven, Mandela was dressed for the first time in a pair of trousers—his father's trousers, cut off at the knee and held at the waist with a piece of string.

It was on his first day at the school that the name, Nelson, was bestowed upon him by his teacher. He has no idea why that name was chosen, except of course for its obvious imperial associations with the great admiral on top of the column in Trafalgar Square. No doubt, too, the white missionaries habitually assigned simple English names to the children because it was too much trouble to learn to pronounce their actual African names. This was a Methodist school and young Nelson too was baptized into the Methodist Church.

Leabie recalled that her father had died when Mandela—Bhuti, she called him, meaning brother—was aged ten. Later, she told Mary Benson that her father had died in 1930, when Bhuti was aged twelve. Mandela himself has also said in the past that his father died in 1930. But in his memoir he puts the memory of his father's dying when he was aged nine, which would be 1927, just a year after the elder Mandela was sacked. The dates can probably never be fully reconciled.

Henry Mandela had of course referred to his bad health during the hearing and Mandela has given a vivid, if brief, account of his father dying during a visit to Qunu—he routinely circulated among his wives—when he found him lying on his back in his mother's rondavel, coughing endlessly. Mandela believes he was dying from a lung disease, cancer perhaps, but there was never any formal diagnosis. He stayed there for several days, after which his fourth wife came to look after him, along with Mandela's mother. He called for his tobacco and was reluctantly given a pipe, which seemed to soothe him—and then he died. Mandela could not remember any feelings of grief, more a sense of being "cut adrift."

Leabie said that her father called the acting paramount chief, Jongintaba—the man he had earlier helped to promote—to his deathbed and asked him to take care of his son. "I am giving you this servant Rolihlahla. This is my only son. I can see from the way he speaks to his sisters and friends that his inclination is to help the nation. I want you to make him what you would like him to be; give him education, he will follow your example."

Mandela's sister claims to have heard Jongintaba give his assurance that he would do as Henry Mandela wished. She tells Benson, "The Chief bought him clothes and he became a human being"—an odd expression, as if he was not human until he donned Western dress.

After a period of mourning, Mandela left Qunu and was walked by his mother across the hills to the Great Place at Mqhekezweni, where he was delivered into the charge of Jongintaba. "We travelled by foot and in silence until the sun was sinking into the horizon," he says of the journey.

Mandela was dazzled by his first look at the Great Place, from the bright white of the lime-washed walls on the seven rondavels and two rectangular houses, to the sizeable herds of cattle and sheep grazing contentedly on the rich land beyond the gardens and ploughed fields. And here comes the paramount chief, Jongintaba in his Ford V8 motorcar, the nearby men jumping to their feet at his approach and shouting, *Bayete a-a-a Jongintaba*—"Hail, Jongintaba!" He is a confident man in a smart suit, the owner of many such suits, which Mandela will take a particular pleasure in pressing.

"Children from poor homes often find themselves beguiled by a host of new temptations when suddenly confronted by great wealth. I was no exception . . . The slender foundation built by my parents began to shake,"

Mandela recalled. Still, he felt that the king and his wife, Noengland, accepted him as if he were their own child.

So much did they love him and respect him, he told Richard Stengel, his ghost-writer (it does not appear in his memoir), that they refused to allow him to return to Qunu when he was homesick and wanted to visit his mother. "They thought that there I might be under a wrong influence and I would then not want to come back... they were so attached to me that they didn't want me to leave."

Mandela did not see his mother again for many years.

There is no reference, anywhere in Mandela's memoirs, to the illusory nature of the chief's wealth, the fact that he had trouble with money and alcohol.

Mandela seems unconcerned by these aspects of his new guardian, seeing him instead, as others saw him, as the embodiment of royal authority, the very centre around which life revolved. Mandela's admiration was especially focused on the paramount chief's grand V8 car and his suits. No one else in the area had a car, which can only have heightened the wonder of it to Mandela.

The magistrates' archive makes no reference to any womanizing by Jongintaba but notes an £800 debt he had incurred and the consequent court proceedings he faced around 1930, at just the time Mandela had joined him at the Great Place. The magistrate observes that "much of this is the result of extravagance," the chief being "unable to resist buying as long as credit is extended to him." His car was "a particular burden."

The magistrate is not overtly racist or even harsh in his comments about Jongintaba. Indeed, he observes, with some sympathy, that the chief's predicament is "unfortunate as the chief is of great service to this office and loyally and efficiently assists in executive work, but owing to judgments and writs against him he has to avoid coming to Umtata."

But in 1935, Jongintaba upset the magistrate by trying to borrow an additional £60, which he said was for school fees to send his children (Mandela included, no doubt) back to educational institutions. He incurred further wrath by making the same request again a year later. The magistrate protested at the "gross extravagance of his style of living," noting that Jongintaba, who continued to face constant civil actions for debt and occasional impounding of his herds, "has the habit of intemperance."

Mandela became close to Jongintaba's son, Justice, who was four years older than Mandela and, it would appear, a chip off the old block, inheriting some of his father's less appealing traits. After initially being unfriendly towards the new arrival, Justice took a liking to Mandela and treated him as a younger brother.

When Mandela first knew him, Justice was already at the high school, Clarkebury Boarding Institute in Engcobo. Mandela followed him there in 1933, when he was fifteen, after he had completed his primary education at the village school just beyond the Great Place and spent one year at a school in the nearby town of Qokolweni.

The chief kitted him out with a suit and a pair of boots and drove him to Clarkebury. He introduced Mandela to a church minister who was the governor of the school. The minister held out his hand to Mandela—the first white man he had ever shaken hands with.

Jongintaba told the minister, "I am bringing this boy here so that he can have a proper education, because I am grooming him as the councilor for Sabata the future king and I would like you to take a special interest in him." Sabata was the heir to the throne, then still a baby. Jongintaba, his regent, had often told Mandela of his intended role: "It is not for you to spend your life mining the white man's gold, never knowing how to write your name."

Mandela noted how the minister treated Jongintaba with great deference and assumed he too would be on the receiving end of some respect as a member of the royal family. But once the regent had left, after giving Mandela a pound note, the most money he had ever possessed, Mandela was treated just the same as everyone else. He later thought this had been a good lesson as he suspected that he had been "a bit stuck-up" back then.

He could not be stuck-up for long in his new boots, which he barely knew how to walk in. He crashed clumsily across the wooden floors at Clarkebury and was teased by a pair of young female students as a country boy not used to wearing shoes. He rushed at the girl who made the remark, wanting to choke her, but she screamed and ran. They eventually became friends and he discovered that she too was determined to get a good education.

There was also, at the school, a black African woman teacher who was one of the first, if not the first, African woman in the country to get a BA, a Bachelor of Arts degree, though when he first heard this, Mandela did not even know what a BA was. He still had a lot to learn.

Three

AFTER A YEAR at Clarkebury, Mandela returned to Mqhekezweni to undergo the ritual of circumcision—an elaborate coming-of-age ceremony. In his later years he could take impish pleasure in turning world leaders ashen with his frank descriptions of the brutal procedure by which the foreskin was finally cut.

In his memoir, Mandela recalls that the ceremony was arranged for Justice, who must then have been twenty years old—he was four years older than Mandela who recalls his age at circumcision as sixteen. Just under thirty boys took part altogether, a mixture of young royals and commoners who stayed together—for two months altogether—in two huts in a remote area beside the Mbashe River at a place called Tylahara, the traditional setting for the circumcision of the Thembu kings.

According to custom they crept out and stole a pig, a deliberate last act of boyish mischief before becoming a man. Mandela recalled that they lured the pig away from its farmer, "...so you then catch it, slaughter it and make a fire and eat it. Oh it's a lovely thing, man. The meat has never tasted like that again. It was nice to roast a pig."

On the eve of the circumcision the boys' heads were shaved and they took part in a dance attended by young women who sang and clapped a slow beat to which the boys moved, gradually becoming faster and more frenzied.

The next morning an audience of friends and relatives gathered to watch from a distance while the boys bathed in the river and then sat down in a row wearing just a blanket, with a drum beating. Mandela was tense, hoping he would not shame himself by crying out or flinching at the cuts to come. The *ingcibi*, the circumciser, advanced down the line, swishing his assegai (spear), the boys crying, *ndiyindoda*, "I am a man," as their foreskins fell away.

Mandela described it thus:

> He then takes your penis, pulls the foreskin and then with the assegai, no anesthetic, he does this... (once forward)... one back, and he cuts off the foreskin and then you say *ndiyindoda* and then another man who is behind the expert who circumcises you, he says, tie that foreskin, with the edge of your blanket, and you tie it in, and then they bind the wound with a type of leaf which has got little thorns but it is a very good leaf and it has got healing properties. They tie it around your penis and then they take you to the hut when everybody has been circumcised. At the hut there they build a fire but they make sure that there must be wet wood so that it should make smoke because there was a theory that smoke makes it, the wound, heal quicker. So you sleep, and also when you sleep you must sleep in a particular way. You sleep on your back, one leg is flat on the ground and the one other like this... yes, bent like this, you see, but you are on your back and this one is straight. The idea is that you should not, there should be no pressure on the wound, on the penis. The legs must be separate... and if you make a mistake, and do this, the attendant beats you with a stick so even if you have been asleep and you slip up—you immediately wake up and straighten your one leg and keep this one in this position. So then at midnight the attendant wakes you up, one by one, and says go

> and bury this a distance away from here and it was very dry, you dig and it is dark and you are alone and you dig and bury it and then come back and then ask the next boy to go and bury the foreskin.

The attendant, one of the *amakhankatha*, also painted the bodies of the young men, now known as *abakwetha*, or initiates into manhood, in white ocher. In his memoir Mandela says the pain of the two cuts was so intense that he momentarily forgot to cry out *ndiyindoda* and felt ashamed afterwards that he had not been stronger. The men remained in the huts, in quiet contemplation, while their wounds healed, then they bathed again, washed off the white ocher and were painted anew with red ocher.

When the ceremony was completed, the huts, and everything in them, was burned, to symbolize the destruction of their last links with childhood. They were supposed to walk away and not look back, but Mandela would tell in later life that he had broken with custom and sneaked a backward glance.

Mandela was presented with two cows and four sheep as tokens of his manhood and then took part in a final ritual where he heard a memorable speech by a brother of Jongintaba, Chief Meligqili, who warned the young men that the promises of manhood were all an illusion because they were a conquered people, slaves in their own country. They were chiefs who would never rule, or young men who would go to the city, live in shacks and drink cheap alcohol, while they ruined their lungs in the mines so that the white man could live in unequaled prosperity.

The children of Ngubengcuka, the flower of the Xhosa nation, were dying.

While the chief may have meant his words as a wake-up call, a warning, perhaps even a call to arms, Mandela detected that the other young men felt as he did—angry not with the white man, but with the chief for spoiling their great day with his ignorant remarks. As Mandela then saw it, the chief had failed to appreciate the value of the education and benefits that the white man had brought to the country.

Still, Meligqili had sown a seed inside him and over time it began to grow. He later realized that the ignorant man that day was not the chief but himself.

Meanwhile, now that he was a man he was entitled to a new Thembu name and was given Dalibunga, which became the preferred term of address, even in future years, for his relatives as well as other visiting chiefs and guests from the eastern Cape. A friend and colleague, Joe Matthews, could recall groups of traditionally dressed visitors appearing outside Mandela's home in Orlando in the 1950s and calling *a-a-a-Dalibunga!* by way of greeting.

Living at the Great Place under the guardianship of the paramount chief, being groomed as a royal adviser, coming to manhood, having his own small herd of cattle and sheep all served to reinforce Mandela's sense of himself as a privileged young Thembu, albeit one whose destiny remained in the Transkei. Clarkebury introduced him to students from across southern African, young men and a few women from different tribes, but he still saw himself then as part of the elite tribe, the Thembus.

It was at Clarkebury that he first began to show promise as a student, completing his junior certificate in reduced time over two years instead of the usual three. So, by the good grace of his indebted guardian, he went on to Healdtown, the Methodist college located at Fort Beaufort, which was once an outpost of British forces during the Frontier Wars as they advanced into Thembuland and imprisoned Xhosa warrior leaders on Robben Island.

The school was like a little slice of England, with a thousand students and a staff of all races, presided over by a Dr. Wellington. Proud of his Britishness and of his relation to the Duke of Wellington, he would boast about his forebear in speeches to the student body, telling them how his ancestor had saved civilization both for Europe and for the natives. (The students would all applaud, never then objecting to being called natives.) The African students would sometimes be derided as "black Englishmen" but, Mandela admitted, that really was their aspiration, amid the school's strict, unforgiving regime.

It was at Healdtown that Mandela discovered the two sports that would sustain him through his adult years, running and boxing. He was tall and lanky then, more suited to the former than the latter. He had his first taste of leadership too, as a prefect, in charge of a group of boys responsible for cleaning windows, sleeping in the same dormitory with them and seeing them properly turned out for parades.

In his early days at the school it seemed to Mandela that the different tribal groups kept to themselves and there were few interactions across tribal lines. So Mandela and others were amazed when a popular Sotho teacher married a Xhosa woman from Umtata. Mandela himself became pleased to make friends from other tribal backgrounds, though he remained a proud Xhosa and won the Xhosa essay prize in 1938 for his writings on a long-since forgotten theme.

He would never forget the day when the renowned Xhosa poet, Mqhayi—a poet laureate of the African people, in Mandela's view—came to give a talk at Healdtown. Mqhayi was a nomadic figure who traveled around creating and sharing his poetry. He had written the lyrics for the anthemic "Nkosi Sikilel' iAfrika."

Mandela had seen him once at a distance when he passed through Mqhekezweni and was thrilled now to be hearing him speak. The day was declared a holiday at Healdtown. At first, when Mqhayi appeared on stage carrying two assegais, Mandela was disappointed at this average-looking man with sunken eyes. His first words seemed like a struggle too, not the poetic outpourings Mandela had expected. Then, as he talked, one of his assegais caught the curtain wire across the stage and he seized on this as symbolic of a clash of cultures, African and European. Today, he said, it was a clash producing no results, only a stalemate, but the day was coming when the African culture would prevail.

Mqhayi segued into his well-known poem about the division of the stars, gesturing to the skies with his assegais and offering the Europeans the biggest cluster, the Milky Way, because they were full of greed and envy and fought over plenty, but offering different stars to other nations, races and various tribal groups, before finally becoming still and saying, now come, you, House of Xhosa, I give you the Morning Star because it is the most important star, the star for counting years, the years of manhood. He dropped down on one knee as he spoke these last words and the students, the Xhosas at least, exploded into applause, Mandela not least among them. He was learning to embrace all the African tribes, and become African himself. But he was still a Xhosa and was inspired by the message of defiance.

By now Mandela had not merely caught up with his older "brother" Justice, but had overtaken him. Justice remained at Healdtown, still studying for his Junior Certificate, when in 1939 Mandela, aged twenty-one, became an undergraduate at the University College of Fort Hare, just a few miles away in the town of Alice. Justice enjoyed playing more than studying, says Mandela, and was an indifferent scholar.

Fort Hare was the leading college for black Africans in southern Africa—Oxford, Cambridge, Harvard and Yale all rolled into one, as Mandela has said—and many future leaders from across the region were educated there: Seretse Khama, Kenneth Kaunda and Robert Mugabe among them. Here too battles had been fought during the Frontier Wars, before the missionary college had been created there by Scottish Methodists in 1916. The first two Africans graduated in 1924.

It was indeed an elite institution, with just 150 students in Mandela's time, and the seniors sometimes lorded over the new arrivals, the freshers. In spite of the privileged backgrounds of many of the students, there was a spirit of dissent at Fort Hare, perhaps fostered by the likes of Professor Z. K. Matthews, one of the leading black scholars of his generation, who had studied the early African-American civil rights activists such as Booker T. Washington and his book *Up from Slavery*. Like Washington, Matthews could be seen as a moderate campaigner in comparison to the radicals of the 1960s and later, but in his day he was a ground-breaking, influential figure and, in lectures, often an outspoken critic of the racist government.

Mandela himself was no stranger to controversy during his time at Fort Hare. Early on, he took on a leading role in a minor rebellion, trying to establish a democratically elected House Committee to challenge the status of the seniors. Mandela was mocked by a senior at a meeting as a backward country boy who couldn't even speak English properly. The same senior later broke down and cried when the freshers tried to punish him for disobeying the rules their committee had created. Mandela had no qualms about the action as he was certain it was right. It was not personal or vindictive—well, not entirely, as Mandela was well aware that he had been ridiculed.

Mandela studied English, anthropology, law—and native administration, a subject that would have rendered him employable within the Native Affairs department up in Pretoria, or in one of its many local branches. It was a realistic goal in those days and Mandela saw himself becoming qualified as an interpreter between Xhosa and English, perhaps working with a magistrate.

Mandela first met Oliver Tambo, his highly religious future law partner and ANC colleague, when they played football together at Fort Hare. When Mandela was not playing football he was invariably on a long-distance run. Another student, slightly older, was his own cousin, later to become his political adversary and love rival: K. D. Matanzima, a thin, handsome man known to Mandela and his family as "the Cigarette," because of his slender physique. Matanzima could be a querulous character, inclined to take issue, and was particular about rules and regulations. He was also quite regal, like Mandela, and liked to be well dressed. "The two of us were very handsome young men and all the women wanted us," the Cigarette told Fatima Meer.

There was a wide range of musical activities at Fort Hare from church choirs to ballroom dancing, which Mandela took to. "We spent hours learning to dance graciously. Our hero was Victor Sylvester the world-champion of ballroom dancing." As he said, it was all very well learning to waltz and foxtrot but the places they might go to show off their steps were all out of bounds. So they put on their suits and sneaked out to the village hall in nearby Ntselamanzi, where Mandela graciously selected an attractive young woman and invited her to dance. They moved well together and he casually asked her name. Mrs. Bokwe was the wife of one of his masters, a leading African intellectual, whom Mandela now saw at the side of the dance floor, in conversation with Professor Z. K. Matthews. Mandela returned his master's wife to her husband's side and the incident was never mentioned.

In late 1940, a year after his arrival, Mandela became involved in a new dispute at the college when elections were called for the Students' Representative Councils. He and others planned a boycott in protest against the poor conditions at Fort Hare, especially the bad food and the lack of power wielded by the Student Council.

Perhaps Mandela was inspired by his role as John Wilkes Booth, the assassin of Lincoln, in a Fort Hare drama society production. It was a small but crucial role, laden with tempting symbolism about the dangers of standing up for what you believe in — the only play in which Mandela ever participated, before prison. (He was once the king in *Antigone*, on Robben Island.)

When the Student Council elections were called, only around twenty-five students turned out to vote, the rest observing the boycott. Mandela was one of the six students elected in the minority vote, all of whom promptly resigned as part of the protest. The principal tried to outwit them, saying that instead of voting in the hall they could vote again, during that evening's communal dinner when all the students would be present.

Once again only the same twenty-five voted and the same six students were elected. But now there was uncertainty, as the full electorate had been gathered together, even if most had not participated. Mandela consulted Matanzima, who advised him, "No, you must resign, it's a question of principle." Mandela told the others he would not take up the position, but as they all agreed to stand he was now isolated.

The principal called him to his office and told him that if he refused to serve he could not come back the following year. Mandela was frightened but still Matanzima told him he must stand firm on the principle. Mandela says he was, if anything, more afraid of Matanzima than the authorities, so he again went back to repeat his refusal to the head of the college. He was effectively expelled, told he could not return unless he agreed to serve on the Student Council. Although Mandela could not bring himself to compromise, he still left for home thinking uneasily of the consequences, worried that he was sacrificing his academic career to an abstract position.

Back in Mqhekezweni, that December 1940, the regent, Jongintaba, neither understood nor valued Mandela's protest and insisted he would have to return to Fort Hare for the New Year. Justice was in Mqhekezweni too. He had finished school altogether and had been living, perhaps idly, in Cape Town. Possibly this troubled Jongintaba as well. He had two problems on his hands, who were both kicking their heels at the Great Place. The regent called them together to a meeting, told them he was going to die soon and proposed to see them both married. In fact, he had chosen their brides already. Justice was to marry the daughter of a Thembu leader and Mandela's bride would be the daughter of the local priest. Mandela says he protested that he was still at school but Jongintaba brushed that obstacle aside, saying he would look after the wife, while Mandela went back to Fort Hare.

Mandela went to the queen and told her he wanted to marry someone else, one of the queen's own relatives, but only after he had finished his studies. He had in fact never dated the girl in question but was simply trying to find a way out of a difficult situation, made more complicated by the fact that the young woman chosen for Mandela by the regent was actually in love with Justice and had been having an affair with him—a matter about which Jongintaba was quite unaware.

The queen was sympathetic and would have backed Mandela's alternative choice, but the regent would not compromise. He had already agreed and paid *lobola* (bride price), he said, and there was no turning back. As neither Mandela nor Justice wanted to marry, the two decided to run away and hatched a plan to escape to Johannesburg.

The other side of this story emerged during a visit to Mqhekezweni in the summer of 2008. There in the Great Place was the rondavel that Mandela and Justice had shared as boys, and before it a new-built, redbrick house, paid for by the kindness of Mandela himself and occupied by the widow of Justice, Nozolile Mtirara, a friendly, though tired, elderly woman who spoke no English but was happy to talk through an interpreter.

Nozolile was the poor bride that Justice had run away to escape. She had no memory or knowledge of a prospective wife for Mandela, she said. So far as she was concerned, she was the only proposed bride. She had never met Justice and knew nothing about him when she was assigned to become his wife, but that was not strange to her; it was the custom. The regent saw her, decided she was suitable to be his daughter-in-law and that was that.

She believed that Justice and Mandela had run away to defy the tradition of arranged marriages. Nozolile was just twenty when she was chosen and had no option then but to sit and wait for her husband-to-be to return. She could not even go to school. Justice eventually came back and married her in 1945, four years after he had run away. (Mandela, of course, never returned to his chosen bride, if she ever existed.)

According to Nozolile, it was not long after they married that Justice returned to his old ways and ran away again, only this time he did not go to Johannesburg, but remained in the eastern Cape, womanizing. As Nozolile put it, repeating it for emphasis, "He really was a womanizer." They had six children between them and Justice never took any more wives, but he was very different from Mandela, apolitical and interested only in having a good time.

On one occasion, before he went to prison in 1962, Mandela had come to the Great Place and found the house closed up, both Justice and Nozolile gone. Justice was off with a woman in East London and Nozolile had returned home to her family as a protest because she could not feed her children without her husband to support her. As Nozolile understood it, Mandela had told Matanzima, who was by now the chief minister in the Bantustan government at Umtata, that Nozolile must go back to her marital home. She had been ordered to return, although, in that patriarchal world, no one thought to order Justice to return to his responsibilities.

Nozolile said the old chief, Jongintaba, had been heartbroken when his son and Mandela had run away and he had died little more than a year later, as his health quickly deteriorated.

His photograph was on the wall above Nozolile, alongside images of his father, Dalindyebo, the man who had nominated Henry Mandela to become headman; Justice himself; and his brother, Sabata, who had become paramount chief and had also been active in the struggle against apartheid.

The old chiefs had been wealthier, said Nozolile, and the role had changed. Back then the chiefs had worked for the people; nowadays they wanted the people to work for them. Nozolile's grandson was the current chief but the traditional herds were much reduced in size and value. When Mandela was released from prison in 1990, said Nozolile, he used to visit with groceries because they were all poor now. It was his way, she thinks, of thanking the old people who raised him at the Great Place.

Of course, Justice and Mandela had no material wealth when they hatched their plan. They needed money so they stole two of Jongintaba's cows, sold them to the local trader and hired him and his car to drive them, with what few clothes they had, to the railway station at Mbityi.

They had plotted carefully, waiting until the Bhunga, the local puppet parliament, was sitting at Umtata. The chief would attend the sessions, starting on Monday mornings and remaining there for the week, only coming home for the weekends.

According to Mandela, it was usual for the chief to take one of the two young men with him to the town, apparently fearing what they would get up to if left alone together. He routinely took Justice and was happy to leave Mandela behind, in charge, but the week before the escape, he had taken Mandela instead.

For some reason, the following Monday morning Jongintaba went off on his own. Justice and Mandela were packed now, with all their clothes in a single suitcase, and were ready to go when the chief suddenly and unexpectedly returned. They ran off and hid in the cornfields. He asked after them and was told they were somewhere around. He said he had only come back for his Epsom salts, which they thought was a suspiciously inadequate reason to return, sure now that Jongintaba knew something was going on. After he drove off, they came out of hiding and waited until his car had disappeared over the hills before they began their journey.

When they got to the railway station, they discovered that Jongintaba really was one step ahead of them. The stationmaster told them he had been instructed not to sell them tickets as the chief believed they wanted to run away. They were stunned that he knew but would not give up. They persuaded the trader to drive them on to the next station in the town of Butterworth, a journey of some fifty miles across the Mbashe River.

There they caught the train to Queenstown but could not continue to Johannesburg as they did not have the necessary native passes (the pass laws required black South Africans to carry an identity book which restricted their rights and their movement). They had planned to visit a clansman there and seek his help. As luck would have it, they bumped into a relative of Jongintaba, himself a chief, who said he would take them to the chief magistrate of Butterworth to get the passes. The magistrate was just completing the paperwork when he decided to make a courtesy call to his opposite number, the chief magistrate at Umtata, to tell him he was issuing passes for two young men from his area. Jongintaba was there with the magistrate and soon explained what they were up to. "Arrest those chaps, bring them back here now." The Butterworth magistrate was furious at them for their deception: "You are crooks, you come and tell me lies here, go away from my office." Mandela and Justice agreed that they had lied but tried to plead that they had committed no offense. Nonetheless, they were thrown out with no passes, though thankfully spared arrest.

They went instead to a friend of Justice's who they thought might help as he worked for an attorney. By chance the attorney's car was being used on a trip to Johannesburg so the friend offered to arrange a lift for them. The white attorney's mother, who was going to the city to visit her daughter, sat in the front beside the driver while Mandela and Justice sat in the back, Justice behind the attorney's mother, which for some reason made her uncomfortable. She seemed frightened of Justice and made him swap seats with Mandela, keeping an eye on him throughout the journey.

Mandela conceded that Justice could be wild and exuberant, and he had no fear of whites, but even so, he could not explain the woman's attitude. Evidently he was not yet used to the common racist fear of the black man, felt by many white people in South Africa, then and now.

After this awkward journey of a few hours they finally reached Johannesburg. It was Wednesday, April 16, 1941 (Mandela later recorded the date in the papers for his divorce from his first wife), and he was twenty-three years old.

Four

ON THEIR ARRIVAL in Johannesburg, Justice and Mandela headed straight to Crown Mines, one of the larger gold mining complexes on the reef. The mine was already expecting Justice as his father had earlier made an introduction for him, while the chief had been pressing Mandela to return to Fort Hare.

Justice told the mine foreman, known as an *induna*, or boss-boy, that the chief wanted him to give Mandela a job too. They might have got away with that deceit, if they had not told a friend who was also working there that they had actually run away. The friend went straight to the *induna* and told him the truth. The next day the *induna* summoned Justice and Mandela to his office and demanded to see their written permission from the chief to seek work. The supervisor showed them the telegram he had received from the chief: send Justice home at once!

The *induna* said he was going to collect the money for their fare and send them back to the Transkei. They left the mine and went to see a family friend and associate of the chief, Dr. Xuma, then the newly appointed president of the ANC, who in turn passed them on to a contact, Mr. Wellbeloved, who worked for the organization that represented the whole mining industry. Mandela tried to impress the man, telling him he wanted to work while he continued his studies for a BA. Mr. Wellbeloved said, in that case he would send them for jobs at Crown Mines.

So back they went to the mine, where they were accepted by a different official. But while Justice was given a trainee position in the office, Mandela was told he would have to start as a watchman. He was given a round helmet-like hat, a knobkerrie nightstick and a whistle.

They stayed at the home of the compound manager. Mandela thinks he served for a week at the most, sitting on duty at the compound gate, monitoring the comings and goings, before another telegram arrived from the chief that went to the *induna*, who did not know that they had returned and begun work. When he found them at the mine he ordered them to leave immediately.

Mandela went back to the house to collect their suitcase and as he was leaving, being helped by another man, unnamed, he was stopped by a guard who wanted to search his luggage. Mandela had an old revolver in the case that had belonged to his father and of course the guard found it. He blew his whistle and other guards came, but instead of arresting Mandela they arrested the man who was with him. Mandela followed them along to the police station where he showed his Fort Hare student papers and explained that the gun had been his father's. He claimed he had only brought it with him because he was afraid of gangsters, having been told that Johannesburg was rife with them.

The police released Mandela's friend and charged him instead. On the Monday morning he went to court and was given a small fine.

Mandela now went to stay with a cousin, Garlick Mbekeni, for a few days and told his relative of his ambition to become a lawyer. Mbekeni said he would take him to meet a very clever fellow, "one of our home boys." Together they went to a suite of offices, Sitha Investments, at Barclay Arcade on the corner of West Street and Commissioner Street in the business district of the city. There they sat and waited in reception while Mandela watched an African woman secretary—the first he had ever seen—speedily type a letter.

After a while the secretary took them through to the inner office where

Mandela was introduced to a "light-skinned, colored-ish" looking chap ("Colored" was an apartheid definition for people of mixed race) who appeared to be in his late twenties but seemed kind and wise beyond his years. He was wearing a double-breasted suit. Mandela didn't know it then but the man had a white father.

He found it hard to believe later when he asked his cousin what degree the man had and was told he had not been educated past Standard Six. How could that be? "He has knowledge and skills from the university of life," Mandela's cousin told him, "and Johannesburg is a good place to learn."

The man was Walter Sisulu, real estate agent, activist and communist, later to become Mandela's greatest political influence and mentor.

Sisulu had been in Johannesburg since 1928, when he arrived at the age of sixteen—pretending to be eighteen—to work at Rose Deep Mine. At first, he lived in a dormitory with his kinsmen and was mortified, after a while, to discover that homosexual sex—sodomy—was commonplace among the laborers. He gradually reasoned that it was an inevitable consequence of the pattern of labor migration forced on young men by poverty and poor expectations in rural South Africa. Deprived of a normal family life, they sought solace and release with one another.

Johannesburg had initially sprung up as a miner's camp in the late nineteenth century, to cope with the rush that followed the discovery of gold in 1886 on the Witwatersrand (the name of this low ridge of hills, running across central southern Africa, is often abbreviated to the rand or the reef). The camp evolved into a city, its narrow, downtown streets a tribute to the way the area was finely divided, to squeeze in the maximum number of small plots for excavations.

Miners came to the area from all over the world but it was the British and the Boers who fought for control of the region, later to become the Transvaal state and eventually a province of the Union of South Africa, formed in 1910.

The formation of the Union signaled the beginnings of the system that would later be formalized as apartheid. Anti-slavery legislation had actually enfranchised black Africans in some areas of southern Africa in the mid-nineteenth century, but those voting rights were eventually removed and restrictions on movement were effected as the colonials sought to claim the best of the region for themselves. There were early pass laws for black Africans, supplemented by restrictions for the Indians too, who had arrived in substantial numbers as indentured laborers.

The Natives Land Act of 1913 made Africans aliens on their own land, sometimes overnight in rural areas, as they lost all rights in places where they had been living and farming since time immemorial. The Act created territorial segregation between the races, forcing black people into reserves that amounted to less than 10 percent of the total area of the country and denying them the right to own land elsewhere. A succession of laws followed—the Native Affairs Act of 1920, the Natives (Urban Areas) Act of 1923, the Native Administration Act of 1927—each reinforcing the oppression of Africans and further asserting the authority of the white minority. The restrictions, the repressive laws, just kept coming.

Migration from the rural areas to Johannesburg—Egoli, City of Gold, as it came to be called—accelerated throughout the first half of the twentieth century and few men resisted a stint in the mines with the regular income it promised. Young boys like Sisulu were swayed by the prospects. His biographer and daughter-in-law, Elinor Sisulu, described how the returning migrants "boasted about the glitter and bright lights of distant cities and proudly displayed their clothing, watches, radios and other items bought from the town to the awe and admiration of their listeners, among whom was Walter."

Like Mandela, Sisulu was born in the eastern Cape. His mother Alice worked as a domestic servant, perhaps in Umtata, which is where research places his father, Albert Victor Dickinson, a white man who was working for the chief magistrate, possibly as an assistant magistrate.

Alice returned home to give birth to her son, Walter, in 1912 but must have gone back to Dickinson as, four years later, she gave birth to a second child by him, a daughter. They do not appear to have lived together as a couple—interracial marriage would have been socially unacceptable and later became illegal anyway—but neither does Dickinson seem to have entirely abandoned his responsibilities, paying some money to support his children.

Being a child of mixed parentage did nothing to inhibit Sisulu's sense of injustice at the hardships imposed on black Africans and from an early age he was politically aware and active, involved in industrial action against poor labor conditions. There is some evidence, however, that his racial make-up may have influenced him to become a mentor to Mandela rather than the leader of the ANC, as he believed that many people would never accept a man of mixed race.

Acting as a real estate agent for black people in Johannesburg in the early 1940s was quite unlike being an agent in the West half a century later. According to Elinor Sisulu, her father-in-law acted more like a social worker, enabling Africans and Indians to buy and build their own homes in the township of Alexandra. Because it had already been established as a "native location" in 1912, Alexandra was excluded from the strictures of the 1913 Land Act, which prevented Africans buying or owning property in white areas.

A German businessman provided the loans, and a law firm, Witkin, Sidelsky and Eidelman, registered the bonds that indemnified the loans. Sisulu sourced the clients for a commission and must have noted that the law firm had no problem employing communists. Two were on the staff as clerks: Gaur Radebe, an African, and Nat Bregman, a white Jewish Marxist who was also a stand-up comedian who sometimes did turns on the radio.

When Mandela told Sisulu he had been forced to leave Fort Hare in the middle of his BA, following a protest, the older man realized that Mandela "was someone who would go far and should be encouraged. He was the kind of young man we needed to develop our organization." No doubt, Sisulu meant the African National Congress, not the Communist Party.

Mandela told him he wanted to study law and Sisulu wished to encourage him, so they went along to Witkin's where one of the partners, Lazar

Sidelsky, agreed to take him on as a clerk while he studied law to become an Articled Clerk—a lawyer's assistant—and completed his BA degree by correspondence with UNISA, the University of South Africa.

Back in Mqhekezweni, Chief Jongintaba certainly did not abandon his efforts to force Justice and Mandela to return. A few days after he had seen Mandela for the first time, Sisulu was contacted by the ANC president, Dr. Xuma, who warned him against helping the two escapees. It was too late now, anyway, but Sisulu decided to ignore the warning.

Finally beyond the chief's reach, Mandela was free to settle down and found digs in Alexandra, at 46 7th Avenue, a typically overdeveloped stand, or plot, full of higgledy-piggledy rooms added on to a small central dwelling, with no electricity or water. (Such amenities were still forty years away, only finally being plumbed in and switched on in the mid-1980s. It was the lack of electricity that prompted Alexandra's nickname, Dark City.) Mandela found the darkness an uneasy contrast with nights in the eastern Cape, as the shadows in Alexandra hid all manner of unsavory activity on the narrow, unmade, overcrowded streets: the illicit drinking dens, or shebeens, where home-brewed beer was sold, the police raids, the gangsters, the arguments, the fights, the gunfire.

"Exhilarating and precarious" was how he characterized the life of Alexandra in his memoir.

He described it vividly in a letter to someone he had known there, in 1970.

> Alexandra! That is a remarkable place. To some it is a township with a dubious reputation: famous more for its notorious gangs, slums, braziers and smoke. To others it is a perfect haven, where a person may build a dream house on his own plot of ground and be lord in his castle.
>
> To me it is my other home. Alex introduced me into many of the intricacies of town life. It nursed and toughened me for the rough career to which I was subsequently drawn. Then my total income was £2 a month out of which I had to pay a monthly sum

> of 13/4 for rent. For some time I lived literally on plain bread and cold water.

Mandela must have been highly motivated, as he buckled down to complete his degree in trying circumstances, as well as studying for his Articles at Witkin's. He had rented his room in Alexandra from the Xhoma family, John and Harriet, who had eight children. According to one of their daughters, Gladys, they embraced Mandela as one of their own, liking him even more than their own son. Gladys was only six or seven when Mandela came but remembered that, whenever they went to his room to take food or return washing or ironing, he was always reading and writing, by candlelight. Their father told them he was studying to be "a liar"—a lawyer.

Mandela always dressed formally for work and would take the bus to the city every day. Back home he was sometimes left in charge of some of the children and would read them stories and play games with them. He would smack them if they were naughty but they didn't mind because they knew that if he did, they had done wrong.

Behind the Xhomas' home was a small Anglican church, where Mandela used to worship and sing in the choir. The minister was the Reverend Mabutho who, according to Gladys, had brought Mandela to their home in the first place. In fact, the minister was a fellow Thembu who knew Mandela's family so he was only too happy to put him up in his own home when Mandela first arrived. But Mandela had neglected to tell him the truth of why and how he had left the Transkei. When the minister discovered the whole story, he felt deceived and made Mandela leave, but not before arranging a room with the Xhomas. Mandela, who maintained contact with the minister and his wife, remembered Mrs. Mabutho's disapproval when he started dating a Swazi girl. Although the relationship did not last long, the minister's wife still made it clear she thought he should be dating only young Xhosa women.

Another one of Gladys's most vivid recollections was of Mandela's interest in her sister Didi who used to wash his clothes but refused him when he asked her out, saying he was more like a brother to her.

Mandela remembered her as a very beautiful girl working as a domestic servant. He would see her when she came home at weekends and he was keen to make love to her but she already had a boyfriend. In any event, Mandela felt inhibited by his own appearance, as he had only one old suit and one shirt, which he wore day in and day out. "I didn't look tidy at all."

Fearing rejection, Mandela did not propose a relationship to Didi as he could see she felt superior to him and did not want to give her the greater pride of saying no. Instead he tried to encourage her to go back to school, which she had left, she said, because she was bored. He urged her to think beyond her beauty and her many admirers, and to complete her education so that she could find independence in a professional job.

Poignantly, Mandela recalled how Didi and her mother came to his own law offices some years later, seeking help. Didi, heavily pregnant at the time, had been abandoned by her boyfriend and wanted to take action against him for breach of a marriage contract. Mandela couldn't help thinking that if she had taken his advice she might have been saved from the humiliating experience.

But back then, he was very conscious of his own depleted appearance, noting how Didi's boyfriend had well-tailored clothes in the American style with a waistcoat and a hat. He would hook his thumbs in his waistcoat pockets and stand in the yard looking really superior, greeting Mandela as if he were a nobody. Many young men, Mandela noted, used to go to the city to steal and come back to sell their booty in the township so they could have the smart, American-style clothes. Mandela would never forget another dapper young man in a hat who came to sit next to him on a bus and with evident disdain asked Mandela to move up so there would be no contact between them, so that his coat would not touch Mandela. "And at that time it was painful, you know, it was painful."

Even his one suit had been a hand-me-down from his employer,

Sidelsky, and Mandela had to get it patched to maintain it. One day when he was walking in town he saw a woman, Phyllis Maseko, who had been a student with him at Healdtown and Fort Hare. He was so ashamed of his appearance that he crossed the street to avoid her, but of course he was not so invisible. She saw him anyway and called out, "Nelson! Nelson!" The incident ended happily as she invited him to visit her home in Orlando and fed him well.

Another friend from Healdtown would give him groceries while he was living poor in Alexandra and he relied on the Sunday plates of pork and vegetables he would be served by his hosts, the Xhomas. Sometimes he would walk the five or six miles to work at Witkin's to save the bus fare. Even then he would not have money to buy food.

Some young men in Alexandra did not trouble to go to the city to steal but went robbing on their own doorstep. They formed gangs, of which the Msomi were the most notorious. A friend warned Mandela to watch out for the Thutha Ranch gang as they were operating around his area. *Thutha* meant collecting and taking away, and this gang were renowned for clearing people's homes while they slept. One night Mandela woke up and heard voices in the yard outside his room. They were arguing: "No, let's go in" and "No, man, this chap has no money, has nothing, he's a student." Some wanted to break in but the dissenter was tough: "Leave the student alone, leave him alone." Someone kicked the door so hard that the bolt snapped and they could have entered easily but instead they just passed. Mandela moved his bed against the door and slept like that afterwards, very grateful for his narrow escape.

Walter Sisulu's daughter, Beryl Simelane, recalled that Mandela came to live with her father in Orlando because gangsters were after him in Alexandra, but in his own narrative Mandela says he left after just a year or so and spent a couple of years living in mining compounds where he had free accommodation. The chief, Jongintaba, visited him at one compound. Mandela was surprised to find that he was no longer disapproving or demanding his return, instead seemingly accepting of his new life. Feeling rehabilitated, Mandela could at last stop considering his homeland with the indifference he had affected to excuse his escape as well as to ease his sense of loss of the world in which he had been raised.

That feeling of being reconnected to his past did not, however, prevent his experiencing "stabs of guilt" when the chief died not long after his visit. Mandela was concerned that his own behavior, flouting the chief's authority, running away to the city, might have hastened the chief's end. Jongintaba can only have been around fifty-three when he died, but no doubt his lifestyle had taken its toll. Furthermore, according to Nozolile Mtirara, the poor bride that Justice had run away to escape, Jongintaba had been heartbroken when his son and Mandela had run away and, as a result, his health deteriorated.

It is tempting to consider that Walter Sisulu knew just what he was doing when he took Mandela along to be articled at Witkin's. Having sensed his new friend's potential, he may also have been aware that placing him alongside fellow clerks who were active communists might hasten his induction into radical politics.

Mandela was certainly influenced by Gaur Radebe and Nat Bregman even if he was still bound by the courtly manners he had learned as a regal Thembu and as a "black Englishman" at school. When he joined the law firm a typist told him there was no color line; they all took tea together. She said she had bought new cups for him and also for Radebe. In reality, of course, the woman had bought the cups so that the white staff would not have to share their own cups with the Africans. Mandela realized this was the color line the woman had denied existed.

When he told Radebe he saw how his expression changed. Radebe told Mandela to follow his lead when it was time for tea at eleven. Mandela watched as Radebe ignored the two new cups and took one of the others, making great show of adding sugar and milk, pouring the tea and stirring it before drinking. Mandela did not want to disappoint Radebe but neither did he want to upset the typist, so he went without tea altogether, saying he was not thirsty, and used to have coffee on his own in the kitchen.

Like Sisulu, Radebe had little formal education but seemed to Mandela to be wiser than many graduates of Fort Hare. Surprisingly, although his employer Sidelsky did business with the former and employed the latter, he cautioned Mandela against getting involved with both men, warning him that they were troublemakers and rabble-rousers. Radebe would speak to Sidelsky as if he were personally responsible for the suffering of Africans, telling him that one day the tables would be turned and "We will dump all of you into the sea."

Radebe was actively involved in the politics of Alexandra and it was through him that Mandela took part in his first protest, during a march of 10,000 to support a bus boycott against an increase in the fare. Mandela attended some Communist Party meetings with Radebe and also with Bregman, whom he would think of as the first white person to become a friend. Mandela remembered how Bregman had once taken a sandwich from his packed lunch and offered it to Mandela to break in half so they could share it. Years later, Bregman did not even remember this moment; to him it meant nothing. He was not a racialist and just accepted Mandela for who he was: a fellow human being, if also then, in Bregman's eyes, a bit of a provincial, a backwoods country boy who was very serious about what he was doing and seemed determined to take the opportunity to make something of himself.

Bregman, who later became an attorney and started his own law firm, was never heavily involved in politics, being more interested in show business. Although he remained "one of the minnows," in his own words, he used to go to meetings and took Mandela along.

Mandela was fired both by a growing recognition of the injustice Africans were suffering and by intellectual curiosity. He realized the communists were fighting a struggle based on class, but for him race was the foremost issue and class warfare seemed almost irrelevant while there was racial oppression. The gatherings he went to with Bregman were his first taste of the multiracial world in which he would soon be immersed. He had never before seen so many whites, Indians and Africans together in one room, on equal terms, and was intimidated by the company as well as by the high-flying conversations. It is hard to credit, now, but he was too shy then to speak up at meetings.

Bregman remembered introducing Mandela to Michael Harmel, who was a leading party theorist and would later become a good friend of Mandela's. Bregman told Mandela that Harmel was lecturing at Wits—the University of the Witwatersrand in Johannesburg—and had an English MA from Rhodes. Mandela could not believe his eyes. Harmel's disheveled appearance was legendary and Mandela could not understand why he wasn't wearing a tie. That was not how he had been taught to behave at Fort Hare.

While Mandela was no more vocal at meetings of the ANC and gatherings of activists that he attended with Gaur Radebe and Walter Sisulu, they awakened in him a new sense of purpose, a kind of calling, that he recognized and embraced. There was no question now of him ending up in the Native Affairs department as an interpreter or playing adviser to a Thembu chief.

When he finally completed his BA at the beginning of 1943, he borrowed the money from Sisulu to buy a new suit and returned to Fort Hare for his graduation. He spent some time with his cousin, K. D. Matanzima. Matanzima was pursuing a different destiny, seeing himself remaining in the eastern Cape as a traditional chief. He accepted Mandela's legal ambitions but urged him to return to work in Umtata where he was needed.

Mandela knew he could be of service there but it was no longer what he wanted. The daily grind of oppression in Johannesburg had opened his eyes. He was looking to a future in politics and identified the ANC as his natural political home, even as he became aware that the Congress leadership was looking weary, self-satisfied and out of touch with the new generation of activists, both educated and uneducated.

Although it was already three decades old, with a history of challenge and protest, the ANC had struggled to become the popular voice of its people and had yet to mount any determined resistance to racist oppression. No white newspaper had reported the 1912 conference in Bloemfontein at which several hundred African leaders and delegates agreed to form a new umbrella organization that would apply political pressure to the Union government and act as a forum for their views and grievances. It was named the South African Native National Congress and would not become the African National Congress for another eleven years.

In 1914 the Congress had been at the forefront of protests against the new Land Act and when their petition to the prime minister, General Botha, was ignored they decided to send a delegation to the king and parliament in London. This too had no effect, but that did not prevent the Congress suspending protests at the outbreak of the First World War and declaring support for the Empire.

Complaints against the Land Act continued to be aired during the war at meetings and tribunals, as many African organizations still appeared to believe they could change the direction of government policy by conventional means of debate. They turned up to give evidence to select committees and sought representation on government bodies established to consider "native affairs." The Natal Native Congress called for a national convention of all races and representatives to determine the country's future.

Africans might reasonably have expected some reward for their loyalty at the end of the First World War, but of course none was forthcoming. In reality, they only became even more disenfranchised, both politically and economically, prompting the first signs of unrest with a series of strikes and demonstrations that were quickly and severely quelled by the authorities.

There were signs of frustration at the ineffectiveness of the Congress. Some African women, in the Orange Free State, an independent Boer republic, organized an anti-pass protest. The first African campaign of passive resistance began in 1919 on the reef, a year after the war had ended. It had surely been influenced by the protests of Gandhi a decade earlier, when Indians had felt similarly betrayed after supporting the British government during the Boer War. In return for their loyalty, Indians had faced restrictions and enforced registration. Gandhi's campaign of mass defiance, which began in Johannesburg, was known as satyagraha—devotion to the truth—and lasted for seven years, during which thousands of Indians were imprisoned, whipped and occasionally shot for refusing to comply with registration laws.

Defiance would sustain the ANC for many years to come but in 1919 it was still a new concept to Africans. Even though they showed the same discipline and order as Gandhi's followers, they were subject to an even harsher response as white vigilantes joined police in breaking up their demonstrations.

Nothing changed, disillusion set in and new protest organizations sprang up, although the Congress continued to hold the greatest potential for mass support. There was a renewed petition to the king in London, seeking royal intervention in South Africa. One of the senior Congress figures, Solomon Plaatje, had been part of the first delegation to London and remained there to write *Native Life in South Africa*, which was considered a vivid account of the difficulties created by the 1913 Land Act.

There was a further significant publication, *The Black Problem: Papers and Addresses on Various Native Problems*, by the first African professor, D. D. T. Jabavu, who lectured at Fort Hare. It was not a call to action so much as a summary of concerns, advocating the training of "well-educated African leaders" to represent the people. Most of the Congress leaders were middle class and well educated already and were sometimes seen as a remote elite, out of touch with the grass roots.

Black African protest was muted in the 1920s when white mineworkers launched sometimes violent strike action in support of the privileges they wanted over black African workers. Of course the white workers won their cause at the expense of the Africans who were once more relegated to inferior jobs and opportunities. The National Party, which found a franchise among the poor white Afrikaners, became increasingly powerful and aggressive in pursuit of African repression. The 1930 Riotous Assemblies Amendment Act enshrined new powers to suppress protest. The focus was constantly directed towards solving the "native problem."

There were still African voters in the Cape province, some of whom had hoped this could be a springboard to a wider franchise for Africans, but by the mid-1930s it had become clear that this would never happen and the last Africans with voting rights would soon be gone. Instead the government created a Natives' Representative Council as a purely advisory forum with some elected Africans and some Africans chosen by the government—all under white leadership. This body was abolished only in 1951 and for a long time it was supported by the ANC as a way of influencing public policy.

The ANC had periodically accepted co-operation with other organizations and, even briefly, with white communists but it was a predominantly African group that assembled, back in Bloemfontein, on December 16, 1935. This was the anniversary celebrated by Afrikaners as the Day of the Covenant for a famous nineteenth-century victory over the Zulus. It had been declared an annual public holiday at the formation of the Union in 1910.

At the time, and over subsequent years, that day would be provocatively marked by the ANC and others. In 1935 it became the focus for the formation of a new body, the All African Convention, which was a fresh voice of unity for the mounting of grievances against government repression. It may have sounded like a strong challenge but of course it was blunted by lack of force and a delegation to the government was politely rebuffed.

How much longer could black South Africans continue turning the other cheek?

The ANC seemed to be sleeping through much of the mid to late 1930s but there was renewed hope with the appointment of Dr. Xuma as president in 1940. The document it produced in 1943, *Africans' Claims in South Africa*, was a confident assertion of rights by the older generation of ANC leaders. It had been inspired by the wartime Atlantic Charter, created by US president Roosevelt and British prime minister Churchill as a vision for a post-war world in which all people would be free from want and fear, and entitled to self-determination.

By 1943, however, the ANC's national conference of the previous year had also called for the formation of a youth league. Young activists resented the timidity of their elders, the way they tried to bargain with the government while cozying up to other races and organizations, and generally betraying themselves by seeming to accept the status quo.

There was too a growing sense of nationalism, or perhaps chauvinism, among some of the young lions of the ANC, such as Anton Lembede. They were influenced by the political philosophy of Jamaican-born Marcus Garvey, who promoted a "back to Africa" campaign for those who had been taken as slaves as well as supporting the idea of Africa for the Africans.

Xuma was on the left wing of Congress but even he was seen as conservative by the younger generation and was, like many, especially suspicious of South African communists as potential agents of outside influence. His letters to colleagues were said to be full of hostile references to communists.

At the 1943 ANC conference, the formation of a youth league was still the subject of fierce debate, a year after it had first been raised. Xuma was warned that such a thing would bring about his downfall, but the young lions had been canny in lobbying Xuma before the conference, encouraging him in the idea that he could be one of its initiators. His presidential address duly included a call to youth and a resolution in favor of the league was carried.

Dr. Xuma had a stylish house and surgery in the heart of Sophiatown—it is still there today, one of only two properties that survived the destruction of the township by the apartheid regime in the 1950s—and Mandela was among the young men who called there one evening in late February 1944 to push his acceptance of the Youth League's draft constitution and manifesto.

Mandela was struck by how grand Xuma's home was. Xuma had revived the ANC, regularized membership and subscriptions, and brought money into the coffers, yet he represented the old way of doing things: delegations, statements, committees—gentleman politics in the British tradition. As a man so recently being groomed to become a "black

Englishman" himself, Mandela understood how all that worked. But now there were new voices around him, offering a more militant approach, putting his own upbringing in a different perspective.

There were informal meetings at Sisulu's office, at the ANC and elsewhere as a nucleus was formed and the concept of a youth league began to take shape. In his memoir Mandela recalled Walter Sisulu's home, 7372 Orlando West, as a place where young radicals would gather and talk, sustained by the home cooking of Walter's mother, Ma Sisulu, who seemed able to produce a pot with enough food for everyone, even ten or twelve hungry young men. But the first plate, the one with the most generous helping and the tenderest, juiciest piece of meat, would be for her son.

She would look after them all, but she was not going to deprive her son.

Oliver Tambo was among the young men who went to Xuma's home, having also fallen under Sisulu's influence. He too had found a place to take his Articles, at a downtown law firm just a block away from Mandela at Witkin's. Anton Lembede, perhaps the most radical and gifted in the group, was already a lawyer. Joe Matthews, the son of Z. K. Matthews, remembered Lembede once beginning a speech with the provocative remark, "As Karl Marx said, a pair of boots is better than all the plays of Shakespeare." It caused uproar in the audience.

Lembede was close to Ashby Peter Mda, usually known as AP, who started out as a teacher and later became a lawyer, following the same trajectory as Tambo. AP was also an articulate champion of nationalism though not so inclined towards communism. The young lions were not clones and struggled to find an agreed line both on multiracial politics—or non-racial politics, as they called it—and on communism. Sisulu himself initially supported a more chauvinistic nationalist approach—that is, exclusive and not open to co-operation with non-Africans—but he softened his stance over time.

That was true too for Mandela who, perhaps influenced by Lembede, also took a more Africanist approach early on and was hostile to other groups, such as Indians and communists, especially when they were both, even as he himself was developing close friendships with Indian communists. Then, and later, it was difficult to find the right way forward. It was these issues that would cause the most painful divisions in the liberation movement.

Other key figures included Jordan Ngubane, a journalist at the popular African newspaper *Bantu World* who had been an early supporter of a youth movement. "As the circle in which I moved in Johannesburg widened," he wrote, "I realized that the ferment in me was in everyone else." A teacher, Congress Mbata, and a medical student, William Nkomo, were also closely involved and took part in the delegation to Xuma's home. Here too, even among the young lions, was an educated elite, only the presence and influence of Sisulu pointing to a more egalitarian mix.

By all accounts, Xuma reacted angrily against the Youth League's manifesto, which Mandela had helped to draft, with its open criticisms of the ANC for its failure to advance the national cause, its weaknesses of organization and constitution, and its "erratic policy of yielding to oppression, regarding itself as a body of gentlemen with clean hands."

The proposed Youth League constitution revealed a sleight of hand that muted the nationalistic fervor. Membership was open "to all African men and women between the ages of twelve and forty" but it would also be open to "other sections of the community who live like and with Africans and whose general outlook on life is similar to that of Africans."

Anton Lembede later made clear in an article that he regarded non-European unity (that is, solidarity between African, Indian and colored people) as a fantastic dream with no basis in reality, beyond occasional convenient co-operation with Africans as a single unit. He made blunt assertions: "Africa is a black man's country," "Africans are one," "the leader of the Africans will come out of their own loins."

Sisulu remembered how Xuma spoke sarcastically to the delegation of their "high learned manifesto" and attacked them for usurping the authority of the ANC national executive. In spite of his opposition to its manifesto, however, Xuma could not afford to make his disapproval of the Youth League public. It was, after all, a cause that he himself had championed at the last conference. He had been outmaneuvered by the young men and could do no more than offer his blessing, after being reassured by them that the ANC itself would remain the dominant body.

On Easter Sunday, April 9, 1944, the young men gathered together to found the African National Congress Youth League, the ANCYL. They were joined by one woman, Albertina Thethiwe, who was engaged to be married to Sisulu. The meeting took place at the Bantu Men's Social Centre (BMSC) on Eloff Street Extension in the heart of Johannesburg. The BMSC was one of the most important venues in the city and, like that of many Africans, Mandela's life was closely linked to the building.

It had been built on former mine land—mining had encroached upon the very middle of the city—and had been financed with funds raised from public donations that had been called for by the Johannesburg newspaper, *The Star*, to support the families of black people who had been murdered during the white miners' riots on the Witwatersrand in early 1922. Just over £1,000 remained after £1,280 had been paid out. It was this sum that was used to create the center as "a nucleus for social intercourse for natives employed on the Witwatersrand." Some might describe it as a sop to the "natives," to keep them happy, but it certainly became a place of significance, hosting meetings, dances and boxing tournaments, while offering plenty of opportunities to participate in everything from perusing newspapers in the reading room, "whilst enjoying a cup of tea or music over the radio," to billiards, draughts, PT (physical training) and boxing.

The BMSC was "a beacon lighting the way for migrant labor coming to the city" and "with a slogan of Body, Mind, Spirit and Character it has continued to struggle and to impress those of our fellow beings who have accepted its coming with a feeling of one-ness."

Mandela had very personal memories attached to the BMSC and wrote to his wife Winnie from Robben Island in 1970:

> By the way, the other day I dreamt of you convulsing your entire body with a graceful Hawaiian dance at the BMSC. I stood at one end of the famous hall with my arms outstretched ready to embrace you as you whirled towards me with the enchanting smile that I miss so desperately.
>
> I cannot explain why the scene should have located at the BMSC. To my recollection we have been there for a dance only once—on the night of Lindi's wedding reception. The other occasion was the concert we organized in 1957 when I was courting you, or you me. I am never certain whether I am free to remind you that you took the initiative in this regard.
>
> Anyway, the dream was for me a glorious moment. If I must dream in my sleep please Hawaii for me. I like to see you merry and full of life.

By 1944 the BMSC was also home to the Jan Hofmeyr School of Social Work, where the woman of Mandela's dreams, then a beautiful but naive young girl, Winnie Madikizela, would arrive a decade later, to begin her studies.

Mandela thinks there were about 100 people at the BMSC for the formation of the Youth League, while Sisulu's biographer puts the figure at around 200. To Mandela they were an elite group, many of them graduates of Fort Hare, and not exactly a mass movement, but under the leadership of founding president Anton Lembede they became a powerful force for change. That Easter Day was certainly the start of a new era in South African politics, even if Mandela was not yet a leading figure himself in the Youth League or, indeed, the liberation movement. He was a man on the rise, who had done enough to earn himself a place on the Youth League executive.

Three months later, on July 17, 1944, he was back at the Bantu Men's Social Centre, as best man at the wedding reception of Walter and Albertina Sisulu (which followed a civil ceremony and a traditional ceremony back in the Transkei). The speeches were many, and no doubt long, by Mandela, Dr. Xuma, Lembede and others. There was dancing to the jazz band, the Merry Blackbirds. Among the bridesmaids was Evelyn Mase, so soon to be a bride herself. For Mandela was about to take a wife too, a woman who seems to have gone missing from his life story, a woman who is entitled to, and overdue, some restoration.

Five

IN MARCH 2009, the Soweto Heritage Trust opened Nelson Mandela's former township home on the corner of Ngakane and Vilakazi Streets as a museum. Number 8115 Orlando West is now officially known as Mandela House. White people were once banned from entering Soweto; later they became too afraid to go there; now they arrive in organized groups on tourist buses.

To enhance the displays, the curators of the museum decided to originate audio-visual material and conducted a filmed interview with Winnie and her daughters Zindziswa and Zenani (more familiarly known as Zindzi and Zeni) during which Winnie insisted that she had been the first and only Mrs. Mandela to live in that house, following her marriage to Mandela in June 1958. Her daughter Zindzi revealed not long after that she had always thought that too and had only just discovered it was not actually true. She and Zenani had always been told that story by their mother, but were now keen to see it corrected for the sake of accuracy.

The incident was not only indicative of a tendency to rewrite history but was also a pointer to some of the ill feeling that has arisen in recent years between the offspring of Mandela's first family from his marriage to Evelyn, on one side, and the family of Winnie Madikizela-Mandela on the other. The Nelson Mandela Foundation, which represents Mandela's interests as well as arranging his business affairs and charitable concerns, sits somewhere between them, not always easily.

Among the first family there is a feeling that they have been dispossessed, written out of Mandela's life. Among Winnie's family there is a sense that his first family have sometimes wanted to exploit Mandela's name for their own ends, be it financial or political.

The tensions between the two families have occasionally boiled over into open hostilities, most notably at the time of his son Makgatho's death in January 2005, which was followed by the public proclamation that he had died of HIV. It occurred again during Mandela's ninetieth birthday celebrations in 2008; and most recently, a year later, over Mandela's two controversial public appearances in support of Jacob Zuma and the ANC during the 2009 election campaign.

These tensions have their origins way back in the family history and are perhaps an inevitable consequence of Mandela's devotion to the liberation cause. Mandela has often expressed his guilt at the suffering he inflicted on his family as a result of his involvement in the ANC's struggle against apartheid. Certainly, not all the bitterness felt by the two sides of the family is aimed at the other. Much of it, especially from the first family, is directed towards Mandela himself.

As one of his granddaughters said, "I feel that men like him who sacrifice their families for the better good of everyone shouldn't have families because their families pay a heavy price, as we've paid."

These are sensitive, delicate personal issues, not only involving Mandela but others too—they speak of hidden tragedy and blighted lives—and I can only write about them because people have been open with me, wanting to see the truth aired at last. From the beginning, I was encouraged by those around Mandela to write about him as a human being. Don't write about the icon, came the plea; he knows he is not a saint, he has flaws and weaknesses just like everyone else.

* * *

After residing in Alexandra and then the mining compounds, Mandela lived for a few months at the home of Walter Sisulu at 7372 Orlando West, which must have been among one of the earliest batches of completed properties in a newly created township in the heart of what would later become known as Soweto.

African families, especially those from rural areas such as the eastern Cape, accepted their responsibilities to extended family and friends from the homelands and would rarely refuse anyone in need of a meal or somewhere to sleep. People might have come to the city looking forward to new opportunities, but they would look backward too, in most cases, and never forget their origins or seek to erase their past.

While he was still a schoolboy back home, Sisulu had shared classes with Sam Mase, who was distantly related to him through marriage. Sam got caught up in the religious fervor that swept through the young men in Qutubeni, the town where they lived. His faith remained unshaken all his life and was already in place when he moved to Johannesburg and stayed with the Sisulus. There, he became politicized and, in spite of his faith, perhaps even a communist. Sam was even an early influence on Walter, introducing him to left-wing literature.

Sam's younger sister, Evelyn, also left the eastern Cape and she too came to stay with the Sisulu family in 1939 when they were still living on Orlando East. Evelyn had been entrusted to the care of Sam after the death of their mother when Evelyn was twelve. Sam was the eldest survivor of six children, but three had died in infancy, following the premature death of their father, a mineworker. Their mother was his second wife. Evelyn began training to be a nurse, as her mother had wanted, and became friends with Walter's future wife, Albertina. Walter left the house to Sam when he moved to a new, larger house at 7372 Orlando West.

As Evelyn would later tell the story, her brother became ill and could not carry on paying her school fees. She therefore began her nursing training at the non-European Hospital in Hillbrow where she was paid £1 a month and enjoyed a half-day off every fortnight, when she would go to the bioscope, or cinema—segregated of course—to watch Fu Manchu films.

When the Sisulus moved on, Evelyn continued living with her brother but would visit the new Sisulu home. It was there that she met Mandela. Evelyn told biographer Fatima Meer, "I think I loved him the first time I saw him. The Sisulus had many friends. They were such genial, generous people and Walter had many friends who came to their home, but there was something very special about Nelson. Within days of our first meeting, we were going steady and within months he proposed. Nelson spoke to my brother and he was overjoyed, the Sisulus were overjoyed. Everyone we knew said that we made a very good couple."

They were radiant, she said, on the day of their wedding at the Native Commissioner's Court in Johannesburg on October 5, 1944. Mandela was twenty-six and Evelyn was twenty-three. They could not afford a wedding feast and there was no traditional element to their celebrations—Mandela never even paid *lobola*.

At the time of Mandela's release from prison, in 1990, Evelyn was back in the eastern Cape, running a store in the village of Cofimvaba, with a notice pinned to her gate asking the media to leave her alone. One reporter, Fred Bridgland, eventually penetrated her defenses and found her fuming gently at the manner in which her ex-husband's release was being compared to the second coming of Christ.

"It's very silly when people say this kind of thing about Nelson. How can a man who has committed adultery and left his wife and children be Christ? The whole world worships Nelson too much. He is only a man."

As has become clear in the writing of this book, Evelyn's bitterness had been simmering for many years. She felt ill treated and abandoned but even in spite of all the years of perceived neglect, it was not hard for her to conjure her feelings of thirty-six years earlier when she met this handsome, charming man who made her laugh, who flirted and said he would come to see her at the hospital. He had kept his word and they quickly became lovers.

"I thought he was beautiful."

Of course, the young couple had little money and Mandela must have been under increasing pressure as he tried to work and study, while supporting his new wife, with children soon to come. Evelyn said that from the start they had "many, many problems and most important was the house problem. There was literally not a house, nor a room to be rented within reasonable distance of my work and Nelson's." So they took a room with Evelyn's other surviving sibling, her sister Kate, whose husband was a clerk at City Deep Mines. Kate stayed at home looking after her own two children. The newlyweds did not have to pay board and lodging, but simply shared what they had, which wasn't much, with Mandela only working part-time and Evelyn still only bringing in a few pounds a month from her nursing.

Yet they were happy together, she said, and they were both excited when she became pregnant. Mandela had arranged for her to be admitted to Bertram's Nursing Home and his joy was there for all to see when their first child, a boy, Thembekile, was born on February 23, 1946. Mandela came to see her loaded with nighties and baby clothes and, when she brought Thembi home, there waiting for them was a beautiful cot that he had bought.

The arrival of Thembi must have entitled the family to their own place as they were now allocated a two-roomed house in Orlando East where they lived for a few months before moving to 8115 Orlando West at a monthly rent of 17s 6d in or around early 1947.

It is not clear exactly when Mandela first moved into number 8115 but it was certainly at least a decade before Winnie joined him there in June 1958. There would have been documentation recording his lease and rental payments, but all the paperwork was stored at the West Rand Administration Board and that burned down in the mid-1970s.

Mandela has said he moved there as a young married man with a child in 1946 but his first wife, Evelyn, told Fatima Meer that they moved there in early 1947, which seems the more likely date.

One possible clue is a surviving file of correspondence relating to an application that Mandela made at this time for a loan from the Bantu

Welfare Trust. He wrote to them on December 30, 1946, using a PO box number as his reply address. He wrote again on May 28, 1947, this time from 8115 Orlando West. It therefore seems likely he moved to the house in between those dates.

Number 8115 was the place of Mandela's dreams, often referred to by him later in letters from prison, as in this evocative letter to his daughters Zindzi and Zenani in 1969, written to support them after their mother Winnie had been arrested:

> It may be many months or years before you see her again. For long you may live like orphans without your own home and parents, without the natural love, affection and protection Mummy used to give you. Now you will get no birthday or Christmas parties, no presents, no new dresses, no shoes or toys. Gone are the days when, after having a warm bath in the evening, you would sit at table with Mummy and enjoy her good and simple food. Gone are the comfortable beds, the warm blankets and clean linen she used to provide.
>
> She will not be there for friends to take you to bioscopes, concerts and plays, or to tell you nice stories in the evening, help you read difficult books and to answer the many questions you would like to ask. She will be unable to give you the help and guidance you need as you grow older and as new problems arise.
>
> Perhaps never again will Mummy and Daddy join you in House no. 8115 Orlando West, the one place in the whole world that is so dear to our hearts.

In his memoir he suggested the modest scale of his dreams: number 8115 might not have been much, but it was his. In fact it was not even his, but was rented:

> The house itself was identical to hundreds of others built on postage-stamp sized plots on dirt roads. It had the same standard

tin roof, the same cement floor, a narrow kitchen and a bucket toilet at the back. Although there were street lamps outside we used paraffin lamps as the homes were not yet electrified. The bedroom was so small that a double bed took up almost the entire floor space.

It was the opposite of grand but it was my first true home of my own and I was mightily proud. A man is not a man until he has a house of his own.

The name Soweto (an acronym based on the first syllable in each of the three words in South-Western Townships), where the Mandelas and Sisulus lived, was not officially adopted until 1963 as the collective name for the locations that had been established on land inconveniently positioned on former farms some distance beyond the southwestern edges of Johannesburg and conveniently—for whites who didn't have to look at it—hidden from the city by mining mounds.

The city did not want black people living in the inner urban areas such as Sophiatown and hoped eventually to forcibly remove them to the outer locations. The original settlements had sprung up to accommodate the Africans who had flocked to the city during the gold rush, both as miners and as general workers: domestics, flat boys, houseboys and so on. Assemblies of shacks and tents had gradually been transformed into thriving slums, continuously swelled by new arrivals. At the turn of the century all the races had been thrown in together, but with the advent of segregation, black people began to be shipped out to Klipsruit, the first of the southwestern locations next to, if not quite on top of, a sewage farm.

Orlando—named for the then chairman of the Native Affairs Committee, Councilor Edwin Orlando Leake—was first envisaged in the early 1930s as the "biggest and finest township in the Union of South Africa." The first homes were basic constructions with a bucket for a toilet and soon became known as "matchbox houses," but that did not stop the city council from marketing Orlando East with photographs captioned, "Happy township residents."

During the Second World War there was a new wave of arrivals in Johannesburg from the rural areas and Orlando East struggled to cope with the increased overcrowding. There was conflict between the newcomers, many of whom had nowhere to sleep, and the older residents. A campaign arose for new land and housing, led by the so-called horseback "messiah" of Soweto, James Mpanza. On March 20, 1944, he led a famous march on his horse from Orlando East across the river to Orlando West, where he set up a squatter camp with shacks made from sacking material called *masakeng*, which gave the camp its name, Shantytown Masakeng. Mpanza controlled the camp and collected rents.

The city council responded by offering shacks of its own at cheaper rates. But by 1942 only 750 houses had been built there and thousands more were needed. Indeed, part of the problem to begin with had been the slow pace of progress at its proposed development of Orlando West

Number 8115 was part of an accelerated building program of 2,350 new homes that began in 1944. The first fifty were handed over the following year to selected tenants from Orlando East, Shantytown and elsewhere. The work continued in the shadow of threats by impatient squatters to take over the properties. At one stage some half-built homes were invaded by several hundred families and building work ground to a halt.

The tender was very specific that the newly built homes should be "sub-economic in character" with a maximum shelf-life of around forty years. They were three-roomed and four-roomed properties within a single-story rectangular design and would include provision for

> cooking (coal or wood burning stoves only); food storage; sanitary requirements (water-borne sewage will not be available for a considerable period. Competitors are asked to include in their plans a future WC to each house); ablutionary requirements (facilities provided should be of a character most suited to low-cost installation and maintenance).
>
> Stoeps or porches may be included at the [tender] competitor's discretion but the economic factor must here, as elsewhere, be

> constantly borne in mind. No electrical work to be allowed for, either in the plans or the estimate of cost.

The city council tried to get the properties occupied as soon as they were ready, which suggests that the three-roomed corner site at Stand 8115 must have been finished and ready at the end of 1946.

In later years, as the various locations became established, residents would dub them with names that parodied posh white areas. Beverly Hills was one, while Mandela's corner of Orlando West became known as Westcliff, after the area in Johannesburg overlooking Zoo Lake. Archbishop Desmond Tutu moved in down the road.

The Mandelas had a second child in 1947 and named her Makaziwe, a Xhosa name that means "She Must Be Known." She was ill from birth and never recovered, dying after nine months in 1948. Mandela does not give her illness a diagnosis in his memoir but Evelyn has said the cause of death was meningitis. Her grave at the family burial site in Qunu has this inscription: "From the scented garden of his earthly creations, God plucked the sweetest blossom from his heavenly abode."

After the sudden death of Thembi in a car crash, in 1969, at the age of twenty-three, Mandela must have thought back to the first Makaziwe and wrote that he ought to have been better prepared, for Thembi was not the first child he had lost:

> Way back in the 1940s I lost a nine months baby girl. She had been hospitalized and had been making good progress when suddenly her condition took a grave turn and she died. I managed to see her during the critical moments when she was struggling desperately to hold within her body the last sparks of life which were flickering away. I have never known whether I was fortunate to witness that grievous scene. It haunted me for many days thereafter and still provokes painful memories right up to the present day, but it should have hardened me for similar catastrophes.

One wonders, too, at the effect, on both Evelyn and their relationship, of such a difficult loss, during a period when their lives were already encircled by hardship. Mandela said his wife was distraught. He had outlined something of the state of his affairs in his application to the Bantu Welfare Trust in December 1946, in which, with exaggerated formality, he had stated how pleased he would be if they would kindly consider his application for a loan of £250.

He was about to leave Witkin's, he said, where he had been working as an articled clerk at £8 10s a month, and become a full-time student at Wits where he would be studying for his final year of his Bachelor of Laws course—the LLB—to become qualified as an advocate. He needed the money to pay his university fees and buy the necessary textbooks.

> I may well mention sir that I have faced and am still facing considerable financial difficulties. For the last two years my studies at this university have been done under very strenuous and trying circumstances. My only source of income is the salary I receive from this firm. It is out of this salary that for the last two years I have been able to pay for my university fees and to support myself and my family and in view of the high cost of living in this city I have found it almost impossible to make ends meet.
>
> I have no father and my mother whose financial position is very humble indeed has done her utmost to assist me towards my education and has exhausted all her resources and can do nothing more for me.

He was not discouraged, he told the Trust, and was determined to continue his studies until he completed the course.

He got the loan, but was refused when he asked for an additional £150 five months later, in May 1947. He applied yet again that September ("At the risk of seeming unreasonable...") only this time asking for just £102, which, for some reason, found favor and was granted.

Mandela had enrolled at Wits in 1943 to begin his LLB in the hope of becoming an advocate. It was a part-time course and he was then the only black African in the law faculty. There had never been a black barrister in Johannesburg.

Mandela's enrollment at Wits marked the beginnings of his political associations and friendships with people from other races. It was through the university that he met Joe Slovo, Ruth First, Bram Fischer, George Bizos, J. N. Singh and Ismail Meer, among many others. Like Mandela, nearly all these people had been raised within narrow racial confines, but were commingled by their interest in the anti-racist politics of the left.

When Mandela first knew him, Meer, a South African of Indian descent, was in an interracial relationship with Ruth First, a very glamorous, sharp-witted young white woman who was already an active young communist and at the beginnings of a career in radical journalism. People who knew them said they made a striking couple, but Meer's family disapproved of the relationship and it did not survive.

If they had married, they would have been criminalized anyway, by the Prohibition of Mixed Marriages Act of 1949 and the Immorality Act of 1950.

On the rebound, as some believe, from Meer, Ruth First got together with Joe Slovo and they were married in 1949. She and Meer continued to move in the same circles and it sometimes seemed that they still had feelings for each other. Amina Cachalia remembers them dancing together at a party years later and how it was evident that there was still a connection. Ruth was quivering when she came to Amina. What should she do about her reawakened feelings for Ismail? Amina told her to go out, take some deep breaths, come back in and talk to her husband.

Ruth and Joe were not always faithful to each other, their volatile marriage—which has been characterized as an open one—punctuated by many flirtations and affairs, sometimes with the husbands and wives of comrades. The Slovos were famous too for their multiracial parties.

Meanwhile, Ismail Meer was living in a rented apartment at 13 Kholvad House, around the corner from Kort Street where could be found the best Indian restaurants in Johannesburg, such as Kapitan's and Azad's.

The flat, which became a popular venue for political and social gatherings, was later occupied by another young Indian activist, Ahmed Kathrada. Mandela was a regular visitor, and would sleep over if he stayed late and missed the curfew for Africans. Meer's future wife, Fatima, recalled the beginnings of their friendship.

> We were just courting at the time. My husband was rather proud of me and wanted to introduce me to Nelson so he brought him to my parents' home in Pinetown. I was a teenager, about seventeen, at high school, so neither of these two young men were taking me very seriously, they were both treating me like a teenager, which I was resenting. I felt patronized. They were not treating me as an adult, as an equal. They were teasing me. Nelson liked teasing people. He has a wonderful sense of humor.

Indian communists and radicals from the South African Indian Congress were more highly motivated than the ANC at this time. They looked back to Gandhi's satyagraha campaigns and mobilized widespread support in 1946 for the first post-war protests of passive resistance against the Asiatic Land Tenure Act, which Indians called the Ghetto Act as it sought to confine them to specific areas.

Ironically, Mandela's growing friendship with white and Indian communists and radicals coincided with the rise of his ANC Youth League nationalism. While he was personally close with many white and Indians, he was suspicious that many of them felt themselves to be intellectually superior and would take over if the ANC tried to work with them. And Mandela believed that the struggle was the struggle of black Africans, first and foremost.

When Ruth First wrote to invite the Youth League to become affiliated with the Progressive Youth Council (essentially young communists), the ANCYL wrote back with a sniffy rejection: "We fear there is a yawning gap between your policy or philosophic outlook and ours. We are devoting our energies to the preparation for the greatest national struggle of all time, the struggle for national liberation." Co-operation could only "result in chaos, ineffective action and mutual jealousies, rivalry and suspicion."

The fiercest and most articulate nationalist was the ANCYL's leader, Anton Lembede. But he died following a brief illness in 1947, his loss creating "a gaping wound in one's soul for a lifetime," as one Youth Leaguer wrote. Mandela and Sisulu had come across Lembede writhing in pain in his office. They called a doctor and he was quickly sent to hospital but died there two days later of "cardiac failure."

A. P. Mda took over at the head of the ANCYL and the position was slightly softened. Mda, according to Mandela, was able to separate his resentment of racism or white domination from white people themselves and he was not so rabidly anti-communist. Soon after he was appointed, Mandela became the body's secretary.

As the Youth League sought to exert greater influence, both Mandela and Sisulu were elected into positions in the mainstream ANC, which meant their devoting even more time to politics and spending even less at home. Mandela later reflected that he hardly ever went out with his wife. He could count the occasions when he had done so on the fingers of one hand. However, when he was at home he changed nappies and participated in childcare. He had brought his younger sister Leabie from the eastern Cape to their home and she went to school in Orlando. Evelyn had never previously met Mandela's mother, Nosekeni, when she too came to stay with them in the late 1940s. Mandela himself had not seen her for some years. She was supposed to be unwell and was weak on arrival but Evelyn saw that she recovered rapidly once under their roof. Evelyn told Fatima Meer that she thought her illness was the result of her missing her son.

It is notable how little Mandela saw of his mother after he left Qunu and went to live with the regent, Jongintaba, at Mqhekezweni all those years earlier. Was he too busy or too poor to see her? Was he too caught up in city life or was he, in some way, embarrassed by this illiterate, pipe-smoking woman with narrow horizons—a reminder of his own humble beginnings? Apparently she once answered the door to one of his Indian comrades and told her son that a white man had called for him. On being corrected that it was in fact an Indian, she asked, "What nationality is an Indian?" There were no Indians in the rondavels of the eastern Cape.

During her stay, Mandela's mother was helpful in the home, affording Evelyn some freedom to take an active part in politics. Evelyn would often be characterized later as apolitical and uninterested, having time only for her faith. In the mid-1950s she did become a devout Jehovah's Witness—probably influenced by the strong faith of her brother, Sam—but in truth Evelyn was far from apolitical.

Ruth Mompati, an ANC member, remembered Evelyn in the ANC Women's League and would see her alongside Albertina Sisulu at branch meetings in Orlando West. As Evelyn herself told the reporter Fred Bridgland, she used to dress in ANC colors—black skirt, yellow blouse, and green-and-white scarf—to go to Women's League meetings across the Witwatersrand at townships like Springs, Evaton and Atteridgeville. "I was shy but I spoke."

Furthermore, Evelyn told Fatima Meer that she was "roped into" the Nursing Union by Adelaide Tsukudu, a fellow nurse who would later marry Oliver Tambo. "Adelaide was vivacious and very persuasive," said Evelyn. "She and Gladys Khala had strong feelings about the rights of nurses and particularly about the discriminatory wages of black nurses. I shared those feelings and I threw my weight in with them. We held meetings at the General Hospital and at Darragh Hall. Nelson was pleased with my involvement and very supportive."

Evelyn liked the house to be busy with visitors from home, such as K. D. Matanzima, who always turned up with an entourage. She wanted all her guests to feel the house was their own. It seemed to her that they were a happy, crowded family. Mandela himself was highly organized and "very regular in his habits," always up at the crack of dawn to go jogging, before a light breakfast. He was glad to do the family shopping and even, according to Evelyn, enjoyed bathing the babies and sometimes "taking over the cooking from us women."

Perhaps Evelyn was putting a gloss on their lives together, to emphasize the great hurt she believed was done to her later, or maybe those early years, once their initial housing problems were solved, really were as simple and contented as she implies. You would look in vain through Mandela's memoir for any suggestion that his wife was ever politically motivated herself or saw politics as anything other than his own "youthful distraction." He represents the beginnings of the end of their marriage as a struggle between her religion and his cause, but that is not quite the whole story.

Throughout this period they must, at the very least, have been under continual financial strain. The Bantu Welfare Trust periodically reminded him of the need to repay his loans and he mostly ignored their letters. When they eventually threatened to go to his sureties for the money (these included Sisulu), he quickly replied, with an apologetic promise to begin repayments—a promise he did not keep.

His financial position cannot have been helped by his inability to complete his LLB at Wits. It must, to some extent, have been a vicious circle, a trap in which his impoverished, overcrowded home life, coupled with the diversions of his burgeoning political activities, conspired to intrude on his studies. The more his studies suffered, the more his financial status was affected as he could not move on. He apparently still hoped to become an advocate. When he wrote to the Dean of the Law Faculty at Wits in December 1949, pleading for one last chance to retake his final examination, he had been studying for the LLB for seven years and had failed the final year three times.

A retake, technically, was known as a supplementary examination, which Mandela wanted to schedule for the following month, January 1950. He told the Dean that, over his seven years at Wits, he had incurred considerable expenses, totaling £472 17s, by purchasing textbooks and traveling between Orlando and the city with a monthly second-class train ticket.

"Early in 1945 it became clear that I could not continue with my studies unless I was in possession of sufficient funds and with this end in view I sold my property and for some time I was able to continue with the course." This is the only reference to any property owned by Mandela. So far as is known, he never owned any.

The letter continued:

> Soon thereafter these funds were exhausted and I was forced to apply to and received from the Bantu Welfare Trust Johannesburg the loan of £301 [actually it was £352] . . . part of which I used towards my fees and the balance in the maintenance and support of my family.
>
> This amount was also exhausted and for the years 1948 and 1949 I had to draw upon my last reserves which had been accumulated with considerable difficulty by means of personal savings. This reserve has now been exhausted leaving me almost destitute and stranded.
>
> Besides I have a number of pressing accounts which I am unable to meet and in view of the gradual rise in the cost of living in this city, it shall be impossible for me to continue my studies for a further year and it would greatly assist me if I could be permitted to present myself for the supplementary examinations in January next.
>
> I should also add that during the whole of this period I studied under very difficult and trying conditions. I was a part-time student and resided (as I still do) in Orlando Native Location in a noisy neighbourhood. In the absence of electric light I was compelled to study in the evenings with a paraffin lamp and sometimes with a candle light. I wasted a lot of time travelling between Orlando and city and returned home after 8pm feeling tired and hungry and unfit to concentrate on my studies. Even during the examinations I was compelled to work in order to maintain the only source of livelihood that I had. It is my candid opinion that if I had done my work under more suitable conditions I could have produced better results.

It is not hard to visualize the contrast between Mandela's world and that of the majority of students, who must have come from the white middle class and had comfortable homes in the garden suburbs—and black domestic staff to maintain them.

Mandela's letter was considered by the Dean and his six colleagues on the faculty board at a special meeting on December 14, 1949, at 5 p.m. at the Chambers of Advocate Pollak. They considered three applications to take supplementary examinations and granted two of them. The board regretted that it could not accede to the request of N. R. D. Mandela as he had failed in three courses in his final year.

George Bizos had first met Mandela the previous year when he too began studying at Wits. Like Mandela, Bizos had arrived in the city in 1941, as a refugee from Nazi-occupied Greece. He was concerned by the oppression of black people and their unequal treatment on the Wits campus so was at a protest meeting where Mandela spoke on behalf of a student activist facing expulsion.

Bizos would himself become one of the greatest advocates in South Africa and a prominent defender of the oppressed. In his view, the Dean of the Law Faculty, Professor Hahlo, was a racist at heart and had "drunk deep into the cup of apartheid."

Mandela later disclosed to Bizos that the Dean had told him that becoming a barrister was beyond the ability of black people. To be a barrister, the Dean had said to Mandela, you must be part and parcel of the mores and habits of the people—meaning white people—so in his opinion Mandela should really drop his personal ambitions and become an attorney, which did not require an LLB but a diploma in law, for which the Dean would give him credit but which would still require another two years of study. (A South African attorney can only appear in court in minor cases and instructs advocates/barristers in major cases.)

Mandela never did become an advocate.

He does not make much of these events in his memoir and was apparently reluctant for the subject to be aired when his letter came to light during research by a Wits historian in the post-apartheid era. But Evelyn, his first wife, would recall, many years afterwards, how significant the incident had been.

"Nelson had not spoken about politics when he courted me. Now he talked often about the oppression of our black people. He was particularly upset when he found people at Witwatersrand University were blocking him from becoming an attorney [surely she must have meant to say advocate] because of the color of his skin." Evelyn clearly believed it had been a turning point in Mandela's commitment to the struggle, a personal motive for his fight against apartheid.

The first black advocate in Johannesburg was not called to the Bar until 1956. His name was Duma Nokwe, and he used to have to hang his robe in Bizos' rooms, as the Natives' Urban Areas Act made it illegal for him to have Chambers of his own in the city and no one else would have him.

As Mandela struggled at Witwatersrand, a new political order was being established across South Africa. By the time of the general election of 1948, there were schisms in white politics between the Afrikaner Nationalists, many of whom had sympathized with and supported the Nazis, and Jan Smuts' ruling United Party, which had taken the country to war on the side of the British. Though himself an Afrikaner long committed to racist policies, Smuts had reservations about post-war South Africa as a segregated country. By contrast with the blinkered, isolated South Africa of the next forty years, he was an outward-looking prime minister who played a key role in the formation of the League of Nations, a precursor of the United Nations, the very organization that would later impose sanctions on South Africa.

Smuts' reaction against segregation may have been practical—he had commissioned a report that suggested it was unsustainable—but it certainly appalled the majority of Afrikaners, who looked to the Nationalists to protect them from the prospect of a united South Africa of equal opportunity. The "Nats" campaigned in 1948 on a nakedly racist platform, introducing the newly coined concept of apartheid, which came from the Afrikaans word for "apartness." Of course, the policy was not so much one of separation as subjugation. Apartheid appealed to the white electorate.

In May 1948, as the apartheid era began, Daniel François Malan became prime minister and the United Party merged with the Nationalists as the National Party. The laws that defined apartheid flowed thick and fast through parliament over the next decade. The first was the 1949 Prohibition of Mixed Marriages Act that outlawed mixed marriages, followed a year later by the Immorality Act that prohibited interracial sex.

The Population Registration Act of 1950 categorized everyone in the country by racial classification and introduced the pass system for the different racial groups. The Group Areas Act of the same year determined where the different races could live, naturally enough securing the best urban locations for the minority white community.

If "petty apartheid," as it was known, was the segregation of facilities such as restaurants, public toilets, buses, trains and all other municipal services, as under the Reservation of Separate Amenities Act of 1953, then "grand apartheid" was the political separation envisaged by the Bantu Authorities Act of 1951, which ordered the creation of the Bantustans, the territories where it was hoped all black South Africans would reside. Black South Africans were no longer legal residents of their own country, only citizens of their homeland, or Bantustan. Mandela's home, of course, was the Transkei, now the "Republic of the Transkei," with its capital and administrative headquarters in Umtata. Kaiser Matanzima was soon to become the first and long-serving president of the puppet state, with Columbus Madikizela, the father of Winnie, as his minister of agriculture. For many Africans, accepting these roles was a sell-out.

By 1960 more than twenty major Acts of parliament had been passed in the pursuit of the permanent suppression of black, Indian and colored people. No aspect of life—home, education, employment, leisure—remained untouched, or free. "South Africa belongs to us once more," Malan had said in his 1948 victory speech. The Nats were determined not to give it up ever again. They imagined apartheid as lasting for all time.

For the nationalist Africanists of the ANC Youth League, then and later, there were awkward comparisons between the two brands of nationalism, African and Afrikaaner. Of course, the Africans did not exactly want to oppress and exploit others on the basis of their race, but they did share with the whites a kind of chauvinism and desire to be at the top of the heap. The Youth League was initially unmoved that the ANC itself, under Dr. Xuma, was forging ever closer links with other groups. The so-called doctors pact of 1947 had Dr. Xuma and his Indian counterparts, Dr. Yusuf Dadoo and Dr. G. M. Naicker, agreeing to work together to campaign for votes and an end to discrimination.

But as the National Party came to power, Mandela and the Youth League held some joint discussions of their own with Indian Congress activists. Though there was to be no direct co-operation between them for a while longer, the Africans were learning something from their Indian colleagues and were newly radicalized by the prospect of the apartheid state.

A year later the Youth League drew up a Programme of Action. The document was to redefine the ANC, asserting the ANCYL's commitment to African nationalism while acting as a blueprint for resistance and protest, which, for the first time, would take the ANC activists outside the law and oblige them to court arrest. This was the moment for the ANC to stop being a pressure group and lead the way to mass action.

Mandela, Walter Sisulu and Oliver Tambo went to Sophiatown to present the program to Dr. Xuma for his approval, determined that it should be accepted by the ANC. All were ready to blackmail the president that they would support his re-election at the annual conference only if he supported the program. "We told him that gone were the days when the choice of leader depended on his status as a doctor or lawyer. It now depended on whether he could muster the support of the masses of the people," Mandela said in an interview with Elinor Sisulu.

When they told Xuma how Gandhi and Nehru had built organizations of mass protest by going to jail and wanted him to do the same, Xuma obviously felt he was being addressed by upstarts. "What do you know about Gandhi and Nehru? You come to lecture me here?" When they presented him with their ultimatum—endorse the program or be deposed—he became even angrier, accusing them of blackmailing him and of being young, arrogant and disrespectful.

Mandela could see that Xuma was not about to throw away his comfortable existence as a doctor by going to prison. He refused to back the program and sent them away, out into the late-night curfew with no means of getting home. They had to find beds nearby at the house of a friend of Sisulu's.

That was the end of Xuma. At the Bloemfontein conference, his presidential speech was received with "hollow clapping." A vote of no confidence was proposed and seconded by members of the Youth League. "A shock wave went through the hall. Never before had a president been criticized," a Youth Leaguer, Diliza Mji, told Fatima Meer. The ANCYL had won the vote but lacked experience themselves to put forward a suitable candidate to be president, so had to find a stand-in (a regent, you might say) and chose Dr. James Moroka with Sisulu elected as national secretary.

The Programme of Action was adopted and a national strike was called for June 26, 1950, in protest against apartheid. The ANCYL soon discovered the caliber of their new president. He hosted a meeting with the Indian Congress and the Communist Party, only to agree to support a rival national protest, a stay at home, two months before the ANC's own strike, on May 1, 1950.

The Youth Leaguers were furious.

Political friction between Indian and African mirrored the social unrest that had broken out in January 1949, when long-standing tensions turned to violence after an incident in Durban in which an Indian retailer was alleged to have beaten an African youth caught shoplifting. In the hierarchy of the oppressed, Africans always felt themselves at the bottom of the pile, and many resented the merchant class of Indians who, they believed, exploited them. Of course, the vast majority of the Indian community were working class too, with their own struggles. There were social divisions among the Indians who came to South Africa. The so-called passenger Indians, who had come freely to work and prosper, might see themselves as superior to the indentured laborers; plus, of course, they had brought with them the status of their caste.

Africans often went to the Indian locations to shop and sometimes ill feelings arose. As a result of the incident in Durban, many Indian shops and homes were burned, with a death toll of 137—fifty Indian and eighty-seven African.

Sisulu and Ismail Meer were among those who went there to try to quell the riots. Some Youth Leaguers were slowly being persuaded of the need for unity, and now, in calling a rival "stay away" protest, the Indians and the communists were trying to thwart them. Mandela, and once or twice even Sisulu, tried breaking up communist meetings. On one occasion, which they would joke about later, Mandela hustled Yusuf Cachalia from a platform where he was speaking.

Years later, the Pan-Africanist Congress would rise from the ashes of the Youth League, looking back to the Programme of Action as the true statement of African resistance (rather than the 1955 Freedom Charter). The PAC leader, Robert Sobukwe, himself a former Youth Leaguer, would hark back to 1950 and refer to the May 1 strike as a communist stunt.

Already, the African nationalists of the Youth League feared that the Programme of Action was being undermined by ANC support for the May strike. Mandela's attempts at disruption were just one measure of the open hostilities.

Paul Joseph, then a young Indian communist, remembered being thrown out of a Youth League meeting at the time—"Sorry, this meeting is only for Africans"—but saw Mandela there and noted that even though he was not yet prominent there was something about him. "He had charisma, he was articulate, very dapper. A good statesman and highly regarded by the Indian community."

Ahmed Kathrada became incensed by the Youth League's opposition to the May strike and confronted Mandela when they met in the street. They exchanged initial pleasantries and then Kathrada challenged Mandela to defend his position on a joint platform, saying, "I'll stand with you and I'll beat you." They parted angrily, but Kathrada was glad to have defended the position of his Indian colleagues and anticipated that he would have their support when Mandela stood to complain about him at a later meeting. As Kathrada later recalled, "I am there as a driver, standing at the door, and Madiba gets up and complains about the disrespect this youngster showed towards him. I'm expecting my mentors Ismail Meer and J. N. Singh to be friendly to me. Meer got up and said, this was Kathrada's fault, he's an impetuous, hotheaded youngster." Indeed, Kathrada had neglected to consider the importance of age and seniority. Mandela was eleven years older.

Like Paul Joseph and Kathrada, Mosie Moolla had been active in bringing out support for the May 1 strike and he too saw the tension between the two communities, African and Indian. They were forgetting who the real enemy was—white domination and white oppression; they were all in the ghetto; none of them could vote; none of them could choose where to send their children to school. They were all second-class citizens.

In spite of all the ANCYL's efforts to prevent it, the May 1 strike went ahead. Mandela and Sisulu were on the street, watching a spontaneous gathering in Johannesburg, when the police opened fire and they had to seek shelter. Altogether eighteen people were killed, all of them African. Paul Joseph remembered the recrimination afterwards when a Youth Leaguer attacked an Indian activist and assaulted him, saying, "You Indians killed my people."

The Youth League decided to turn its own June 26 strike call into a day of mourning but the response was not quite as widespread as they had hoped. Sisulu (naturally enough, being a communist himself) believed there should be greater co-operation between the ANC and communists. He proposed a campaign of national civil disobedience against the many new laws being enacted.

Mandela agreed with the idea of a campaign but was still thinking on separate lines and argued that it should be African-only. He was outvoted. After its December 1951 annual conference, the ANC issued an ultimatum to the government to repeal the new laws, by the end of February 1952, otherwise a major campaign of defiance would begin.

It was around this time that Mandela's friendships across the racial and political divide finally began to wear down his resistance to cooperation with the communists. He had high regard for ANC communists such as Dan Tloome and J. B. Marks (even though Mandela's Transvaal branch had once tried to expel Marks because of his communist beliefs) and would spend long night hours arguing with Moses Kotane, who would challenge him to accept that they were all fighting the same enemy and that the communists had no desire to take over the ANC.

When the government passed the Suppression of Communism Act in 1950, the Communist Party of South Africa disbanded and later re-formed as the South African Communist Party—an underground movement with a structure of secret cells. The Act was widely regarded as a blow against all opposition, as the law's definition of communism was so broad that it encompassed virtually any protest.

There had been a joint conference to consider how to protest against the Act (not long after the contentious May 1 protest in 1950) at which Mandela had agreed with Yusuf Dadoo's call for a united front and Tambo had said, "Today it is our Communist Party, tomorrow it will be our trade unions, our Indian Congress... our African National Congress." They had issued a joint statement. The conference was later recalled by prominent white communist Rusty Bernstein as the meeting where the foundation stone was laid for the ANC coalition that would dominate the decades to come. It was the meeting where hatchets were buried.

Feeling ill informed about Marxist philosophy, Mandela acquired some books and began studying the likes of *Das Kapital* and *The Communist Manifesto.* His memoir contains a brief but considered reflection on dialectical materialism and his recognition that a classless society is not so far removed from the communal life of a rural African community. The call to revolution, he said, was music to the ears of a freedom fighter, and there was no conflict between communism and the struggle against racism. So he "amended his view" of communists and opted from now on to embrace them in the liberation movement.

This was not a position shared by the more determined nationalists of the Youth League who remained suspicious of any communist influence that might dilute African ideals. They even went so far as to form an underground "watchdog committee" to monitor communist leanings and push the nationalist cause.

The divergence of opinion among the Youth Leaguers was a sign of the greater divisions to come within the ANC.

Six

DESPITE BEING FORCED to abandon his ambition of becoming an advocate, Mandela was beginning to attract attention, both for his growing role as a political activist with potential for leadership, as well as for his appealing personality and well-groomed appearance. His regal bearing, allied with his fondness for tailored suits, gave him the appearance of affluence. Perhaps starting work meant he had more money to spend. The Bantu Welfare Trust loan was still sitting there, unpaid.

Joe Matthews, the Professor's son, recalled Mandela at the previous December's annual conference presenting the plan for the Defiance Campaign. Mandela was dressed in his favorite double-breasted suit, according to Matthews. "You know the two best-dressed chaps in the movement were Madiba and [Yusuf] Cachalia on the Indian side. You would look at a suit that Madiba was wearing and you would go all over and say, 'I want a suit like that one.' The tailors would tell you, 'There's no such suit.' He was really a great dresser."

In December 1951, at the ANC's annual conference, Mandela presented the plan for the Defiance Campaign, a series of protests that would be unleashed if the organizations demands were not meant. Although they had been inspired by the passive resistance of the Indian activists, Mandela and the majority of the Youth Leaguers had no wish to emulate their spiritual devotion to passivity. For them, non-violence was a tactic, not a way of life as it had been in the days of satyagraha under Gandhi. The son of the Indian leader was there as an observer at the ANC conference and listened to their plans for the campaign. He asked for permission to speak but annoyed many with his comments that Africans were not ready for defiance as they did not understand the principles of satyagraha, such as non-violence and discipline.

The conference agreed to send a letter to the prime minister, warning him that their campaign would begin if he had not repealed the apartheid laws by the end of February. In an echo of the phrase that would soon become the rallying slogan of the ANC, "Freedom in our lifetime," the letter spoke of the ANC's aims for "democracy, liberty and harmony in South Africa" and said they were "fully resolved to achieve them in our lifetime."

Back home after the conference, Mandela and Sisulu drafted the letter, which then needed to be authorized and signed by their president, Moroka. Although suspicious of communists, Moroka liked and trusted Mandela, who was deputed to take the letter to Moroka in Bloemfontein, a journey of several hours from Johannesburg.

In Mandela's version of events, he was asked to take the letter because he was the only one who could drive, having just passed his test a few weeks earlier. Not many Africans took the driving test and even fewer could afford a car, though at this stage Mandela was driving only a borrowed vehicle. During the journey, Mandela accidentally knocked a white boy off his bike and although the boy was not badly hurt the police were called. The Afrikaner sergeant told him, *Kaffer, jy sal kak vandag*—kaffir, you will shit today—and Mandela retorted in English that he would shit when he pleased and not when ordered to by a policeman. They searched his car and found a copy of the newspaper *New Age: Wragtig ons het 'n Kommunis gevang*—"My word, we've caught a communist." He was eventually released, only to run out of petrol and so had to humble himself on the doorsteps of white farmers—"My *baas* has run out of petrol"—to obtain some fuel. He eventually reached Moroka and got the letter approved.

Evidently, Prime Minister Malan was much offended at the "impertinent" tone of the letter, which sought to put the ANC on equal footing with the government. He did not reply personally but got his private secretary to sign a lengthy and patronizing riposte, representing the government's apartheid policies as a "programme of goodwill" to the hapless Bantu.

"The laws are largely of a protective nature. Even those laws which are regarded as particularly irksome by the Bantu people have not been made in order to persecute them, but for the purpose of training them in the performance of those duties which must be fully observed by all those who wish to claim rights."

The letters were publicized, which helped to feed anticipation as the Defiance Campaign approached. No one knew what was going to happen, whether or not the people would turn out in large numbers to support the protests and how the government would respond if they did.

Mandela was now president of the Youth League and a growing influence on the ANC executive—and his trademark confidence was coming increasingly to the fore. He had a leading role in the first round of protests, which took place all around the country on April 6, 1952—on the very day that Afrikaners were celebrating the 300th anniversary of the arrival in the Cape of their founder, Jan van Riebeeck. There were mass rallies at numerous locations that attracted crowds of thousands, with over 30,000 attending the largest protest in Port Elizabeth. It looked as if the ANC and their colleagues had caught the mood of the moment.

The ANC and the "Joint Planning Council" met in Port Elizabeth in May where a National Action Council was formed. Mandela earned a prominent position, being appointed volunteer-in-chief to orchestrate and oversee the acts of defiance. That evening, after the council meeting, there was a farewell dinner for Professor Z. K. Matthews who was going off to New York for a year to take up a post as a visiting academic at Columbia

University. Mandela spoke at the dinner and surprised the old guard of the ANC when he said he looked forward to becoming the first black president of South Africa. Joe Matthews recalled there was quite a lot of criticism of the speech afterwards. "How could the leader of the Youth League, in the presence of his elders, make such a statement? He was a very cheeky fellow, you see, Madiba."

Professor Matthews was an influential ANC figure and his departure on the eve of a historic campaign was not great timing, raising suspicions that he was avoiding the risk of arrest. However, his presence in New York helped the ANC to present its case to the United Nations (which would soon be setting up a commission to examine the "racial situation" in South Africa), as well as forge links with emerging community leaders such as Dr. Martin Luther King and older activists such as the singer Paul Robeson, who was much loved by Mandela and his colleagues. Just as there was international support for the ANC's campaign, so the policy of defiance would influence activists elsewhere in Africa, in India and in the Caribbean, and would help to shape the non-violent civil rights movement in the United States.

Meanwhile, Special Branch had begun monitoring the activities of their political opponents. Their records, contained in the National Archives of South Africa, give some insight into the growing power of Mandela's oratory as he sought to stir the spirit of protest in his audience. On May 25, just before the trip to Port Elizabeth, he addressed a crowd of ANC activists in Johannesburg. Clearly, the idea of black majority rule (perhaps with himself as ruler) was already taking shape.

> We know that when the Nationalist Party is destroyed by the forces of the people we African people will rise and rule the country. I say this fully aware of the consequences. I am sure that when we are in power our government will name Swarts, Strydom, Malan and Donges as the enemies of liberty...In spite of our unity and support of the world, Dr. Malan has made laws. It is time you must raise your hands and say this will happen over our dead bodies. See

> the assault of innocent men and women by the police at the city hall steps yesterday. They are only rehearsing and preparing for the coming forces.

Sisulu was by now a full-time official of the ANC but was much impressed by Mandela's commitment, as he traveled around addressing meetings yet still seemed to be in the ANC office every day, while simultaneously supposed to be working nine to five as an attorney (Mandela had joined an all-white firm in 1952 after finishing his studies). They both escaped the first round of banning orders, as the government tried to clamp down on the leadership in advance of the main protest.

The Defiance of Unjust Laws Campaign officially began on June 26, 1952, a date later enshrined as Freedom Day in the history of the ANC. In an age before mass communications it was very nearly a masterpiece of planning, with coordinated acts of defiance beginning in the early hours in Port Elizabeth, where a group led by Raymond Mhlaba were arrested for going through a whites-only entrance at a train station.

Across the country, crowds gathered around the volunteers chosen to show defiance and the African anthem rang out, alongside cries of *Mayibuye, iAfrika!* Come back, Africa. Mandela worked closely with Yusuf Cachalia, both starting their day at the ANC office in Johannesburg. They were becoming good friends, though often in opposition too. Mary Benson, a future Mandela biographer, recalled seeing him for the first time in the offices of the Indian Congress, in the middle of a furious argument with Cachalia. "Quite embarrassed, they broke off to answer my questions about the Defiance Campaign. Neither he nor Yusuf remembered the incident and he had long ago learned to control his hot temper."

Mandela did indeed have a hot temper, which he could not always contain. Yusuf Cachalia was doing well to have forgotten about it. For others the experience of being a witness to, or a recipient of, Mandela's fury—albeit rare—was not something to be easily shrugged off. If such anger was a sign of stress, then Mandela was surely a man in the thick of it, in June 1952, with a young family at home, his career to be nursed and his role at the center of a national protest campaign that would inevitably result in his going to prison.

On the eve of the Defiance Campaign he had been the main speaker at a "Day of the Volunteers" rally in Durban. Volunteers were asked to take a pledge. Mandela's influence can be detected in the last line of the oath, when the volunteers acknowledge, "It shall be my duty to keep myself physically, mentally and morally fit." Mandela was nothing if not holistic.

He had found himself in front of 10,000 people. As he said in his memoir, "I had never addressed such a large crowd before and it was an exhilarating experience. One cannot speak to a mass audience of people as one addresses an audience of two dozen." That day in Durban he told the crowd, which must have been a very mixed group, "We can now say unity between the non-European people in this country has become a living reality."

No doubt, Mandela was profoundly committed to the liberation movement, making his way to its center by the sheer force of his personality and political acumen. But perhaps too, as some members of his own family have articulated, it was not all entirely selfless and there was an element of personal ambition too, which found its footing at this moment, around June 1952, when he took center stage for the first time and tasted the potency of leadership.

At the very least it must have fueled his self-confidence and self-belief. Though he is rarely described as arrogant, it was acknowledged by many that Mandela's vanity went deeper than his double-breasted suits and he was clearly seldom troubled by issues of low self-esteem.

As he directed events from the ANC offices, he was obliged to call on Walter Sisulu to be arrested much earlier than planned, as a replacement for a church minister who had a last-minute change of heart about going to jail. Mandela was keen to ensure that the campaign involved senior figures so that everyone could see they were prepared to lead from the front. Sisulu agreed to stand in and changed out of his suit at Mandela's concern that such smart clothes were "impractical dress for prison." Then Sisulu and an Indian activist, Nana Sita, led a group of fifty volunteers in their act of defiance, attempting to enter a township in Boskburg, a few miles east of Johannesburg, without permission.

Mandela and Cachalia also traveled to Boksburg, to hand a letter to the magistrate, notifying him of the act of defiance. As they had hoped, a group of journalists and photographers were watching as they presented the letter. They then went to the township to watch the protest unfold. The police had locked the township gates and for an hour both sides seemed to stand, frozen. No one knew what the police were up to, or what tactics they had been told to adopt. Would they stand aside or start shooting? It could go either way. Then the gates opened and as the volunteers stepped forward with Sisulu and Nana Sita at their head, a police whistle blew and they were all arrested.

Mandela and Cachalia went back to Johannesburg where another group planned to invite arrest by remaining on the streets after the eleven o'clock night curfew. Mandela left a council-of-war meeting at midnight and unintentionally walked straight into the curfew defiance. "No, Mandela, you can't escape," a policeman called out. No sooner had he been arrested than Cachalia was as well, and they were on their way to the Marshall Square police station along with many others, all singing the ANC anthem.

Years later, Mandela recalled the incident in a letter to Amina Cachalia, who remembered taking food to them the next day, at Marshall Square. Mandela had shared a cell with Yusuf, which made the differing treatment they received all the more ridiculous. Then and later, prisoners received, for example, the best food if they were white, middling provisions if they were Indian, and food that was barely fit for human consumption if they were black: "In the morning an orderly brought him [Yusuf] eggs, buttered bread, chips and coffee. He offered me porridge and I protested vehemently. 'Eat your food, man, you are not a white man!' he said. I retorted, 'Is he white?' at the same time pointing to your man [Yusuf]. The orderly surveyed him closely and apparently being unable to classify him snapped at me, 'Shut up. You talk too much. That's why you are here,' and off he went."

Though the prisons and police jails were to become the settings for many acts of cruelty, violence and torture by the forces of the state, Mandela himself never suffered much physical abuse. But on his first night at Marshall Square he took a kick on the shins.

> As we were jostled into the drill yard one of us was pushed so violently by a young European constable that he fell down some steps and broke his ankle. I protested whereupon the young warrior kicked me on the leg in true cowboy style. We were all indignant and I started a demonstration. We drew their attention to the injured man and demanded medical attention. We were curtly told that we could repeat the request next day. And so it was that this man, Samuel Makae, spent a frightful night in the cell, reeling and groaning with pain. Only next day was he taken to hospital.

The campaign had caught the popular imagination and hundreds were being arrested across the country. There was a much repeated protest song, "Hey, Malan! Open the jail doors, we want to enter," and it was no surprise when the police acted to quell the ongoing campaign by arresting many of its leaders, including Mandela, who were charged under the Suppression of Communism Act.

There were twenty accused altogether and for the preliminary hearing at Johannesburg magistrates' court, a crowd said to be in the thousands gathered outside to support the defendants. It was the first time such a mass protest had been made at court and this too marked a new development in the struggle as freedom songs rang out, such as one that began, *Thina sizwe, thina sizwe esinsundu*—"We Africans! We Africans! We cry for our land. They took it. They took it. Europeans. They must let our country go..."

They were so many and so noisy with their songs and their slogans and the ululations of the women that the magistrate had to ask the ANC president, Dr. Moroka, to make them disperse, which he duly did. The crowd had comprised not just ANC and Indian Congress activists but Indian schoolchildren and white students from Wits.

Alas, the accused themselves could not stand so united. Dr. Moroka hired his own attorney to run a separate defense and when Mandela tried to talk him out of it he said the campaign had been organized without him and he was not going to stand alongside communists. During his testimony in court he actually started pointing out the communists he knew among the accused before the judge stopped him. All of the defendants were convicted of furthering the objects of communism but received suspended sentences, as the trial judge Franz Rumpff noted that they had consistently called on protesters to follow a "peaceful course of action and to avoid violence in any shape or form."

The prosecution had incidentally sought to prove that the new freedom songs, the cries of the ululating women, were themselves calls to violence. A white musicologist had to be called to explain that the vibrato sound was a "typical African expression of joy or sorrow."

As the Defiance Campaign continued, its popularity was reflected by a huge surge in ANC membership, from around 20,000 to over 100,000. The membership fee at the time was 2s 6d, which ought to have made the ANC rich but, of course, most people could not afford the subscription and regular collection was haphazard.

The numbers of those who actually paid were far smaller.

Still, 10,000 defiers had been called for at the start of the Defiance Campaign, and 8,577 had responded by the time the campaign began to falter in October when riots broke out in the eastern Cape. Mass rallies had been banned but when special permission was granted for an ANC "prayer-meeting" in East London, the military moved in and eight Africans were killed, with dozens injured. In the aftermath, enraged protesters went looking for revenge. Two white people were attacked and killed, one of them a nun whose body was mutilated. The rioting spread, nearby at first, to Port Elizabeth, but later northwards to Kimberley, and eventually reaching Johannesburg, with ever more lurid press coverage, which focused on the six white deaths among a total of forty, with hundreds injured.

Mandela and other leaders tried to prevent further trouble, speaking directly to those involved. Mandela gave a speech at the Denver Hostel in Johannesburg where the residents had rioted four days earlier, saying that they had made a mistake in attacking the police and that their actions had resulted in three more killings. "If everybody stood together and remained united there would come a time when we would repay for the blood of those killed."

The leaders had never once called for or incited violence, and there was plenty of evidence of provocation by the authorities, but such serious incidents inevitably undermined the peaceful intent of the campaign, opening the way to negative publicity.

"For a while primitive Africa ruled," said the *Die Burger* paper in Cape Town, "stripped of the varnish of civilization and free from the taming authority of the white man." Others attempted to link the protesters with the ongoing Mau Mau insurgency, a violent uprising by Kenyans against British colonial rule.

The government passed strict new laws under which defiers could face flogging and much longer prison sentences. Mandela and his fellows organizers realized they could not ask people to face such harsh punishments. By now, the campaign was beginning to run out of steam and in January 1953 it was called off. There was no doubt, however, that the campaign had been a triumph, in the way that it had redefined the ANC and ushered in a new age of protest to challenge the authorities. It had created a new leader, too, though by no means all the influential Youth Leaguers had gone with Mandela on this journey across the racial and political divide. A. P. Mda wrote that Indians and white communists were taking over the ANC, while Jordan Ngubane turned on his former ANCYL colleagues Mandela and Sisulu, saying they were becoming "mere puppets" of Dr. Dadoo, the Indian leader.

Indeed, there was significant opposition from members of the Youth League, both to the Defiance Campaign—articulated by a group calling itself the "Bureau of African Nationalism"—and to Mandela himself, who was challenged for the presidency of Transvaal ANC by the leader of a faction that called itself Bafabegiya—those who die dancing—after an elite group of nineteenth-century Zulu warriors. The Bafabegiya complained of financial irregularities within the Transvaal ANC and were unhappy with the cozy relationship between the ANC, Indians and communists. The Bafabegiya themselves were mainly ex-communists who had hardened into an Africanist clique. Their candidate was defeated in the election against Mandela in late 1952 and they gradually faded from significance. Still, it must have been apparent to all concerned that many Africans would never be won over by the idea of a multiracial alliance.

But among the defiance organizers there had been disappointment at the lack of participation by white people. After discussion, the campaign leaders decided to call a public meeting for sympathetic Europeans at Darragh Hall in Johannesburg. Around 200 people heard Sisulu and Tambo tell them that if they did not stand up to be counted, Africans would think they all supported apartheid.

The meeting led the following year to the creation of the Congress of Democrats, formed by white anti-racists, most of whom were communists and had been involved in the Springbok Legion, which had been formed during and after World War II by left-thinking Jewish soldiers to promote troops' welfare and a wider range of socialist values. Others later formed themselves into the beginnings of the Liberal Party. The divisions between the radicals and the more woolly-minded whites had been apparent at the Darragh Hall meeting. One liberal had suggested lobbying for better facilities for black people in the white suburbs, such as open spaces where domestics could go to relax. The suggestion was shot down by the communist Rusty Bernstein: "We have been challenged to take a principled stand against apartheid and the status quo," he said, adding, "a park for nannies is a dismal and insulting response."

Within the ANC there was general despondency at the dismal and insulting performance of their president, Dr. Moroka, who compounded his sins at the annual conference by using his presidential address to express his loyalty to the king of England, the institution of the monarchy and the Commonwealth. By contrast, the head of the Natal ANC, Chief Luthuli, had become universally popular after sacrificing his title to the cause. He had been called to the Native Affairs department and ordered to resign from the ANC or lose his chieftaincy. He had been dismissed as chief of Stanger on November 12, 1952, and issued a famous riposte: "Who will deny that thirty years of my life have been spent knocking in vain, patiently, moderately and modestly at a closed and barred door?" He was not a militant figure, supporting the new political alliances with both Indians and whites, but his statement openly expressed the "new spirit... that revolts openly and boldly against injustice." In a stand-off against a rival candidate at the December conference, he was elected to replace Moroka as president-general and Mandela became one of four newly created deputy president-generals.

That same month, Mandela achieved his first mention in the London *Times*, which reported in a two-paragraph article, headlined "Attorney Prohibited" and datelined "Johannesburg Dec. 11"; that "Nelson Rolihlahla Dalibunga Mandela, an attorney, president of the Transvaal branch of the African National Congress and national 'volunteer in chief' of the defiance campaign, has been prohibited by the Minister of Justice from attending any gathering in the Johannesburg magisterial district for six months. He is also prohibited for six months from living in any area of the Union except the Johannesburg magisterial district." The article explained that the notice had been issued under the Suppression of Communism Act and the Riotous Assemblies Act, which could be deployed against the "promotion of feelings of hostility between Europeans and non-Europeans."

The ban did not just prohibit political gatherings, but all gatherings. Mandela could easily break the law in his own home, with his own family. All social events and business meetings could be included. It was not easy to practice as a lawyer when you were banned. Indeed, following his earlier conviction, the Transvaal Law Society tried to get him struck off its roll altogether, complaining that his leadership of the Defiance Campaign "did not conform to the standards of conduct expected from members of an honorable profession."

He had been defended at a hearing of the Supreme Court by the chairman of the Johannesburg Bar, Walter Pollak. The court accepted that there was nothing dishonorable in an attorney identifying himself with his people in their struggle for political rights, even if his activities infringed the law. Mandela won the case and the Law Society was ordered to pay his costs.

In the middle of the Defiance Campaign he had opened his own law practice with an Indian secretary. Technically speaking, the Urban Areas Act prevented Africans renting offices in the city without the express permission of the authorities. Sisulu had battled long and hard with the help of white lawyers to obtain premises for his estate agency.

Mandela found rooms at Chancellor House through the amenable Indian owner, but never got further than a temporary permit, which soon expired. He described what happened in his speech of mitigation at his trial in November 1962, in which he outlined the impact of racism on his life and career.

> I discovered for example that unlike a white attorney I could not occupy business premises in the city unless I first obtained ministerial consent in terms of the Urban Areas Act. I applied for that consent but it was never granted. Although I subsequently obtained a permit, for a limited period in terms of the Group Areas Act that soon expired and the authorities refused to renew it.
>
> They insisted that my partner Oliver Tambo and I should leave the city and practice in an African location at the back of beyond, miles away from where clients could reach us during normal working hours. This was tantamount to asking us to abandon our legal practice, to give up the legal service of our people for which we had spent many years training. No attorney worth his salt would agree easily to do so. For some years thereafter we continued to occupy

premises in the city, illegally. The threat of prosecution and ejection hung menacingly over us throughout that period.

Since leaving Witkin's, on becoming an articled clerk, Mandela had worked at a succession of white law firms. There were no African legal partnerships at all, then. He had spent a year at Terblanche & Briggish and then gone to a more liberal firm, Helman and Michel, where he studied for the exams that would qualify him to practice as an attorney. He liked Helman's because they did not charge higher rates to African clients, as many firms did. After passing his exams, he went to H. M. Basner as a newly qualified attorney, apparently already planning to branch out alone. Hymie Basner, a former communist, still enjoyed a radical reputation for supporting cases arising from the struggle and was tolerant of Mandela's own political activities.

Mandela had needed a testimonial from his first employers, Witkin, Sidelsky and Eidelman, before he could join the Transvaal Law Society and begin to practice as an attorney. Lazar Sidelsky, who had once cautioned Mandela against mixing with troublemakers and rabble-rousers, evidently now regarded Mandela as one of them and was tempted to refuse him the testimonial, warning him to keep his nose out of politics.

"You'll end up in jail, sooner or later," Lazar told him.

"For the benefit of my people I must carry on," said Mandela.

"You'll do more for your people if you set an example to them. Let your people become educated. Don't worry about politics."

Some years later, Sidelsky was on his uppers after a business failure had brought him to the brink of ruin. As he stood waiting for a bus one bleak night, a vast car glided to a halt beside him and there was the handsome attorney, Mandela, offering him a lift home. During the journey Mandela mentioned some money he believed he owed Sidelsky but his former mentor dismissed the matter as long forgotten. A check for £75 arrived in the post for Sidelsky soon after.

An Afrikaans secretary left when Mandela joined Basner's, as she refused to take his dictation. She was replaced by the Indian Zubeida Patel, who went with Mandela when he began practicing on his own. He had by then formed a close bond with Oliver Tambo, who had qualified as an attorney not long before Mandela and was working for another downtown white law firm, Kowalsky and Tuch.

Mandela would visit him there during the lunch hour, where a white secretary observed how he would deliberately seat himself in a whites-only chair in the waiting room. Africans were expected to stand, humbly waiting to be spoken to, but that did not work with Mandela. He would call out, "Mr. Tambo, please!" with the emphasis on the Mr., as it was normal for black people to be addressed by their surname only, if that.

Tambo had already completed his Bachelor of Science degree at Fort Hare when he was sent down (expelled) in 1942 after playing a central role in that year's strike, which, bizarrely, centered on the students' rights to use facilities on Sundays. It was a matter of principle, apparently not one that clashed with Tambo's religious values. Many people who shared Tambo's strict faith would not have been advocates for entertainment on the traditional day for churchgoing. He had been a Christian since childhood and maintained a regular routine of prayer and church. He was also a keen and talented choral singer, as well as a skilled practitioner of the traditional Xhosa art of stick-fighting.

Struggling to find work with his record as a troublemaking strike-leader, he was eventually accepted as a teacher at the mission school St. Peter's in Johannesburg where, some years earlier, he had been a pupil and head prefect. He had been a popular figure at the school, respected and admired by staff as well as pupils, as a man with firm beliefs and a strong sense of fairness. At the age of thirty-one, in 1948, and with the help and encouragement of Walter Sisulu, Tambo had begun his Articles with a sympathetic white law firm.

He was considered a studious, reflective character, very thorough and serious in all he undertook, perhaps sometimes a little too thorough and serious, and not as easy to get to know as his more open comrades, Sisulu and Mandela. He was a painstaking lawyer and sometimes a frustrating legal partner who took too long with cases. Tambo suffered from childhood with asthma, an affliction that he bore with quiet stoicism when it occasionally and inconveniently took him to the point of collapse.

Tambo accepted Mandela's invitation to go into partnership and within a few months, in early 1953, they had taken offices without a permit on the first floor of a building opposite the magistrates' court on Fox Street. Their joint names were etched on the glass in gold-leaf lettering, which Tambo described as standing out like a challenge. According to Tambo's biographer, Luli Callinicos, the two young African attorneys shared a vision of a black law firm where black clients would not feel intimidated or inhibited by barriers of culture and language.

By 2008 the names in the glass had long gone and the building was in a very poor state of repair, scarcely a monument to the towering figures of South African history who had once worked there. Outside, a line of washing, predominantly socks and smalls, was strung between the pillar of the building and the nearest lamp-post while, inside, a number of otherwise invisible families were squatting. The building appeared to have been damaged by fire and there was no evidence of its former use almost half a century ago. It could be said that it had been squatted then by two lawyers without a permit.

For much of the 1950s it had been the only black African law partnership in South Africa, a place of hope and refuge for black people who would travel there from all over the country to get legal advice and representation. Everyone who ever worked with Mandela or visited him at Chancellor House agreed that the place was never less than overrun with clients. When the office opened in the morning there would already be a queue of clients on the stairs. Winnie recalled that, when she visited, she would sit reading quietly in the lobby area, shoulder to shoulder with clients, as she waited on Mandela to go for lunch or finish his day's work.

To be a black African at the height of apartheid was to negotiate an impossible minefield of petty offenses that might land you in jail. Chief among the obstacles, of course, were the pass laws. It was a common sight in the city to see groups of African men standing handcuffed together on a street corner, or sitting in a line on the curb, or being marched through the commuter crowds to jail, having been arrested for pass offenses.

The figures rose exponentially throughout the decade. By 1958, for example, there were 396,836 convictions under the pass laws. But 1959 saw the greatest number of prosecutions in history, a total of 1.8 million, not just for pass offenses, but also for possessing or making "Bantu liquor," as home-brewed alcohol was called (Africans were banned from buying alcohol themselves), and for trespassing, that is, being some place they were unauthorized to enter. No doubt there were thousands more arrests that never reached court. The black population of South Africa was, broadly, around 10 million, out of a total of around 15 million, of which just 2 million, the ruling minority, were white. The rest comprised Indian and "colored" people.

Mandela originally agreed with Tambo that he would focus on the political work while Tambo took care of the legal firm, but those boundaries soon became blurred. Mandela was banned and could not leave the area of Johannesburg, leaving Tambo to make the court appearances around the country, representing clients. Sometimes the clients had traveled hundreds of miles to Chancellor House, preferring that journey to a shorter one to the nearest white lawyer.

In later years, before the fall of the apartheid regime, Tambo described how

> to reach our desks each morning Nelson and I ran the gauntlet of patient queues of people overflowing from the chairs in the waiting-room into the corridors.
>
> South Africa has the dubious reputation of boasting one of the highest prison populations in the world. Jails are jam-packed with Africans imprisoned for series offences—and crimes of violence are ever on the increase in apartheid society—but also for petty infringements of statutory law that no really civilized society would punish with imprisonment.

> To be unemployed is a crime because no African can for long evade arrest if his passbook does not carry the stamp of authorized and approved employment. To be landless can be a crime, and weekly we interviewed the delegations of grizzled, weather-worn peasants from the countryside who came to tell us how many generations their families had worked a little piece of land from which they were now being ejected. To brew African beer, to drink it or to use the proceeds to supplement the meager family income is a crime, and women who do so face heavy fines and jail terms.
>
> To cheek a white man can be a crime. To live in the "wrong" area—an area declared white or Indian or Colored—can be a crime for Africans. South African apartheid laws turn innumerable innocent people into "criminals."
>
> Apartheid stirs hatred and frustration among people. Young people who should be in school or learning a trade roam the streets, join gangs and wreak their revenge on the society that confronts them with only the dead-end alley of crime or poverty.
>
> Our buff office files carried thousands of these stories and if, when we started our law partnership, we had not been rebels against apartheid, our experiences in our offices would have remedied the deficiency.
>
> We had risen to professional status in our community, but every court case, every visit to the prisons to interview clients, reminded us of the humiliation and suffering burning in our people.

Ruth Mompati joined the firm later in 1953. At the time she had been married a year and was then known by her married name, Ruth Matsoane. (Mompati was the first name of her first-born son, which she began using as a surname after going underground in the 1960s.)

She had arrived in the city just after the Defiance Campaign of June 1952, from her home in the Cape-province, west of Johannesburg. By 2008 the district in which she had been raised had been renamed in her honor and she was the mayor of the town of Vryburg. She had just turned eighty-three but was still "dignified and reserved" as others remembered her from all those years earlier. She had a warm personality and fine features, evidence of the beautiful young woman she once was.

In the summer of 1952, Ruth was already a member of the ANC but a prisoner of her profession, she said, having been a teacher, salaried by the government, and prevented from being politically active.

She remembered, though, how the lowly white shop assistants would call all African men "boy"—"Yes, boy?"—or "John," while African women, Ruth included, used to be "Annie." "Yes, Annie, what do you want?" She used to get incensed by this and had once joined a group of young women teachers to teach the shop assistant a lesson.

"Yes, Annie, what do you want?"

"Yes, Sarah," they had replied, "I want a loaf of bread."

The white assistant was enraged. "Sarah? Who's your Sarah? Who's your Sarah?"

"Well, I can ask you the same question, who's your Annie?"

The year that saw the founding of Mandela & Tambo, 1953, also saw the introduction of the Bantu Education Act, which ended the mission schools where generations had studied, while introducing new basic Bantu education, which was hopelessly under-resourced. Any pretext of "goodwill" was gone by now; only naked racist intent remained.

The new prime minister, Dr. Verwoerd, explained the system to parliament in September 1953. "I just want to remind honorable members that if the native in South Africa today, in any kind of school in existence, is being taught to expect that he will live his adult life under a policy of equal rights, he is making a big mistake." He made it even clearer later, in a statement to the senate: "There is no place for him in the European community above the level of certain forms of labor... for that reason it is of no avail for him to receive a training which has as its aims absorption in the European community... Until now he has been subject to a school system which drew him away from his own country and misled him by showing him the green pastures of European society in which he is not allowed to graze."

Bantu education was an adjunct to the Bantustan homelands. Verwoerd wanted the natives to "stand with both feet in the reserves," enjoying an education that should have its roots "in the spirit and being of Bantu society."

Ruth was one of many teachers who left the profession at the introduction of Bantu schooling. Some tried to work in the informal, illegal ANC schools that began to be set up as alternatives. Ruth went to a private secretarial college to retrain as a shorthand-typist.

> Freed from her professional obligations, she had begun attending ANC branch meetings with her husband, near their home in Orlando. Mandela would be at the meetings too, in spite of the banning order that was supposed to prevent his attendance. He and Ruth first met at the home of friends and later she saw him at branch meetings.
>
> She had a friend working at Mandela & Tambo who planned to return to her medical studies. Her friend had told her it was a very busy firm where you worked from the moment you took your seat and the phones started ringing. The clients who came in needed a lot of help because they did not always understand much. It was the type of job you could only succeed in if you loved and cared for your people and for their liberation. As Ruth said, it was not the type of job you took for money.
>
> Ruth went for an interview with Mandela and got the job. She soon found out how right her friend had been. "When you got in the doorway the phone was always already ringing so you literally had to run to the switchboard and sit down." When she climbed the stairs to open up the office in the morning, she would often have to thread her way through a throng of potential customers.
>
> "Mandela & Tambo, good morning!" she would chirrup, answering the phone.
>
> "Mandela & Tambo, good morning!"
>
> Her friends used to tease her for that.

At this point, Ruth's husband moved to Durban to work as a health inspector, but came home now and again. This has led to some speculation. "Mandela was my boss, my leader, my friend," Ruth said, adding, perhaps just a little disingenuously, "I never know what people want me to say."

A journalist had asked her once if they'd had a relationship. "He said that Nelson Mandela was a ladies' man and he wanted me to say I was one of the ladies." Ruth thought the journalist was rude and took exception to his questions. Being dignified, reserved and in her early eighties did not make her very open, or easy to approach with inquiries on personal matters, but I persevered. She wagged a finger at my tape recorder and asked me to turn it off.

The Defiance Campaign was not just the defining moment in the development of the ANC as a mass movement; it was also the point at which women began to take a more prominent role. There was some history of protest by women against earlier pass restrictions and since 1943 there had been an ANC Women's League but it had never held a national conference and struggled to make its mark. This all changed in the Defiance Campaign, when there were designated "women's days" and thousands of women volunteered to take part.

Sisulu's wife, Albertina, was disappointed to find that, when she turned up to volunteer at the ANC offices in Johannesburg, she was turned away because her husband, at that stage, was already in jail. Many married women, such as Albertina and Mandela's wife, Evelyn, were the mainstays of their families, and it was not so easy for them to make the same sacrifices as their husbands, even when extended family networks were there to help. For many years they were cast in a supporting role. The Women's League was best known for catering and fund-raising.

However, the 1952 campaign, and the greater emphasis on the multiracial alliance, led to the founding of FEDSAW, the Federation of South African Women. Many joined from the Women's League and it was designed, from the start, to take a more radical and active stance, especially against the pass laws and against Bantu education. Many women tried to set up informal schools. Albertina Sisulu organized one at her home as the ANC tried to encourage a boycott of the state's "Bantu" schools.

One of the founders of FEDSAW was Lilian Ngoyi who had been inspired to go into politics by the Defiance Campaign, which prompted her to join the ANC Women's League. Ngoyi had no education but was a vibrant, animated, effervescent character who quickly discovered a natural gift for rousing oratory.

"When she spoke from a platform she could do as she wished with her audience; they laughed with her, wept with her," said the white activist Helen Joseph. They became close friends and now share the same burial plot.

Ngoyi spoke for many when she said, "My womb is shaken when they speak of Bantu Education." She was then already in her forties, living in Orlando as a widow with two children while also working as a seamstress in a clothing factory.

Fatima Meer remembered her as a strong attractive woman who'd had a rough personal life. Meer guessed that Mandela was attracted to her strength and leadership.

By 1953, Fatima and her husband, Ismail, were living in a two-roomed house on Umgeni Road in Durban and remembered meeting Mandela's wife Evelyn for the first time when she came to Durban from Johannesburg to study midwifery at the King Edward VII Hospital.

Quite why Evelyn went to Durban rather than remain in Johannesburg is not entirely explained. By now she and Mandela had a second son, Makgatho, born in August 1950, and an established life in Orlando. It seems in part that she was motivated by personal advancement, as Fatima Meer explains that Evelyn had always wanted to become a midwife but marriage, babies and lack of finances had conspired to deny her the opportunity. By 1953, things were becoming easier: Thembi was six and had started school; Makgatho was a toddler; and Mandela's mother was there to help. Mandela had started work as an attorney and the family was no longer entirely dependent on her income.

Evelyn was, she would say, happy in her love for her husband and secure in his love for her. Fatima recalled that Mandela and Ismail Meer would come to collect Evelyn from the nurses' quarters, where she was staying at the hospital in Durban, and take her back to the Meers' home for snatched weekends with her husband. The Meers would give up their one bedroom to offer their guests some privacy.

Fatima Meer also remembered those weekends when she found Evelyn "a simple person, a good person, nice, very sociable; very easy to get to know and very easygoing." Meer believed Evelyn had come to Durban because that was the only place she could get access to the course she wanted to take. She was not aware of any tension between Evelyn and Mandela; it seemed an easy-going relationship.

There must have been something still between them, as Evelyn was pregnant again when she returned to Orlando towards the end of 1953. Their daughter, born the following year, was named Makaziwe, in tribute to the daughter who had died in infancy five years earlier. Evelyn said that her early Anglican beliefs had weakened during her marriage. According to her, her husband was not keen on religion, but she had prayed to God for a daughter to replace the one she had lost. The arrival of the second Makaziwe restored her faith and brought her back into the Anglican Church. She gave Makaziwe a second name, Phumla, meaning God Has Rested Her Soul.

Returning to Johannesburg from Durban, Evelyn initially believed she was returning to a committed marriage and family, but gradually began to realize that things had changed. Mandela started staying out all night, claiming he was on ANC business.

When she questioned him about it, he said, "No policeman asks questions like you."

Seven

MANDELA'S AUTOBIOGRAPHY, *Long Walk to Freedom*, was first published in 1994, the year he became president of South Africa, but it owes its origins to events on Robben Island twenty years earlier. It was in 1975 that his friend, comrade and fellow inmate, Ahmed Kathrada, first proposed a memoir to boost the growing cult of Mandela and inject some momentum into the stagnating battle against apartheid. Mandela would be sixty in 1978 and the plan was to publish the book to mark his birthday. It would have to be written in secret on the island prison and concealed until it could be smuggled out by Mac Maharaj, who was about to be released.

The enterprise began in typically disciplined fashion. Mandela would write during the night in his usual longhand and each morning he would pass the finished pages to Mac, who would copy them in miniature using a ballpoint pen to reduce the text, so that he could get between eight and ten pages of Mandela's expansive script onto one side of business paper. Mac would leave margins around the lines and cut the sheets into strips for ready concealment. Mac would then hand Mandela's original to Kathrada, who would read it and make notes, then pass it on to Walter Sisulu, who would do the same. Mac would raise queries with Mandela too, and corrections would be noted on both the original and the copy.

Mac eventually left Robben Island with sixty sheets of miniaturized text sealed inside the covers of books, notebooks and a large clip file. The originals were buried in tins in the Robben Island garden, where some were discovered by warders in 1978. Mandela, Kathrada and Sisulu suffered a lengthy loss of privileges as a punishment.

Meanwhile, the memoir, as written on Robben Island, was never published. So far as can be ascertained, it was not much supported by Oliver Tambo, the ANC leader in exile, and it was also criticized by the Slovos and the Indian leader Dr. Yusuf Dadoo. Mac says Joe Slovo did not feel it gave him due credit for his role in starting the military wing known as MK. The actual copy that Mac smuggled out was lost and has never been found. An incomplete version that had been put on disks was used by Mandela as the basis for *Long Walk*.

When Mac was asked whether readers would have learned much about the real Mandela if they had been able to read the original, he said, no, that was part of the problem: Mandela's reluctance to give of himself. Mac used to joke with him about that on Robben Island.

"Madiba, this thing is shaping up to be a fucking political instrument."

Mandela asked, what do you want?

Mac said, this is not a biography—the man, the person has got to come out.

Mandela said, what do you mean?

Mac said, well, your wife, what kind of persona was she, what did you do after your first marriage broke up, before it broke up?

Mandela said, no, I refuse.

Mac pushed him.

Mandela said, no, I don't discuss that with young boys like you. (Mac was then around forty.)

Mac went to Sisulu and appealed to him to intervene, saying, he's got to start talking, he's got to write about it. After some discussion Sisulu agreed that Mac had a point and went to speak to Mandela.

A few nights later Mandela wrote a note to Mac that said, in that section where I write about the break-up of my marriage, insert the following sentence: "And then I led a thoroughly immoral life."

Mac read the note the following morning and went to Mandela.

What is this?

Mandela said, what I told you.

Mac said, I want to know who you led this immoral life with.

No, said Mandela, I won't talk about that.

The reader will search high and low in *Long Walk to Freedom* for any reference to Mandela's immorality. History had been revised. By the time it was published, he was on his way to becoming South Africa's first democratically elected leader and was already widely regarded as the world's elder statesman—perhaps our greatest living beacon of moral authority. An admission of immorality might have detracted, or at the very least distracted, from his heroic reputation—especially when the "immorality" began during and not after the end of his marriage.

There is no doubt that this reputation has at times been irksome to members of his family. It is possible to detect in the newspaper interview that Evelyn, his first wife, gave to Fred Bridgland after Mandela's release in 1990 a desire to do him in, by telling the world what he was really like, about the Mandela she had known, as opposed to the Mandela of near sanctity that he had by that time become in the popular imagination.

Evelyn would certainly be justified in thinking that *Long Walk* was rather more generous and forgiving towards Mandela than it was to her. Understandably, perhaps, the book is neither open nor honest about these highly sensitive, personal matters.

Evelyn later told Fatima Meer and Fred Bridgland that after her return from Durban, Mandela started bringing home his secretary, who would follow him into the bedroom. Although the secretary was unnamed, it was in fact Ruth Mompati. There was also an unidentified other. That other "other woman" was Lilian Ngoyi.

> I could not put my finger on it at first, nobody would tell me. Then the gossip reached me. Nelson, I was told, was having an affair with

a woman member of the ANC. I knew this woman and admired and liked her. She visited us often and I got on well with her. I did not believe the rumor at first but, unable to bear it, I turned to Nelson. Who else could I have turned to? He was angry that I questioned his fidelity. The woman [Ngoyi] was an important ANC leader and that was all there was to it, he said. The gossip continued and there were those who tried to console me by claiming he was bewitched.

There was also another woman [Mompati] and this one started coming home, walking into our bedroom, following him to the bathroom. What was this all about I demanded and declared that I would not allow it, that if she had work to discuss with him she should confine it to his office and not pursue my husband into my house in that unseemly manner.

In fact, as she explained to Bridgland, Evelyn warned Mandela she would pour boiling water over Ruth Mompati if she came to the house again. "Nelson was enraged. He moved his bed into the sitting room. He grew increasingly cold and distant. I was desperate. I went to see Walter. I don't think he ever forgave me for that. He accused me of broadcasting our problems. He stopped eating at home and took his washing to a cousin. Then he started eating out."

Evelyn told Meer that when the rift between her and Mandela became public, she was embarrassed and deeply pained. His sister Leabie and his mother Nosekeni, who were both still living with them, were also feeling the strain. Nosekeni went back to the Transkei. Several people have reported that she was very disapproving of her son's conduct at this time.

I don't think she could bear to see our family torn apart. I went to see my brother who was then living in Orlando East. He spoke to Nelson and then said to me, "If the man has stopped loving you, if someone or something has killed that love, there is nothing you or anyone can do about it." I realized for the first time I was losing my

> man if I hadn't lost him already. Yet I made one last attempt. I went to see Kaiser Matanzima. Nelson admired him and was close to him. If Nelson would listen to anyone I thought he would listen to him. KD spoke to Nelson but Nelson's reply was that he no longer loved me.

Leabie spoke to Fatima Meer, telling her how painful it was to see the two people they respected turning on each other. "It was like the ground below us was breaking and we were falling." Leabie believed it was *ubuthi*, as she called black magic.

There is some dovetailing between the events as Evelyn described them and the brief account given by Mandela in his memoir. He identified the period after the birth of the second Makaziwe in 1954 as the moment when Evelyn first turned to the Jehovah's Witnesses, although it appears that in fact what she experienced was a revival of her allegiance to the Anglican Church. "Whether this was due to some dissatisfaction with her life at the time I do not know," he says, never, of course, intimating that his own infidelities might have had something to do with it.

Evelyn began handing out the Jehovah's Witness magazine, *The Watchtower*, and wanted Mandela to commit to God too, he writes. They often argued about her desire to live back in the Transkei. It was her faith versus his struggle and he was becoming convinced the marriage "was no longer tenable." They struggled for the "hearts and minds" of the children too. While she sought to enroll them in her own beliefs, Mandela had decorated the house with photographs of political heroes and heroic events—Roosevelt, Churchill, Stalin, Gandhi and the 1917 storming of the Winter Palace. He taught the two boys about politics, prompting Thembi to join the Junior ANC, the Pioneers.

Mandela acknowledges that he went out early and came home late but suggests that Evelyn was wrong in suspecting he was seeing other women. "Time after time I would explain what meeting I was at, why I was there and what was discussed. But she was not convinced." In 1955 she told him he must choose—his marriage or the ANC.

He concedes that he was short with Walter, who tried to speak to him on the subject, and suggests that Evelyn's brother Sam was pompous and touchy when he also raised it. According to Evelyn, Mandela was angry with her for "broadcasting their problems" to friends and family.

Finally, says Mandela, two weeks after he was arrested in December 1956—at the start of what would become the four-year cycle of the Treason Trial, when he and scores of others were accused of plotting to overthrow the government—he returned home on bail to find the house empty and silent. Evelyn had left with the children and had even taken the curtains. "For some reason," he writes in his book, "I found this small detail shattering."

But so far as I can tell, that scene never happened and, in any event, is far from being the whole story. Evelyn told Fatima Meer that the brooding silence between them had come to a head over a row involving Thembi's small daily allowance. It all exploded in a torrent of words.

Meer has said she believed the neighbors had once had to intervene when there was "friction" between Evelyn and Mandela. Evelyn told Bridgland about the row over Thembi. "Later after another argument Mandela grabbed me by the throat and shook me and shouted at me. Some elderly neighbors heard the noise and came in to break it up."

According to Evelyn, Mandela told her he was leaving and wanted a divorce. It is part of first-family legend that she eventually found out Mandela was divorcing her only when it was reported in the newspapers.

In fact, it was Evelyn who first began divorce proceedings against Mandela before he later took action against her. Two files have been released that comprise the record of their divorce. They contain a statement made by Evelyn, known as a Particulars of Claim, in support of her petition for separation lodged at the Native Divorce Court in May 1956. She alleged that Mandela had assaulted her on a succession of occasions over the previous ten months.

The allegations were never tested in court and Mandela made it clear he would have denied them, but they are dated and described in some detail in the files of Case 342. Mandela told Richard Stengel that Evelyn had distorted things in interviews. He denied the allegations outright to Ahmed Kathrada and said he had only ever held her when she threatened him with a red hot poker, and then only to twist it from her hand.

Surprisingly, Evelyn made no allegation of adultery against Mandela when she filed her petition. Her reasons could be many: perhaps she lacked conclusive evidence; or perhaps her lawyers advised her that the allegations she had to make were serious enough on their own to make her case. She claimed he had deserted her in February 1955 and had since "cruelly ill treated and repeatedly assaulted her."

In July 1955, four weeks after the historic Freedom Charter conference in Kliptown, Evelyn alleged that Mandela had assaulted her by "hitting her with his fists in her face and knocking her to the ground and causing serious injury to her eye." He had again assaulted her by "striking" her in August 1955 and then had hit her once more, in October 1955.

In February 1956, according to Evelyn's statement, Mandela had given her a week to leave the house. When she refused,

> he wrongfully, unlawfully and maliciously assaulted her by hitting her with his fists and choking her and attempting to kill her by strangling her. The Defendant [Mandela] further inflicted severe injuries to Plaintiff's face and throat during the said assault. Plaintiff was compelled to take refuge with her neighbors who, after some difficulty, obtained possession of her clothing as at the time of the assault Plaintiff was dressed only in her nightdress.

In March 1956, Evelyn's petition claimed, he had ordered her to leave the house and

> threatened to kill her with an axe unless she left the house, in consequence of which Plaintiff [Evelyn] was compelled to take refuge with her neighbours and thereafter went to live with her brother, Samuel Mase at no 5818 Orlando East.

> By reason of the aforesaid assaults and unlawful conduct of the Defendant [Mandela] further cohabitation and living with him has become dangerous and intolerable and Defendant has moreover, refused to allow Plaintiff to return to the common home or to have access to her children.

When she ran to the neighbors on March 25, 1956, she had left the children behind. She was now seeking custody, a formal separation and maintenance of £50 a month for her and the children, plus the return of the furniture and other goods she had contributed to the marriage.

Mandela responded with his own petition that August—he had Nat Bregman as his attorney and Joe Slovo as his advocate—in which he denied the allegations of assault. He also announced his intention to defend the action, together with a counter-claim for custody and "restitution of conjugal rights failing which a decree of divorce on the grounds of Respondent's malicious desertion." He claimed Evelyn had left him to live with her brother, taking with her their daughter Makaziwe. She had, he said, agreed to allow the boys to remain with him but had since changed her mind and taken them from him.

He argued that they would be better off with him as he had his mother at home to look after them while Evelyn worked full time. He had seen the children several times at her brother's home, looking dirty and neglected. Samuel's house he described as "congested" enough already, with his wife and their four children, forcing Mandela's own three children to share beds and couches with their cousins. Besides, the boys' school—he seemed to be making no claim to Makaziwe—the Seventh Day Adventist School, was just 150 yards away from his home at number 8115, while it was two miles away from Evelyn in Orlando East.

A hearing was arranged and postponed. Then a second date was put back until November, with a provisional arrangement for Mandela to retain custody of the two boys, and give access to Evelyn. On November 5, 1956, Evelyn withdrew the case altogether, with no explanation given. That date was a month before Mandela's Treason Trial arrest, and six weeks before his release on bail when, according to *Long Walk to Freedom*, he came home and found Evelyn gone and the curtains removed. In actual fact, she had finally left in the middle of the night, in March, ten months earlier, presumably leaving the curtains behind. It is just possible she went back and took the curtains down while he was remanded in custody.

As to why she withdrew the petition for separation, there could be any number of reasons. It seems most likely, however, that the couple simply reached an understanding. It appears that Evelyn was hoping for reconciliation. The allegations of violence might have been politically awkward for him, as he was achieving ever greater public prominence as an ANC leader. In those days, divorce hearings could be reported and no doubt he must have been keen to keep certain details out of the court and the press.

In the account she gave to Fatima Meer, Evelyn made no mention of domestic violence nor of her petition for separation, but instead related that Mandela had come to see her at her brother's home, asking her to forget about the incident and return to number 8115. She did so, as she was desperate to save the marriage even if it meant clutching at straws.

> But there was no thawing of the freeze. That chilling, unbearable distance continued. I realised that I had no marriage. I moved out and went to live in the nurses' quarters. Perhaps I imagined that if I reversed the situation, and I walked out, instead of him, he would come to his senses and that he needed me to keep the family together. If that was my feeling I was totally mistaken. Nelson never came to see me at the nurses' home nor did he send any messages to me. I had initiated the separation. A year later I moved in with my brother.
>
> Perhaps if I had been patient, if I had tried to understand why he had turned away from me, perhaps things may have been different and I would still be his wife. He was the only man I ever loved. He was a wonderful husband and a wonderful father.

It is hard to reconcile Evelyn's account with the dates in her court claim. Perhaps she moved back home around the time the petition was withdrawn. She suggests she lived at the nurses' residence for a year, but there is no mention of this in the court papers so it seems likely that the move came later, in 1956, as the "unbearable distance" continued.

Evelyn went on to explain to Meer that the children would go back and forth between their two homes. Maki—the shortening of Makaziwe—was only two and too young to understand or be affected, and Makgatho at five was young enough not to be bothered. But Thembi, she says, was older—he was ten in 1956—and suffered intensely.

Mandela agrees, in *Long Walk*, that Thembi was troubled, describing how he lost interest in studies and became withdrawn. "Man, that chap is quiet," Sisulu had once said to Mandela of Thembi after taking him out. Mandela said Thembi took to wearing his father's clothes sometimes after the separation as "they gave him some kind of attachment to his too often distant father." Thembi was eventually sent away to school, opening up an even greater distance between them. In her book, Meer refers to the frost that settled in Thembi's heart after his father had parted from his mother. At the time of his death in a car crash in 1969, Thembi had never visited his father on Robben Island, even though he was living just a boat-ride away in Cape Town. He had become a "bootlegger" there, in the words of his daughter Ndileka, running a shebeen together with Ndileka's mother, Thoko, selling alcohol illegally to Cape Coloreds on 7th Avenue in the southern suburb of Retreat.

Not one of Mandela's children from either marriage ever followed him into politics, though both Zenani and Zindzi, his daughters with Winnie, have played a political role, making statements and public appearances from time to time.

Meanwhile, Evelyn was continuing to delude herself, she said, that since there were children from the marriage, there was still a marriage. That changed, a year or more later, when a friend pointed to a notice in a paper. "Your husband is divorcing you," said the friend.

Evelyn said she had heard "vaguely" that Mandela was dating a social worker from Baragwanath Hospital but had thought it was just one more woman whom he would discard as he had the others. She went to see a lawyer and did not oppose the divorce, she said. "Since Nelson had never paid *lobola* he did not have rights over the children according to African law. That distressed him very much and he arranged with my brother to pay the *lobola* and my brother said since he had ill-treated me, he would accept it. So Nelson did one of those rare things, paid *lobola* after the marriage had ended. In fact he *lobola*'d the children."

When the divorce was finally granted and the marriage was formally dissolved on March 19, 1958, it was at the instigation of Mandela. He had begun the second round of proceedings on January 2, 1958 and a summons was served on Evelyn a week later, on January 9, leaving only a slender window of opportunity for her to have read in the newspapers that she was being divorced, as she later used to tell her family had been the case.

The terms of the settlement, which were promptly agreed with no exchange of accusations this time, gave Evelyn custody of all three children, with Mandela contributing £15 a month to cover their maintenance and their school fees. Evelyn kept the property that she had contributed to number 8115: two wardrobes, two beds, one dressing table, a dining-room suite of table, six chairs and a sideboard, a radio and a coal stove. Mandela also agreed to give her a lump sum of £50 and the title deeds to a plot of land he had bought back in Umtata. He was allowed to keep the sitting-room suite and "kitchen scheme" (all except the coal stove) at number 8115.

By then, Mandela had met Winnie and was keen to clear his way to marry her. Winnie has said she was too shy to ask Mandela about his marital status. He was practically twice her age, an elder, and it wasn't easy to have personal conversations with him. For a long time it has generally been believed, as some members of the first family believed, that Winnie must have been the cause of the breakdown of Evelyn's marriage to Mandela. From the start, Winnie faced some resistance, even hostility, from some members of Mandela's family and friends, because of her supposed role, and perhaps for other reasons too, such as her enviable youth and exceptional beauty. It was true that falling in love with her had prompted

Mandela to seek a divorce, but of course his marriage was long over by then.

The dates that mark the beginnings of Mandela's relationship with Winnie are still not entirely clear. Winnie said that Mandela and Evelyn had been separated for five years by the time they got together, which is not true; it was more a matter of months than years, but still, it is clear there was a gap. Winnie was not to blame.

In *Long Walk*, Mandela does refer to Evelyn as a very good woman, charming, strong and faithful and a fine mother. Mac Maharaj, who probably knows Mandela as well as anyone left alive, says he was always keen to speak of Evelyn afterwards with respect. When Mac told me this, I felt bound to point out that he had not apparently always treated her with respect at the time. Of course, it is entirely possible that Evelyn imagined all those stories of assault, out of malice or revenge, but the fact that she alluded to them outside the divorce papers, and that the neighbors were involved, lends at least some credence to her account.

Then too, remember, they are only one side of the story.

You may wonder whether Mandela ever reflected on those events afterwards and felt guilty about his treatment of his first wife. He has certainly expressed his guilt in recent years at not being there to support Winnie. Fatima Meer, who even at eighty remained an eloquent and incisive observer of her old friend, conceded she was not sure that he would feel guilty, as he was self-righteous, a patriarch—very patriarchal, in fact—so he wouldn't feel guilty. He would always feel, in general terms, that he had done what he had to do and what was right at the time. She did not see him as a man to have regrets.

Fatima Meer put it neatly in her book *Higher than Hope* when she described Mandela as extremely attractive to women and easily tempted by them. In her view, he probably did not believe a passing liaison would place his marriage in jeopardy, perhaps expecting Evelyn to be more tolerant and less puritanical. But those extramarital relationships cannot be dismissed as "passing liaisons" that a wife—even a 1950s wife—should have tolerated. Though Ruth Mompati denied it, people close to Mandela are confident in asserting that she had a child by Mandela during this period.

In 2008, when Mompati was interviewed in her home town of Vryburg, the town where she was then mayor, she was as wise and friendly as any octogenarian you could wish to meet, so it is not easy to now take issue with her. Nor is it the intention here to cast her as some kind of scarlet woman or mere decorative appendage to the Mandela story. She fought long and loyally for the ANC and made great personal sacrifices, leaving her home, her family and her children to go underground and be among the first women to receive military training for Umkhonto we Sizwe. In 1962 she went to the Soviet Union for training in the handling of guns and bombs to become a military instructor. As a result she did not see her two sons again for eight years and hated the fact that white South Africa had forced her to choose between her children and the ANC. Then both children died only months apart in terrible and unrelated circumstances.

However, once the difficult subject was raised and the tape recorder was turned off, she said that she knew people would say she had had a son with Mandela, but it was disrespectful to her then husband—they separated not long after—as well as simply not true. She did not, in so many words, deny the affair but she clearly stated that there had been no son. But there are others who are equally positive that there was a child. In fact, there is reliable oral testimony that Ruth used to speak about it herself—almost boastfully, it was said—while she was living in exile in the Zambian capital of Lusaka.

A significant clue may be buried in her own narrative of how her two sons died, four months apart, either side of Christmas in 1997. Her youngest son, Tebogo, had a brain tumor and died not long before his fortieth birthday. Her older son, Mompati Neo Matsoane, asphyxiated suddenly. Although not epileptic, he choked to death on his tongue.

His mother was then the South African ambassador to Switzerland. When she had spoken to him on the phone that final afternoon, they had been laughing and he had said, "Oh, you don't know how handsome your son is this afternoon." Ruth guessed he was up to some mischief. He died that evening. Unlike the death of his brother, the passing of Mompati Neo Matsoane was announced in a press release issued by the ANC. That I believe was the son of Mandela, born April 25, 1955, died January 7, 1998. Apparently he looked like his father.

The story is known within Mandela's family and there are suspicions there could be other women and half-siblings as well. Mandela's daughter Zindzi has said that she thought of her father as a player when he was younger, with his cigarettes and his snappy dress, and she could certainly testify to his charm, as that was the first thing that struck her about him when they first met during her adolescence on Robben Island.

Zindzi recalled an earlier Winnie in her father's life, Winnie Matyolo, who is mentioned in Mandela's memoir as one of his first girlfriends. The daughter of the Methodist minister by the Great Place in Mqhekezweni, she had loved Mandela then in spite of her older sister who ridiculed him as a barbarian, backward boy who was still learning to eat with a knife and fork. In his memoir Mandela had said they eventually went their different ways and drifted apart, but Winnie Toni (her married name) gave an interview to a Johannesburg newspaper, describing how they had reignited their relationship. This occurred after they were both married, when she was living in Johannesburg working as a nurse, and they would "steal moments of togetherness" when Evelyn was not around. Evidently, he had smuggled her into number 8115 during his first marriage.

There were other women too, some with names that do not appear elsewhere in the record, stories that hinted at, rather than proved, affairs. At an ANC conference around 1953/54, a beautiful activist, Mrs. Malopo, was accused of not supporting the regional Transvaal president—Mandela—and stood up to deny the charge: "The president has been at my home," she said, "and not only that, *evile a siya katiba yahae ko lapen*" (he left his hat at my house). It seems unlikely that anyone in the hall doubted the meaning of the euphemism. The Transvaal president must have had some public reputation in those days as a "ladies' man."

Amina Cachalia describes Mandela as very tight-lipped about these matters even now and says that, in spite of their sixty years of friendship, he will not readily spill the beans. "If I ask him he denies it. When I asked him about Ruth he said, 'Don't talk nonsense.' And about Lilian, 'You were my friend, she was my friend.'

It has been said, though not by Amina, that he had a "glad eye" for her too, although their friendship had always remained just that. She was another beauty, politically active and married, of course, to Mandela's close comrade, Yusuf Cachalia. She and Mandela would go around together sometimes. He once took her out to lunch in the suburbs near Bloemfontein and when they got there Lilian Ngoyi turned up too. Amina had the strongest feeling that the two of them had arranged the lunch and that Mandela had only brought Amina along as cover for the set-up. In spite of his tight-lipped denials, Amina has no doubt he had quite a few girlfriends.

It appears that there was an occasion when Evelyn had returned home to find Lilian Ngoyi having supper with Mandela at their table. Unsurprisingly, Evelyn had been very upset. Ngoyi, according to Fatima Meer, was not among those beautiful women whom Mandela liked to charm and be around. Meer had seen her once with Mandela and he had introduced them to each other. Meer had observed that Ngoyi was a strong, attractive woman, but not feminine like, say, Winnie Madikizela-Mandela. "Lilian wasn't very feminine, she was statuesque, one might say manly."

Fortunately it seems that, even for Mandela, looks weren't everything. Ahmed Kathrada recollected having been at his Kholvad House flat once with Mandela when they had a visit from a striking young woman, a *Drum* "cover girl"—*Drum* being the vibrant African magazine that captured and reflected the culture and politics of black South Africa in the 1950s. Kathrada struggled now to remember her name, but he had not forgotten how he and Mandela had been aroused by her presence, and then crestfallen when she asked them who the singer was that they were listening to on the gramophone. Anyone who didn't recognize the baritone Paul Robeson was unworthy of their attention.

Another bikini-clad *Drum* girl was the singer and actress Dolly Rathebe who came from Sophiatown. She was a contemporary of Miriam Makeba and her band, the Skylarks. When Abigail Kubeka, a former member of the Skylarks, was asked in 2008 about Dolly and Mandela, she leaned out of her chair at her elegant Soweto home, pretended to lift up the edge of the carpet and sweep that story underneath it, putting her finger to her lips and saying "Sssh." That was all she was prepared to say.

It appears that Dolly, who was ten years younger than Mandela, was among those who carried a torch for Mandela through the prison years and had hopes he might come to them after his release in 1990. By then, most people assumed, the game was up for Winnie, and Mandela would be looking elsewhere for comfort and companionship. Although Amina never said this herself, others suggested that she also might have had hopes in that direction. Evelyn's granddaughter, Ndileka, noted that her grandmother never remarried, rarely spoke ill of Mandela, and always affirmed her continuing love for him. So perhaps she too was hopeful. Dolly, Amina, Evelyn and who knows who else? However, Mandela thwarted and surprised them all when he divorced Winnie and married Graca Machel instead, on his eightieth birthday in July 1998.

A couple of years after Mandela's release, Evelyn married a fellow Jehovah's Witness, Simon Rakeepile, and became a Pioneer, creating an extra level of devotion to her religion. Her new husband was insistent that she took his surname, which, her family surmised, was because he did not want to live in the shadow of that "big name." Both Dolly and Evelyn died in 2004.

No one could ever accuse Mandela of not having lived life to the full. With hindsight, it rather looks as if he outgrew Evelyn as he soared professionally and politically, ascending to the peak of his young powers just as their marriage fell apart.

There are those who will say that, far from being chauvinistic, Mandela was an early advocate of feminism, supporting the development of women in politics and encouraging the increasingly active role that many women began to play in the struggle. Others noted his weakness for women, the particular way he would respond to them, especially the pretty ones, the manner in which he liked to charm them and, of course, the ways in which they used to fall at his feet.

Whilst he might have left behind the rural African society of his origins, he carried with him the values of that world, which had its roots deeply embedded in hundreds of years of patriarchy, where men were free to have as many wives as they could afford and often sat around talking under the trees or in the kraal, making the big decisions, while the women did all the hard work. Men who were not tribal chiefs were still chiefs in their own domain and had been raised from boyhood to assume the superior role, while the girls stayed close to their mothers. No wonder the ANC Women's League took charge of catering in the early days.

Mandela was a revolutionary in many ways, but not as a husband or father. He had ingrained conservative values that he could not shrug off, even as he sought to bring down the government and smash the apartheid state. Ruth Mompati took exception to Mandela being described as old-fashioned. "Old-fashioned, what does that mean?" She said the ANC had championed women's rights from 1953.

But Amina Cachalia recalled that Winnie had once said to her that if Mandela had not gone to prison, if he had been home all the time, they would have been long divorced because of his old-fashioned habits.

As he rose steadily in the world, Mandela was still getting letters from the Bantu Welfare Trust, asking for its debt to be honored. In their fourteenth debt-chasing letter to Mandela in March 1954, signed by one Quintin Whyte, the Trust reminded him of its loan in 1947 and his undertaking to commence repayments in 1948:

> On looking through our records I find that no payments have been made against your account and the secretary informs me that he has written several letters to you without avail. As this loan has been outstanding for a considerable time I am writing to inform you that unless we receive a substantial sum which will bring your

> monthly undertaking up to date in accordance with the terms of your contract with the trustees I shall be obliged to call upon your sureties to honor their undertaking.
>
> These loans are made on the understanding that they will be repaid so as to enable the trustees to continue assisting other deserving Africans and your failure to repay your loan makes this impossible.

That was the last letter in the file, but Mandela did not finally begin repaying the Trust for a further six months, when he sent them £15 in September 1954, eight years after the first loan, with a promise to pay off the rest in installments. In his covering letter, he wrote: "May I be permitted to convey my sincere appreciation of assistance given to me by your Trust."

In spite of his failure to pay his debt in a timely manner, he was in so many ways a controlled and disciplined character. Mandela did not gamble, as far as is known, only ever drank a little and is supposed to have admitted he had tried *dagga*—marijuana—just the once. He didn't like it and never touched it again because he said it made him feel silly. He still had a weakness for a little pomp and flash, however.

Makgatho remembered for Fatima Meer the impact of his father's presence as he would set off from Orlando for the city in his big car, which Mandela called his "colossal Oldsmobile." Two-tone green, it was smooth on its springs over the bumps of the unmade township roads, a rare and extravagant vehicle outside the white suburbs. "He was very popular where we lived. When he would leave the house and get into our car the children would come running and they would shout 'Afrika! Mayibuye!' We would feel so proud. Daddy would explain the meaning of the words to us. He would tell us that they were not just words, that when the people called 'Mayibuye! iAfrika' they meant that they wanted what was theirs returned to them." Come back, Africa.

Adelaide Joseph and her husband, who would ride in that car too in Orlando, also saw how everyone knew and greeted its driver. Adelaide would say that was when she first knew for certain he would become a leader. There was something about him that made you want to look at him.

There went Mandela, heading for the city in his car. He must be wearing a suit from Alfred Khan, the Jewish tailor. Kathrada had seen him wearing those smart clothes, especially that brass-buttoned, double-breasted jacket with the ANC emblem sewn into the breast pocket. Thinking he must have one for himself, he had demanded of Mandela, where did you get that jacket, and then gone and ordered it without regard to the cost. He nearly choked when he went to collect it, the price was so high. Who did Mandela think he was, Harry Oppenheimer? Khan made Oppenheimer's suits too.

And of course, even when he put on the blazer, Kathrada could still never be quite so smart as his friend as no one wore clothes quite like Mandela. They were part of his ego and his self-respect, as George Bizos sees it. When Mandela was imprisoned he wore regulation shorts like all the other African prisoners. When asked whether those shorts had a great impact on Mandela's dignity, Bizos conjures a rich phrase in reply: "No, nothing is going to deprive Mandela of his evaluation of himself."

He was, as others saw him, tall and handsome, beautifully dressed, dapper but not dandy, stately, particular about himself, smiling often and listening carefully, usually cool and controlled in the face of provocation, but not always. There is a story Winnie once related to Paul Joseph of Mandela stopping his car to assist a white woman whose own car had stalled. Telling her to get back in, he pushed the car back to life, at which the woman offered Mandela a sixpence. He smiled and refused, then refused again when she tried to insist. Finally she got annoyed. "What do you want, a shilling?" But still Mandela stayed calm.

Then one night in the early 1950s he was out in a car with Sisulu and Amina Cachalias' husband, Yusuf. Some or all of them had been drinking. They saw two white Afrikaners beating up an African man with a horse and cart. They stopped and got out, all fired up and ready for a fight, but the situation was defused and they were denied the ruckus.

Some people won't hear a word against him; he is truly sanctified in their eyes. One such is AnnMarie Wolpe, who says there are no "buts" with Mandela, no "He's lovely, but..." "He is just totally charming, a man of stature, a very impressive person. I was very conscious of that," says AnnMarie. "I liked him enormously, enormously."

At dinner at the Wolpes' one night he said he had just been turned over by ruffians—*tsotsis*—on the road in Orlando, who had knocked him to the ground and started to beat him. Suddenly they stopped. "Wait! It's Mandela." They lifted him up and dusted him off and sent him on his way with a profound apology. Mandela told the Wolpes that night, privately, that he feared personal violence and especially feared the threat of it in prison.

The drive to the city in the big car usually came to an end at his law office, which opened for business at eight, invariably with a queue, closed at five, and often shut down for an hour in the middle of the day when the two partners stepped out for a lunchtime curry. A fresh queue sometimes formed during that hour. On one occasion Jack Hodgson was waiting impatiently outside when Ruth Mompati returned from her own lunch. He was quite angry.

Have a heart, Ruth said, we must have our break.

Mandela was an effective lawyer, according to Bizos, if not a lawyer's lawyer. That would be Tambo, who was reserved and careful, where Mandela was flamboyant, a showman in the court. The courtroom was the last refuge of the oppressed, where there could still be some hope of a fair hearing and a black lawyer could be the pride of his black client, playing his small part in attempting to stem the overwhelming tide of prosecutions linked to the apartheid laws.

That did not mean, of course, that the court did not harbor racists. One weekend Mandela called on Bizos for his advice as an advocate, visiting him at a house in a white suburb where Bizos was staying as a guest. Even the act of arriving at this house was fraught, as Mandela shocked the children of the host family by parking his sedan on their drive and knocking at their front door.

He told Bizos about the provincial magistrate, Dormehl, who had clearly taken exception to having a black lawyer in his courtroom. He seemed determined to make life as difficult for Mandela as possible. Mandela was famous enough by then and everyone involved in the law knew who he was. But, as Bizos observed, magistrates and prosecutors had a tendency to see Mandela as "uppity." His customary self-confidence and commanding presence rubbed up against the white folks' idea of how a black man should behave.

The Dormehl had been absurdly hostile to Mandela, threatening to jail him for impertinence and refusing to proceed with the case until his certificate—his right to appear in court—was produced.

Mandela returned with the document and the case commenced, only for Dormehl to begin interrupting his attempts at cross-examining witnesses with objections that his questions were irrelevant. Mandela was icy but calm and persisted with the procedure, which merely further inflamed Dormehl. The magistrate now dropped all the usual niceties of the court and started barking at Mandela, not using his name, but by calling him, "Hey, you." "Hey, you, sit down," he had ordered Mandela as he tried to ask a question. "Hey, you, I have warned you before." They broke for lunch and after the adjournment the face-off continued as Mandela stood once more to question the witness.

"Hey, you, sit down." Mandela sat down. Dormehl ordered the witness to leave the box. Mandela stood to say he was not finished. "Hey, you, I told you to sit down. Will you sit down. I will count up to three and if you are still standing when I have counted three I will call the orderly to eject you from the court. One... two... three... Get this man out.

Only when the orderly was practically on top of him did Mandela sit down. He said he would have to withdraw from the case, but his client, a clerk accused of minor corruption, refused to let him and insisted he wanted only Mandela. After talking to Bizos, Mandela agreed to petition the Supreme Court for the magistrate to withdraw as he had objected to having a black attorney in his court.

By the time the case came before a Supreme Court judge, Dormehl had presented an affidavit, along with supporting statements from others, to the effect that he had appeared in court with his hands in his pockets and behaved in such an arrogant manner that the magistrate could not believe he was an attorney. The affidavit did not refer to Mandela by name but called him *die natural*, "the native." The judge ordered the magistrate to step down.

Bizos tried to persuade Mandela to return to Kempton Park to see his moment of triumph but Mandela was not interested, now that he had the result. Justice had prevailed, as it sometimes did.

Ruth Mompati remembered another occasion, closer to home, when an African bellboy in a hotel came into the office at Chancellor House, looking for Mandela's help. He had embarked on a relationship with the hotel manager, his white female employer, and they used to have sex together in her room when he had finished his shift. Another member of the staff had told the police, who had burst into the room and arrested the bellboy under the Immorality Act of 1950. They had not arrested the white woman.

Immediately after he was freed on bail, the bellboy came to Mandela & Tambo for help. He was very worried and had every right to be. As Ruth knew, it would be a difficult case to defend. Ruth watched Mandela and the bellboy leave the office and head across the street to the magistrates' building, a journey of no more than a few yards. Ten minutes later they were back. So soon? They had won. Mandela had succeeded in having the case thrown out. The white woman had helped by refusing to give evidence.

A future comrade, Denis Goldberg, would listen to Mandela recounting tales from the bench too, and was not always happy with what he heard. Mandela told him how he had defended a black man accused of rape by cross-examining his alleged white victim in deliberate detail. Was there penetration, did he remove your underwear, did he actually put his penis into your vagina? She couldn't answer because he was a black lawyer and for a racist white woman that would be a renewed violation. Mandela's client went free. Goldberg said he didn't know whether to applaud his legal skills or not.

Mandela knew what he was doing, playing on racial fears and turning a trial into a show with his theatrics, often for the benefit of the township crowd in the gallery who sometimes came to court to see the fun. Once, while defending an African servant accused of stealing her employer's clothes, Mandela hooked a pair of allegedly purloined panties on the tip of his pencil and held them up for the white woman to see. "Madam, are these yours?" he asked. She was too embarrassed to say yes and the case was dismissed.

As time went on, politics began to dominate Mandela and Tambo's lives. It became harder and harder for their firm to operate effectively as lawyers and they started to struggle financially. Bizos remembered Tambo expressing his concerns to him in the late 1950s, worrying about Mandela's recent expensive wedding to Winnie.

"I don't know how he could afford it..."

Eight

IT IS DIFFICULT to grasp the impact upon Mandela of the strain that he must surely have been under in the mid-1950s as he negotiated his way, daily, through an ever more complicated existence. He shared with all African men the many routine humiliating and emasculating strictures of apartheid and, additionally, contended with the renewed banning orders that were designed to further inhibit him. Mandela also faced a mounting burden of responsibilities. He was juggling a young family and an unhappy marriage with a hectic love life; he had his own business in which the hours were long, the work was constant, and he would never get to the end of the queue of needy clients; he had a modest budget with which to finance his expensive tastes; he was deeply immersed in the leadership of the ANC, shaping policy, attending meetings, making speeches, campaigning on any number of different causes from the forced removals of black families from Sophiatown to the bus boycotts in Alexandra, from the resistance to Bantu education to the growing clamor for a Freedom Charter.

White radicals were becoming increasingly important to the struggle and the Africanists resented their presence. Cracks were opening up in the movement and Mandela was trapped in the middle. He was among a small group of senior ANC figures who had transformed a lobby group into a mass movement and, as a consequence, now carried the hopes and expectations of the general population of black Africans. The threat of jail was never far away. He often sounds overheated in his speeches during this period. One can only wonder how he managed to fit everything in.

Late in 1953 the ANC was still transfixed by its success in the Defiance Campaign and the resulting "upsurge in national consciousness," as Mandela called it in his speech as Transvaal president to the regional conference. Since he was banned from addressing crowds, the speech had to be read for him. He said he and others who were banned had been "exiled from their own people."

The speech is remembered now for its introduction of the so-called M-Plan, the Mandela-Plan, which has since been trumpeted as a means of enabling the ANC to operate underground. With its leaders banned, and the Communist Party banned too, it seemed only a matter of time before the ANC itself would also be shut down. The M-Plan appeared to offer the basis by which the ANC could function as a secret organization with cells.

In fact, the M-Plan was not so much a secret strategy as an attempt to create a tighter and more efficient ANC in keeping with the swelling ranks of its membership. The "cells" were part of that trickle-down structure, with cell-stewards in charge of cell-blocks, which were in fact simply several houses grouped together on a street. Streets were managed by wards and wards by branches with a central committee at the top. The center wanted closer control of the regions, which did not always fall into line. The regions, in turn, were suspicious of the plan. The concentration of power would create dictators, they said.

Mandela's speech envisaged the plan as the machinery for a modern ANC, rather than one still reliant on "public meetings and printed circulars." He urged local action and called, "Never surrender!" He spoke of the enemy within, the "shady characters, political clowns, place-seekers, splitters, saboteurs, agents-provocateurs, informers and policemen" who masqueraded as committed activists but were simply trying to create internal strife to wreck the Congress. His obsession with those "politically backward individuals" in this keynote speech was testimony to the internal divisions that continued to hinder the struggle. Old-guard conservatives did not always appreciate the upstart Mandela and his continuing drive to militancy.

He assured the speech its place in ANC history when he quoted—but did not attribute to its source—something he had read by the Indian leader, Jawaharlal Nehru:

> You can see that there is no easy walk to freedom anywhere and many of us will have to pass through the valley of the shadow [of death] again and again before we reach the mountain tops of our desires. Dangers and difficulties have not deterred us in the past, they will not frighten us now. But we must be prepared for them, like men in business who do not waste energy in vain talk or idle action. The way of preparation [for action] lies in our rooting out all impurity and indiscipline from our organization and making it the bright and shining instrument that will cleave its way to [Africa's] freedom.

"No easy walk" was Nehru's phrase, not Mandela's. He later told writer Anthony Sampson that he had often used the writings of Nehru without acknowledging them, which, he said, "was a silly thing to do." But, he added, "when there is a paucity of views in you, you are inclined to do just that."

The ANC adopted the M-Plan but always struggled to implement it. At least the plan offered some platform for continuity when the ANC was finally banned, after the Sharpeville massacre in March 1960.

Meanwhile, some eight years ahead of the formation of Umkhonto we Sizwe (MK), the military arm of the ANC, Mandela was already anticipating the necessity for armed conflict. At the time of his "no easy walk" speech, Walter Sisulu was on a mission abroad, with fellow ANC communist Duma Nokwe. They were part of a broader South African delegation to the Youth and Student Festival in Bucharest, the capital of the communist state of Romania. Sisulu was looking to establish links with other African activists, as well as communists in Eastern Europe and elsewhere. The trip took Sisulu to London en route to Romania and then on to Moscow, where he took the trans-Siberian train to Peking.

Mandela had supported Sisulu's trip and persuaded Chief Luthuli to agree to it. Before Sisulu left, Mandela had asked his friend to take soundings in China on their support for a turn to violence by the ANC. "Though we believed in the policy of non-violence we knew in our hearts it wasn't going to be a satisfactory answer," Sisulu has said of this early development. When he asked the Chinese, they warned him that revolution was a very serious affair, not to be embarked on lightly. The ANC should not be misled by slogans, he was told, and should analyze the situation carefully before reaching a decision.

Sisulu discovered on his return that there was quite widespread speculation that he had been abroad to try to procure arms, so evidently Mandela's militaristic intentions were already getting some circulation. Also, back in South Africa, he and Mandela faced hostility from those who suspected Mandela of misusing funds to finance the trip without authorization. Chief Luthuli claimed he had never been asked to authorize it, which did not help.

The anti-left element within the ANC was finding its focus within the Orlando Youth League, which would be the wellspring later of the breakaway Pan-Africanist Congress. They resented all white, Indian, and communist involvement. One of the most vocal supporters of "Africa for the Africans" was the League's newly elected chairman, Potlako Leballo, who satirized the ANC left-wingers as "Eastern functionaries" and nicknamed Sisulu "Mao Tse Tung."

A quiet, studious young academic from Fort Hare named Robert Sobukwe had also started to influence the Orlando Youth Leaguers. Although not flamboyant or commanding in the style of Mandela, he was thoughtful, eloquent and inspiring. He had begun lecturing at Wits, traveling daily to the city from the township on the train, where he would often be mocked—ironically, for an Africanist—by other young men, gangsters known as *tsotsis* mainly, for being a "black white man" (an echo of Mandela "the black Englishman") because of his tweed jacket, gray trousers and briefcase.

Sobukwe was just one of the hardcore Africanists who were still pushing the 1949 Programme of Action that had stimulated the revival of the ANC five years earlier and been trumpeted, by Mandela among others, as a nationalist doctrine. But Mandela had moved on; the struggle had moved with him and the clock could not be turned back. That was essentially what concerned the Africanists and many others within the ANC: the all too eager willingness to forge interracial alliances. The conservative forces of the apartheid government feared a communist takeover—as did the Africanists.

There was by now an alliance of congresses (not yet formally a Congress Alliance) in which the ANC and the Indian Congress were joined by SACTU—the South African Congress of Trade Unions, the newly formed SACPO—the South African Colored People's Organisation, and the Congress of Democrats, where many of Mandela's friends and comrades—the Bernsteins, the Slovos, the Fischers, the Wolpes, the Hodgsons and so on—among the white communist community could find a legitimate political home.

Mandela addressed the Congress of Democrats' meeting in Johannesburg in late 1953, defying his ban to tell the whites that for Africans to submit to *baasskap* (the policy of absolute domination of the native peoples by white settlers in South Africa) would be not only to surrender their honor but also to betray the trust and confidence placed upon them by the ANC. "Our first concern is to strengthen the congresses and to make them in theory and in fact the fighting organization of the people. If we carry out this task earnestly and diligently the clique of small and frightened men that rule South Africa today will never be permitted to work their wicked ways upon us. If we make action the cornerstone of our political activities the people of South Africa will ultimately achieve victory and finally defeat the racial policies of the government."

This alliance of congresses might have been a step too far for the Youth Leaguers of Orlando, but it was not broad enough for others. To those who complained of Sisulu's trip to the Eastern bloc, Mandela had pointed out that no one objected when Professor Matthews had gone off to America, to teach and to absorb himself in the history of the civil rights struggle.

Matthews, or the Prof, as he was widely known, had returned brimming with energy for campaigns that would reach out across the country and "capture the imagination" of the people. During a meeting at his home near Fort Hare in Alice in the eastern Cape, the idea had emerged of a nationwide appeal for a vision of a future South Africa. A series of public meetings would culminate in a national convention to approve a manifesto for the way forward. That was the origins of the Congress of the People (COP) and the Freedom Charter. Even white Afrikaner racists would be asked to contribute.

Professor Matthews brought the idea to the organizers of the regional ANC conference in August 1953 and later drafted a memo to define more clearly his ambition for a "dream" of freedom for all, a blueprint for a democratic, non-racial South Africa. Oddly, he then took little or no further part in the exercise, never even laying eyes on the draft charter that was drawn up and failing to attend the conference. He claims in his memoir that he was too busy with other matters, taking over as acting principal at Fort Hare around this time, but others have suggested he felt sidelined and excluded from the process that he had set in motion.

The campaign fell into the hands of a National Action Council, which immediately offended the Africanists by being neither exclusively African nor giving sufficient prominence to the ANC. Indeed, their fears that the whites would take over, given half a chance, seems borne out by the way in which the charter was eventually drafted by Rusty Bernstein: the draft constitution for black rule in South Africa was authored by a white communist.

But first the raw material of the charter had to be collected. Here, too, Bernstein played a key role, writing the leaflet that became the nationwide call to participate, and in the process coining the phrase, "Let Us Speak of

Freedom!" This was a grass-roots action, as the leaflet circulated and "Freedom Volunteers" went out among the people at meetings and rallies, on street corners and from door to door, to collect their grievances, demands and wishes so that they could be fed into the creation of the charter. It was reported how they came "flooding into COP headquarters on sheets torn from exercise books, on little dog-eared scraps of paper, on slips torn from COP leaflets." Bernstein remembers that the fragments were all stuffed into an old cabin trunk while the council set about organizing the congress.

Alongside these council meetings, Mandela was also involved in the campaign against Bantu education, setting up informal schools and promoting a boycott against the new apartheid schools. Then too he was among those trying to defend Sophiatown against the government's plan to bulldoze its streets and turn it into a white suburb.

Sophiatown had risen to prominence as one of those overpopulated anomalous urban locations, a "freehold township" where black people could actually own properties. Perversely, it had been built at the turn of the century as a white suburb, by a developer named Herman Tobiansky who had christened the network of streets after his own family (his wife's name was Sophia).

Not long after whites had begun buying the first stands (plots), the town council decided to site the sewage works next door, so Tobiansky started selling stands to anyone who would buy them. All sorts of properties made of all sorts of materials, predominantly brick and corrugated iron, went up there, and for a while Sophiatown was truly multiracial with white families living among black, Indian and colored families. The whites soon started complaining of the social and moral dangers their children faced from the intermixing. While those claims were obviously false, the township genuinely posed health concerns: water wells were quickly contaminated by the sewage, and disease followed on the heels of overcrowding as stand owners sought to maximize their income by building "barracks" on their plots. One infamous stand—little bigger than an ordinary housing plot—had sixty families living on it.

There was limited employment and not much money, so people cast around for alternative methods of making an income. Women took in washing or brewed beer; men turned to crime and formed gangs of pick-pockets, robbers, black marketeers and protection racketeers. Every street in Sophiatown had at least one gang and some, such as the Americans and the Berliners, became notorious far beyond the boundaries of Sophiatown. The gangsters lurked in the numerous shebeens, such as the 39 Steps, the Man in the Moon or the House of Truth, where they mingled with activists, musicians, writers and singers. Sometimes the gangsters helped themselves to the singers, literally, as they attempted to kidnap or carry off the likes of Miriam Makeba.

Abigail Kubeka, who sang with Makeba in the Skylarks, remembered that they often performed for free at fund-raisers for the ANC, perhaps at the Bantu Men's Social Centre, or even at the Odin Cinema in Sophiatown itself. Afterwards they would go on to the 39 Steps where the gangsters would buy them drinks and maybe ask them to sing, over and over again, the same song. They would do whatever the gangsters wanted, until they left at 5 a.m. and went to sleep nearby at the home of the Skylark who lived in Sophiatown.

Makeba also sang with the jazz vocal group, the Manhattan Brothers, before she stepped out on her own. The Brothers' Joe Mogotsi relates that they had once saved her from being taken by a gangster by saying they needed her up early for a rehearsal. Mogotsi claimed the gangsters' style and even their name had originated with the Brothers who invented their own American-influenced dress with tight, sharply creased trousers that were known as *tso*, as in "sharp," and so the trousers and the wearers came to be called *tsotsis*.

The jazz culture looked to America for its style but was distinctively African too, with songs performed in Xhosa, and lyrics that were often about love and lost romance but might also lament the laws of apartheid or mock its practitioners. One popular song, written by Vuyisile Mini who was later hanged for his role in MK, taunted PM Verwoerd, *Verwoerd Pasopa naants' indod' emnyama*, "look out, Verwoerd, here come the black people."

People called Sophiatown by its affectionate name, Koffi, and it was widely romanticized as a place of excitement and adventure, a melting pot for many cultures and an inspiration to writers and musicians. The shebeen was a place where you could drink away your dreams, as some did, such as the gifted *Drum* writer Bloke Modisane, while beyond the shebeen doors lay a grim, unlovely existence, hedged in by apartheid, poverty and the ever present threat of violence. At the Church of Christ the King—one of the few original buildings that still survives in Sophiatown—the much loved white priest, Trevor Huddleston, initiated a junior jazz band and gave a talented young boy, Hugh Masekela, the chance to play the trumpet that had been donated to him by Louis Armstrong.

Despite its vibrancy, Sophiatown was a slum and the political pressure to clear it was unrelenting. Even many of the 11,000 people who lived there wanted to live elsewhere but, for many years, the authorities had nowhere to relocate them to. It was the Group Areas Act of 1950 that marked the beginning of the end of Sophiatown. Residents would be removed to the southwestern townships, in particular Meadowlands, out beyond Orlando. By now, the destruction of Sophiatown had some appeal. It was a seat of trouble and resistance as well as an urban eyesore, a "black spot" on the landscape. The removals were set to begin in February 1955; the bulldozers would move in and the properties would be destroyed, with only the most basic compensation for the owners. A new white suburb would rise up, called Triomf.

The ANC was determined to stop the removals and Mandela was one of several leaders appointed to galvanize resistance. A "Let the People Speak Committee" was formed and there were weekly rallies in Freedom Square in Sophiatown. In March 1954, a full year before the eventual clearance, Mandela addressing a meeting:

> When the people rise and demand their freedom, heavens will reciprocate. The time is bound to come for action. What concerns the people of Sophiatown most is their removal from here... I will tell you that [Prime Minister] Malan has decided to remove you

without consulting any of your leaders. He will throw you in the open veld... We cannot avoid a major crisis... I know that when we are forced to the clash between the forces of liberation and fascists the forces of liberation will triumph. On that day all of us will be in Sophiatown... We know that there are many people and even educated Africans who are telling people that you are backwards and that the police and the army will crush you if you rise against them... there is nothing superior about the white man. He can be fought as he has been fought before... if we can stand together we can sweep everything before us.

This is the question you must ask yourself in Sophiatown. You must rally everybody and protect your families and property. I can speak on behalf of the leaders in this province, that on that day we will all be here. If you in Sophiatown can stand together against the government you cannot be removed. You have the support of the South African Indian Congress. The writing is on the wall when we will crush the forces of reaction and defend our houses and prevail over the forces of reaction.

Forty ycars later Mandela was giving a round of additional interviews to gather fresh material for his memoir. The interviewer was Ahmed Kathrada and Mandela told him about the failures of the Sophiatown campaign.

We held a series of meetings in Sophiatown every Sunday in which we tried to mobilize the community against removals and several of us, you see, appeared in those meetings—you appeared, I appeared, people like Trevor Huddleston, the chairman was Robert Resha, people like Walter, and we mobilized the people against these removals.

But of course we were against terrible odds because the government was saying, especially to the tenants and they fell for it, you are being exploited here by the owners and. property owners, we are moving you to a place where you will not live in such filthy conditions, where you are going to have your own house, your own garden.

And eventually this particular tactic beat us and because tenants were really being exploited and they were living under very overcrowded conditions of filth and squalor and eventually that beat us. But the issue here was one of not accepting the principle that blacks should have freehold rights. Especially in the urban areas that was the issue. And that is what we were really defending. Not the exploitation of people by the landlords, we were against that, but we were defending the principle.

As the date for the start of the removals approached, the campaign became more desperate for success. The ANC was committed to resisting the removals and now realized it faced a significant, humbling defeat.

The rhetoric became increasingly inflammatory and the slogan "over our dead bodies" gained currency. It did not take much to stir the angry young men of Sophiatown and the prospect of a bloodbath began to seem all too likely.

Mandela's own speechifying got the better of him one day—he was lucky Special Branch missed it—when he told the Freedom Square crowd to be prepared to use violence before long. He then pointed at a line of police and began singing an ANC song with the refrain, "There are our enemies." He was reprimanded by the ANC executive but he was not the only one anticipating or inciting violence.

It was the speech of another firebrand, Robert Resha, after the removals had begun that caused no end of trouble later. A bugging team in a room adjacent to ANC headquarters recorded Resha in May 1956 as he addressed a meeting, explaining to them what a volunteer was:

Volunteers are those people who do and die. Volunteers are those people who...when they are given leaflets to do they go out and distribute those leaflets...A volunteer is a person who is

> disciplined... When you are disciplined and you are told by the organization not to be violent, you must not be violent.
>
> If you are a true volunteer and you are called up to be violent you must be absolutely violent. You must murder. Murder! That is all.

Forced to defend the speech, Resha claimed his words were born in the rubble of Sophiatown, which was at the time in ruins, "like a bombed city." The ANC had succeeded in taking Sophiatown to the brink, but had no intention of tipping it over the edge, nor, really, any plan of what to do or where to go.

Sisulu remembered a meeting of senior figures from the various congresses at which the white communists Jack Hodgson and Cecil Williams had wanted to meet force with force, while others proposed putting up barricades. These ideas were dismissed as unrealistic and tempers became frayed with "personal insults of cowardice" being thrown around. The best the ANC could agree on was to offer alternative homes with ANC families to those who did not want to accept the government's flimsy new builds in Meadowlands.

"It was coming for sure, we all believed it," said the Sophiatown poet-gangster Don Mattera. The residents were waiting for the call to revolution from the ANC, but it never came. Instead, they were stood down by Joe Modise who confronted the crowd and told them that they were in no position to take on the army and the police.

As Anthony Sampson said, that did not deter the world's press from descending on Sophiatown at the beginning of February, hoping for some action. Sampson at first thought they might get their wish when he arrived at dawn to the sound of *tsotsis* hitting telegraph poles, the "battle cry of Sophiatown." But there were many hundreds of police on the streets and an emergency banning order had been issued by the minister of justice the day before. The minister said the police had reliable information that "the Natives in Sophiatown have in their possession a number of machine guns, revolvers, pistols, hand grenades, home-made rifles and home-made dynamite bombs."

If, indeed, they had assembled that sizeable an artillery, the people of Sophiatown never used it. The first 150 families went off without a fuss; the removals began and continued without any significant resistance. Eventually all the houses were emptied and the bulldozers moved in. Dr. Xuma's home and the Huddleston church were among the handful of sites left intact. Like a white flower, Triomf sprang up through the rubble. Fifty years later, Triomf is Sophiatown once again, in name if not yet in spirit, but any resident digging in his garden on a Sunday afternoon might chance across some bulldozed fragment from the ruins of the old township, that "black spot" that had been eradicated from the city.

The ANC's education boycott was no more of a success than the Sophiatown campaign, so hopes rested on the Congress of the People, which was set for two days in late June 1955. Each of the white political parties was invited to take part, the Nationalists included, but none accepted. The Liberals withdrew, apparently because they did not like the communist company they were keeping, though within the ANC there was the suspicion that, in fact, the Liberals' real problem was their reluctance to be led by black people.

The organizing council struggled to find a venue where all races could gather freely—no easy matter under apartheid—and finally had to accept the offer of a bumpy, makeshift soccer field with oil drums for goalposts on the outskirts of Orlando, in Kliptown. The site was cleared and a fence erected, enclosed with hessian sacking. Delegates had been appointed from all corners of the country and many hundreds arrived for the start of the two-day congress on June 25, 1955.

The trunk containing the people's messages had been opened just days before, as Rusty Bernstein was handed the task of hurriedly shaping the raw material into a draft charter for approval by the congress. Bernstein later described how volunteers helped him sift through and organize the thousands of messages, dividing them into individual piles based on themes such as labor, land, civil rights, votes, education, living standards... Some of those were then further divided into subgroups.

Many messages were simple demands, or statements that defied the categories: "freedom and equality," "justice for all," "no more racialism," "we're not moving," "life too heavy."

Bernstein recalled eventually being left alone with the scraps and giving them a last look through before returning them to the trunk. The trunk and its contents later vanished, and have never been traced. In their place came Bernstein's imaginative distillation of the themes, which he transformed into a draft charter, finally topped and tailed with an "oratorical flourish" that he came to regard as "considerably overblown."

Bernstein seems skeptical that anyone ever actually read and agreed the draft before it went to press in time for distribution at the conference. The historians Thomas Karis, Gwendolyn Carter and Gail Gerhart claim it was read by Mandela, Sisulu and Joe Matthews, son of the Prof, as members of the ANC working committee, while also suggesting it was by then too late to make changes as "thousands of copies had already been reproduced."

Professor Matthews was not alone in never seeing that draft. The ANC president was never shown it either. Chief Luthuli was banned and still back in Groutville, recuperating from the stroke he had suffered some weeks earlier. In earlier times, surely, such a vital paper could not simply have been printed and sent off without first being chewed over and put to the vote at executive committees and conferences of the ANC. The history of the creation of the Freedom Charter carried with it an unspoken sense that power was changing hands at this climactic moment; of Luthuli and Matthews stepping back, or being gently elbowed aside, while Tambo, Sisulu and Mandela came forward to take charge. It was the moment too that the alliance with white communists was set and sealed. Bernstein recalled the initial resistance he sensed from Tambo, whose faith did not favor communists, but they found common ground and became friends and colleagues.

Did the triumvirate ever stop to consider that truly bizarre, thoroughly awkward paradox: that it had taken a white comrade to articulate the hopes and dreams of a black nation? It seems likely at least that Mandela was alive to the political sensitivities. He must have known exactly who wrote the Freedom Charter, but in Mandela's memoir Bernstein's name does not figure in this context. Instead, he emphasizes that "the ANC branches contributed a great deal to the process of writing the charter" and that regional drafts were circulated for comments and questions before "the charter itself was drafted by a small committee of the National Action Council."

A committee of one, in fact.

Perhaps because he had never been consulted, Chief Luthuli did not mind acknowledging that the charter was open to criticism. "It is by no means a perfect document. But its motive must be understood, as must the deep yearning for security and human dignity from which it springs."

Not many of the principal players were actually on the platform at Kliptown—they were all banned from speaking in public. Even the man who had written the charter, Rusty Bernstein, was banned, along with his wife. They traveled out to the site and stood on a pile of coal against the fence for a while, peering over, until they attracted the attention of the police and went home. Mandela and Sisulu stood on the roof of a shop owned by Jada, an Indian friend of Sisulu. Later, Mandela put on a modest disguise and walked a little among the crowds. Bernstein had found the spectacle disappointing—drawing fewer people than he had anticipated after all those months of planning—but Mandela thought it was impressive, "both serious and festive," as the reading and approving of the charter took place alongside songs and speeches, with food being served and children dancing.

There was a "peace pavilion" and many stalls with banners, posters and leaflets bearing the slogans of various shades of left-wing political opinion. Even the Africanists had set up there, selling a special edition of their publication, *The Africanist*. Potlako Leballo later claimed he had got into a physical fight while he was at the congress.

The police were present and kept a careful note of proceedings, useful later as a record of what occurred. After the opening frills, the Freedom Charter was read, first in Zulu, then in Sotho and finally in English. Each section was presented as a resolution to be adopted, punctuated by many cries and choruses of *Mayibuye! Mayibuye!* And *Afrika! Afrika!* The police record noted that when people were not addressing the crowd in English, they were "speaking in native."

At some point, late in the proceedings, the records tell us that the organizers announced that there were 2,884 delegates, comprising 2,186 African, 320 Indian, 230 colored and 112 white people. That actually totals 2,848, so perhaps a digit got transposed somewhere along the way. Of that total, 721 were women.

On the second day, the police were still standing around, taking notes and photographs, creating an intimidating presence. Yusuf Cachalia turned to Sisulu and said, "The dogs just stand there and do nothing." At that precise moment the police barged forward, swarming onto the platform or lining up before it with their peaked, strapped hats and their Sten guns. An officer announced over the microphone that treason was suspected. Special Branch officers set about seizing every document they could find, including a treasonous sign saying, "Comrades. Tea 3d. Tea and sandwich 6d."

The organizers of the congress had been unable to arrange any lighting, but the police set up hurricane lamps over table tops and began collecting thc names and address of everyone there, as darkness fell. The crowd began singing the African anthem. Mandela briefly considered offering himself for arrest but thought better of it and slipped away back to the city.

The Congress of the People took its rightful place as a defining moment in the story of the struggle and the bumpy field at Kliptown was consecrated. It became ANC "holy ground," as Robert Resha had called it in a closing speech on the last day. The date of June 26th would be Freedom Day forever more. Although the congress adopted the Freedom Charter, that did not quell the fierce controversies that swirled around the document and surged into the breach it created in the movement, from the opening words onwards:

"We, the people of South Africa," Bernstein had written, "declare for all our country and the world to know, that South Africa belongs to all who live in it, black and white, and that no government can justly claim authority unless it is based on the will of the people."

In the mid-1950s, when a tiny minority of whites still held the black majority in their grip, the notion of togetherness was perhaps too woolly, resembling more the loose thinking of a white liberal perhaps than a black political party at the forefront of the struggle. For the Africanists, the country did not belong to all who lived in it; it belonged to black Africans and the whites were there only as uninvited guests. That was the single, central, unpalatable proposition at the heart of the charter, for the nationalists of the Orlando Youth League as well as for many others who were not necessarily so extreme as the Africanists, but who still wanted their country to themselves or were suspicious of white people and did not feel they shared in that country too.

The resonance of the Freedom Charter has never gone away. Many, maybe even most, black South Africans—Mandela's own daughter Zindzi declared herself among them—felt at times resentful after 1990 that the (relatively) peaceful transition to majority rule had denied them the fight they had hoped for, their moment of revenge, the chance to "drive the white people into the sea."

There is no doubt that Mandela's triumph was to avoid a bloodbath. By his own example of forgiveness and reconciliation, he had shown a way forward from a seemingly impossible position. In those later years he embraced that aspect of the Freedom Charter and drove it forward into government by the sheer strength of his character and his moral authority. He held the line between hope and chaos.

As its end-of-year conference approached, the ANC was tying itself in knots, trying to find a way to adopt the Freedom Charter—a stable door closing after a bolted horse, if ever there was—without usurping the voice of the people that had spoken at Kliptown.

Bernstein said he had tried his best to keep his own prejudices out of the charter but there were still a number of left-wing values embedded in it that were equally difficult to manage. No one was going to argue with "The people shall govern" or "The people shall share in the country's wealth"—they were vague enough and desirable enough aims to please everyone—but the prospect of mass nationalization envisaged by the phrase "the mineral wealth beneath the soil, the banks and monopoly industry shall be transferred to the ownership of the people as a whole" sounded distinctly Marxist.

Perhaps to avoid an immediate and lasting schism, the ANC put off adopting the charter to a special conference the following April. Nevertheless, the controversy still dominated the annual gathering in December 1955, where Africanists were outraged at the suppression of a letter from the former ANC president, Dr. Xuma, that complained that the new leadership was forgetting its old values and was too quick to join with other races who could more easily be "making sacrifices themselves." The ANC was losing its identity, Xuma wrote. ANC officials refused to read out the whole letter as it would be too damaging. Africanists tried to shout down speakers, calling out, "Africa for the Africans!"

There was even greater scuffling and squabbling at the special conference four months later, in April 1956, in Orlando when the Freedom Charter was finally adopted. One of Mandela's former close colleagues on the ANCYL, A. P. Mda, wrote a bitter article for *The Africanist*, reminding readers of what they had once stood for, as "from our inception we saw the burning need of ridding the ANC of foreign domination." He said, "No white man has ever impressed us."

He was way out of step with Mandela, who sought to explain the Freedom Charter in an article of his own, published in *Liberation* in mid-1956. He was asked to "correct the assumption that the Freedom Charter was the embryo of a socialist state." And, indeed, he did stress that trade and private enterprise would flourish while explaining that "the Charter strikes a fatal blow at the financial and gold-mining monopolies that have for centuries plundered the country and condemned its people to servitude."

Others were poring over the Freedom Charter too, finding treason in its terms and in the unuttered idea that its aims could be achieved only by violence against the state. Before the year was out, the Police would be ready to act.

* * *

In late 1955, with life in full swirl, Mandela's latest ban expired. He suddenly decided to take a trip home to the eastern Cape, saying it was to assess the political state of play in the provinces, but also to reconnect with the countryside and his old friends and comrades. Some city friends gathered at number 8115 to mark the occasion and he was seen off, after midnight, by a song from Duma Nowke. Mandela liked driving into the dawn and often adopted that time of departure. Perhaps also it was a tactic to avoid the attention of the police. The car radio was tuned to Radio Bantu and the popular show *Rediffusion Service*, which played songs from Miriam Makeba, Dolly Rathebe, Dorothy Masuku and "the smooth sound of the Manhattan Brothers." The African music went straight to his heart, he said.

He drove through Natal into Durban, stopping for meetings, and then southwards following the line of the coast before turning inland towards Umtata and his former family home at Qunu where he visited his mother, Nosekeni.

He had not been home for many years, although his mother had been staying with him in Orlando periodically since the late 1940s. As Evelyn had claimed, Mandela's mother had returned home because of the domestic unpleasantness at number 8115.

In Mandela's memoir, his arrival at his mother's home is recorded as if it were a reunion following many years apart. He describes how he felt guilty seeing her poor and alone, and tried to persuade her to come back to Johannesburg, but she refused and swore that she would not leave the countryside she loved. But Mandla, the son of Makgatho, argued this could not be correct as Nosekeni often went and stayed with Mandela in Johannesburg. Mandla speculated that her refusal to leave Qunu may have been a gesture of disapproval, because of his conduct towards Evelyn. Perhaps, in fact, he had gone there to try to persuade his mother to return, as he needed her help with childcare. On the other hand, it was also the case that he had not made much effort to visit his mother while she was in Qunu. According to Evelyn, Nosekeni missed her son. Mandela said he had not been to Qunu for thirteen years, but it may well have been his first trip back there since he had run away in 1941. He had left on a wrong note, as Mandla put it. The idea was also expressed in simple, traditional terms by Mandela's cousin Sitsheketshe. He said it was true that Mandela had not returned home for a long time, which was not right because as a man you worked for your family, you went to work and then you came back to your family.

Mandela recalls in his memoir that he neither hugged nor kissed his mother. "That was not our custom," he said. Others in his family have noted his difficulty with being physically demonstrative. It is said that he appeared to find it easier to embrace a stranger than to express physical affection with one of his own family. During the additional interviews he conducted with Ahmed Kathrada, Mandela elaborated on the question of custom, saying that it had been his practice in the past "not to kiss your mother and so on," but he had got used to it now and would do it with family, though it was not something he was raised to do. He conceded that he had tended to neglect his family, something that really only changed when Winnie came along and made him do things differently. Previously he would send home an occasional lump sum with "one of our fellows who was going down home." Winnie had told him, no, that's not the correct way, because his mother just used that money and finished it. A regular payment was better.

When he arrived in Qunu it was already night and his mother was asleep. She woke up and at first looked as if she was seeing a ghost, he writes. "And, to show the conditions under which she lived, she got up and whilst I was talking to her she got stuck into the groceries. I brought some chicken for her and fruit and other pieces of meat and sugar, tea. I bought a stove for her, you know, brought paraffin with me, and milk. As she was talking to me she got up and started lighting the stove, preparing tea for herself and, I don't know, the way she was eating, you see, I didn't think there would be space for the tea." What Mandela may have been describing was seeing his mother so hungry that she gorged herself on the food and it made him uncomfortable, perhaps even embarrassed, as he sat watching her.

He spent a couple of weeks in the area, moving between Qunu, Umtata and Mqhekezweni where he was reunited with the wife of Jongintaba who had been like a mother to him after he left his own mother in Qunu. He felt renewed affection for his past but also sensed the ways in which he had moved on and embraced new ideas while others had stayed put. He was glad he had not returned there, as his cousin Matanzima had urged him to do, after graduation twelve years earlier.

Matanzima—whom Mandela knew as Daliwonga—was immersed in the new Bantu Authority that would soon be established in Umtata, with Matanzima at its head. Mandela, of course, was profoundly opposed to these government-imposed pretend-parliaments, and he and his cousin would never be reconciled because of them, even though their family ties kept them close. When they debated the Bantustans, Mandela hoped to persuade his cousin to resist them, but Matanzima explained how he planned to use them to restore the status of his own royal house, which had been destroyed by the British many years earlier. He too wanted freedom, but found common ground with the government that it was achievable through "separate development." Matanzima believed the ANC could bring only bloodshed and bitterness. They ended up talking until dawn without ever shifting their positions. Mandela felt grief for the "loss" of his former mentor.

He continued his journey, driving west to Cape Town via Port Elizabeth, where he met Govan Mbeki for the first time. He was then still running a co-operative store but was about to have a change of career and begin work as an editor at the left publication *New Age*. People would be suspicious, later, that Govan had seemed to ascend so rapidly within the ANC, without ever paying his due in terms of bannings and arrests. He could also be fierce and disagreeable.

Mandela was in Cape Town in late September when the police launched a widespread series of raids and arrests under the Suppression of Communism Act. He was heading up the steps of the *New Age* offices when he heard the police moving around inside and turned away to avoid being arrested himself. He would not be so lucky next time.

He returned to Johannesburg and a renewed banning order. By now it was 1956 and his wife Evelyn was petitioning for a separation.

Elsewhere in the city a young woman was about to start work as the first black pediatric medical social worker at Baragwanath Hospital near Orlando. She would commute daily by bus from the Helping Hand hostel where she lived, downtown. Sometimes she would be waiting a while by the hospital bus stop. Soon Mandela would notice her there as he drove past, be drawn to her beauty, as others were. The young woman claimed not to know she was beautiful. No one had ever mentioned it to Winnie Madikizela back in Bizana in the eastern Cape.

Nine

ACCORDING TO WINNIE Madikizela-Mandela, she was a country girl from Pondoland who knew nothing of the big city when she arrived there for the first time in 1953, round about the age of eighteen. She had never seen a train before she boarded the one that took her to Johannesburg, entrusted by her father into the care of some men he knew, illiterate tribesmen in traditional dress who were on their way to work in the mines. Her home, her entire horizon, was the one-street village of Bizana and she had previously only ever left it to go to Shawbury High School, a few hours away in Qumbu.

It was at Shawbury that she had first heard of the fighting in Johannesburg and the leaders who were inspiring people to protest. One of them was Oliver Tambo, who also came from Bizana. Another was Nelson Mandela, a name that meant nothing to Winnie. She herself had been caught up in a student rebellion at Shawbury, the small beginnings of her own political awareness.

She had the teachings of her paternal grandmother, too, who was bitter at the way white people had barged into Pondoland and taken over the region—including the trading store her grandmother had run. Her grandmother had been horrified at some of their habits. Normal people went to the toilet in the forest, but not whites. They went to the toilet in their houses. Can you imagine! She gave them a special name, meaning People Who Toilet Inside Their Own House.

Winnie's mother, Gertrude, who had died when Winnie was ten, had been a teacher, like Winnie's father. Gertrude's mother-in-law resented her for being light-skinned, and she disparaged her own grandchildren as being related to those whites. She could be cruel, whipping their ankles with her stick, but Winnie and her siblings loved her anyway, in spite of that piercing pain.

Winnie's father, Columbus, had been strict. He later became an entrepreneur but was then the head of the local school. His family treated him at home just as they would at school, standing if he came into the kitchen while their mother was preparing a meal and not sitting in his presence. Winnie did not have a home life where her parents got down and played games with her. He wouldn't hug his children, but he would stroke them sometimes and talk to them with a wise air. He was old-fashioned in some ways and a modernizer in others—not unlike Mandela perhaps—as he had rejected the role of chief, preferring instead to be the school principal, while encouraging independence in his daughter, whom he had named Winifred because he admired the industrious ways of the Germans, and Nomzamo, which meant One Who Will Endure in the Face of Trials.

It was Columbus who had identified the caring nature of his daughter, seeing her bring home local children who needed support with school fees. He would always help them but he dissuaded her from an early ambition to be a doctor because, he said, she would only be treating people for money. If she really wanted to help people, Columbus advised Winnie, she ought to become a social worker.

Many fathers would have wanted to keep their daughters close, pending a suitable marriage, but Columbus found Winnie a place far away where she could continue her education. Her grandmother, she says, was only too glad to be rid of her. The Jan Hofmeyr School of Social Work had been operating out of the Bantu Men's Social Centre in Johannesburg since the early 1940s. The first graduation ceremony had been held there in 1943.

When Winnie stepped off the train at the city's Park Station in 1953, she hoisted her suitcase on to her head, carrying it down the platform as she was used to transporting containers of water from the river back home, balanced with the aid of coiled cloth. She had been warned about the city *tsotsis* and didn't dare carry the case in her hand for fear it would be snatched.

She could not miss the look of horror in the face of the white woman, the wife of the school's Professor Hough, who was waiting to meet her. If she had not already felt like a naive girl from the country, that look would have done it for her. She was taken to stay at a hostel on Hans Street, the Helping Hand for Native Girls, where she soon befriended another resident, Adelaide Tsukudu, and found that she was dating her "brother" from Bizana, Oliver Tambo. Adelaide and Winnie shared a room together and often wore one another's clothes.

Esme Matshikiza, whose husband Todd was a well-known jazz musician and composer, had herself graduated from the Hofmeyr School and would pass Winnie sometimes on the way to work, noting how her style of dress, even the way she carried her bag, marked her out as a girl from the backwoods. She would see Winnie occasionally at BMSC dances, often with a young man, Barney Sampson, whom Winnie dated for a while. Barney would be dancing with exuberance, smiling all over his face with pleasure at being with this country beauty. Later, when Winnie became a social worker too, she and Esme would sometimes have professional meetings to discuss cases and Esme would be most impressed by how serious and particular Winnie was.

Winnie's course at the Jan Hofmeyr School was somewhat removed from contemporary social work training. She studied all the things one might expect, such as problems of family life, public health problems and administration, personal health and hygiene, law and social legislation and modern penology. But in addition there was native administration, biblical introduction and Christian social teachings (Winnie had been raised as Methodist by her fanatically religious mother), folk dancing, storytelling, PE and, for all women students, those two essential prerequisites for good social work intervention: cookery and needlework.

For practical experience during her course Winnie returned to the eastern Cape where she took a three-month internship collecting case studies. While she was going out and about, she came across the local chief, Mandela's cousin, K. D. Matanzima. She made such an impression on him that without ever asking her whether she liked him or not, he decided she would make a good wife and sent a deputation to her father to open negotiations for her hand in marriage.

Her father wanted to know what was going on. Who were these people? He sent the deputation away and said he would wait to hear from Winnie. A more traditional father might have been flattered by the approach and might not even have bothered to consult his daughter. Winnie could only tell him that while she had been practicing in this chief's area he had taken an interest in her but there was no relationship between them. From Matanzima's perspective, his conduct was perfectly normal and customary. However, Winnie knew he had wives already and had no intention of becoming wife number three or five, or whatever it was.

She returned to Johannesburg, graduated and started work at Baragwanath Hospital while continuing to reside at the Helping Hand. One day, in 1956, Winnie was at Park Station with Adelaide to meet Oliver Tambo. As they sat in the car a tall man came up whom Tambo introduced as his partner in his law firm. The two men talked for a while about legal matters. That was the first time Winnie met Mandela. Nothing came of the meeting.

Winnie used to catch a morning bus to Baragwanath and would wait at the bus stop on the other side of Park Station. She often saw Mandela, driving past, either picking up somebody or dropping them off—she never knew who or which it was. She was unaware whether he noticed her or not (he would later say he had) and didn't check to see whether he was looking her way as she always had her nose in a book. She especially liked reading biographies.

Once, her bus was late. She was standing there waiting when Mandela pulled up and offered her a lift, which she accepted. He dropped her at the hospital. Still nothing further happened between them and perhaps never would have done, if it had not been for a bizarre encounter some time later.

Out of the blue, K. D. Matanzima wrote to her at the Helping Hand hostel to say he was coming to Johannesburg to visit a relative and wanted to see her at an address in Orlando. It was clear to Winnie that Matanzima still wanted her for a wife. She resolved to go to the house in Orlando to refuse him and settle the matter. When she knocked at the door, she nearly fell backwards when it was opened by Mandela. The house was number 8115. Mandela was startled when he saw her. Matanzima had told him he was expecting a visitor but without saying who it was. Winnie was embarrassed and so too, it seemed, were the two men. Everyone sat awkwardly through a hurried meal, no one able to say anything, before Winnie was taken back to the hostel by a driver.

She met Matanzima the following evening at the home of another of his relatives in Killarney. There she told him politely that she would not become his wife. It seemed to her that he had never been turned down before.

Seeing her at his home must have triggered something in Mandela as he called her at the hospital soon after and asked whether she would meet him to discuss something in relation to the Treason Trial. Winnie said Mandela did not pick her up himself from the hostel but sent his comrade, Joe Matthews, instead. In fact he never came to the hostel, she could not say why. Joe Matthews was younger, she said, so perhaps that was more comfortable for Mandela. It was a girls' hostel and Winnie herself was still young, perhaps twenty-one at the time, while Mandela was approaching forty. He was like an elder, so she called him Tata.

Joe Matthews collected her in Mandela's Oldsmobile and took her to the law offices where she sat while Mandela finished his work. She would learn subsequently to sit quietly with a book in the waiting room, elbow to elbow with clients. That first day she was nervous, the country girl with this famous man she had heard about at school, who was even a patron of the Jan Hofmeyr School of Social Work. They drove out past the hospital into the veld and went for a walk. If she had been a city girl she might have worn sneakers but instead she wore sandals. When the strap broke, he took her hand to steady her, as a father might a daughter, according to Winnie.

Mandela was smarter then, smarter than the man people knew later, she said. He was young and energetic. He was serious, humane, kind, gentle, compassionate. Not once did Winnie ever see him charging clients, for whom life was vicious. Winnie could see that, even though Mandela thought social work far inferior to the world of the law, he had some of the instincts of the social worker. Mandela would sit patiently, listening to each of his clients and their individual concerns; no problem was too small to solve.

He invited Winnie during their date to become involved in organizing the Treason Trial fund-raiser, which she did, along with Ruth Mompati and one other. The function was held at the Bantu Men's Social Centre, with a performance by the Manhattan Brothers. There was trouble at some point between some gangsters and the bullets started flying. Mandela was not present—he was banned and could not attend gatherings.

Winnie places the date of this dance in 1956, which does not fit as the Treason Trial only started, abruptly, on December 5, 1956, following the 156 arrests. Even more confusingly Winnie says she graduated from the Jan Hofmeyr School in 1955 and began work at Baragwanath Hospital early in 1956 when she first met Mandela. The graduation certificate that was awarded to Winnie is clearly dated December 9, 1955, but in the archives of the magazine *Drum* there is a photograph of Winnie taken at the Bantu Men's Social Centre during her graduation ball and that photograph is dated a whole year later, December 1956. When shown the photograph, Winnie could not explain the disparity in the dates but immediately recalled that the white dress she was wearing at the ball had later been worn by her room-mate Adelaide at her engagement party to Oliver Tambo.

It seems likely that Mandela and Winnie had that awkward dinner and then their first date early in 1957 and that the Treason Trial fund-raiser took place on Friday, March 29, 1957, at the end of yet another dull week of hearings at the trial itself.

Z. K. Matthews wrote regularly to his wife, Frieda, during the trial and she reproduced the letters in her slender memoir, *Remembrances*. On Wednesday April 3, 1957, he wrote to tell her about the function he had attended at the Bantu Men's Social Centre the previous Friday night:

> It was held to raise funds for the Treason Trial and was well attended. Over 200 pounds was raised which was alright [sic] for the Fund but there were so many tsotsis present that it was obvious that there would be trouble before the end. The Manhattan Brothers were performing and that part of the affair was OK, but when the dance started I told Chief Luthuli that we had better depart as some of the tsotsis were playing about with revolvers. Shortly after we left the shooting started and several people were injured by stray bullets. Bakwe [their son, Joe Matthews] had not attended as he is banned and our lawyers had instructed all banned people not to attend any gatherings. This place [Johannesburg] is such a terrible place that one never knows what might happen to one.

This must be the same dance that Winnie organized, with gun-toting *tsotsis* and none of the banned leaders in attendance. Winnie claimed it had raised £25,000, but £200 sounds considerably more realistic.

Further confirmation is to be found in the 1970 letter from Robben Island that Mandela sent to Winnie, in which he described how he had dreamed of her "convulsing your entire body with a graceful Hawaiian dance at the BMSC." It reminded him, he said, of the concert they had organized there in 1957 when they were courting.

Mandela's application to divorce Evelyn was finalized on March 19, 1958. Two months later, on May 25, 1958, the engagement of Nelson Mandela and Winnie Madikizela was reported in the African newspaper, *Golden City Post*. It was the week's "No. 1 social announcement," proclaimed the *Post*. "The party is being held at the home of Mr. and Mrs. P. Mzaidume at Orlando West." They were Winnie's aunt and uncle, and she had by now left the hostel to live with them. In an unpublished photograph taken at Mandela and Winnie's engagement party, he is wearing a blazer with polished buttons, while she looks resplendent in a long green dress he had bought for her.

When it came to their marriage, there was no conventional proposal, not even a traditional approach to the bride's family. It has been written before that Mandela simply pulled the car over one day and asked her to marry him but, according to Winnie, even that was an exaggeration. He had in fact spoken to her while he continued driving, not asking, but telling, her that she was going to be taken by her uncle, Alfred Mgulwa, to Bizana on Saturday so that she could report to her father that she was getting married and ask him to arrange a date. Mandela then gave her a slip of paper with an address and told her the woman would make her wedding dress. This turned out to be Ray Harmel, the wife of Mandela's white communist colleague, Michael Harmel. "He never asked me!" Winnie said. "But it was part of the life. I enjoyed it."

Nor did Winnie ever ask Mandela whether he was free to marry her. She was unsure of his marital status, she said, but just assumed he couldn't come to her if he already had a wife. She couldn't ask him, and never did ask him, but in time, when he saw that she was concerned, he did speak to her about it.

Others around her were not so easygoing. She recalled how Oliver Tambo had warned her. "Zami," he had said (that was her home name; even Mandela called her that), "Zami, just make sure you are not hurt. The life you are embarking on is going to be an uphill road. I want you to take a decision yourself if you want to go through with it."

Fatima Meer has written how Winnie's boyfriend, Barney Sampson, took it badly when she gave him up for Mandela and attempted suicide with an overdose, but Winnie claims she had long finished with Barney by then. He was just a young boy and she had been taught to be wary of young men. "That's how I ended up with this old man." It was her grandmother's lore—the young boys in Johannesburg were *tsotsis*.

Fatima Meer described Winnie reaching Bizana and talking first to her father's second wife, showing her one of her photographs of Mandela, dressed for boxing, and saying, this man wants to marry me and I have come to get your approval as I also want to marry him. When she told her stepmother his name, she inhaled sharply. "I hope it is not Mandela of the ANC?" Winnie's stepmother told her she was mad.

Her father, she said, seemed happier that her husband-to-be was older and thought that Mandela would protect his young daughter. But he took his time to give his approval after Winnie's older sister rebelled against the relationship and shared the view of their grandmother, who warned her, "You are going to look after that man's children. All he wants is a maid to look after his children while he's in prison." As Winnie said, they were all prophetic and Winnie knew everything they said was bound to happen but she had become hooked on the struggle too. "I had no dreams of a castle where I would live happily thereafter with my prince. It was a cause and I think the reason for that was the brutal, bitter apartheid that rendered us nobodies; and the fight for dignity, the fight for your worth, was much bigger than your personal life," she recalled

With permission granted, Mandela sent two relatives to negotiate the *lobola* over freshly slaughtered meat and beer with Winnie's male relatives.

Even then, in those early days, Winnie provoked strong and widely differing opinions in all who met her. It certainly seems that people were often threatened or distracted by her looks. When Mandela introduced Winnie to some of his comrades at the Treason Trial, Ahmed Kathrada told him afterwards, "Such beauty does not go with a revolutionary." Mandela reported the remark to Winnie, who thought the idea was nonsense. Until she came to Johannesburg, she said, she had not known she was supposed to be beautiful. Back home in Bizana, her family were always making adverse comments about her appearance, insulting her for not having the looks of a true African.

Mandela sent Winnie to meet the Meers in Durban. When Fatima went to collect her from the station, she saw a beautiful young woman emerge from the compartment. Winnie was vivacious and bubbly but shy, and she had a handbag full of photographs of Mandela, which was how Meer knew there was a romance brewing. Meer never understood at the time why Mandela had sent Winnie to see her but some months afterwards was able to ask Winnie herself when they were detained together during the state of emergency. "Didn't you know?" said Winnie. "He sent me to stay with you to get your approval as he was thinking of marrying me." He had never mentioned that to the Meers.

Ruth Mompati has said that she did not detect any shyness in Winnie and recalled her as politically aware but not particularly active at first. Yet it seems Winnie was soon involved alongside the ANC women, the wives of Mandela's comrades. The journalist and activist Joyce Sikhakhane said that Winnie was very militant, carrying herself like a queen, and none of the "old girls" liked her. She broke with the usual way of doing things. (Maybe Sikhakhane was muddling the young Winnie with the later Winnie and the terrible controversies that enveloped her.)

In spite of everything that happened later, everything Winnie might have done or been involved in, Adelaide Joseph never lost the great respect and regard for Winnie that she had formed from their first meeting in 1958. She was lovely to look at, shy and humble. Having to grow so quickly and take so much on must have been hard for her. Adelaide recalled that Winnie would address meetings at Gandhi Hall in Fordsburg and would stand among the women of FEDSAW. When she walked into a hall, people would start singing songs about her and Mandela, making up songs in praise of them, right there.

A group of women including Winnie, Adelaide and Amina Cachalia had gone for "lessons" in public speaking from their white comrades, Hilda Bernstein and Helen Joseph. Adelaide always felt uncomfortable with Hilda, the wife of Rusty, who seemed to feel intellectually superior and could put others down with ease when she chose to. One day the black and Indian women had rebelled, asking why they had to be taught to speak by white people when they were the ones who were oppressed and could learn to speak for themselves. The white women didn't like it.

Amina Cachalia suspected that it took Winnie a while to get used to Mandela's interracial world, that she was not used to mixing with white or Indian people. Amina remembered the public-speaking classes too and how Winnie would sit leafing through a fashion magazine while the rest of them talked about subjects like Lesotho. Hilda Bernstein would ask, what's wrong with Winnie, why isn't she interested? Amina did not think she was uninterested, just gauging her position.

Mandela began taking her to Sunday lunch at the home of Michael (Mick) Harmel, whose wife, Ray, made Winnie's wedding gown. The Harmels' teenage daughter Barbara sometimes worked at Mandela & Tambo during the summer holidays. Barbara had been a red-diaper baby, as she put it, the child of communists. She did not find life at home very easy, had a difficult relationship with her mother and was all too aware of the tensions in her parents' relationship. Barbara describes it now as "a shit marriage." Her parents had been a total mismatch, Ray from a working-class family and Mick from the bourgeoisie. He told his daughter he had only married her mother because he was romantic about the working class. Her friend Ilse, the daughter of Bram Fischer, used to call Mick *loskop*—"loose-headed." He was all over the place, he had flings and many felt he treated his wife abysmally, though Barbara saw both sides and was aware that he was often on the receiving end of her mother's harsh criticisms.

Suddenly, Barbara found she had a soul mate in Winnie who appeared to have no time for the political conversations at the dinner table. Barbara was looking for an escape too. She would always feel tongue-tied and shy around Mandela and the equally urbane, charming Bram Fischer. So the two young women would slope off upstairs to Barbara's bedroom where they would lie on the bed and talk, or pore over "girly stuff" such as the postcards and letters from Harmel's pen pals around the world—from communist countries, naturally. Winnie seemed to adopt her, like a ready-made big sister, picking up on Barbara's troubles. She would often call during the week as well, and would always remember the names of Barbara's teachers or the school friends she had fallen out with. Barbara describes Winnie then as a sweet young woman, shy, though not naive, and for a while their friendship was the most divine thing in Harmel's life.

Barbara Harmel remembered being with her mother and father at Winnie and Mandela's engagement party in Orlando, the three of them the only white people there. Barbara had been invited to the wedding in Bizana but her parents said she couldn't attend, because it was during term time. Still, she remembered the bridal gown and the pre-wedding photographs that Comrade Eli Weinberg took of them all in June 1958. Weinberg, a white Jewish communist banned for his activism, lived across the road from the Harmels and was trying to scratch a living as a photographer for African weddings. He had a studio at home, so there were always cars outside delivering African wedding parties. Barbara used to wonder how people who were poor could spend so much on their weddings. Mick told her that when you have nothing there are specific occasions you go to town on: weddings and funerals among them.

The photographs Weinberg took were not conventional ones shot at the event, but staged before or after the ceremony. In the case of Mandela and Winnie, they were taken at the Harmels' home, with the Harmels in the photographs too. Mandela is sitting in the center; on one side of him is Winnie and on the other side Ruth Mompati.

Ruth was at the wedding in Bizana on June 14, 1958, making the journey as one of a group who shared two cars to pool the petrol costs. Duma Nokwe and his wife, Tiny, were with her, as was Lilian Ngoyi. Amina Cachalia was invited but couldn't go. Fatima Meer must have been at the wedding as she gives a dazzling, first-hand account of the festivities in her biography of Mandela, beginning with the party traveling down from Johannesburg after Mandela has been granted a six-day reprieve from his banning order, leaving just enough time for five days of feasting and celebrations.

Winnie was ill—it sounded like stress—and took a day or two to recover before finally taking the ritual hot bath and slipping into her wedding dress. Relatives leaped into a joyous dance as she stepped out into the morning sun. The ululations of Winnie's grandmother led the chorus as she left for the church in a car decorated with the colors of the ANC.

The service was thoroughly African with Xhosa hymns and a minister dressed in animal skins. The celebrations continued with dancing and singing at the family's ancestral home, at the burial ground beside the kraal. Mandela presented head cloths to the older women in Winnie's family as they danced up to him in turn to receive their gift, ululating their thanks. The bride's party walked around the kraal led by young women to emphasize the bride's virginal purity. Mandela's group formed a parallel procession while Winnie's grandmother danced energetically with "sweat trickling down her cheeks and nose" in what appeared to Meer to be a final tribute to life and fertility.

A lament was intended to signal the sadness of Winnie's departure from her family but she was too happy to respond with tears.

"How can she cry?" said her sister-in-law. "She has found a prince."

Dinner was served from the three-legged pots by the kraal, a dish of *umngusho*—samp (dried corn kernels) with beans—and salads. The party moved on to the town hall of Bizana where there were speeches. Winnie's father warned the newlyweds that their marriage would be no bed of roses. "Be like your husband," he told his daughter. "Become like his people and as one with them." The cake had fourteen tiers. Fourteen! Thirteen of them were cut into pieces for the guests. The fourteenth tier was wrapped for Winnie to deliver to her husband's ancestral home at Qunu. Events now moved so quickly that the fourteenth tier was never delivered and remained at number 8115, where it was kept in the bottom of a cupboard in a green plastic container with a cream-colored lid. Winnie would bring it out every year on their wedding anniversary and light a candle, her daughter Zindzi relates. It smelled so good, she said, that they couldn't wait to eat the damn thing. No, Winnie, would tell her, we are waiting for your father's release. The cake was destroyed when the community torched the house in the 1980s, at the height of Winnie's infamy.

Mandela's mother had not attended the wedding—possibly as a gesture of disapproval—but was waiting to greet them when they arrived back at number 8115 for another round of feasting just in time to beat Mandela's six-day curfew.

Tribesmen from Mandela's clan later came from the eastern Cape and gave Winnie a welcoming new name, Nobandla. Within a few weeks of the wedding she discovered she was pregnant. She went back to work at Baragwanath Hospital while Mandela resumed his role as a defendant in the Treason Trial. Winnie was about to join him in the criminal justice system.

She was arrested for the first time in her life that October, after joining the ANC women from Orlando at a public protest against passes for women outside the Native Commissioner's office in Johannesburg. Some 2,000 women assembled and over two days more than 1,200 were arrested, most ending up in the police cells at Marshall Square. Winnie was held there herself for some two weeks.

"I have married trouble," Mandela told his advocate friend George Bizos. He had not tried to stop Winnie from taking part, but had warned her of the potential consequences. He was almost proved right—she did lose her job as a result and it looked as though she might lose her baby too, as she started bleeding in the cells. Albertina Sisulu, one of the leaders of the protests, together with a nurse, both took care of her and the bleeding eventually stopped.

They were relieved when Zenani (meaning, What Have You Brought?) was born at Baragwanath on February 5, 1959. Mandela was at the Treason Trial in Pretoria at the time, but at least he had been there to take Winnie to hospital the night before. In a letter to Zenani, he later described how he had come home late and "found Mummy highly restless." He and Aunt Phyllis had taken her to a maternity ward.

> Your birth was a great relief to us. Only three months before this [it was actually longer] Mummy had spent fifteen days in jail under circumstances that were dangerous for a person in her condition. We did not know what harm might have been done to you and to her health and were happy indeed to be blessed with a healthy and lovely daughter. Do you understand that you were nearly born in jail? Not many people have had your experience of having been in jail before you were born. You were only twenty-five months old when I left home [at the end of March 1961] and though I met

you frequently thereafter until January 1962 when I left the country for a short period, we never lived together again.

Winnie found a new job as a social worker at the Child Welfare Society and went back to work when Zenani was five months old. She became pregnant again and suffered an early miscarriage, which Mandela attributed to the "acute tensions" of the trial.

"I still remember one Sunday as the sun was setting I helped mum out of bed to the toilet," he wrote to Zindzi in 1980. "She was barely twenty-five then and looking loving and tasty in her young and smooth body that was covered by a pink silk gown. But as we returned to the bedroom she swayed and almost went down. I noticed that she was sweating heavily and I discovered that she was more ill than she had revealed. I rushed her to the family doctor and he sent her to the Coronation Hospital where she remained for several days. It was perhaps one of her first dreadful experiences as a wife." It would have been a baby boy and he was as tiny as Zindzi's fist had been when he left her, Mandela wrote.

Winnie became pregnant for the third time soon after and Zindzi was born at the Bridgman Memorial Hospital on December 23, 1960. Of course, Mandela was elsewhere at the time; it was the Christmas break in the Treason Trial and he had been called to the eastern Cape to see his son Makgatho, who was ill at school there. According to Winnie, he had contracted tuberculosis. Mandela broke his ban to drive through the night to collect his son and bring him back to Johannesburg into the care of Evelyn.

Mandela did not know until he got home that Winnie had gone into premature labor. The baby was fine but Winnie was weak. Mandela remembered a story told by the Xhosa poet, Mqhayi, who returned home after a long trip to find his wife had given birth and suspected another man was the father. He rushed in with his assegai, ready to kill them both, but saw that in fact the baby looked just like him: *u zindzile*, he had said, meaning, you are well established. Mandela's baby was well established too, hence her name Zindziswa.

Her father went on the run, three months after Zindzi was born. She had no memory of him at all before her first visit to Robben Island in the mid-1970s. Zindzi was almost thirty when her father was freed but still entertained hopes that they could at last have the normal family life she had never known. She soon realized that was impossible. She accepted that people don't really miss something they've only ever fantasized about.

But how she had longed for that normal family, through all those years.

Even before her father was freed, she was refereeing arguments between her two parents at visits and meetings. Heated exchanges. They both had foolish pride. He could be very angry and also very stubborn. One of his greatest weaknesses, said Zindzi, is that the first person who comes with a report is right. "I used to say, what type of lawyer is this?" What type of politician, too, one might ask. Mandela, a true democrat, was renowned for his listening skills, taking everyone's opinion into account. In domestic matters, by the sound of it, he took a more dictatorial stance.

Once Zindzi accepted that her parents could not be reconciled, it became easier for her to welcome Mandela's third life partner, Mama Graca—Graca Machel, the widow of Samora Machel—into their family. Graca had made it clear to Zindzi, quite openly, the first time they met, that she would never occupy Winnie's place in Madiba's heart. That was something everyone is agreed on, even now—that Winnie was the great love of his life. But the new relationship had at least provided some members of the family with a stable emotional base. Graca was warm and affectionate, said Zindzi, while her father, though loving, was physically undemonstrative.

Stability was notably lacking in all their lives. No wonder, as Zindzi said, "All of us—Madiba's kids—have had rocky relationships. I filed twice for divorce, tried again, it fell apart. My sister was also having difficulties, she's separated now. Makgatho also had a second marriage. There's a pattern here."

Zindzi embraced Graca but still blamed her father for the troubles her mother had endured, holding him accountable for the unhappiness she had known herself throughout her disrupted childhood, through the years of isolation and harassment.

Others have said they believed Winnie had suffered breakdowns, that she had a brother and sister who had experienced long-term psychiatric illness. Zindzi was sure her mother had suffered, and that she still struggles, with depression. It was hardly surprising.

Winnie had done her best to shield it from her children, always maintaining a veneer of optimism around them, according to Zindzi. She was determined to be strong and expected the same of her children, too. "I don't want to see you cry, especially in front of the enemy. Never show them you're weak." No tears, no therapy: that was not their way. "I fall apart in the shower but emerge with my head held high," was how Zindzi put it.

She could see the pain behind her mother's mask and felt her father was responsible. There was a period after his release when Zindzi did not have contact with him for two years. "I was really upset with how he was treating my mum. We can sit together and talk about things now. He's mellower." But when people ask her, how can he make it up to you, she says she wants things that can never happen, a walk in the park, a playful roll around on the grass. At least when she sees him with the grandchildren, that completes something for her. She has learned to define her life not by how much she has endured, but by how much she has overcome.

Winnie had done much to shape her children's view of the world, trying to be both parents at once, while keeping their father alive in their imaginations. He loomed large, said Zindzi, but was never real to her. They knew he was in prison for a good cause and they became politically aware from an early age. Their education was affected as they moved from one school to another, disguising their identities and even sometimes their appearance.

Perhaps to compensate, or as Zindzi suggested, to protect them, Winnie always tried to make out that all the relationships in the family were rosy. She would never bad-mouth Mandela's former wife, Evelyn, and told her own daughters they had two mothers, encouraging them to call her predecessor Mama Evelyn. Winnie would suggest it was an echo of Mandela's father's four wives, so that, like them, Madiba had also grown up with more than one mother.

Winnie claims that, contrary to what she has read in books, she had a very good relationship with Evelyn. "He [Mandela] would write to me and tell me to go and look after his children. Even his first wife's adult children, he would write to me and scold me if they were not in school. He was that type of person. He cares for everybody and it wouldn't even occur to him to send the letter to his first wife. No, he does not consider things like that. And then of course he's naturally very authoritarian."

The stepchildren, she said, were practically as old as she was at the time, but in fact Thembi was just thirteen when his father married Winnie in 1958. Makgatho was eight and Maki was four.

Zindzi was surprised to discover in 2008 that Evelyn had actually lived at number 8115. Winnie had never made that clear. Even then, Zindzi thought that Evelyn had lived there only briefly before the separation, whereas in fact it had been her home for nearly a decade. It was also not until she was older that Zindzi became aware of the tensions and resentments between the two sides of the family. Behind the scenes, the world of Mandela's family was not so rosy, after all.

Zindzi had little memory of Thembi, who had died in the 1960s, but she recalled sitting on Makgatho's lap, listening to jazz, which he had introduced her to. He would read her stories by James Hadley Chase. He and his sister Maki would sometimes collect the two girls and take them to Evelyn's house in Orlando East for the weekend. It seemed to Zindzi that they spent the whole time praying with Evelyn and grew up waiting for Armageddon.

Those were not unhappy memories; she was just too young to understand what was really going on.

The Sisulu children knew that things changed after Evelyn and Mandela divorced. Lungi remembered how they stopped going to number 8115 where they had formerly felt so welcome and at home. He was *bhuti*, brother, to Makgatho and Thembi. Lungi's sister Beryl continued to believe that Winnie had been the catalyst that ended Mandela's first marriage. Perhaps Albertina Sisulu had thought so too. It was never chummy between Albertina and Winnie, said Beryl. Of course the Sisulus were distantly related by marriage to Evelyn and were bound to be sympathetic to her position.

Albertina Sisulu, by all accounts a kind, loving, open-hearted woman, must have hidden her feelings for Winnie, tending to her when she began bleeding during her first imprisonment after the pass protests, and working closely with her over the years.

However, it is said that she had never forgiven Winnie for what she believed to be Winnie's role in the events connected to the killing of Dr. Abu Asvat, at the Soweto surgery where Albertina worked, on January 27, 1989. Albertina had unwittingly let the two young gunmen into the surgery and was in the next room when the doctor was killed by a single gunshot. Asvat had been the last person outside Winnie's circle, the members of her Mandela United followers, to see thirteen-year-old James Moeketsi Seipei, better known as Stompie, who was probably killed on January 1, 1989. The suspicion was that Asvat had been assassinated because he was a witness to the ill-treatment of Stompie that had taken place at Winnie's home and could give evidence that pointed to the teenager's murder.

Winnie was subsequently convicted of four charges of kidnapping and a charge of accessory to assault. She was given a five-year prison sentence but never served any time. The assault charge and the sentence were both overturned on appeal. The case was heard after Mandela's release and he announced their separation in 1992, between the conviction and the appeal: "Ladies and gentlemen, I hope you appreciate the pain I have gone through."

Clearly, Winnie was involved in terrible deeds and was quite possibly implicated in murder, actions far beyond excuse or justification. It seems that she spiraled out of control and became a party to savage violence. Savage, not in the racist sense, but in its purest form, like the behavior of the white English public-schoolboys in *Lord of the Flies*. Savagery is what happens when we have been stripped of our humanity, when the primitive instincts inside us all are laid bare. That was the brutalizing effect of apartheid, allowing for the special importance that the white regime had placed on destroying Mandela's wife—that naive, country girl from Pondoland.

Back in the days of relative innocence, the Sisulus certainly believed that Winnie had treated Evelyn's children differently than her own. Thembi had never seen eye to eye with her and there is little warmth between Winnie and Maki, now the sole survivor of the first-family children. Beryl, Walter Sisulu's daughter, said she had access to photographs showing Winnie's own children, wrapped up in warm coats, while Maki was in just a little jersey, in the middle of winter. Maki apparently believed that Winnie had tried to keep her away from her father. She was bitter, but not just towards Winnie. "Bitter" may barely do justice to the great pain Maki must be carrying.

Maki would not agree to be interviewed for this book, apparently because it would cause her too much hurt (though others of a more Machiavellian view think it may be because she wants to tell her own story, in her own book, one day) but a close relative, her niece Ndileka, the daughter of Thembi, agreed to talk. There is no doubt that Fatima Meer was right when she had written of the frost that settled on Thembi's heart, following his parents' divorce.

In an account for Meer, Makgatho spoke of the difficulties the first-family children had faced after their parents' separation and how he had sided with his father, while Thembi, he thought, had sided with their mother.

> In 1958 Thembi was home from school. We used to go to daddy's office and we would drive to Orlando with him. Then one day we stopped somewhere and we picked up Winnie. She was very friendly I thought. What a pretty lady. She was talking and her eyes were shining. I liked her. We met her many times after that, usually at daddy's office. I thought nothing about it. Then one day daddy told us that Winnie was going to be our new mother. That seemed

> strange to me. I talked about it with Thembi later. I said to him, daddy is going to stay with Winnie and Winnie is going to be our new mother. It upset Thembi, but he said nothing.
>
> Then when I went to visit daddy in Orlando West at our house, I heard my aunts and my grandmother talk about daddy's wedding. They were all very excited and they were making big plans.
>
> I continued visiting daddy after his marriage and to spend weekends with him. Winnie was okay to me. I regarded her as my mother, like my father wanted me to, and this upset our mother. She didn't want me to go there at weekends, but I went.

According to Ndileka, her father, Thembi, believed Mandela had treated Evelyn very shabbily. Money loomed large among the issues between them all later. Not knowing the detail of the divorce settlement, Thembi believed his father had not given his mother "a cent out of his purse." According to Ndileka, there was once a physical fight between Thembi and Winnie and there was no love lost between them. Of course it is not unusual for a child to resent her father's new partner, especially in such strained circumstances. Winnie denied any fight with Thembi—their relationship had always been close, she said.

When Thembi moved to Cape Town it was certainly not to be closer to his father on Robben Island. He married Thoko in 1964, soon after she became pregnant with Ndileka, who was born in February 1965. Together they ran the shebeen and the profits were used to support his family, in particular, says Ndileka, to educate and clothe Makgatho and Maki, Thembi's brother and sister.

Ndileka went to live with her grandmother in Cofimvaba in the eastern Cape. She was running a store there, which she had called *maliyavusa*—"money leaking" or perhaps "the scent of money." It had once been run by a white German but the introduction of the Transkei Bantustan Homeland had closed the area to all but Africans who had been born there. The pickings were plentiful, for those who were happy to join in. K. D. Matanzima—the Homeland chief minister himself—had evidently driven Evelyn around and told her to pick any store she fancied.

As Ndileka said, Evelyn, being highly religious, was deeply disapproving of Thembi's business as a bootlegger and took the attitude that no granddaughter of hers was going to grow up in such a dissolute environment. But she could not refuse the proceeds of the shebeen, because she needed the money, while Makgatho and Maki were being educated in Swaziland.

The first family, those who survived, believed that Winnie used to be given money by Mandela for all five of his offspring but it never migrated through to the first-family children. Even in later years, when Ndileka and her sister were studying, they would struggle to get money via Winnie that was supposed to be coming to them from Mandela. According to Ndileka, she gave up her studies in frustration at not being able to obtain the money, whilst her sister Nandi would have quit business school in Cape Town if not for the support of Ndileka and Evelyn. What the first family could not have known was of the very real difficulties Winnie herself faced obtaining any money at all to support the whole family.

As a child, Ndileka spent time around the shebeen during visits. She could recall how it would stay open until midnight serving illicit wine to Cape Coloureds out of big bottles that would have to be hidden under the house when the police came.

In July 1969, Thembi was twenty-four and had yet to visit his father on the island across the water from Table Bay. Thembi was driving back from a trip to Durban where he had just bought a plot of land for a house. Next to him in the passenger seat of the car was Thoko, while the wife of Thoko's brother Leonard was asleep on the back seat of the car. They were nearly at the end of a ten-hour journey through the night, just crossing the river by Beaufort West at around 9 a.m., when three cars collided. Seven people died, including Thembi. Thoko was the sole survivor.

The loss of their first-born son prompted the only contact that ever took place between Mandela and Evelyn after the separation. Evelyn said she had earlier tried to visit Mandela in prison in Johannesburg, following his arrest in August 1962. He had refused to see her and she had gone away, humiliated. Now Mandela wrote to Evelyn, a letter composed in formal terms, in stark contrast to the letter he wrote on the same day to Winnie.

To Evelyn he expressed his sincere condolences, knowing how devastating the cruel blow of Thembi's death must have been to her. It was apparent from the letter that he had not seen or heard from Thembi in five years (he had last seen him in 1964 at the Rivonia Trial) and had not received a reply to a letter he had written to him two years earlier. He acknowledged Thembi's financial support for his family, adding that he had looked forward to more correspondence between them and to meeting Thembi and his family when he left Robben Island. "All these expectations have now been completed shattered."

He articulated his feelings far more openly in the much longer letter to Winnie, which reveals just a hint of the distance that had opened up between father and son. "During the Rivonia Case he sat behind me one day. I kept looking back nodding to him & giving him a broad smile. At the time it was generally believed that we would certainly be given the supreme penalty & this was clearly written across his face. Though he nodded back as many times as I did to him, not once did he return the smile."

Mandela's mother had died ten months earlier, in September 1968, aged seventy-seven. He had been denied permission to attend her funeral and was again denied permission to attend Thembi's funeral. Meanwhile Winnie had been imprisoned herself. The overall burden, he wrote to her, was too heavy for one man to take. "But I do not at all complain, my darling."

Ndileka's mother, Thoko, never recovered from the psychological impact of the crash. She remarried after two or three years, to Phineas Nkosi, and had a third daughter, before Nkosi died of kidney failure in police custody in Johannesburg in 1982.

Mandela's daughter-in-law, Thoko, had first attempted suicide after the fatal car crash. Following the death of her second husband, she tried driving off a cliff, taking her third daughter in the car with her. Thoko suffered a knee injury, while the daughter was unharmed. She tried again to kill herself and failed, finally succeeding at the fourth attempt, drowning herself by jumping from the docks into Durban harbor in 2002. She had fought depression for a long time and Ndileka, who had become a nurse, was disappointed in herself at the end, for missing the signs that Thoko was about to try again to end her life. "But it didn't matter—she had made up her mind."

Beyond the depression she had been a real character, said Ndileka, a bubbly person who could laugh happily, a laugh that rose up from the bottom of her stomach.

If Makgatho had, as he said, sided with his father in childhood, that did not last through the years as he came to adulthood and struggled to shape his life around his father's unrelenting scrutiny.

It looked as if he had lost his way after being expelled from school, apparently for organizing a student strike. He initially appeared to have remained close to Mandela, describing to Fatima Meer how he had first visited Robben Island in 1967, when he was sixteen, after leaving school in Swaziland. He remembered how he could relax at Mum Winnie's and play his records there, no doubt the same jazz records that Zindzi had sat and listened to with him. It had been Mum Winnie who had arranged and paid for his trip to the island. He had enjoyed seeing his father but was only allowed thirty minutes, which was too short. His father had asked him to stand back so he could look at him and said how tall and good-looking he had become. (Someone outside the family has described Makgatho as looking like his father—only without the charisma.)

He had visited Mandela regularly on Robben Island after that until the mid-1980s when, he claimed, he got lazy. Meer suggests it was not laziness but his father's constant urging to return to school that put him off. She cited a letter Mandela had written to a friend—Meer herself, perhaps—in 1974, complaining how Makgatho had lost his sharpness, could not pass his matriculation and was finding it hard to resist the attractions of city life. Mandela was keen to reawaken his son's ambitions.

Makgatho got married, to Rennie, and the couple had a child. When Rennie returned to full-time education in 1978, Mandela wrote to Maki, Makgatho's sister, in the process betraying his view of his errant son: "The fact that Rennie is at school and her own decision will make Makgatho realize that he will be the only black sheep in the family. Keep writing and urge him to think of his future and to go back to college."

The black sheep.

Makgatho tried to return to college in 1979 but could not get in without his matriculation. According to Meer, he was deeply frustrated and full of pain. It was around this time, perhaps, that he started drinking.

There was disagreement between Maki—who wanted Makgatho in the eastern Cape with their mother, out of the way of the city temptations—and Mandela, who wanted him back in his studies. Mandela told Maki in a letter that Rennie's success in education was all down to Mum Winnie, "who is keen to do everything in her power to help all the children attain their ambitions." In truth, perhaps, they were not the son's ambitions, but the father's.

Makgatho's marriage foundered. He remarried and had another son. Ndileka says he was a broker at an insurance company for a time, while continuing to drink too much. She did not think he was an alcoholic by that stage but he sometimes indulged heavily. The family, with the help of Matanzima, got him back to Cofimvaba and the care of his mother, where he helped her to run the store.

Seemingly more settled, he finally returned to study, taking up law at the University of Natal. He qualified and began working with the law firm of family friends. It was while he was doing his LLB, said Ndileka, that he finally descended into alcoholism and eventually went into rehab.

Was it perhaps too much, doing law? No, said Ndileka, that wasn't it.

"He skipped through his law degree, he could get high marks without a battle." She believed it was the internal struggle provoked by his father's release that most affected him.

"He perhaps thought he could pick up where they left off but there was this big void between them. My grandfather telling him how he wishes he was as strong as Maki and how he can't say a thing to him because he's an alcoholic. That really eroded Makgatho's self esteem."

Ndileka's view of Mandela is that he embraces weakness in others and takes strength from it. Thembi and Maki had their mother's fighting spirit, something Ndileka believed she had inherited too, and could stand up to him. Makgatho did not have that strength. Mandela did not want to understand that alcoholism is a symptom of something, did not want to look at the root cause of his son's problems. "He landed in that hospital bed because of my grandfather."

Ndileka does not know how long Makgatho had been HIV positive but she had known for about four years when he went into hospital at the beginning of December 2004. She recalled the Sunday lunch—a first-family tradition—just before his admission when he had suddenly seemed so unlike his usual self. Normally he would be the first to forgive Madiba, to say, "I think Tata has taken care of all of us equally," but that day he had seemed very angry, perhaps over some dispute that had denied him a car that Madiba had agreed to buy him. "I don't think Tata has taken care of us," he said. He meant the offspring of the first family.

So far as Ndileka was concerned, he went into hospital suffering complications from his alcoholism. He had contracted pancreatitis back while he was studying in Durban but now there were other problems too that were beyond fixing with surgery.

He just deteriorated and there was nothing anyone could do. As the family gathered at his bedside, both Ndileka and her aunt, Maki, who were seeing the same therapist, wanted to try to bring Makgatho and his father together before he died. The therapist suggested that when Mandela was at the bedside, they take his hand and place it over Makgatho's, because Mandela was unlikely to reach out himself in a physical gesture. As Ndileka said, "He's not the person to say I love you."

When Mandela came to Makgatho's deathbed, accompanied by Graca, Maki took his hand and guided it over Makgatho's hand, so that they were physically touching, as the therapist had suggested.

Mandela slid his hand away.

"He was frozen," said Ndileka who was there watching. "He just could not accept his own feelings. Grandad can be affectionate with strangers but he is completely cut off from his family. He'll confide in his housekeeper about things he's unhappy with but never to us. He's an African man and to show feelings would be a weakness and he can't do it."

Ndileka was angry that Mandela announced Makgatho's HIV status to the world, in proclaiming that he had died of HIV AIDS. He might have been wanting to destigmatize the disease but that was his thing; it was about Mandela, not about his son, whose disease it was. So far as Ndileka was concerned, HIV might have been a contributing factor to Makgatho's death, but it was not the whole story. The whole story was not something Mandela would have wanted out there.

In other ways, too, Makgatho's death had brought family tensions to a head.

"Tensions were so high after Makgatho died that we didn't even allow them to come and accompany the body. At the funeral we were like salt and water, chalk and cheese." Ndileka says that the younger generation—Mandela's younger grandchildren and great grandchildren—met afterwards and wanted to understand why there was so much ill-feeling. The first-family children tried to explain to the second-family children who, reportedly, said that they had never heard those stories from their mothers. The first family replied that they could not deny their own experiences.

There was talk of arranging a meeting between all the generations but, at the time of writing, that meeting has yet to happen. "We would be willing to meet and have an honest open debate," said Ndileka. "The tensions are simmering but if you think they are simmering now, wait until he dies. Then they will come to boiling point. The fight for the soul of Rolihlahla has not even begun because the ANC claims he's theirs, the Foundation say he's theirs..."

As part of Mandela's private celebrations for his ninetieth birthday in 2008, Maki and the first family organized a party at his ancestral home, in Qunu in the eastern Cape. They had earlier devised a Mandela family logo—apparently a bee or a wasp, the design was Makgatho's and he was inspired by the name Rolihlahla—as if it were a marque or a brand and attached it to the invitations they sent out, as well as to labels for the wine they were to serve. Mandela wine. That was widely perceived as exploiting the family name. Neither Winnie nor her daughters, Zindzi and Zenani, attended the party.

During the election campaign in 2009, Mandela was twice wheeled out onto the ANC platform to support the campaign of Jacob Zuma, who has since become the country's president. Both incidents involved Makgatho's son Mandla, who was himself seeking a position with the ANC—the first Mandela to do so since his grandfather.

The Mandela Foundation and the second-family daughters did their best to prevent the appearances, fearing they had been poorly organized and would be detrimental to Mandela's declining health. There was no open discussion about the appearances beforehand. After the second appearance, in Johannesburg, there was a stand-up row at Mandela's home between Mandla and Zindzi, who had rushed there earlier that day, just too late to physically stop Mandela being taken out by Mandla.

Just as the wine label logo was perceived to be exploiting the name for commercial gain, now it seemed as if Mandela was being exploited and made vulnerable in his old age, for the political gain of others. That, at least, was how it looked to the Foundation and to the second family. Mandla would argue that he was entitled to make decisions concerning his own grandfather, and who would stop Mandela from supporting the ANC?

Among the first family, there is resentment towards the Foundation and those around Mandela who seem to stand between them like a barrier. Ndileka said her grandfather had created a prison around himself and was too old now to break it down. Mandla feels the Foundation have failed to represent Mandela in the way the family would have liked and were too caught up with him as an individual. Maki, apparently, has tried to become involved in the Foundation and has been refused a role.

Mandla said that, for a long time, people would never have known Mandela had other children, beyond Zindzi and Zenani, which in many ways goes to the heart of the problem: the first family felt invisible after Winnie and her children came along, and especially so during the struggle years while Mandela was on Robben Island.

Mandela had given enthusiastic support to Mandla when he became installed as local chief at Mvezo, the community where Mandela's own father had been deposed, sixty years earlier. It may have looked as if Mandla was using this modest power base as a platform for his own political ambitions. No doubt Mandela has been waiting all his adult life for someone in the family to follow in his footsteps. During Mandela's twenty-seven years in prison, it had been Winnie and Zindzi in the main who had kept the family name alive. The first family were never involved in either a public or a political role, partly at the wish of Evelyn.

Meanwhile, there had been times when Maki could not help herself and allowed her bitterness and private hurt to seep into the public domain, particularly around the time of her father's release. She told *Femina* magazine in 1990 that she and Makgatho, who was then still living, were from the neglected side of the family, overshadowed by Winnie and her daughters. She had had limited contact with her father after the divorce from Evelyn and never developed a father-daughter relationship. "I really know him very little that way." She said she's had moments of real bitterness and anger towards Mandela for not being there.

Fatima Meer says that she believes Maki had "inherited" her mother's bitterness towards Mandela. In that *Femina* interview, Maki acknowledged that Evelyn had been bitter and angry towards her father too.

Maki could not understand why Mandela had to go to prison. Why couldn't he just have gone into exile, as many others did, and why did he have to come back, when he knew he was bound to be caught? She questioned his motives. Perhaps he was not as selfless as the saintly image suggested. In her view, his motivations were a mixture of the self-aggrandizement that afflicts people in liberation struggles and the simple ambition that she could recognize in herself.

"I doubt that my father wanted to become a hero. I think he felt that with the exodus of ANC leaders somebody had to stay behind and be the galvanizing force inside the country. How could the struggle survive if they were all living elsewhere in exile? I think he decided to make that sacrifice and risk a prison sentence or even death.

"Of course there is a price-tag attached to the decision in terms of the effect on his family but it was something he was prepared to do."

After he went to prison, if the children ever needed anything, he would say, go to Mama Winnie, but, Maki said, things never happened with Mama Winnie the way her father thought they happened. This caused friction. Meanwhile, her own mother had been sidelined. He ought to have known better. "You know my grandfather had four wives. My father knows full well what happens in that situation. You can't delegate one wife to see to everything concerning all the other children as well as their own. You are creating problems."

Maki said she had learned to channel her anger with the help of spiritual beliefs. She would try to talk to herself and tell herself, well, at least he believed it was for a good cause; or, he's not perfect, he has weaknesses too. Her mother was highly religious, she said, as a Jehovah's Witness while Maki would go to church but was no longer really a full member.

In the Wits archive is a letter Mandela wrote in the late 1970s to his friend and white liberal comrade, Helen Joseph, asking her to support Maki but warning her that Maki was a *Watchtower* follower and passionately religious: "I have always believed that religious values should be quietly observed and not publicly advertised."

He must have been thinking too of Evelyn, who used to go door to door in Orlando with *The Watchtower*, when she was still living in Orlando East after the divorce, before her return to the eastern Cape. Ndileka recalls being dragged round with her and having no choice in the matter, as Evelyn locked up the house behind her when she went out so they could not stay behind. She was a disciplinarian and morally strict, denying her children such leisure activities as going to see films because they were too worldly.

Although Ndileka did not recall Evelyn being openly negative about her ex-husband, she would, however, betray her feelings with little comments, such as letting them know when she felt she was being abandoned, if the children and grandchildren went off to see Mandela at Christmas. "Oh, Rolihlahla is very lucky, he sees you people just grown up." Whilst some bitterness was there, Evelyn did her best not to pass it on.

It appears that Maki's outpourings of discontent at the time of her father's release, while naturally human and perhaps understandable, had been politically awkward, creating doubts about her reliability and motives. It certainly seemed as if the first family were looking for reparations, in some way, and Mandela had sought in his last years to make provision for all his offspring. But, as Beryl Simelane said, what's done is done, and cannot be undone.

While some at the Foundation would admit to having made mistakes and were therefore trying to improve their role, there was no doubt that they were also trying to rise above political and familial sensitivities and act objectively in Mandela's own best interests. There were closer links between Foundation staff and Winnie's daughters but the Foundation were still trying to reach out to the first family, while sometimes meeting suspicion, even outright hostility.

In many ways, of course, the same losses that Zindzi could articulate in terms of her longing for the father she never had were the losses the first family had known too.

Ndileka could have been speaking for Zindzi when she said that it had taken her a long time to be reconciled to her relationship with Mandela and how much she had wanted it to go beyond what it is. "Through therapy I learned to accept that it will not go further. I was looking for a grandfather I could go and talk rubbish with, go and consult, go to a restaurant. That just didn't happen."

It is now too late and too hard for Mandela to get beyond cursory inquiries about how she is doing at work. His short-term memory has gone and he has a few tales that he tells his grandchildren, already many times over. They always pretend it is the first time that they have heard them and laugh at the anecdotes. Zindzi's experience has been the same. No doubt the first and second families got to hear the same stories.

He had given his best years to the struggle, and this was all that was left now, for his family: the same harmless yarns replayed many times over by Mandela while the triumphant narrative of his life was being endlessly recounted by others who never stopped to think of the sacrifices and the hurt he had forced on those around him. Mandela made his own choices—he did what he did with his eyes open. It could be said that Thembi, Makgatho and Thoko were unwitting martyrs to the cause. Thembi, Makgatho, Maki and their children might have been the invisible Mandelas in the struggle for liberation but they were not uninvolved, after all. The price was high for them. Higher than most.

Ten

MANDELA MUST HAVE been proud of his young bride and was evidently pleased to be able to invite friends and comrades to share his new and improved domestic circumstances at number 8115, even if he was not always sensitive to Winnie's feelings, as she learned to run a home on their dwindling resources while struggling to get used to her husband's ways. She had known what she was getting into when she married him, of course, but even so, it was hard to accept that family was so unimportant in the scheme of his life."You just can't tear Nelson from the people, from the struggle," she would later say. "The nation came first. Everything else was second. But in the little time we had together, he was very affectionate."

He would leave the house early, often after going for a run, and come back late with a group of colleagues, unannounced, whom he expected her to feed. "Darling, I brought my friends home to taste your lovely cooking." There might be ten people with him and one chop in the fridge. "I used to be reduced to tears," Winnie wrote in her memoir, *Part of My Soul*, "and he would laugh and run around looking for a packet of tinned fish from the local shops. He is just like that. He never had a banking account. He couldn't possibly have one."

She became the butt of his dry—dare one say, old-fashioned—sense of humor, as she would recall, on occasions when people asked where he had found this little girl. He might tell them that he was Winnie's political savior or, worse, that he had married her only because she had promised to bring him some compensation cases for his law practice. "He pulls those jokes with a very straight face—you would have to know him to understand."

Rica Hodgson recounts a meal she and Jack, her husband, had gone to at number 8115 not long after Mandela and Winnie were married. He was mad about her, Rica remembered. When the Mandelas were dining at the Hodgsons' apartment in Hillbrow, Rica had said she'd never eaten an African meal and wouldn't he offer them an African meal one day. Sure, he had said, come for lunch on Sunday, or whenever it was. So Rica and Jack had made a rare white foray into Orlando and found themselves eating roast chicken, roast potatoes and vegetables, followed by fruit salad and cream. That's not an African meal, Rica had complained, you could have had that at my place. Come on, Rica, said Mandela, what did you want me to do, go out and dig grubs for you?

Winnie complained of losing her identity, becoming "Mandela's wife," and perhaps sought to reassert her independence in the car, during driving lessons with her husband. "Impatient teacher" meets "headstrong pupil" was how Mandela characterized it. During a particularly fraught lesson he got out and stalked home.

But perhaps the most significant source of stress in the Mandelas' young marriage was the Treason Trial. The mass raids began on December 5, 1956. The arrests had been very carefully planned, with Dakota military planes waiting in Durban, Port Elizabeth and Cape Town to fly those arrested up to Johannesburg where they were all imprisoned together at the Fort. There were 144 arrests on the first day, among them Mandela himself, who was in bed when the police knocked on the door of number 8115 before dawn. They woke everyone up and searched the house after telling Mandela he was charged with "High Treason," according to the warrant, and should pack a few things as he was being taken into custody.

He knew the arresting officer, Head Constable Rousseau, and teased him as they drove into the city, Mandela sitting unrestrained in the front passenger seat: "What would happen if I seized you and overpowered you?"

"You are playing with fire, Mandela."

"Playing with fire is my game."

Mandela was obliged to strip and line up with his fellow detainees against the wall. They stood in the cold for over an hour, awkwardly naked, young and old alike, including Chief Luthuli who had been brought from Natal and Professor Matthews. Mandela recalled for Anthony Sampson that M. B. Yengwa got hold of a blanket to wrap around himself and began singing a praise-song honoring the nineteenth-century Zulu leader Shaka. Luthuli, himself a Zulu, said, that *is* Shaka! He began singing too and dancing, and they all then joined in. A white doctor appeared and asked whether any of them were ill, which they weren't. They were ordered to dress and locked into communal cells.

Within a week there were 156 detainees, comprising 104 Africans, 44 whites and Indians, an almost even number of each, and 8 coloreds. They organized themselves into an instant society, a congress of the people, fittingly, since the charges arose from the Freedom Charter, with sessions of physical exercise, lectures, debates and inspiring sessions of communal singing led by Vuyisile Mini.

Mosie Moolla relates that Oliver Tambo, who was also a renowned singer, helped to organize the Fort choir in an impromptu performance of the "Hallelujah Chorus," conducted by Tambo himself with Mini's glorious baritone soaring above the throng. Joe Slovo, who was among the white accused, recalled that the defendants were divided by race within the cells, with the whites being given more space and better bedding than the others. There were three drums of food at mealtimes and each had a sheet of paper floating on the top as a label: Congress One was the pot for whites with well-cooked chunks of beef or pork; Congress Two for the Indians and coloreds was porridge or vegetables with some fatty pieces of meat, probably the offcuts from the whites' pot; while Congress Three was the African pot with no meat in it at all, just a mixture of pap and beans. Slovo was among those in the white section who, he said, lay idly in their beds listening enviously to the singing from the African cells.

When *Regina versus Adams* (Faried Adams was Accused No. 1) and 155 others finally reached court, the inmates famously found themselves penned in by a wire cage, to which one of them attached a note, "Do Not Feed" (or perhaps "Don't Feed"), as a reminder, if any were needed, that they were being treated like animals. The initial hearings were held at the Drill Hall in Johannesburg. To begin with, there were large crowds gathered outside in support. On the first day the police opened fire and, inside, the accused held their breaths at the sound of shooting. There were twenty-two reported injuries but no one was killed.

In spite of the seriousness of the alleged offenses, bail was readily granted, albeit set on a sliding scale of £250 for whites, £100 for Indians and coloreds, and £50 for Africans. As a result, Mandela and all but a few of the accused were home in time for Christmas 1956, no doubt blissfully unaware of the long haul that lay ahead for the small proportion of them who would go to a full trial. The prosecution had estimated the case would take "six to eight weeks" but in fact it sprawled across fifty-one months, only finally coming to an end—with a full acquittal for all or withdrawal of charges—in March 1961.

The state had spent months preparing the prosecution, assembling some 12,000 documentary exhibits and dozens of witnesses whose evidence occupied most of the subsequent year. In December 1957 the attorney-general withdrew charges against sixty-five of the accused, for lack of evidence.

The defense attempted to have the charges against the remaining ninety-one defendants dismissed but, the following month, the court decided that there was a case to answer against them and the trial should go ahead. Potentially, Mandela and the other remaining defendants all faced the death sentence.

By the time the trial proper had begun in August 1958—a couple of months after Mandela's wedding—the proceedings had shifted to the Old Synagogue in Pretoria. The Crown hoped to prove a conspiracy but seemed uncertain and obfuscating when it came to defining its nature, a weakness the defense lawyers were highly effective in exploiting.

To all intents and purposes, the case was withdrawn altogether in October 1958 and wild celebrations erupted. The defense lawyers were carried out on the defendants' shoulders, Rica Hodgson remembered, kissing Oliver Tambo who was taken aback at being kissed in public by a white woman. Ruth First called a spontaneous party that night at her home.

As her husband, Joe Slovo, said, at a purely personal level their lives were very little different from those of the other middle-class whites who inhabited the "half-acre plots of posh suburbia." The Slovos had servants, two cars, a gardener and a comfortable income swelled by the generosity of First's parents, Julius and Tilly. Short of exile, he said, there was no way out of the trap of white privilege, nor any easy way to eliminate the social separation between the Slovos and their black comrades.

Still, the Slovos could bring everyone together in a close approximation of equality at their parties, which were renowned for their music such as jazz and *kwelas*, the dancing and the free-flowing alcohol. As Rica Hodgson said, you never knew what tomorrow held, so you went out and had a marvelous bloody time.

That night, said Slovo, their house was bursting at the seams by eight o'clock. Among the guests were the bishop of Johannesburg, Ambrose Reeves, and Trevor Huddleston who, like Rica Hodgson, was involved in the Treason Trial Defence Fund. Slovo said they should all have guessed the state would be keen to hit back after their humiliation at the trial. Sure enough, just before midnight, the police swarmed in through the windows and doors, bringing with them reporters from the Afrikaner press who later described the decadent scene that greeted them.

"Many colors at party" was the headline in *Die Burger*. "A party at which whites, natives and Indians were present was held in a Johannesburg suburb last night. There were about 200 people present. White and non-white drank, danced, sang and chatted together. The police appeared at 10.30 p.m. In many of the cars white women rode with natives."

According to Slovo, the police went away empty-handed as none of their black guests was caught with drink. Many had poured the contents of their glasses into a large vase that Slovo had bought with the proceeds of a poker win. Mosie Moolla, an enthusiastic participant on the social scene, had been dancing when the police came in. "It was a lovely party, man."

This was the mixed racial world of the Treason Trial that was shaping Mandela's cultural landscape, just as it was defining his political development. It was a unique existence within the racist, segregated society of South Africa. Many white South Africans would not even share a pavement with black Africans and would cheerfully push them out of the way as they passed, if they didn't voluntarily move.

Out there, on the streets of the apartheid state, the worlds of white and black were almost entirely polarized, for the benefit of the whites. Black Africans were denied access to many places and institutions that the white minority preferred to keep to themselves. Not so, however, the white communists, and a few others, who opened their lives and their homes, sometimes uncomfortably but invariably with the best of intentions, to their comrades across the color line.

Mandela had once taken Winnie to a dinner party at a white comrade's flat, high up in one of Johannesburg's most famous apartment buildings. Okay, they had been obliged to ascend in the *nie blankes* service lift, as they were not allowed to step inside the main lift, which was for whites only, but still, they had been welcomed and accepted once they arrived at the door of Cecil Williams' apartment.

Mandela had sometimes been to dinner with the lawyer Harold Wolpe and his wife AnnMarie, who described how readily she had accepted Mandela into her home. It was no different from anyone else, she said breezily. However, some days later she admitted—to her great credit—that she had thought long and hard and the truth was that there had been a frisson, part awkwardness, part thrill, at having a black man at her dinner table.

Like all children, the children of the white middle-class communists did not want to stand out from their peers, but of course they did not blend in at all, because their parents had black people as house guests, not just as servants. As Toni, the daughter of Rusty and Hilda Bernstein, put it, "Africans weren't considered people by most of white South African society." She remembered overhearing a conversation on a bus once where a white madam was explaining that she had been forced to move home after catching her maid having a bath in her bathroom. Toni recalled coming home with a schoolgirl friend and finding Mandela sitting in the living room, having tea with her father. It was deeply embarrassing as black men just weren't supposed to sit in one's living room. She hustled her friend into her bedroom and explained that the black man was actually a chief.

Barbara Harmel relates how, as a child, she hated her parents mixing with Africans, all except the Mandelas, whom she adored. She had school friends who were banned by their parents from visiting Barbara's home, because they had Africans there. Neighbors would say, "How can your dad have lunch with natives?" Barbara just wanted to be like the other children. "Please don't do this to me," she wanted to say to her parents.

AnnMarie Wolpe says that, even though "crossing the color line" was difficult, that did not stop everyone flirting at parties. It was sexually exciting and just became the norm without ever leading anywhere, in most cases. The women would be sitting lined up against the wall and the men would approach them. The older ANC women, such as Albertina Sisulu, would keep themselves apart from these goings-on.

AnnMarie remembers dinners with the Slovos and the Mandelas, Winnie sitting quietly while the men told jokes and legal anecdotes. Ruth First was rude about AnnMarie's cooking, which devastated her when she had spent hours "looking at the fucking cookery book." Ruth was dominant, and for years AnnMarie felt excluded by her from conversations, as if she was unworthy of Ruth's attention. Joe Slovo would tease AnnMarie and flirt with her, especially at the whites-only tennis parties, which many of the communist comrades used to attend.

AnnMarie could remember the Sunday-afternoon pool parties at the Fischers (the Bernsteins had a pool too and open house on Sundays) where she would try to avoid getting caught in conversation with some of the deadly comrade bores, whom she refused to identify, even all these years later.

Ilse Fischer, the daughter of Bram and Molly Fischer, could not remember many Africans at those pool parties; there were more guests from the Indian community, many she didn't know. Complete strangers would still come up to her sometimes and say they had been at her pool. Amina Cachalia would take her children there and could picture the ANC crowd around the pool, basking in the sun.

Bram Fischer had built the pool from the profits he had made fighting a case for a tobacco company and he always seemed completely at ease in mixed company. Paul Joseph, an Indian communist who was as alert as anyone to the casual racism of the times, thought the Fischers on a par with the Mandelas, a rare white couple, Bram having made huge sacrifices of his own to the struggle.

Although the Mandelas were not often at the bigger gatherings, the Sisulus would be. Once, when Paul's wife, Adelaide, was being harassed a little by frisky African colleagues, Walter Sisulu came over and called them off. "Don't behave like that, it's not nice."

Joseph knew that some people complained that the whites were always trying to make up for the guilt they felt. He remembered talking to a Cape Town colleague during the Treason Trial who said you couldn't set foot at a party without the whites rushing over to offer you food and drink. The colleague told him how unhappy some black, Indian and colored colleagues had been when a white activist, Lionel Foreman, had got married and held two parties, one for the riff-raff and the other for the select few. The "riff-raff" (those who were not white) had decided to march on the second party in protest. Paul told the Cape Town man that their action was wrong, that the activist had probably just wanted his family there and shouldn't have to have his loyalty tested.

In Joseph's view some colleagues were so damaged by racism that they regarded having sex with a white woman as some kind of triumph, a form of getting one over on them. He was shocked when he heard that one or two of their women comrades had had affairs with Dennis Brutus, an

African colleague. Ruth First was mentioned, which upset Joseph because she was a dear colleague. Whom she slept with was her business, and it was wrong for Brutus to be going around talking about it.

Latent resentments sometimes spilled over during drink-fueled moments, such as the occasion when after drinking in the shebeens, Robbie Resha and an Indian comrade had made their way to a party at the home of white Jewish activists, Ben and Mary Turok, in the Johannesburg suburb of Orange Grove.

As the story was related by Mac Maharaj, the hosts gushed over the pair arriving from the shebeens, who were keen to carry on drinking and went straight to the bar, only to discover that the well was dry, the spirits having all been consumed. They decided to leave but the Turoks pursued them down the drive. Comrades, please don't go, the party's still alive.

The Indian, none too sober, turned back, and said, yes, *baas*, to Ben and, yes, missus, to Mary. Ben went to Sisulu to complain about the Indian's "racist" behavior. Sisulu, ever the diplomat, calmed Turok and said he would speak to the offender, who "blew his top" and couldn't see why there was a problem. Sisulu told him they did not want unnecessary friction among colleagues. OK, said the Indian, according to Mac, but tell me, was I not right with those bloody white arrogant bastards? OK, OK, said Sisulu, but just don't say it.

Ahmed Kathrada said there were often gatherings at his apartment in Kholvad House on Saturday nights and though he could not buy his own liquor he had a white comrade who would get it for the parties. AnnMarie Wolpe says that the supplier of spirits was her lawyer husband, Harold. On this particular night there was some brandy left over from the Friday-night session the night before. Suddenly vice squad cops turned up, around fourteen of them. Kathrada was carted off to Marshall Square and charged with possessing alcohol. He knew it was just political harassment and the case was dismissed when the vice officers admitted they had been put up to it by Special Branch.

Joe Mogotsi remembers that he used to go to mixed parties where he might have to stand in the kitchen pretending to be a waiter if the police came. There would be white women and African women there but not many Indian women. The Indian men would get involved with the women but the guys with Mogotsi would say, bring your own. Where are the Indian chicks?

Mogotsi was on stage playing the second male lead at the opening night of *King Kong*, the musical, on February 2, 1959. The first ever musical—a jazz opera—with a black cast, it raised the roof in Johannesburg, then went on tour in South Africa, and again later in London's West End. Normally a white and a black audience could not have shared the same theater. But on this special occasion, at the great hall on the Wits University campus, they had been allowed to sit in alternate rows. Esme Matshikiza was in the first non-white row, three rows from the front, with her husband, Todd, who had composed the songs. This had come about through a song he had written, "Sad Times Bad Times," to mourn the premature deaths of friends. What had they done to deserve their fate? asked the song. It had been performed by Joe Mogotsi's group and was heard and remembered by *King Kong*'s producers.

Esme said that Mandela was not then the world celebrity he later became and so was sitting even further back in the audience with his young wife Winnie, who was pregnant. During the drinks interval they stood chatting on the non-white side of the segregated foyer. Mandela told Todd how much he liked "Sad Times Bad Times" with its Xhosa lyrics and how clever it was of him to have written about the Treason Trial. What had they done to deserve their fate? Todd stole a glance at Esme. That was not what the song was about at all, but never mind, it seemed to fit.

The mid-1950s bus boycotts in Alexandra and elsewhere were intended to resist fare increases. In reality, they posed a wider threat to the economy as literally thousands of people opted to join the boycott and walk several miles each day, to and from their jobs. Though the boycotts were led by an alliance of community representatives, Mandela was frustrated that the ANC could not offer clearer leadership and feared the Africanists were trying to manipulate the boycott towards a violent confrontation with the government that they could not hope to win.

Unable to take command himself, Mandela eventually pushed for an end to the boycott and a compromise acceptance of the modest subsidy offered to keep the fare prices in check. It was a poor solution, dictated by leaders far from the "front line," and it cost the mainstream ANC a considerable loss of popularity, which the Africanists were able to exploit.

The Africanists were still looking to the 1949 Programme of Action, which had been promoted by the ANC Youth League as a declaration reclaiming the land for the African people. As they would say, the Freedom Charter was in "irreconcilable conflict" with the 1949 Programme. At the 1955 Congress of the People, the land that was theirs had been auctioned for sale by the ANC. Now, suddenly, the land belonged "to all who live in it."

Some Africanists still hoped to turn the ANC in their direction while others wanted to break away and form a new organization. Meanwhile the core issues had ceased to be harmless political differences and had begun to descend into vicious rivalry with an encroaching air of violence. There was a struggle for power within the ANC—the entire future direction of the liberation movement was at stake.

By mid-1958, it looked as if the issue of the multiracial Congress Alliance would split the ANC. The historians Karis, Carter and Gerhart later said it was impossible to gauge with any accuracy "the extent to which Africanist hostility to the multiracial front actually reflected the sentiments of Africans either inside or outside the ranks of the ANC. The Africanists were convinced they were closer to the mood of the masses than were the Congress leaders."

The Africanists had chosen the Transvaal ANC—where Mandela had once presided—as their battleground, because it was their own heartland, from their Orlando base, and because the branch was beset by problems. They had tried and failed to gain control of the branch and again met resistance when they attempted to dislodge the incumbent local leaders. Just when it seemed they might succeed, the chairman closed the meeting and began singing the African anthem. There was some fist-fighting in the hall and, later, a raiding party of Africanists broke into the ANC offices and drove off with the official ANC car. Two of the leaders, Potlako Leballo and an Alexandra activist, Josiah Madzunya, were expelled from the ANC.

Leballo worked at the Information Service of the US Embassy (USIS) where he often used their facilities to make copies of papers and perform other simple administrative tasks for the Africanists. His role there would give rise to the suggestion within the ANC that the Africanists were being manipulated by the CIA. There is no evidence this was true, but it was the height of the Cold War and any anti-communist activity would have held some appeal for the United States.

While Mandela worked with Tambo and Sisulu to try to reorganize branches and eradicate local corruption, they had also planned a three-day stay at home to protest against the general elections of 1958. "The Nats Must Go!" was the slogan. However, the Nats won the election and the stay at home was ignored, so that the ANC were forced to call it off after the first day. This was the latest humbling failure to galvanize popular support and it strengthened the hand of the Africanists.

In his memoir, Mandela played down the events that led to the formation of the Pan-Africanist Congress, perhaps preferring not to incite further bloodshed by dwelling on the violent mood that overtook the ANC during this period. His book characterizes the breakaway leaders as motivated by personal grudges or disappointments and feelings of jealousy or revenge. "I have always believed that to be a freedom fighter one must suppress many of the personal feelings that make one feel like a separate individual rather than part of a mass movement. One is fighting for the liberation of millions of people not the glory of one individual."

These were high-minded sentiments but, in the late 1950s, across Africa, the tide was with the Africanists, as Ghana and Guinea led the way to independence for black Africa, without the help of white people or communists. There was a dream of a United States of Africa, but that too did not include white people. As Mandela would soon find out, it was he who was then out of step with history, not the Africanists.

Matters came to a head over the first two days of November 1958 at the provincial conference of the ANC, chaired by Oliver Tambo and held in Orlando Communal Hall. Chief Luthuli made the opening address and blamed the re-elected Nationalists for injecting the "virus of prejudice and sectionalism" into the African community. Some Africans, he said, were trying to emulate the Nationalists and claim exclusive control of their country, which was encouraging them backwards, towards a mentality of tribalism. The Africanists, around 100 of them armed with sticks, heckled the mainstream ANC speakers from the back of the hall, while backing their own speakers with much foot stomping and cries of *Afrika!*

The Africanists hoped to take over the conference and vote in their own representatives. At a meeting beforehand they had agreed to take violent action if necessary—a near unanimous decision, with Robert Sobukwe the only voice of dissent. According to Benjamin Pogrund's biography of Sobukwe, the Africanists had actually planned to kidnap Mandela, Luthuli and the other leading ANC figures the night before the conference started. They had been dissuaded but Sobukwe went to the conference still fearing bloodshed.

As the conference progressed the atmosphere became increasingly threatening. Pogrund, who was there as a reporter, was the only white person in the hall. He left after being warned that he was about to be attacked. His support for Sobukwe and their friendship were no protection.

At the end of the first day, Tambo concluded that the only way to defeat the Africanists was to meet fire with fire. He rounded up a posse of thugs of his own who appeared on the Sunday, armed with lumps of wood, sticks, iron bars and truncheons. There were rumors that he even had a stash of guns in the back room, just in case. Tambo himself stood at the door with his menacing-looking gang. The Africanists backed down from a confrontation and left, believing that they were about to be murdered.

As the conference proceeded with the elections, the Africanists returned to deliver a letter, which they handed over at the door. The letter declared that they were waging a political battle against the oppressor and were not a "para-military clique, engaged in the murder of fellow Africans." They had come to a parting of the ways and were "launching out openly on our own as the custodians of the ANC policy as it was formulated in 1912 and pursued up to the time of the Congress Alliances."

The Africanists returned to the Orlando Communal Hall the following April for the inaugural convention of the Pan-Africanist Congress. The hall was bedecked with placards bearing slogans such as "Africa for Africans, Cape to Cairo, Morocco to Madagascar" and "Forward to the United States of Africa." There were cables of greetings from Kwame Nkrumah and Sekou Toure, the respective heads of state of independent Ghana and Guinea.

In spite of his quiet presence, Sobukwe had revealed himself as the intellectual heart of the new movement and from his opening address it was clear he would become its leader. His inspiring speech spoke of the new scramble for Africa, which was being wooed and flirted with by both America and the Soviet Union. Sobukwe did not agree with the idea of South African "exceptionalism" and made common cause with those who had achieved—as well as those who were still seeking—independence in Africa. He agreed with Kenya's Tom Mboya who rejected both Western imperialism and Soviet hegemony.

Less appealing were Sobukwe's racist views towards Indians, pandering to the stereotype of the Indian merchant class who, he said, "have become tainted with the virus of cultural supremacy and national arrogance." It had not been that long since there had been murderous race riots in Durban. His words lived up to the fears of many in the ANC and the wider congress movement who believed the PAC would "play the race card."

Mandela knew Sobukwe well, had represented him in court, and admired and respected his intelligence. He told Fatima Meer that he kept trying afterwards to obtain a copy of that speech and that Sobukwe became evasive: "Nel, I've got it at varsity" or "Nel, as soon as I have a moment I'll get it to you." Mandela said, "Robbie was always cautious, playing his cards close to his chest, but very honest."

If it was true that Sobukwe was honest, he must have been manipulated by others within the PAC as they sought to present their new organization as attracting mass appeal while, in truth, it was failing to gather widespread support. The PAC was constantly trying to upstage the ANC and seized its opportunity in early 1960, after the ANC began organizing a new anti-pass campaign that was to begin on March 31, 1960 and culminate on Freedom Day, June 26th, with a bonfire of the passes.

On March 18th, Sobukwe called for a mass pass defiance to take place three days later, on March 21—ten days ahead of the ANC campaign. It was short notice for such a campaign and anticipated that followers would go to jail on the "no bail, no defense, no fine" slogan. He wrote a letter to the Commissioner of Police, promising a disciplined approach and seeking to avoid violence. He also wrote, asking the ANC to join them, but they refused, saying it was a sensational action that was ill prepared and had no prospect of success. Mandela claimed the ANC had asked the PAC to join their campaign and never had a reply.

On March 21, Chief Luthuli had just taken the stand in the Treason Trial at the Old Synagogue in Pretoria. Mandela was in the dock listening as Luthuli testified to the ANC's non-violent stance while, back in Johannesburg, Robert Sobukwe was at the head of a procession of anti-pass protesters, marching to offer themselves for arrest at the Orlando police station.

There was a further protest at Vereeniging, a few miles outside Johannesburg, in the location of Sharpeville. Benjamin Pogrund had never heard of the place before, when he learned of the crowd of several thousand who had assembled there to march on the municipal offices at the entrance to the township. Later the police would say 20,000 people had gathered, but the organizers claimed the crowd numbered some 5,000. Police reinforcements were brought in with Saracen armored cars.

There was no order to open fire and it has never been explained what prompted the police to start shooting. There is no evidence that the police faced any threat, other than a large crowd of peaceful protesters. In London, the South African High Commission claimed that 20,000 "Natives" had attacked the police with assorted weapons including firearms. That was not true, according to all the first-hand accounts. Pogrund had arrived in his car a few minutes before the shooting happened and was lucky to escape with his life as the crowd became enraged by the massacre and turned on him with sticks and stones.

The reporting of Sharpeville came from *Drum* journalist Humphrey Tyler—"a gun opened up toc-toc-toc and another and another. The shots had a deep sound"—with pictures from his accompanying photographer, Ian Berry. Tyler noted that people were laughing at first, perhaps thinking it was a game, with blanks, but they were real bullets flying from police revolvers, rifles and Sten guns, in rounds of volleys that altogether lasted less than one minute. Pogrund says that 68 died and 186 were injured, while pointing out the uncertainty of the precise number. The usual quoted figure is sixty-nine deaths. Most of the victims were shot in the back, forty of them women and eight of them children.

Elsewhere, PAC protests had drawn patchy support—from crowds of thousands in Cape Town to far smaller numbers in Durban. In the ensuing days there were further fatalities amid greater mass demonstrations as a well of anger rose up inside the country and around the world. The government actually relaxed the pass laws in an attempt to prevent further confrontation. The South African stock market wobbled, while the ANC thought the moment might have come when the government could be pushed aside.

On the night of Sharpeville, Mandela, Sisulu, Slovo and Duma Nokwe sat up all night devising a response, which they gave to Chief Luthuli to present to the country. Slovo said it was left to the movement—the Alliance—to pick up the pieces of the PAC's disastrous actions, but in reality the ANC had been outplayed. The effect of the shooting was to catapult Sobukwe and the PAC to the forefront of the struggle against apartheid. The terrible truth was that the tragedy of Sharpeville was the PAC's triumph. Slovo recalled that he and Mandela waited alone together for the others to arrive and the meeting to begin. "We were both depressed and commiserated with each other about the massacre, and about the fact that the ANC national campaign into which so much effort had already been put had been so tragically pre-empted."

Luthuli called for a day of mourning—a day's strike—and he and Mandela and others publicly burned their passes in an orchestrated arrangement. The day of mourning was held on March 28, with hundreds of thousands staying away from work and many taking to the streets in protest. Now the state made its move and on March 30 a state of emergency was declared, habeas corpus was suspended and mass arrests took place. Mandela was arrested at number 8115 in the early hours of the morning. He had known what was coming from a tip-off the previous day. Ahmed Kathrada recalls that he was celebrating Eid with friends when he got a cryptic message from Mandela and went to number 8115 to be told that they were all going to be detained. The leadership decided that everyone should attend the Treason Trial as usual.

Oliver Tambo had left the country three days earlier, to form a leadership in exile. Ruth First crossed into Swaziland wearing a red wig, taking her three children. Most of the other key figures were among the 2,000 arrested, everyone, that is, except Wilton Mkwayi who tried to offer himself for arrest at the Treason Trial that morning and was waved away by the police. He insisted he was one of the accused and ought to be arrested but they didn't believe him. He left South Africa and ended up in China, where he undertook military training before coming home. He would claim that *muti*—African witchcraft—had saved him from arrest.

The ANC and the PAC were banned. Some of the PAC leaders betrayed their commitment by posting bail. Sobukwe had expected a short jail sentence but instead was given three years and ended up in solitary confinement on Robben Island, where his sentence was endlessly extended without further trial, by the so-called Sobukwe Clause.

Sharpeville did little to divert the lumbering passage of the Treason Trial. The jubilation and partying at the withdrawal of charges in the trial back in October 1958 had been short-lived, as the case was soon revived while the number of defendants was streamlined down to a more manageable thirty. After a mere three months of legal argument, the trial proper had begun again in August 1959.

The Freedom Charter was the prosecution's key document, albeit just one exhibit among thousands. According to the prosecutor Oswald Pirow, the aims of the charter necessarily demanded "the overthrow of the state by violence." That proved the "hostile intent" required to make the charge of treason stick. The accused, claimed Pirow, were "inspired by communist fanaticism, Bantu nationalism and racial hatred in various degrees."

Pirow was a Nazi sympathizer who had come out of retirement to prosecute the trial. In an unguarded moment—or perhaps he simply did not care what he said, or whom he said it to—he had told the historian Tom Karis during the trial that he wanted to see the "worst Natives" such as Robert Resha jailed for five years. Separate development, he said, appealed to most "good Natives." But if there was a real threat to white rule, the shooting of 5,000 natives with machine guns would provide quiet for a long time to come.

When Pirow had died suddenly in late 1959, there were rumors among the defense that his death had been forecast, perhaps even caused, by witch doctors attending the trial.

Before the arrests during the 1960 state of emergency, Mandela used to catch a lift each day to Pretoria with Helen Joseph in her car, which they christened Treason Trixie. Joe Slovo, Robert Resha and Ahmed Kathrada would often travel with them. Joseph recalled how they would pick out grand houses for themselves as they drove out through the well-heeled northern suburbs. Kathrada chose a villa with wings for all his Muslim wives.

According to Mac Maharaj, who was not there but heard about it later, Mandela would often attack Slovo and the communists on the journey, complaining that, despite appearances to the contrary, the Communist Party was run by whites and was no beacon of equality. As Mac said, that was an indication of how well Mandela knew the party apparatus.

The trial was an appalling waste of time for all involved. People read, slept, stared into space and did crossword puzzles. Volunteers provided lunch in the walled garden of a nearby vicarage. Days passed. Very little happened. "These proceedings are not as funny as they may seem," the giggling defendants had been warned by a stern magistrate, sometime earlier in the sequence of hearings.

By common consent some of the most entertaining exchanges occurred when the state called a witness to provide expert evidence on the nature of communism. Professor Andrew Murray, a philosopher from Cape Town, was skillfully forced by defense lawyer Issy Maisels to concede that "Native" life was so circumscribed that natives might be entitled to consider themselves oppressed, whether communist or not. And, he was bound to agree, not one of the accused had ever committed an act of violence in the name of their cause.

Murray was led through various writings in an attempt to help the court understand what they were dealing with. He identified one passage as "communism straight from the hip," not realizing it was an extract from something he himself had written.

The prosecution case had only just ended and the defense case begun when the Sharpeville state of emergency was declared and all the defendants were detained. Their lawyers complained to no avail of the difficulty of advising their clients. It was agreed that, by way of protest, all the lawyers would withdraw, leaving the defendants to defend themselves. In a further attempt to undermine the case, each of the accused began calling their fellow accused in turn as witnesses.

With Tambo out of the country, the law partnership with Mandela could not survive. It had, in any case, been struggling financially. Before he left, Tambo had appointed a white Jewish lawyer, Hymie Davidoff, to wind up the practice. Davidoff now won permission from the Pretoria prison commander, Colonel Prinsloo, for Mandela to be freed to assist him.

Instead of returning to jail after court on Friday afternoons, Mandela drove to Johannesburg, escorted by Sergeant Kruger, and went to work at Chancellor House. Kruger might stop at a shop for biltong (sun-dried lean meat) and leave Mandela unguarded in the car. If it was a test, Mandela did not let him down. He considered running off but stayed put and in return—a kind of gentlemen's agreement, as Mandela put it—Kruger allowed Winnie to visit him at the office and others, such as Amina Cachalia, to deliver curries to him for meals.

Back in Pretoria, many of Mandela's fellow defendants became fed up with the strain of representing themselves in court. Technically they all still faced the death penalty. They turned on Mandela and asked him why he had driven their lawyers away. He reminded them it had been a joint decision. They complained that as a lawyer he was the expert whose opinion they had relied on. Mandela persuaded them to continue. It was a trial of strength, he said, a test of an immoral idea against a moral one. In reality, the prosecution had little evidence of any violence that it could rely on. There was only Robert Resha's statement that volunteers should, if asked, murder. The defense tried to demonstrate that he had simply got carried away and, indeed, it was an isolated example of a call to arms.

The defense lawyers returned to court when the state of emergency was lifted in August 1960. Mandela went home for a final few months, but was still rarely there as he was desperately short of money. He tried to revive his legal practice from the lounge of Ahmed Kathrada's flat. Just as at Chancellor House, Kholvad House was soon overrun with Mandela's clients and Kathrada complained he could find peace only in his kitchen.

The prosecution ended its case in early March 1961, at the end of four months of closing argument, constantly interrupted by the judges asking searching questions that the prosecution could not answer about the ANC's propensity to violence and its part in the communist conspiracy. The defense was ready for what it believed would be a three-month summing-up of its case. Bram Fischer had spent days preparing his own argument, which he believed would last for three weeks. On the third day of his presentation the judges stopped him and adjourned, returning on March 29, six days later, to pronounce a unanimous verdict of not guilty. All the defendants were discharged.

The court was packed with defense supporters who erupted in celebration, singing the African anthem and praise-songs for the lawyers and the defendants. That evening there was a victory party at the Fischers' Beaumont

Street home. Mandela wrote about that night in a letter to Amina Cachalia in 1969.

> You were among those who travelled all the way to Pretoria & who warmly congratulated & cheered us on our discharge, glad to share victory with those with whom you had fought so long & hard for a new order & a new world.
>
> Zami [Winnie] & I met you at the party the same night but you were soon gone. A few days thereafter I bade farewell to Zami & kids & now I am a citizen across the waves.
>
> It was not an easy decision to make. I knew the hardship, misery & humiliation to which my absence would expose them. I have spent anxious moments thinking of them and have never once doubted Zami's courage & determination. And there are times when I even fear receiving letters from her, because every occasion she comes down I see with my own eyes the heavy toll on her health caused by the turbulent events of the last 8 yrs.
>
> Moments in my life are occupied by tormenting thoughts of this kind. But most of the time I live in hope & high spirits.

Amina had retained a vivid picture of the end of the trial. Her husband, Yusuf, couldn't go, but Ruth First said she would pick her up, so Amina went with Joe and Ruth. They arrived with "different feelings," not knowing what the outcome would be. Someone had taken a "lovely photograph" of Ruth and Amina walking into the building, and then they were in the court with those mixed feelings, and suddenly the defendants were free and there was absolute merriment.

"We hugged and kissed and we sat, we stood up, we didn't quite know what was happening."

Amina had no memory of the party, however. She had young children at home, which was perhaps why she left quickly.

Freed from the charge of promoting violence, Mandela was now free to promote violence.

Eleven

IT HAS BEEN written elsewhere that Mandela made some financial provision—six months' rent paid up in advance—for Winnie and his two baby daughters, Zeni and Zindzi, before he left them to live out his last months of freedom as a fugitive. Winnie told me there was no such provision, that Mandela could not have raised six months' rent even if he wanted to, and from the time of their marriage in 1958 they were always in financial difficulties.

According to Winnie, the nice clothes and the seemingly easy lifestyle were all an illusion. Most of the clothes, including the suits from Mr. Khan the tailor, were gifts. Mandela rarely paid for anything. He had bought most of the furniture for their home at 8115 Orlando West on credit from a Mr. Levine. After Mandela went underground, he stopped paying the installments. Levine turned up one day and repossessed the lot, including the carpet. Winnie went to Mandela's former articled clerk, Godfrey Pitje, who had taken over some of the business of Mandela & Tambo, and borrowed some money to go and re-repossess the furniture, this time in her own name.

Of course, from the very beginnings of their marriage, Mandela had rarely ever been home. As Winnie often told her daughters in later years, she was the most unmarried married woman. She never lived with her husband.

Even back then, Winnie felt she was a sacrifice to the cause. Marrying Mandela was marrying the ANC, but unlike others around him who found it difficult and painful, she understood and accepted that role.

He never actually told her he was leaving her to live underground. In Winnie's recollection he came home from the Treason Trial one day in March 1961 as the case was drawing to a close. He stood outside the gate, by the car, talking with comrades Joe Matthews, Joe Modise, and Duma Nokwe. Modise came to her in the house and said, Mama, can you please get me a suitcase and pack a few clothes for Madiba? Winnie had been taught never to ask questions. Whenever her husband went out, she never asked and never expected to be told where he was going.

She took a case and packed a few shirts, a couple of suits, and some underwear. Winnie handed the suitcase to Modise and he took it away. They all got into the car and drove off. Mandela had not even spoken to Winnie, but that was the end of their lives together at 8115. Next thing she knew he was in the papers, making a surprise appearance at the All-In Conference 300 miles away in Pietermartizburg.

Seventeen African countries had become independent in 1960, following the beacon examples of the former Gold Coast, which had become Ghana, and Guinea. Harold Macmillan, the British Conservative prime minister, had caught the mood on his tour of Africa at the beginning of 1960. His address to the South African parliament in Cape Town, on February 3, would pass into history for its use of the phrase "wind of change." It was a long and carefully measured speech, betraying none of the casual, colonial language of racism that was in common usage at the time, especially in his host country. Listeners could detect, in his reserved tone, a distaste for the unpleasant structures of apartheid.

Instead, the speech set out to dignify the independence movement in Africa and warn the Union of South Africa, now celebrating its fiftieth anniversary, not to ignore the pattern of history:

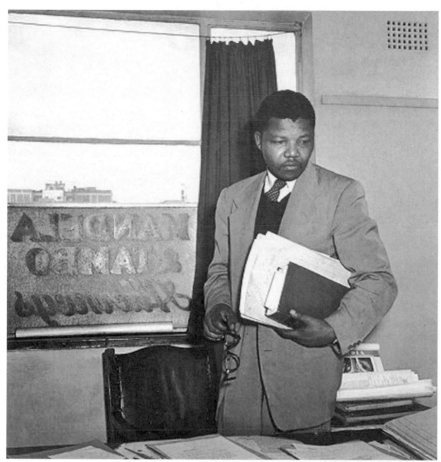

Nelson Mandela in the offices of the law firm he shared with Oliver Tambo, 1953. (Jürgen Schadeberg)

Mandela's guardian, Jongintaba Dalindyebo, the Thembu Regent who raised him on the eastern Cape, following the death of Mandela's father. (Duggan-Cronin Collection)

The rondavel at the Great Place in Mqhekezweni where Mandela lived as a child, in the care of Jongintaba. (Mayibuye Centre/Link Picture Library)

Mandela with his cousin K. D. Matanzima. Their lifelong friendship transcended bitter political differences and rivalry in romance. (Robben Island Mayibuye Archive)

Walter and Albertina Sisulu's wedding party at the Bantu Men's Social Centre, July 1944. Best man Nelson Mandela is at far left and next to him, his first wife, Evelyn; they married three months later. (Elinor Sisulu)

Mandela's first wife, Evelyn, with their two sons, Thembi and Makgatho, in the late 1940s.

Mandela showing off his style as a young man about town in Johannesburg. (Robben Island Museum)

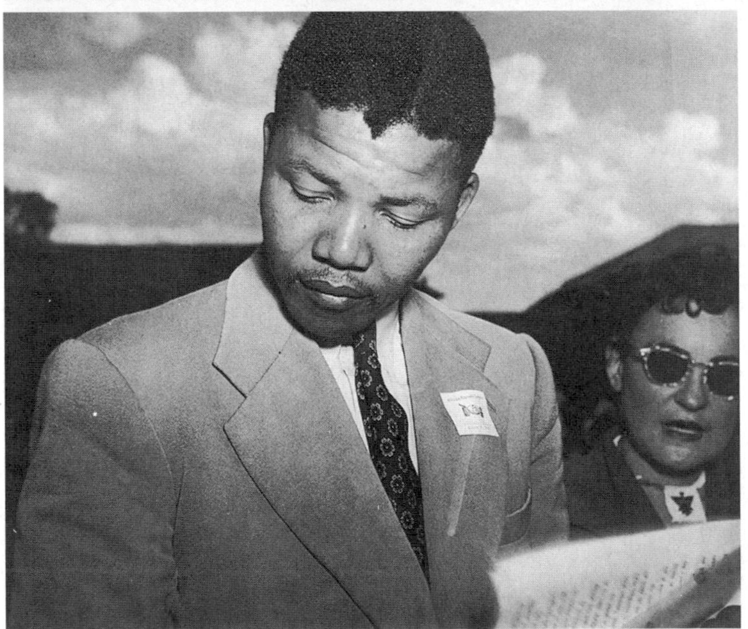

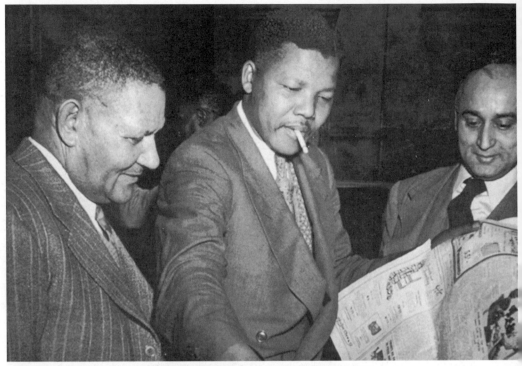

Volunteer-in-chief during the Defiance Campaign in 1952, with Dr. Moroka and Yusuf Dadoo (right). (Jürgen Schadeberg)

Mandela, the increasingly prominent 1950s activist. (BAHA)

The influential scholar Z. K. Matthews at the Johannesburg railway station, with Robert Resha (right). (BAPA)

Mandela at the center of a song of protest, outside the Drill Hall, Johannesburg, scene of the early days of the Treason Trial in 1956. (BAPA)

During the 1950s the ANC worked closely with Indian communists such as Ahmed Kathrada and white Jewish radicals such as Ruth First. (BAPA)

The Treason Trial bus carrying defendants to the court in Pretoria, 1958. In front of Mandela are Patrick Malaoa and Robert Resha (left). (BAPA)

Mandela was always a fitness fanatic and had a passion for boxing. He sparred regularly during breaks from the Treason Trial. (BAPA)

Significant women in Mandela's life, in addition to his two wives, included Dolly Rathebe, the Sophiatown singer and actress (Jürgen Schadeberg); ANC women's leader Lilian Ngoyi (BAPA); and Ruth Mompati, his law firm secretary and an ANC activist. Mompati, here on Mandela's left, was a guest at Mandela's wedding to Winnie, on Mandela's right, in 1958.

Nelson Mandela and Winnie Madikizela. They were married for over thirty years but only ever briefly together. By common consent she remains the great love of his life. (Alf Kumalo)

Nelson and Winnie Mandela with their second daughter, Zindzi, not long after she was born in December 1960. (Alf Kumalo)

Winnie with Zindzi, outside the front of the Mandela family home at 8115 Orlando West. (BAHA)

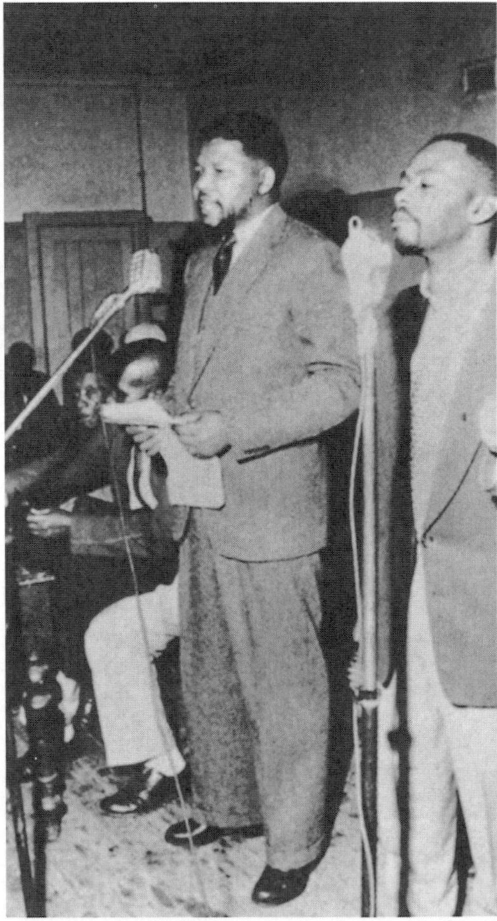

Mandela in a houndstooth suit, addressing the All-in Conference, Pietermaritzburg, March 1961. (Mayibuye Centre)

Nelson Mandela and his MK comrade Joe Slovo outside the Treason Trial, which finally ended in March 1961. (Star)

Nelson Mandela, the "Black Pimpernel," in the famous photograph taken by Eli Weinberg at Wolfie Kodesh's apartment. (Robben Island Museum)

ANC President Chief Albert Luthuli, Nobel Peace Prize winner in 1961, a reluctant participant in the move to armed struggle. (BAPA)

Mandela photographed by Mary Benson outside Westminster Abbey, during his 1962 London visit. (Mayibuye Centre)

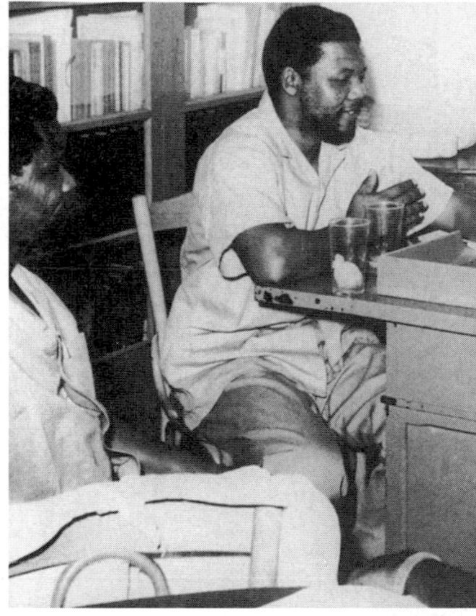

Mandela's newfound role as a military leader came to the fore during his tour of Africa in 1962. (RIM/Mayibuye Archive)

He ended the trip with eight weeks of military training in Addis Ababa in preparation for his role as commander in chief of the ANC's new military wing. (RIM/Mayibuye Archive)

Cecil Williams, who was arrested with Mandela at Howick on August 5, 1962. Seen here with an African student in July 1961. (Times Media)

Mandela poses in a version of the traditional clothes he wore at his 1962 trial. (RIM/Mayibuye Archive)

Liliesleaf Farm, Rivonia, at the time of the police raid, July 1963. (Rivonia Trial Archive/SAHA)

Underground communist leader and lawyer Bram Fischer with his daughter Ilse, 1964. (Times Media)

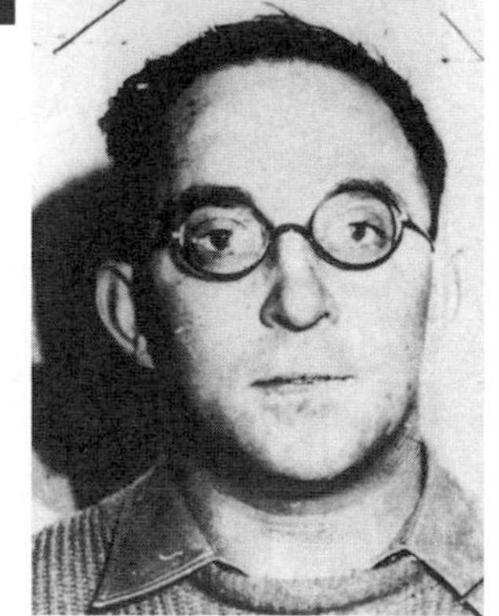

Rusty Bernstein and Denis Goldberg, among those arrested at Liliesleaf. (Rivonia Trial Archive/SAHA)

Winnie Mandela leading Mandela's mother, Nosekeni Fanny, up the steps outside the Rivonia Trial, 1963. (Alf Kumalo)

> In the twentieth century, and especially since the end of the war, the processes which gave birth to the nation-states of Europe have been repeated all over the world. We have seen the awakening of national consciousness in peoples who have for centuries lived in dependence on some other power.
>
> Fifteen years ago this movement spread through Asia. Many countries there, of different races and civilizations, pressed their claim to an independent national life. Today the same thing is happening in Africa. The most striking of all the impressions I've formed since I left London a month ago is of the strength of this African national consciousness. In different places it may take different forms, but it is happening everywhere.
>
> The wind of change is blowing through the continent.
>
> Whether we like it or not this growth of national consciousness is a political fact. We must all accept it as a fact. Our national policies must take account of it.

There was a more palatable message for Macmillan's hosts in his insistence that the Western powers, including South Africa, unite against the rising threat of communism. But the sting was in the tail, when he said, "As a member of the Commonwealth it is our earnest desire to give South Africa our support and encouragement, but I hope you won't mind my saying, frankly, that there are some aspects of your policies which make it impossible to do this without being false to our deep convictions about the political destinies of free men, to which, in our own territories, we are trying to give effect."

The speech was said to have left Dr. Verwoerd and others in his government seething with anger. While it was an inspiring message for Mandela and the ANC, it also created within the liberation movement a false, misguided optimism that the apartheid regime would soon fall. If that was the hope behind the message of Macmillan's speech, the effect was tragically the opposite.

The Union decided it did not want to remain in the Commonwealth and began an independence movement of its own, calling a national referendum on becoming a republic. Naturally, the black, Indian and colored population was excluded from the vote, which was overwhelmingly in favor of cutting the cord with the mother country. The date set for becoming a republic was May 1961.

The Sharpeville incident took place within a few weeks of Macmillan's speech, and, in response, the ANC scheduled an All-In Conference in Pietermaritzburg for March 1961, at which the plan was to call for a national convention, with no exclusions of any races this time, to discuss and plan a new non-racial constitution. Mandela had been banned for five years from public speaking but the order was about to expire and he could, briefly, legally speak at the conference.

The ANC had decided to reconstitute itself as a secret organization. At a committee meeting that he attended in Johannesburg the night before he left for the conference, it was decided that Mandela should become the new underground figurehead, to evade any attempts to impose new banning orders and to be free to organize the national convention. Surprise appearances, like his speech at the Pietermaritzburg conference, would maximize the impact of publicity. Mandela would not return home from the conference.

In a very real sense, the ANC wanted a martyr, and the fall guy was Mandela. Among those at the committee meeting was Mandela's closest colleague, Walter Sisulu, who said later, "When we decided that he should go underground I knew that he was stepping into a position of leadership... we had got the leadership outside, but we must have a leader in jail."

Everyone seemed to understand and accept that Mandela's freedom was now finite, that he was bound to end up in jail, either on conviction at the Treason Trial, or later. That, of course, was not a decision in which Mandela's family had participated or had any say.

He said, later, "This would be a hazardous life and I would be apart from my family, but when a man is denied the right to lead the life he believes in, he has no choice but to become an outlaw."

According to Mandela in his memoir, he went to say goodbye to the children from his first marriage on the afternoon before he left for the conference. His eldest son, Thembi, was by then in school in the eastern Cape, but his son Makgatho and his daughter Makaziwe were both still living with their mother Evelyn at the home of her brother Samuel Mase in Orlando East. He described taking the two of them out on the veld, talking, walking and playing, and finally saying goodbye, not knowing when he would see them again. "The children of a freedom fighter also learn not to ask their father too many questions, and I could see in their eyes that they understood that something serious was occurring."

Behind the scenes of the liberation movement there were ongoing tensions, notably between the PAC Africanists, who wanted no co-operation with white activists, and Mandela and the ANC, who were committed to the Congress Alliance of black, Indian, colored and white organizations. The PAC were initially scheduled to be a part of the Pietermaritzburg conference but then withdrew, along with the white liberals and a church group that cited ANC domination as the problem.

As *Drum* magazine reported, the odds were all against success,

> and yet the outcome was a triumph, an indication of a new spirit of resolve which was emerging among the African people. 1400 delegates from all over the Union got to Maritzburg and many of them slept out in the veld because there was no other place for them to stay. They came by train, by car, by food, by bicycle. They came carrying bundles of food which they shared out as if on a family picnic. Could the [ruling] National Party have achieved this in the face of a banning order, with few cars and very little money to spend?

Mandela came to the microphone on Saturday night, impeccably turned out as ever in a well-cut houndstooth three-piece suit. He was sporting a new, neatly clipped revolutionist's beard. It was his first free speech in public since his original banning order in 1952. Back then he had been one among the many young leaders of the ANC, but in recent months his status had grown significantly and was still rising. Now his appearance was met with "thunderous applause," much punching of the air and long call-and-response cries of *Amandla! Ngawethu!* He was reported to cut a heroic figure as his "familiar boom" filled the hall. *Drum*'s reporter heard a delegate say it was like a state of the nation address by an American president.

Mandela applauded the ANC as the "sword and shield of the African people." Now that it had been suppressed they had two alternatives: either to accept discrimination and humiliation, or to stand firm for their rights. They could remain disunited in the face of the government's arrogance, or they could stand united to ensure that the government's discriminatory legislation did not work.

"Africans," said Mandela, "must feel, act and speak in one voice."

His speech over, Mandela seemed to vanish, as suddenly and unexpectedly as he had appeared. In those brief moments could be found the origins of the romantic legend that would envelop him in the coming months as he remained hidden—while emerging as the ANC's natural figurehead.

The conference appointed him to lead the organizing council for the proposed three-day strike in May 1961, timed to coincide with the declaration of the Republic of South Africa. Mandela wrote a letter to Prime Minister Verwoerd threatening action if the government failed to call a convention of all races to draft a new constitution. Then he returned for the final days of the Treason Trial in Pretoria, which came to an abrupt end in the middle of that same week, with a complete acquittal for the defendants. Mandela now disappeared from public view.

In his memoir Mandela gave an eloquent summary of the outlaw life, describing it as not unlike the shadow world inhabited by any black man under apartheid, dodging between "legality and illegality, openness and concealment." He became a creature of the night, he said, keeping to his hideout during the day and emerging only in darkness. The secrecy that surrounded his underground life was not merely to avoid arrest, though that of course was part of it. The purpose was also to enhance the myth as well as to protect those who had helped him from being sent to jail. One Indian doctor in Port Elizabeth was apparently imprisoned for two years, merely for hosting a meeting between Mandela and fellow African activists Govan Mbeki and Raymond Mhlaba.

The trick was to be invisible—not easy for a man who is blessed with a commanding physique and a regal air. He learned to slump his frame and to speak more gently and with less assurance. He became more passive, less obtrusive, and never asked for anything, but waited—like a good African "boy"—to be told what to do. He abandoned the elegant suits and wore working clothes, overalls and chauffeur's coats.

Mandela went to a safe house in Johannesburg briefly at the end of the Treason Trial and then began a small tour of the western Cape and Natal, taking the opportunity of disguise to gauge the mood among ordinary people—Muslims in the Cape, sugar workers in Natal and factory workers in Port Elizabeth.

He had secret meetings with leading journalists to promote the strike cause and called others from public payphones, using "tickeys"—threepence pieces. It was a strategy that, along with energetic leafleting by supporters, was intended to widen the impact of the strike—but of course the Mandela myth was also being promoted too. Soon he was becoming known as the Black Pimpernel, which he saw as a "somewhat derogatory" reference to the fictional hero of the French Revolution, the Scarlet Pimpernel, created by Baroness Orczy.

For a long time, the strategy seemed to work, though the effect of the stay at home, made necessary when the government ignored Mandela's letter, was less impressive. The South African *Sunday Express* reported in May 1961 that the leader behind "the proposed May demonstrations" had called the newspaper from a public telephone box and told its reporter he did not think he would be arrested before the stay at home began: "So far we have been able to anticipate every move the police have made. I have so much work that I don't even think about arrest. We emphatically deny reports that violence will take place or that the three-day stay-away strike will be extended."

In fact, at an earlier meeting in Durban, Mandela had argued against more militant comrades who wanted to transform the stay at home into a full-blown strike with pickets and demonstrations. A stay at home was an essentially passive device that had been in use since the early 1950s as part of the non-violent strategy of campaigning in the spirit of Gandhi. Some felt the time had come for a more aggressive response, short of actual violence. Mandela argued—perhaps a purposeful criticism of his PAC rivals—that the mass demonstration at Sharpeville had allowed the enemy to shoot down their people. The ANC and its allies had the confidence of the people because it was not reckless with their lives.

Mandela had so much contact with such a wide range of people while he was underground that it seems remarkable he was not betrayed and caught sooner. Not everyone had the keen sense of security exhibited by comrade Wolfie Kodesh. Fatima Meer remembered Mandela arriving at her home in Durban early one morning after a long journey in those early weeks. As she wryly put it, this "underground" business was a new concept and had only one member.

Later, while Mandela was in the bathroom, the Meers' phone rang. "Has Nelson arrived?"

Fatima was shocked—it was highly likely the phone was bugged. "What Nelson? No such person has arrived here."

"We dropped him at your house a few hours ago," the caller insisted—it was an Indian comrade well known to Fatima.

"No one has come here," said Fatima and put the phone down.

Mandela swore under his breath when she told him and said, "Has he never heard of such a thing as tapped telephones?" He briefly worried, wondering whether he should move on, but was tired and decided to stay put for a few days, having yet more meetings, including one with the writer Alan Paton, who was active in the Liberal Party.

Mandela had made the long journey from Cape Town, where he had spoken to an assembly of African church ministers from the townships.

He had been much taken by the opening prayer, which thanked the Lord for His bounty and goodness while taking the liberty of reminding Him that some of His flock were more downtrodden than others and it sometimes seemed as if He was not paying attention. If He did not take the initiative in leading the black man to salvation, the black man would have to take matters into his own hands.

There had also been a meeting with SACPO—the South African Colored People's Organisation—when he had addressed a businessman's fears that a black African government would oppress "colored" people just as much as the whites had done. It is extraordinary that the realistic prospect of a black government was being discussed in mid-1961, some thirty-three years ahead of its time. No doubt that was a tribute to the African independence movement and the Macmillan speech, but it was also a reflection on Mandela's own growing credibility as a potential future leader. Mandela had reassured the colored businessman of the ANC's commitment to non-racial policies and to equality for all, as expressed in the Freedom Charter of 1955.

Mandela began using more militant turns of phrase in his speeches. The future of non-violent tactics was open to question and very much in his thoughts. In his talks with ordinary people he had sensed their frustration and impatience that past tactics had not led to breakthroughs. He characterized the May stay at home as a war with the government, a government that was raiding leaders of the liberation movement, banning meetings, seizing printing presses, passing new laws for detention without trial and mobilizing police and troops.

By mid-May he was back in Johannesburg and was persuaded to give his first ever television interview to Brian Widlake, a reporter for ITN. The interview was arranged by Ruth First and took place—in secret of course—in the sitting room of the home of a white comrade, Julius Lewin, in one of the leafy, white suburbs of the city. Ahmed Kathrada was deputed to collect Widlake and deliver him to the interview. Kathrada got lost on the way and ended up taking a hopelessly roundabout route. When they finally arrived, Widlake congratulated Mandela on the security measures he was taking, not apparently realizing the circuitous journey was unplanned.

The interview betrayed Mandela's inexperience in front of a camera. He was stiff and awkward and his answers did not always have clarity. But the overall message was plain enough: Mandela and his colleagues were determined to secure a vote for the African people.

A week later, on the eve of the strike, Mandela had a near-miss as he drove into a police roadblock, heading to a meeting of ANC leaders in Orlando. He was dressed as a chauffeur and sat calmly while an officer briefly searched the car. When asked for his pass, he said he had left it at home but gave a made-up pass number and was waved through.

Other leaders also went into hiding to avoid arrest during the strike. Amina Cachalia remembered Mandela being with her husband, Yusuf, at her sister's home in an Indian neighborhood. They sat playing snakes and ladders, ludo and cards, to pass the time. Mandela helped create a small garden in her sister's backyard for her young children.

The first day of the strike began with every appearance of success but, as the hours went on, it became apparent that the number of people staying at home was not as high as hoped. "Most go to work: all quiet" was one newspaper headline. The next day, with an even poorer turnout, Mandela announced that the strike had been called off. The government had done its best to suppress it, with a heavy police presence on the streets, while the PAC and the liberals had also played some part in undermining the ANC's plans. But as one Indian comrade, Mosie Moolla, later said, the strike had fizzled out because you can't keep calling people out on political issues. What they are really interested in is putting food on their table.

Bob Hepple, the young white advocate who was also a trade union activist, remembered discussing the failure with Mandela, who had put a brave face on it. Hepple did not believe the issue—South Africa becoming a republic—had really touched the workers' lives. They might take action on bread-and-butter issues that affected them but this was just kind of, oh, well...

Mandela gave another round of press interviews. The journalist Mary

Benson remembered the "excitingly conspiratorial" feeling as she and two male reporters were driven by Ruth First to an apartment block in the less prosperous white suburb of Yeoville. There they were ushered into Mandela's presence in a "sparsely furnished room dimmed by drawn yellow curtains with a single electric light bulb hanging from the ceiling." It was around this time that Mandela went to stay with Wolfie Kodesh at his secret flat in Yeoville-Berea so this might well have been his apartment, which was certainly under-decorated and had minimal furniture.

Benson said Mandela, in a striped sports shirt and gray trousers, was far from conspiratorial and seemed very relaxed, his eyes closing to slits "as laughter reverberated through his huge frame." He tried to spin the strike as a success, given the government's efforts to thwart them. One of the journalists—they were all white—spoke of the moderation of the Africans and was firmly put right: "Moderation is not the appropriate word! Our feeling against imperialism is intense. I detest it!"

But weren't his supporters worried about co-operating with whites? (This was a question that haunted him.) "Once the average African is convinced that this co-operation is genuine and that whites support his claims and aspirations, he gives full support to this policy." He gave some examples such as the priest activists Michael Scott and Trevor Huddleston. "Unfortunately, other countries in Africa misunderstand this co-operation. But I think this will soon be cleared up."

It was time to go, as Benson relates, but at the door Mandela turned to face them and his face was suddenly somber. "If the government reaction is to crush by naked force our non-violent demonstrations, we will have to seriously reconsider our tactics. In my mind we are closing a chapter of a non-violent policy."

The beginnings of violence? There had not yet been any discussion about this within the ANC and Mandela would later be reprimanded for these comments spoken out of turn. But this was Mandela's initiative. He was ready to start the armed struggle.

Twelve

LIKE MOST OF the young white Jewish people who had become involved in the liberation movement, Wolfie Kodesh was a first-generation South African whose parents had been immigrants from Eastern Europe. Wolfie's own father had fled the pogroms in Russia and though many of the new generation gradually constructed comfortable middle-class lives, they also had their own experiences of poverty, struggle and oppression.

Wolfie had been raised for a while in a Cape Town slum and fought the gray-shirt fascists there in the 1930s. Later he signed up to confront the fascists of Hitler and Mussolini in Abyssinia, in North Africa and finally in Italy, as a volunteer in the South African army serving alongside the Allies.

He had been an early activist in the Springbok Legion, many of whose members, such as Wolfie, were already or later became communists. Even though the ANC did not allow non-black Africans as members, he and Mandela became close colleagues, particularly during the early 1960s.

Unlike the militant younger generation of black Africans, many of the Jews had fought in the war and had valuable knowledge and experience to share.

Wolfie was one of the handful of people chosen to look after Mandela while he was underground, ensuring his security, taking care of his transport and finding him places to stay. Ahmed Kathrada was involved in this "underground committee" too, and their role was just one among many hidden clues to the surprisingly intimate bond between the ANC and the communists—a bond fostered by Mandela that troubled many black Africans, inside South Africa and out.

There is no doubt that Wolfie was a tremendously useful ally for secret operations. While he had been sleeping outdoors during the state of emergency in 1960, he had also affected disguises, growing a beard, wearing shabby clothing and dark glasses and even having a false heel built into a shoe so that he was forced to walk with a limp. He soon abandoned the shoe, however, as the limp tended to attract attention. He would use secret signals to communicate with colleagues, have cars left in side streets for collection and practiced techniques, both on foot and when driving, to avoid being followed.

Wolfie grew weary of sleeping on golf courses and in gardens—it was very cold at night—so he decided it was time to rent a flat. He must have looked at a dozen before finding one between the inner city suburbs of Berea and Yeoville, in an apartment building at 52 Webb Street. It had an underground garage with a parking space right next to the steps to the front door of the flat itself, which was on the ground floor. Perfect! Wolfie took the lease, being careful to sign it with an assumed name, Keith Shapiro, because he knew it was common practice to put the tenants' names at the front entrance and he didn't want Special Branch finding "Wolfie Kodesh" written there.

He made the flat his base for many months, coming and going, but always doubling back and taking different routes to evade detection. Then one night he arranged a meeting for Mandela at the nearby apartment of some friends, a couple with no children who were always kind enough to go out and leave their home empty for Wolfie to use, without ever asking questions.

Mandela, wearing a peaked cap, was driven in from a township and was dropped off, to be collected at 11 p.m. after the meeting, which Wolfie recalled as a gathering of the ANC leadership involving Walter Sisulu and others he had since forgotten. Wolfie was already there when the others arrived, walking down the passage to the apartment where the meeting was to be held. Just as Sisulu entered, Wolfie saw an elderly white couple watching from a nearby doorway. A procession of Africans going into a flat was not a common sight. Wolfie heard the old man say to his wife, "Go and phone the police."

Wolfie ran out into the street, ran round to the French windows of the apartment and knocked quietly on the glass. When the window was opened, he explained what had happened and they all quickly left.

Mandela was not due to be picked up for a few hours but there was no time to waste as the police could arrive at any moment. On the spur of the moment Wolfie said, "Well, look here, I've got a place." They all agreed, "All right. You take Nelson." So he took Mandela the few blocks to his flat. When they were safe inside Wolfie explained how and why he had acquired it. Mandela laughed and said, "OK, I'll stay. We'll see what happens."

He ended up being there for a couple of months or more (the precise dates are beyond recall) as he sought to persuade reluctant comrades that it was time to fight and made plans for the military campaign ahead. It was a small apartment with a single bed lodged in the alcove. On that first evening, assuming that Mandela would take the bed, Wolfie retrieved the stretcher from the cupboard and prepared to sleep on that. Mandela said, no, he didn't want to upset Wolfie's routine; he would take the stretcher, and would not be persuaded out of it.

They sat and talked for a while. Wolfie was naturally keen to be prepared for eventualities. There would be cleaners coming in, African cleaners of course, as all white apartments were then cleaned by "flat boys" who all lived in rooms the size of broom cupboards at the top of buildings. (Locations in the sky, they were called, a location being an alternative name to "township" for places such as Orlando and Sophiatown.)

There was a peephole in the front door, but Wolfie wanted Mandela to have a cover story, so they agreed he would pretend to be a student who was waiting to leave the country for further education. Mandela had a ready name, David Motsamayi, which was to be his pseudonym throughout the months ahead.

Mandela never explained why he chose that name—he claimed he could not remember—but it belonged to a former client of his law firm. As he told Richard Stengel, Motsamayi "was a big shebeen boss and he had been to prison a couple of times but nevertheless a respectable chap, and he made his wealth in jail."

After a hot bath, Mandela went to sleep. His feet must have been hanging over the edge of that stretcher. Early the next morning, Wolfie was awakened about five by the creaking of the stretcher. When he looked he saw Mandela sitting on the edge, putting on a vest, followed by long johns, a tracksuit and takkies—gym shoes. Mandela pulled the curtains apart slightly and opened the window a fraction to allow in some fresh air.

Wolfie was worried, as Mandela had told him what a keep-fit fanatic he used to be with his amateur boxing and his early-morning runs around Soweto. He imagined now that Mandela intended leaving the flat to go for a run. What a breach of security that would be.

Wolfie got up to go to the door, intending to remove the key. "What's wrong?" said Mandela.

"You can't go running around here," said Wolfie.

"Who's running around here?"

"Well," said Wolfie, "I thought you were dressing up to go running, like you did in Soweto."

"No!" said Mandela. "I'm going to do my exercises. I'm going to run, but I'm running on the spot."

That's fine, then, thought Wolfie, and went back to bed. He dozed off only to be woken again a little while later by the sound of Mandela breathing heavily as he worked up a sweat, running in place. It seemed to Wolfie that this went on, literally, for a couple of hours, culminating in Mandela doing what Wolfie described as "frog jumps" all around the floor of the flat. Lucky they were on the ground floor.

"Hey, but that's keeping fit!" said Wolfie, from his bed.

"You know what," said Mandela, "come tomorrow you're also going to run on the spot. You're also going to keep fit."

Wolfie, who was not used to such a regime, was nearly dead after fifteen minutes the next morning but gradually built up to a full hour and was grateful for it. "The two of us must have looked an incongruous pair, one a big, broad-shouldered person and me a short stocky guy, both running on the spot. I imagine it must have looked very funny."

After a couple of days Mandela began to settle down to some work, setting himself up at the table by the window, where he could sit hidden from the street by the lace curtains. Wolfie realized his guest was interested in military matters and after an initial discussion he gave him a book about Karl von Clausewitz, the Prussian soldier and theorist. When Mandela didn't know who he was, Wolfie described him as being like the Karl Marx of military science.

As Mandela's reading tastes broadened, he sent out an appeal for books—the kind of banned material that could get people arrested. In London, a colleague in exile whom he barely yet knew, Mac Maharaj, received the requests for literature and was fascinated by them, not knowing who the books were for: works on guerrilla warfare, on partisan warfare and, at one stage, a call for books and articles on successful counterinsurgencies, especially the role of the British in Malaya. This was a joke to Mac, who was something of an urgent revolutionist himself and had been busy making his own studies of the tactics of Chairman Mao and Che Guevara. Here now somebody back home was interested in what the British were up to. (It was only when Mac was sent to Robben Island and met Mandela in 1965 that he discovered who the reader had been.)

Wolfie heard a noise outside that morning and looked through the peephole to see the "flat boy" busy at work. He had not been into the apartment since Mandela arrived and even that could arouse suspicion. After taking a look at the young man, Mandela said it was time to invite him in and talk with him over a cup of tea. So the cleaner was ushered in and Wolfie made them both a cup of tea. He was a Thembu and Wolfie couldn't understand what he was saying, but could see he was dumbstruck by the idea of a white man serving him and then sitting down to share the table with him.

Soon, however, Mandela—who had the great gift, even then, of talking to everyone in the same easy manner—had the young man laughing and relaxed. Within a day or two Wolfie realized that Mandela had begun using the cleaner to run errands for him, posting letters, collecting shopping and so on.

In the years to come, when it was safe—or safer—to talk, Wolfie would tell the story of a couple they knew whose marriage was in trouble. When Mandela heard, he had insisted on leaving his safe house to visit to try to ease their problems. Wild horses would not have dragged that couple's name from Wolfie.

They were, in fact, Adelaide and Paul Joseph, Indian activists who were friends as well as comrades of Mandela. Paul, a communist, had been a defendant in the Treason Trial and Adelaide was sometimes used by Mandela as a courier. He would turn up at the back door of their home in the Indian area of Fordsburg in a boiler suit, leaving a statement for her to deliver to the offices of the *Rand Daily Mail*. She had once opened the back door to throw out a bucket of water and all but sloshed it in Mandela's face as he stood there unannounced. Mandela had a lifelong passion for Indian food and always loved Adelaide's cooking, among others.

The Josephs had married a month after Mandela had married Winnie in mid-1958. Both couples had quickly started families. Adelaide had become pregnant with twins but, by a tragic misfortune, one had been deprived of oxygen at birth and was severely disabled. He would die at the age of eleven in 1970.

The birth of their son put a strain on their lives and Adelaide would get angry when Paul disappeared for days at a time as he became drawn into underground activities. She wouldn't know where he was—he could've been arrested or in hospital or anything—but whenever she asked, she would be told, don't worry, he's fine. Eventually, she said, listen, I've had enough now, I want a divorce, I want to see Nelson, he can be my lawyer.

She chased Kathrada out of the house when he tried to talk to her. "Get out of here, I don't want to see you," she told him. Wolfie came and she showed him to the door too. They sent Molly Fischer as well. "Why does it have to be Paul?" Adelaide wanted to know. "Why can't it be someone who doesn't have commitments, a family, a sick child at home?"

All of this must have got back to Mandela, and a day was picked for his intervention. Wolfie turned up again at the Josephs' home and told them to be ready at a certain time. He came back later, picked them up and drove them to another house in Fordsburg. Adelaide and Paul walked in, holding hands, not knowing what to expect, and there was Mandela sitting in this little room, waiting for them. He got up, cried, "Addie!" and gave her a big affectionate hug. "How are you, how are the children?" They sat together and exchanged pleasantries for a while, before Mandela said, "Well, I'm glad I've seen you and you are fine, now it's OK, you can go home."

The Josephs left, puzzled. What was all that about? Only years later did they discover, from Wolfie, that Mandela had heard stories about them and was concerned for their marriage—not that he mentioned his concerns when he actually met them. Mandela kept his cards close to his chest, rarely discussing his own personal affairs with anyone, and he clearly assumed the same rule followed for the personal affairs of others.

Now, in this new life, he had "too much privacy." Wolfie would recall him being tearful as he talked sometimes of how much he missed his wife and the world he had left behind. Mandela had a vast network of friends across all races and Wolfie would often be called upon to take Mandela out or bring others to him once darkness fell. More than anyone, he wanted to see Winnie. They had many meetings, both at the flat and elsewhere. Wolfie made careful arrangements, instructing whoever was driving Winnie on the importance of switching cars and taking steps to avoid being followed.

One driver was Rica Hodgson, the wife of Jack Hodgson. A Jewish couple living in more humble circumstances than some of their colleagues, they were both deeply committed to the struggle. Rica remembers how poor they all were—her and Jack, Winnie and the Josephs. Rica had brothers who ran a successful stall in Newtown market, where they were known as the "potato kings" or the "apple kings." She would go there on Fridays to pick up unsold boxes of fruit and sackfuls of vegetables, which she would take to Adelaide Joseph's home in Fordsburg. Winnie would be there too and the three of them would divide up the green groceries, for themselves and for others. Rica would then take Winnie over to Wolfie's so that she could have a few hours alone with Mandela.

Rica remembers Winnie's flawless skin—she was *the* most beautiful woman. Men were mad about her. When Rica saw her again in 2008, Winnie was then in her mid-seventies, yet she remained beautiful. "You've still got wonderful skin," Rica had told her.

"That's all I've got left, Rica," Winnie had replied.

Winnie had no doubt that the security surrounding her visits to her husband was necessary, as she "attracted the attention of the enemy" when Mandela went underground and found herself under round-the-clock surveillance. She had a friend who was a doctor in the maternity ward at Baragwanath Hospital. She would go there disguised as a woman in labor, then swap cars and lie down in the well of the car while they slipped away to take her to Mandela.

She would miss him and he would miss her. "It was hurtful to meet under those circumstances, a reminder of the life we never had, a reminder that things were never normal." Sometimes Winnie would bring their daughters, Zindzi, just a few months old, and Zenani, still a toddler but evidently half aware of what was going on. Mandela wrote to her from Robben Island:

> You will probably not remember an incident that moved me very much at the time and about which I never like to think. Towards the end of 1961 you were brought to the house of a friend and I was already waiting for you when you came. I was wearing no jacket or hat. I took you into my arms and for about ten minutes we hugged and kissed and talked. Then suddenly you

> seemed to have remembered something. You pushed me aside and started searching the room. In a corner you found the rest of my clothing. After collecting it you gave it to me and asked me to go home. You held my hand for quite some time, pulling desperately and begging me to return. It was a difficult moment for both of us. You felt I had deserted you and mummy and your request was a reasonable one...your age in 1961 made it difficult for me to explain my conduct to you and the worried expression that I saw in your face haunted me for many months thereafter. Luckily, however, you soon cooled down and we parted peacefully. But for days I was lost in thought wondering how I could show you that I had not failed you and the family.

Walter Sisulu came to Wolfie's flat several times, as did Joe Slovo. Wolfie went out and left them to talk but on one occasion when he returned Sisulu was still there, past midnight when it was too late for a black man to be on the streets, so Sisulu slept over and Wolfie stayed elsewhere.

Mandela took some pleasure in turning up unexpectedly at people's back doors, as he had with Adelaide Joseph. Wolfie remembered taking him to the home of a white Jewish couple, driving straight into their garage and the couple practically passing out with shock when they saw Mandela standing there.

On another occasion Wolfie took Mandela to a house in the white suburb of Parktown for a meeting, perhaps with Winnie (Wolfie could not remember; she was not there anyway when he arrived with Mandela). The man of the house went off to make them drinks and as he came back down the passage they could hear the glasses clinking noisily on the tray. The man's hands were shaking because he was so nervous. Wolfie gave Mandela a look—"We can't stay"—and suddenly affected to recall another meeting they had forgotten. They left quickly. Their host had clearly known he had South Africa's most wanted man sitting in his lounge.

Sometimes Wolfie tried to come up with diversions for Mandela. When a young white woman, an old friend of Wolfie's from Cape Town, came visiting, he said to her, would you like to meet Nelson Mandela? Who wouldn't? Mandela was famous to the woman concerned for his reputation as one of the best-dressed men in Johannesburg, given to wearing beautiful clothes, very handsome and charismatic in his three-piece English tweeds.

Amy Reitstein (later Thornton) was just twenty-nine at the time and worked as a nursery-school teacher, taking advantage of the long holidays to visit her sister in Johannesburg, possibly in June or July 1961. Wolfie came to collect her and she remembers driving into the basement garage where there was an elegant car parked, which she recalled as a Jaguar. Wolfie told her Mandela had been using it. The car belonged to another old soldier turned communist activist, the successful theater director Cecil Williams.

Williams, who was gay, middle-aged and white, had a wealthy guardian angel, the elderly Mrs. Sharp. She bought him gifts and gave him money. It was she who had provided him with a big car—in fact an Austin Westminster, not a Jaguar—which Mandela sometimes used, pretending to be the chauffeur.

Wolfie and Amy parked, went up the stairs to the door of the flat and rang the bell. She heard Mandela take the chain off the door before opening it. Mandela had been asleep and there he was—one of Johannesburg's best-dressed men—in his shorts and a string vest.

They chatted and Amy made some coffee. She thought Mandela a very impressive figure. He told them he had just been out by himself on an arrangement to meet Winnie. Something had gone wrong and he'd taken the risk of driving into Orlando and sending a neighbor's child to fetch Winnie for him. It seemed to Amy that he was very much in love with Winnie and couldn't bear the thought of their date not materializing.

She couldn't stay long—she still had to get home and her sister would be waiting up as she would not entrust a key to Amy. Everyone was so security conscious then. As she was going, Mandela asked her whether she would like to come again and do some typing for him. She agreed, so

Wolfie came to collect her the next morning and for the next three mornings. She would sit with Mandela at the table by the window and they would talk and work. Wolfie would drive her home again each evening. One morning Wolfie bought steaks and Amy cooked lunch.

Mandela spoke openly about the necessity for a change in tactics, an end to passive resistance. He was writing a speech to deliver to the ANC national executive about the turn to armed struggle and Amy typed it up from his handwritten draft. She recalls her cheek in questioning Mandela about the document and telling him there ought to be room in the military campaign for white comrades.

Mandela also told her that he had made the trip to see Chief Luthuli (who was still ANC president) as David Motsamayi. He posed as the chauffeur to a white stranger who was not involved in the struggle and did not know Mandela's true identity. On the way, Mandela saw in the rear-view mirror that the man was becoming ill. As they drove through Natal, Mandela realized that they were close to an Indian doctor who knew him so he stopped there. The doctor, once recovered from the shock of finding Comrade Mandela at his door, was able to treat the man so their journey could continue. Now Mandela saw that the man was watching him in the mirror, finally saying, "I don't know who you are but no doctor speaks to a driver the way that man spoke to you." No more was said. If the man realized who his driver was, he never gave him away.

Mandela finally reached his destination, a poor farm in Natal, where a child was sent to fetch the chief. Amy could see a sudden flash of anger from him as he talked about how he had been "revolted" by the poverty of the rural people. Mandela stood with Luthuli in a cane field, trying to persuade him to give his blessing to armed resistance. Mandela told Amy that Luthuli had eventually said he could not publicly support the armed struggle but would not oppose it.

One minor historical event that Amy witnessed involved a visit from the Jewish photographer and activist, Eli Weinberg, who, struggling to find work in other fields because of bans and restrictions, had become a professional photographer, with a lucrative line in capturing the weddings of black Africans. Indeed, he had photographed Mandela and Winnie in their wedding outfits, in June 1958.

Wolfie and others realized that there was constant talk of Mandela being missing or dead, so they looked for ways to reassure people of his presence. Weinberg came to the flat and took some photographs. There is an image—not much circulated—of Mandela in what appears to be a tribal blanket but is in fact one of Wolfie's bedspreads. The most famous photograph was the one of him wearing a striped T-shirt. He is slightly full in the face, bearded, and his close-cut Afro hair has an artificial parting razored into it, as was the popular style of the time, in an odd sort of approximation of a white man's haircut.

Of course, as Wolfie told the story, Weinberg had to be smuggled into Wolfie's flat for the assignment. Not his flat, but his "hideout."

A copy of the photograph was taken to Mandela later, after his arrest, who signed it and wrote a message on it. The photograph was returned to Wolfie, who kept it framed on his wall when he went into exile in London. "I look forward to many, many years of collective effort on our part. Let strength, initiative and solidarity be our watchwords," was Mandela's wider message for the comrades. On the back he wrote, "Dear Wolfie, I am most inspired by the many messages of solidarity and support which you have sent me. The terrific spirit of the people makes me absolutely confident of the early defeat of the Nationalist government. Yours, very sincerely." It is dated October 25, 1962.

Wolfie says he was always on edge about Mandela being at the flat for too long, feeling responsible for him, as his minder, and always aware that, in spite of all his precautions, he could still be tailed and caught. When he came back one evening after being out all day, Mandela said he wanted to speak to the cleaner, so Wolfie went up to the location in the sky to find him. The cleaner was not in his room but the door to the tiny room was open. There on the bed was a magazine open at a page with a headline in thick lettering, "Black pimpernel still at large!" alongside half a dozen pictures of Wolfie's flatmate. Wolfie found the cleaner in another man's room and told him, "David wants to see you." The cleaner came down and

Mandela spoke to him, Wolfie watching the man nodding and nodding as Mandela talked to him in Xhosa, apparently asking him to run an errand the next morning. As soon as he had gone, Wolfie told Mandela about the magazine and said he thought it was time to leave. Wolfie had already arranged another place for him to stay.

Mandela said, "No. Why must I go? I'm very happy here. That fellow will never give me away." Wolfie felt that Mandela had some intuition or knowledge about "his own people" that Wolfie lacked. He relented but he was unhappy, still fearing Mandela would be betrayed—if only by an accidental remark—or recognized while he was out. Mandela might put on a chauffeur's coat and hat—in fact, he had a choice of two coats, one a white driver's dustcoat and the other a khaki raincoat—but whenever he went out in these disguises, he was still very obviously Nelson Mandela, or so it seemed to Wolfie.

In his memoir, Mandela says, briefly, that the end of his stay with Wolfie came abruptly after two Zulu men spotted the milk that he had left outside to ferment, on the windowsill of the flat. The souring milk would become *amasi*, a thick yogurt-like drink or topping for African dishes. Mandela was inside the flat talking to Wolfie when he overheard the two Zulus commenting. He could not see them as the curtains were drawn but asked Wolfie to be quiet so he could listen. "What is 'our milk' doing on that ledge?" one was saying. They were wondering why a black man was living in a white area. "I left for a different hideout the next night," says Mandela.

His next refuge was the home of Hymie and Hazel Rochman. In 1961, Hymie was a medic, just approaching forty, and had earlier been an intern at Baragwanath Hospital where he had known and been smitten by the hospital's black pediatric medical social worker, Winnie Madikizela, before her marriage to Mandela. Hymie's wife, Hazel, a newspaper reporter, was pregnant with their second child. They knew Wolfie on the network of white Jewish friends and relatives, many of whom, like Hymie and Hazel, were radical and active, if not deeply involved.

The police used to raid the Rochmans' house, looking for banned publications, which were never found because the Rochmans had buried them in a tin trunk in their garden. The list of prohibited books was ridiculous, remembers Hazel, including, for an obvious if nonsensical reason, *Black Beauty*. They used to hide things for Wolfie sometimes. One day he just came and asked whether they would hide Mandela at their home, 21 Nursery Road, in the suburb of Gardens. They did not feel they had a choice, and of course they wanted to help, but that did not mean they weren't scared by the implications of hiding South Africa's most wanted man. They agonized over where to put him, eventually deciding that, for the sake of appearances, he must go in the servants' quarters outside, in the room next to their black maid, Catherine Shabalala.

All the white Jewish couples, even the most revolutionary, like the Slovos, had black "domestics." The Rochmans never discussed their house guest with their maid, and never ever referred to him in front of her as anything other than David. She too only ever referred to him as David, but she in fact was in the ANC and knew all along exactly who he was. As with the cleaner back in Webb Street, she would run errands for Mandela and help him, whenever he asked.

A friend installed an alarm that ran from the study in the main house to the servants' block, so that the Rochmans could warn Mandela if the police turned up. Otherwise, he used the study himself during the day for his readings and writings, and was invariably out at meetings at night. Wolfie would come to collect him, in a dry-cleaning van, Hazel recalled, which he would also use to bring supplies for Mandela, such as books, paper, food and clothing.

If visitors arrived while he was in the house, he would slip out and pretend to be the gardener. Hazel's own father saw him there on one occasion: "My God, who's that?" Her father recognized immediately that it was Mandela and left, afraid they would all be in trouble.

Mandela had dinner a few times with the Rochmans. Hazel remembers sitting with him in their dining room, the one room in the house that didn't have windows, and listening. She was a little in awe of Mandela and a bit tongue-tied in his presence; on the other hand, her truculent husband, Hymie, took on Mandela over the same issue that was raised by Amy Reitstein—the role of whites in the struggle. Hymie knew the ANC didn't want whites and understood why black Africans would not want to end up taking orders from whites at the top. However, he was still not satisfied with the multiracial Congress Alliance and wanted to see all races—black, white, Indian and colored—gathered together in one rainbow organization. Keeping them separate was like mimicking apartheid, Hymie argued. No doubt Mandela sat courteously through his host's onslaught. Multiracial politics was among the most sensitive questions, causing terrible divisions among black activists. Hymie could not have known of the key role being played by some white Jewish veterans, such as Jack Hodgson, as the armed struggle loomed.

Mandela stayed with the Rochmans for some seven weeks, always appearing relaxed and easygoing, but keeping a polite distance. There was no contact between them after he left.

So many times he escaped arrest by the slimmest of margins. Once he pulled up to a robot—as South African traffic lights are called—and saw police chief Captain Spengler in the car alongside him. He would later describe the time it took for the light to change as "The longest day I ever had."

There were many instances in which he was recognized by black policemen who merely winked, or raised their thumbs in salute, or ignored him altogether and let him pass. There were a couple of sympathetic officers who used to go to the house and give Winnie tips on what the police were up to and where they were searching for Mandela.

Mary Benson describes meeting Mandela at a suburban bungalow and his telling her of a narrow getaway he had made. He had been waiting for a lift on a street corner in town, in his chauffeur's garb, and the car he was expecting was late—"It's vital," he told her, "to be absolutely punctual when you are functioning underground"—and he saw coming towards him an African Special Branch detective who looked straight at him. Mandela thought the game was up but instead the officer winked and gave him the ANC salute. It was evidence, he said, of the ANC's hidden support, even within the police.

Pressure on him was mounting now and Mandela could spare Benson only an hour to talk. When the time was up he offered her a lift back to the city and put on his chauffeur's coat and cap before taking her to a car that was, in her view, "very much the worse for wear." She sat in the back like a white madam while they spluttered along, the car frequently stalling, each moment seeming like an eternity before the engine revved back to life. Benson expected a police car to pull up beside them at any second but eventually they arrived at her sister's flat where Mandela pulled over and they parted.

It sounds as though this was the same vehicle that Mandela provided for Winnie, who described how the "crock of a car" he had given her finally gave out. She was told by a comrade to drive it to a particular street corner. When she got there a tall man in blue overalls opened the door and asked her to move over so he could take the wheel—her husband, she realized—and they drove to a garage where he bought her a newer car, trading the old one in part exchange. He then drove to the city center and when he arrived at a stop sign on Sauer Street, with hundreds of commuters all around, he got out and disappeared into the crowds after a brief goodbye.

"So that was the kind of life we led," said Winnie.

On June 26, 1961, Mandela released a public statement as "Honorary Secretary of the All-in African National Council." The lengthy declaration—like many senior comrades he was rarely given to brevity—reassured ANC supporters that the campaign was continuing and that there would be renewed pressure on the "race maniacs who govern our beloved country." The precise form of the contemplated action, its scope, dimensions and duration, would be announced at the appropriate time but at "the present moment it is sufficient to say that we plan to make government impossible."

He was informed, he said, that a warrant for his arrest had been issued and that the police were looking for him. Colleagues had advised him not to surrender himself and he was not going to give himself up to a government he did not recognize. Seeking cheap martyrdom by handing himself in would be "naive and criminal." It was more important to carry out the important program ahead.

"I have had to separate myself from my wife and children, from my mothers and sisters to live as an outlaw in my own land. I have had to close my business, to abandon my profession and live in poverty and misery, as many of my people are doing... Only through hardship, sacrifice and militant action can freedom be won.

"The struggle is my life, I will continue fighting for freedom until the end of my days."

Thirteen

IT WAS NO easy task for Mandela to persuade the ANC leadership and the Congress Alliance that it was time to go to war. Not even the very modest war—not much more than a few minor skirmishes really—that Mandela initially envisaged. There were some, however, who were straining at the leash, who couldn't wait, who in fact did not wait, but began gathering their own guerrilla armies. That too was in Mandela's thoughts: the danger of being overtaken by events, of being left behind in the rush to armed struggle.

At least he had Walter Sisulu to support him. They had first discussed the prospect of violence back in 1952, as doubts set in about the effectiveness of passive resistance. Peaceable protest might have shown the racist authorities their determination to defy, but was it ever going to overturn the government, or force them to break down the barriers of apartheid? Since then, Mandela had been reading, learning the lessons of history and considering the potential power of a guerrilla army.

His first attempt to win over his colleagues had been at a meeting of the Working Committee of the ANC in May of 1961. No sooner had he started his speech—perhaps the speech that Amy Reitstein had typed for him—than Moses Kotane, both a senior member of the Communist

Party and a leading member of the ANC executive, began attacking his proposal, saying it was ill conceived and born of desperation as he had been outwitted by the government and run out of ideas.

According to Mandela's memoir, Kotane told the meeting, "There is still room for the old methods if we are imaginative and determined enough. If we embark on the course Mandela is suggesting we will be exposing innocent people to massacres by the enemy." Mandela could see that the meeting was swayed by Kotane and was disappointed that Sisulu did not speak up to support him. When he complained afterwards to Sisulu, his friend only laughed and said it would have been "as foolish as attempting to fight a pride of angry lions."

Kotane, who was notoriously overbearing and even bullying in his style, was not universally popular with colleagues. Joe Slovo said he was easier to admire than to like and seemed to revel in the image he had created of himself as "no-nonsense, hard and domineering." Sisulu was the diplomat, a canny tactician, and now said he would bring Kotane to meet Mandela privately so they could have a more open discussion.

Kotane's biography makes no reference to Mandela's involvement in the turn to armed struggle and, it follows, does not allude, even vaguely, to these events. But in Mandela's version they spent the day together at a safe house in the township. Mandela softened his colleague with an African proverb: *Sebatana ha se bokwe ka diatla*—"the attacks of the wild beast cannot be averted with only bare hands." He then proceeded to tell him that Kotane's stance was like that of the communists in Cuba under Batista, who kept waiting for the revolution because they were bound by the rigid doctrine of Lenin and Stalin.

People could wait forever for the right conditions, but Castro had shown everyone it wasn't necessary. He had started a revolution without them and it had still succeeded. Havana had fallen to Fidel Castro and Che Guevara thirty months earlier, on New Year's Day 1959. In just two years they had turned a handful of guerrilla insurgents into a triumphant revolutionary force of thousands, an inspiring achievement to Mandela and the armies of the oppressed throughout the world.

Kotane was still stuck in the old ways of the ANC, Mandela told him, and meanwhile people were already ahead of him, forming their own military units, waiting for the ANC to lead them. This time Kotane listened and eventually said he would make no promises but invited Mandela to bring the proposal back to the Working Committee a week later. He did so while Kotane stayed silent, raising no objections or overbearing challenges. Mandela was authorized to go forward and present his proposition to the national executive in Natal.

Now he had to get support, not just from the ANC but also from the Congress Alliance, where there would be committed pacifists among the Indian and colored representatives. Many had been involved at various stages of the recently concluded Treason Trial when those in the dock had successfully argued that they were truly non-violent. How would they cope with the moral switch being asked of them?

But, as Mandela well knew, his toughest opposition would come from Chief Albert Luthuli, the ANC president, who was a very religious man and naturally opposed to violence and also, perhaps, rather gentlemanly, of the old school. He had in fact been dismissed as chief by the Native Affairs department in Pretoria when he refused their order to resign from the ANC.

He continued to be called chief anyway and seems, more than most, to have embodied chiefly qualities, being described by those who had known him as a strong, charismatic, highly principled man with a powerful voice both as a singer and as an orator. Surprisingly, he was close to Moses Kotane in spite of the fact that the latter was a communist. It appears they each respected the other as men of honesty and conviction.

By 1961, Chief Luthuli had been confined to his home in Groutville for the previous two years of his presidency of the ANC, which made it difficult for the rest of the leadership to involve him in decision-making and keep him up to date with events. This tended to make Luthuli himself feel isolated from what was going on elsewhere. He had suffered a stroke in the mid-1950s and appears to have had unspecified health problems as a result. It seems possible he subsequently experienced some form of depression.

In his memoir, Mandela refers to the historic meetings that now took place as being held in Durban, but, so far as can be ascertained, the actual venue was a beach house within the grounds of a vast sugar plantation at Stanger, a little farther north along the coast from Durban, with Groutville conveniently nearby. The plantation was owned by sympathetic Indian sugar magnates, the Bodasinghs, but still the meetings were held during darkness, on consecutive nights: Mandela remained the most wanted man in the country, Chief Luthuli would be arrested if he was found outside Groutville, and others on the ANC national executive were also banned from leaving their areas or attending meetings.

It was the national executive that met on the first night, probably in the early days of July 1961, ahead of a joint meeting with Indian colleagues the following evening. Mandela again faced opposition as he argued that violence was coming anyway and the ANC risked "being latecomers and followers to a movement we did not control." A prime concern was the impact that the decision in favor of violent action would have on the ANC, with fears that it would cease to function as a political body. Even though it had been banned after Sharpeville, there were concerns that the ANC and its remaining unbanned activists would be further outlawed.

According to Mandela, it was Chief Luthuli himself who suggested the awkward compromise that was eventually agreed on. The ANC would not itself fight the armed struggle, nor would it now form its own armed wing—at least, not publicly. A new organization would be started, which although answerable to the ANC would be otherwise entirely independent with its own separate high command. Luthuli also wanted the resolution accepted, and then forgotten. They should pretend they had never discussed it. Their hands would be clean.

As a result, there is almost no trace now of the meeting, outside the versions given by Mandela. Luthuli never mentioned it. In fact, he would later claim, and not that long afterwards either, that it never happened and that he had never been consulted about the armed struggle.

Perhaps he really was ill and experienced some kind of aberrant loss of memory. But it also must have been difficult for him to reconcile his support for an armed struggle with the announcement, just four months later, that he had won the Nobel Peace Prize. Those words "Nobel Peace Prize winner" appear on the cover of his memoir, *Let My People Go*, first published at the end of 1961. It would have been understandably tricky for the winner of the Nobel Peace Prize, a man of God, to be leading a terrorist campaign at the same time. So that was left to Mandela.

Joe Matthews' father, Z. K. Matthews, the Fort Hare professor, was there, however, and must have subsequently discussed events with his son, as Joe has since described how his father stood with Luthuli in the decision to mount the armed struggle from a separate entity.

Joe says it was a very peculiar decision and the manner in which it was made haunted the ANC for years to come, as, in a sense, the Congress remained a non-violent organization, while the new military body was immediately disowned by those who had given birth to it.

There was confusion in the ranks as the ordinary members of the ANC did not know whether the armed struggle was theirs to join, while, of course, it was to them that the military body turned to find recruits. Soon the ANC would be complaining that its numbers were being depleted by members disappearing for military training. Who was in charge? Joe Matthews remembered his father being asked by a colleague, *Yintoni le high command?* Who is this high command?

Eventually, after Mandela and the others had been sent to Robben Island and Oliver Tambo had become the leader in exile, he moved to resolve the confusion by claiming the armed struggle was being fought by the military wing of the ANC.

That announcement brought the struggle home, where it belonged, but the clarification was by then long overdue. The official histories gloss over the awkward period that preceded Tambo's announcement, as if the armed struggle was always pursued by the military wing of the ANC, and they also tend to neglect to mention that half the people involved were white—which was exactly what the ANC had always feared and resisted: white people making decisions for them.

Meanwhile, Mandela took the fudged agreement to the following night's meeting of the Congress Alliance. Many of the Indian delegates especially, who had been raised on the tactics of Gandhi, were fundamentally against ending passive resistance. At the Indian Congress meeting, which was held concurrently with the ANC meeting the previous evening, tempers had become frayed when those who wanted to stay with non-violence were accused, effectively, of being cowards, of being afraid to go to prison. The Indian Congress finally agreed to approach the ANC in the hope of persuading them that there was still time for non-violent action—but they also agreed to support the ANC if it decided otherwise.

That evening, from eight o'clock onwards at the beach house, Mandela was opposed by people he was close to, whose opinions and judgments he respected. He would never forget the words of J. N. Singh: "Non-violence has not failed us, we have failed non-violence." Mandela answered, no, non-violence *had* failed them because it had done nothing to "stem the violence of the state or change the heart of our oppressors."

The meeting must have been frustrating for members of the ANC national executive who had thrashed out the issues the previous evening, as Chief Luthuli opened the second-night session by saying they had agreed to start an organization that would engage in violent forms of struggle, but he hoped the individual ANC members would be free to express their own views during the debate. It was like starting all over again, and it was no wonder that second meeting was still going as dawn approached.

Ismail Meer, like Luthuli, was a pacifist and had aligned himself with the chief to dissent from the move to armed struggle. His wife, Fatima, on the other hand, was a supporter of armed struggle, but she was not at the meeting. Although Mandela was a persuasive advocate, even he was having difficulty overcoming the fears of comrades such as Meer, Yusuf Cachalia and M. P. Naicker who thought a move to violence would give the state the excuse it needed to kill them all.

In the early hours, just as Mandela thought the debate was moving his way, one Indian, M. D. Naidoo, chided his colleagues, saying, ah, you are afraid of going to jail, that is all. All hell broke loose at this repeated slur and it seemed to Mandela they had gone back to square one. Finally, however, as dawn broke a consensus was reached and the resolution was approved. Mandela does not take the credit himself, in his memoir, but it appears he gave the new military faction its name, Umkhonto we Sizwe—Spear of the Nation—often abbreviated to MK. He merely says the spear was chosen as the symbol because it had long been the Africans' simple weapon of resistance.

Winnie relates that Mandela had been inspired to take the name from something Chief Luthuli had said. After Mandela had eventually succeeded in winning his approval, Luthuli had proclaimed: "I am an African. When a man attacks my kraal I take a spear and defend my family. I give blessing to the armed struggle."

Luthuli is also said to have denied he was against violence, with the words, "If anyone thinks I'm a pacifist, let him try to take my chickens and he will know how wrong he is."

The name, and the image it evoked, might have been pure African, but it was a white Jewish artist and graphic designer, Arthur Goldreich, also a communist, who designed MK's spear logo for its public launch on December 1961. His wife, Hazel, remembers Goldreich sitting at a board working on it, when they lived at Liliesleaf Farm in Rivonia.

The chief went back to isolation in Groutville, while Mandela, with no previous experience as a military leader or strategist, set about organizing MK and planning the opening salvos in a campaign of sabotage. He turned immediately to comrades from among the white Jewish communists, especially those who had fought in the Second World War, beginning with Joe Slovo.

There was, quite naturally, no hidden cache of weapons or stockpile of explosives. "Among the lot of us we did not have a single pistol," said Slovo.

The only people with access to guns were the *tsotsis*, the township gangsters, and the only comrade with any real contacts among them was a rising young star of the liberation movement, Joe Modise. He made inquiries but to begin with nothing much was forthcoming.

At least, now, Mandela was free of the restraints of the ANC, which would not allow white people—any non-Africans, in fact—to become members. Since Sharpeville, much of the political talk at the dinners, the parties, the Sunday-afternoon *braais* (barbecues) around Bram Fischer's pool, especially among the "inner circle," had been of the need for a violent response. AnnMarie Wolpe remembered that Mandela had told her, as they left together following a dinner, "It is with a heavy heart that we turn to armed struggle."

The ANC lacked experience and had no idea how to go about starting a military movement. It took Mandela to grasp the nettle, to read the histories of revolution and to bow to the reality: that they could never get off the ground without the support of the white war veterans. Indeed, it now appears that the white communists exerted an even greater influence than has previously been realized. Mandela was present at a secret meeting of the Communist Party in December 1960 when it decided to begin its own armed struggle, six months before Mandela even raised the subject with the ANC.

Bob Hepple, the young advocate and Communist Party activist, says he was then a kind of factotum for the more senior communists and was asked by party leader Bram Fischer to rent a house for a month in December, where a secret conference could be held. He found a house in Emmarentia; rented a marquee, which was erected in the garden, where people could sleep; organized food; and ferried activists to and from the meeting. He remembers that Mandela and Sisulu were there along with Fischer, Joe Slovo and Michael Harmel, a total of some thirty people altogether.

Hepple was there throughout and clearly remembers the meeting's decision to move to a campaign of sabotage. It was not a tempestuous assembly; there was a consensus: no one was yet looking for an all-out guerrilla war, rather low-level acts of sabotage, which would target places, not people. Michael Harmel, the writer and theoretician, argued that the apartheid state was now bound to collapse. He had produced a paper saying that no further progression was possible along the traditional paths or by adhering strictly to the non-violent slogan in a situation where every democratic demand or criticism is treated as an act of rebellion or treason.

Though it appears that it never became very active, at least one unit, a military or guerrilla cell, was formed in early 1960. Perhaps there were others. The initial Communist Party cell only ever went out looking for suitable non-human targets, but it was the beginnings of the structure that became MK. Kodesh described taking the unit out once to a farming area beyond Johannesburg to cut the telephone wires to Swaziland. The men were up in the trees overhanging the cables, armed with shears, when a farmer's lorry appeared and began reversing with his headlights, fully illuminating them. They dropped down into the open rain gullies at the roadside, but one of them was stuck, caught in the headlights. They all thought he was bound to be spotted, but the lorry passed by.

Paul Joseph, a young married man, remembers a meeting in a back room in Johannesburg where Joe Slovo told him, we are going for armed struggle. He never explained the political principle behind the move. There was no need to explain that to Joseph.

Then and later, Joseph had concerns about what he called "white baggage" in the movement, the "negrophile" attitude among white activists, by which Joseph meant a tendency to patronize black, Indian and colored colleagues and see them as somehow less able. He was always uneasy around Wolfie Kodesh and thought he was suffering from an inferiority complex, or something else that Joseph couldn't quite identify. He was too eager to please his leaders and always seemed to be doing their bidding. One day Kodesh went to Joseph, seeming quite harassed, and blurted out to him, it's time the whites took a back seat, we think the blacks should do it now. So there you are, thought Joseph with irony, the whites have been carrying us all along. He said to Wolfie, "Don't think because we are black chaps we can't think for ourselves."

Joseph was none too impressed with Michael Harmel either. Guru theoretician? He was a lazy bastard who had never worked for a living. In Joseph's view, they—the non-whites—fell into the trap of seeing the whites as having valuable war experience, not realizing they had limited know-how, either of explosives and sometimes of actual fighting. Joe Slovo's war had been confined to a few months in the Signal Corps during the last days of Hitler. He had never seen action.

As Joseph said, he himself was a passive resister and no better qualified to launch an army, "but what they were doing was raw and crude and it was dangerous, risky stuff." He thinks Mandela was taken in by the whites too. He had no more experience than anyone else and here were these white communists from the Springbok Legion who had been in the army, fought fascism, and seen their parents suffer under pogroms and Nazism. For a long time, he says, their wisdom was accepted without challenge.

While the Communist Party tried to begin a guerrilla campaign, other disaffected figures were traveling the same road. Monty Berman—a renegade communist eventually expelled by the party and, according to Joe Slovo, disappointed at being overlooked for a commanding role in the armed struggle—went off and formed the National Committee for Liberation. This subsequently became the African Resistance Movement, the ARM, when he linked up with some radical liberals, including the journalist Hugh Lewin. Lewin would later describe how they spent weeks trying to bring down an electricity pylon in Magaliesburg, by cutting through it with a hacksaw.

There was also some rural resistance and violence in the eastern Cape among unaligned young black men. And the PAC—the Pan-Africanist Congress—had a militant faction, Poqo (or Alone—as in, black Africans alone, without whites), which was also being transformed into a military wing.

So when Mandela warned the ANC that it risked being left behind, he was telling the truth but, perhaps, not quite telling the whole story, as MK became not so much a new group as a merger with the communists. Mandela was appointed commander-in-chief, with Joe Slovo and Walter Sisulu on the high command.

Jack Hodgson was given, or volunteered himself for, the task of producing the necessary explosives. Hodgson was a real soldier; he had fought with the Desert Rats under Montgomery and had also handled explosives as a young miner in the copper belt of northern Rhodesia before the war. He had grown up in an orphanage, came from a poor background and had little formal education, but was socially aware and active from an early age as a union organizer. He had been a founder of the Springbok Legion at the end of the war and was, according to his wife, Rica, an absolute communist who never believed in owning anything. He thought you should be able to pack your case with everything you owned and move on. Consequently, they never had two pence to rub together.

Both Jack and Rica were already married when they met and got together soon after the war. From the beginning, Rica remembers, Jack was never in good health. He was well built and fine-looking but he suffered from stress and always had duodenal ulcers. It came from having to make decisions, he would say. Perhaps it was the stress that could make Hodgson seem harsh and uncompromising. Sometimes, his aggressive manner was a joy to behold. Jack's son Spencer remembered being at home once when the police arrived to serve a banning order on his parents. They were all having breakfast at the time. Jack made the police stand and read their notice while the Hodgsons carried on eating.

Jack asked, "Have you finished?"

"Yes," said one of the policemen.

"Then fuck off."

Spencer saw his father as having a natural affinity with black working-class people, because of his own background. He remembered Mandela and Winnie visiting for Sunday lunch, but more than anything, he remembered one evening in the late 1950s when Mandela had collected him—Spencer must have been about ten at the time—and taken him to the Bantu Men's Social Centre to attend a boxing night.

So far as he could recall, Spencer was the only white person in the crowded hall, but that did not trouble him as he was with Mandela, who was already a leader by then and seemed to know and be greeted by everyone. He was a giant of a man. A giant! (Other children remembered him that way too.) Spencer had no memory of being uncomfortable, only excited, thrilled by the evening as the two of them sat together watching the boxing. In hindsight, Spencer wondered whether Mandela had taken him as some kind of test, to see whether his parents really were as non-racist as they claimed. If it was a test, they must have passed.

By mid-1961, when the Hodgsons' small rented flat in Hillbrow became the center of bomb-making operations for Mandela's MK, Jack had already turned fifty. He was very inventive and could do anything with his hands, said Rica. He liked reading but was very fidgety and needed to be busy. He had once said to her that he would go mad if he didn't get something to do with his hands, so she had found him some string and he had started making hammocks, which Rica had given away as Christmas gifts.

She remembered a kitchen drawer stuffed to overflowing with ballpoint pen tubes, which he had bought to experiment with as timing devices for bombs. Wolfie Kodesh occasionally worked with Hodgson on these experiments or was involved in the testing. He recollected how Jack heated the tubes, bent them and then pushed nitroglycerine inside, before connecting them to a container of gunpowder. The nitroglycerine would be forced round the tube and detonate the explosion of the gunpowder. Rica recalled all this experimenting and preparation of explosive materials as taking place at her kitchen table, but Spencer says it was not just in the kitchen, it was in the lounge too. All round the flat, his father would have little experiments going on. Plastic tubes containing acid sat on bedside tables while Jack timed how long it was taking for the acid to eat through the plastic.

Jack took his son into his confidence and soon Spencer, who was then aged around fourteen, was an important member of the bomb factory, grinding crystals of potassium permanganate with a mortar and pestle to make gunpowder. They would store the powder, which was very strong smelling, in plastic bags, which Spencer remembered were a new thing then. Some of the particles would get into the carpet and became difficult to remove.

On one occasion, Spencer was sitting grinding when a school friend came round and sat down to chat. He wanted to help and as he took his turn grinding he asked Jack why they were doing it. Jack fobbed him off with some plausible explanation. The boy said, oh yeah, and carried on for a while before saying, you can make bombs with this.

Spencer knew just what was going on and why. The cause was fed to him in his mother's milk, he says, and he shared his parents' sense of injustice, not least because he had once seen an African man beaten to death outside a shop for stealing some fruit. It wasn't always easy, being a committed anti-racist in the wider world where casual racism was commonplace. Spencer would often be unsure whether to confront his friends over their comments and behavior or just keep quiet.

Like the communist cell that Wolfie Kodesh had led, the initial MK cells in Johannesburg comprised mainly Indian activists. Ahmed Kathrada was among them and remembered going round to the Hodgsons' flat one Sunday afternoon in the company of some friends and being horrified to find Jack sitting at the table, making bombs. Had he not heard of security? Or secrecy? Was it a kind of arrogance, that he could carry on doing this in front of people? Kathrada always had doubts then about the amateurishness of MK and concerns about the risks he was taking. Hodgson was too gung-ho for his liking.

No one now seems sure whether Jack Hodgson was actually on the national high command of MK or merely the leader of the Transvaal regional command, with Wolfie Kodesh below him. The two of them went out together on their own to practice cutting telephone wires. Wolfie would also sit with Jack and Spencer in the flat, working on the bombs.

Hodgson was a polarizing figure. There was no gray with him; it was all or nothing, black or white. He placed great importance on loyalty and would not be talked out of his steadfast belief in Stalinism, even after Khrushchev's famous speech in 1956, which was the first official acknowledgment of the terrible atrocities Stalin had committed, especially during the purges of the 1930s. The speech made it impossible for many communists to pretend Stalin had been the great and compassionate leader of the post-revolutionary Soviet Union. But others, like Hodgson, continued to believe his legacy was the victim of Western anti-communist propaganda.

In 1961, the party in South Africa was still accepting funds from Moscow, using a Johannesburg travel agent as a conduit for the money. Mandela himself never fled from communism, though neither does it appear he was ever actually a party member, more a "fellow traveler," as Senator Joe McCarthy might have called him, had Mandela been around during the post-war witch-hunts in the United States. One or two people have claimed he actually joined the party but Mandela himself always denied it. Others accept he was never formally a "card-carrier"—not that South African communists actually had cards.

There is no doubt, however, that Mandela embraced communism and communists, considering them among his closest friends and political allies, and enjoying the benefit of their support and fellowship, never more so than as he prepared to launch an armed struggle. One day, in the summer of 1961, Mandela got into a Chevrolet sedan with several communists, including Wolfie and Jack, and set off for a remote brick factory.

The car was laden with explosives.

Fourteen

THOUGH WOLFIE KODESH had lived in the slums of Cape Town as a boy, his father had been a successful businessman until he was brought low by the economic depression of the early 1930s that flowed from the Wall Street crash. Then, like a phoenix, Wolfie's father had risen again, so that by the time of his death, while Wolfie was abroad serving with the army during the Second World War, he had created a mini-empire, which Wolfie inherited along with his brother.

The business was based on a number of plots of land or stands around Johannesburg and two brick factories on a substantial site of around twenty acres, including a small wood, which Wolfie described as being located in the triangle between the suburbs of Primrose, Kempton Park and Edenvale.

Returning to Johannesburg after the war, Wolfie had found himself rich, but conflicted, incurring the wrath of his brother and fellow brickworks' owners, first when he had tried to pay his employees a fair wage and then again when he tried to unionize them. So far as Wolfie was concerned, he and his brother were paying slave wages to their African employees, and it was stabbing him in the heart, every payday. As Wolfie himself said, "On the one hand here I am enjoying the good life, having all the luxuries in the world, and on the other hand becoming more and more involved during weekends and during the evenings with the CP people." It was difficult, being a capitalist and a communist at the same time. When he was awarded a special prize of a book for being the best member of the Yeoville branch of the party, Wolfie knew that something would have to give.

The break came after one of the numerous raids, when the police would burst into the brick factories on weekends looking for illegal beer. They would assault the black workers and break up the tins and drums full of liquor with their police-issue iron staves.

One Monday morning, Wolfie heard that one of his workers was actually an undercover policeman who had been going around handcuffing those arrested during the weekend raid, when he thought no one was looking. Wolfie called the man in and sacked him even as he protested his innocence. He subsequently heard the man had returned to the police station where they all had a good laugh at the officer being sacked by Baas Wolfie.

That was it, Baas Wolfie could be a boss no longer. He sold his stake in the business to his brother for a modest £250 and the company car he'd been using. "I arranged with my brother, and I said, 'Look, I'm going down to Cape Town. I'm finished with the brickworks, and you can have my share. Take everything. I'm not interested in that.'"

By 1960, Wolfie was back in Johannesburg and the brickworks were no longer in operation, though still owned by his brother, who was away on holiday. So Wolfie used the site for an underground Communist Party conference. Members converged there from Cape Town, Durban and all over, meeting for a day of talks while concealed by the overgrown grass, before moving on to a house for the second day of the conference.

A year later the site of the brickworks became useful once again, when the fledgling MK, under Commander-in-Chief Mandela, wanted to test some of its bombs and weapons in a safe place where they could go undetected. Jack Hodgson had around a dozen Molotov cocktails and a bomb, which, of course, he had made at his flat in Hillbrow. Keen they should not be caught as the whole operation would be exposed, he emphasized the need for a secure testing place.

Wolfie immediately thought of the brickworks because, even though they were no longer in operation, they were a place where the sound of explosions was not uncommon, as dynamite was often used to loosen the clay to be excavated for the making of bricks. There was a noisy engineering works next door as well, which would help to drown out the sound of an explosion.

Wolfie's brother had never known of the escapade, so far as Wolfie knew. He had taken Mandela there—Mandela had insisted on being present himself—with Jack Hodgson and a sympathetic pharmacist who had been advising them on bomb-making. You could say it was the first MK mission: one black commander and three white comrades.

With Wolfie driving them in his roomy 1948 Chevrolet, they arrived at the seemingly deserted site and parked the car so that it was hidden from view. According to Mandela in his memoir, they went there at night, with only a small light to work from, but Wolfie says that it was in fact a morning expedition, which would make more sense as night-time explosions would surely have been more unusual and more likely to attract unwanted attention.

A figure emerged from the woods. Wolfie recognized him as an African who had worked there years ago and had stayed on as a watchman for his brother, with a *khaya*, a small, galvanized-iron building tucked away in the trees. Wolfie turned back to the others. "No, it's out. Here's a fellow who knows me and he'll talk."

Mandela said, "No. Just wait a minute. Let me talk to him." He told the others to carry on with what they were doing, unloading and preparing the bombs. The watchman spoke Zulu and soon he was deep in conversation with Mandela, who put a friendly arm around the watchman's shoulder. After a few minutes Wolfie saw that the man was going back to his hut. Mandela said, "Come on, it's all right. I've spoken to him. He's going back to his *khaya*. He's not going to see or hear anything." Wolfie always wondered, but never found out, what Mandela had said to the watchman. He never gave them away.

In an interview for an archive project in the late 1980s, Wolfie said they left before they had time to test the petrol bombs, and he and Hodgson went back later, alone, to try them out. In an earlier account, outlined in a pamphlet "Recollections of Nelson Mandela," by an unnamed author who was obviously Wolfie (one section was called "Nelson Mandela in my flat"), he gave a different account in which, as soon as the watchman had left them alone, they began igniting the Molotovs and bombarding them against the wall of one of the disused buildings.

"Every time a bottle exploded and burst into flames, Comrade Nelson shook his head gleefully and smiled the smile of victory. We all joined in his glee and enthusiasm of course. These were the first known explosions of the new era."

After dousing the remaining flames, which had spread over the wall and surrounding scraps of wood and rubbish, they moved away from the buildings to the open spaces to find a pit where the bomb could be placed. The bomb was constructed from a tin can used for paraffin but now filled, Wolfie said, with nitroglycerine. At the cap was a timing device made from the thin tube inside a pen. (It is perhaps worth noting that Wolfie refers to the thin tube inside the pen as the part that was used, whereas Jack Hodgson's wife, Rica, believed her husband threw that part away and used the outer tube. Perhaps he experimented with both parts.) They had calculated that the timer would be triggered after fifteen minutes.

Once the bomb had been set and put in position, they stood as near the hole as they dared and waited and waited but nothing happened. After more than twenty minutes, Wolfie went, with some trepidation, and retrieved the bomb from the pit. Jack Hodgson adjusted the timer. Wolfie very carefully returned the bomb to its position and clambered back out of the hole, the others' hands reaching in to pull him up, just a few seconds ahead of the explosion.

"An almighty bang!" Wolfie said. Much, much louder than any regular dynamite explosion he remembered from the old days when the brickworks had been active. Of course, back then the dynamite was put into small holes and the sound was muffled, whereas this was in a deep, wide pit full of loose soil so that a huge cloud of dirt and dust was thrown up into the air, a miniature version of the mushroom cloud that might follow a nuclear explosion.

They did not hang around but all, Mandela included, instinctively began running back to the car, diving hurriedly into the Chevy to get the hell out of there, Wolfie at the wheel not bothering to take the winding path but cutting a bumpy route straight through the bushes.

They were triumphant. Mandela, elated, could not stop congratulating them, once they were all OK, and telling Hodgson, "Now, Jack, you must go and show everyone throughout South Africa how this thing is made. Now we know we can do it!"

There was considerable secret activity around this time, much of it involving members of the Communist Party, acting either for party interests or the purposes of MK. The party was keen to find an isolated safe house to use as an underground meeting place and headquarters, and a three-man committee had been formed to scout for locations. Ahmed Kathrada, Michael Harmel and another white communist, Dave Kitson, spent some weeks searching and, according to Kathrada, never had any success.

If that's the case, then Harmel must have continued looking alone.

The owner of Liliesleaf Farm, a Mr. D. R. Fyffe, had been trying to sell the place for over a year as he was suffering from ill health and running a farm had become too much to cope with. In those days, it was extremely rural out there in the northern suburb of Rivonia and not to everyone's taste. George Bizos, the city advocate, called it a mink and manure suburb, a hoity-toity sort of place where people wore mink coats and rode horses to pass the time. A comrade who later came up to join them from Cape Town, Denis Goldberg, said it was so barren out there in the wilds that a night trip to Rivonia from the city became a daring adventure, plunging out into the dark with no street lights. There'd be no reason to go, except to get pissed.

Fyffe had been at the farm since 1954. When he bought it, the main building had a thatched roof. It was (and still is) an area at high risk of fierce electrical storms and a thatched roof was vulnerable to fire, in spite of the lightning roads that had been put in position. Fyffe had replaced the thatch with tiles but had not removed the rods—which the police later suspected were not actually rods at all but secret aerials for underground broadcasts.

He was grateful and relieved when a buyer finally appeared, but he found the whole set-up very unusual, to say the least.

First this man calling himself Jacobson had turned up, one Friday in the middle of August 1961, saying he was looking for a place to live for his brother-in-law who was mentally ill. Jacobson had not seemed so stable himself, always badly dressed—sometimes very badly—and sometimes unshaven. He was not, in Fyffe's view, a man of substance.

Even though Jacobson was at all times gentle and courteous, Fyffe said that all along the whole transaction felt phony. Jacobson—badly dressed? Unshaven? This was Michael Harmel, of course—came back the next day for a second inspection, accompanied by two other men. Fyffe caught the name of only one of them and thought he heard Gellybrand. In fact it was Jelliman, an old communist.

Valeloo Percival Jelliman, then in his sixties, later explained that he used to be in the organization Friends of the Soviet Union and had attended lectures by Michael Harmel at the Trades Hall. He had been called into the offices of the newspaper *New Age* and been interviewed by Ruth First before being sent off to see Harmel, who told him he was looking for a man with no dependents whom he could trust to look after a house and smallholding.

Fyffe described Jelliman in his letter as a small, insignificant, elderly man who clutched a grubby white handkerchief and said nothing. The unnamed other, who introduced himself as an architect, was tall, thin, sandy-haired, clean-shaven and approaching fifty. That was Rusty Bernstein.

When Jacobson returned alone to measure for curtains, Fyffe discovered that his mentally ill brother-in-law was named Vivian Ezra. Fyffe was not to know that Ezra was in fine mental health and had been chosen to become the nominal owner of the property as he was a communist but unknown to the police. When Fyffe tried to call Ezra, he could only reach his wife who knew nothing about the whole thing. As Fyffe said, that just seemed like another fragment in the "general insanity" of the sale.

But at least there was a sale, as within a few days a price was agreed at 25,000 rand, which was then around £12,500. Ezra had the purchase drawn up in a company name, Navian (Pty) Ltd., and on September 22, 1961, Mr. Fyffe handed over the keys to the twenty-five-acre site, including house and outbuildings, known as Liliesleaf Farm, Rivonia.

Nearly fifty years later, Ahmed Kathrada could still become agitated at the way in which, as he saw it, history had distorted the truth and people would keep insisting that Liliesleaf had been the underground headquarters of Umkhonto we Sizwe. That, he said wearily, was "another thing that had to be corrected over and over again." It was true Madiba had stayed there, but that was only because the Communist Party bought it and made it available to him, just as they had made it available to others later, too.

Kathrada was caught up with the idea of the party and MK as separate entities, whereas, in reality, they were profoundly enmeshed with each other. Though Liliesleaf may have started out as a Communist Party hideaway, its greater significance came later, when it served briefly as the hub of the country's MK network and a place of anguished discussions during the planning for a violent revolution.

Mandela did not move to Liliesleaf immediately after the purchase. He spent a couple of weeks at the home of Arthur and Hazel Goldreich in Parktown. The Goldreichs, with their two young sons, Paul and Nicholas, moved to Liliesleaf not long after Mandela, to become "the front—the seemingly ordinary, wealthy, white family living in the main house—for the secret activities that went on there."

The Goldreichs, although related to the Rochmans who had earlier put up Mandela, were far more deeply involved in the movement, and were closely connected to the other prominent white Jewish families, such as Joe Slovo and Ruth First, Rusty and Hilda Bernstein, and Harold and AnnMarie Wolpe.

More than anyone else, except perhaps the advocate and communist leader Bram Fischer, Arthur Goldreich was leading a double life.

Indeed, he was leading a double life in more ways than one. He was not just a successful commercial designer on the one hand and an underground activist, at the heart of the struggle, on the other, but also a family man who had other relationships. As his colleague Denis Goldberg put it, quite plainly, "Arthur was a womanizer and Hazel knew and tolerated it. He used to boast about his revolutionary activities to get into young women's pants."

Goldreich was by no means the only person in the struggle leading this particular kind of double life. Mandela himself led a double life for a while. Double, triple and so on... One of his closest Indian colleagues—had a long-standing, parallel second relationship.

Another prominent activist and MK member, Mosie Moolla, explains that he had a "girlfriend" as well as his wife, both of whom used to visit him in prison. (He also describes his reunion with Mandela after 1990, at which Mandela asked after his wife, then leaned in and whispered, no doubt with a twinkle, "And how is the other one?")

Bram Fischer may have been having an affair during, or very soon after, these history-shaping events. The Hodgsons, the Slovos. They all had episodes of "double lives" if that's an appropriate term.

Some say Joe Slovo slept with so many of his comrades' wives that it is more a question of whom he didn't sleep with than whom he did. Maybe that observation is apocryphal. He certainly tried it on with AnnMarie Wolpe who claims she rejected him. He was not, apparently, rejected by everyone. The Slovos' daughter Gillian also wrote about her mother's affairs in her brilliant memoir, *Every Secret Thing*. Even now, some think that was in bad taste and complain about the invasion of her parents' privacy, as if the truth should be varnished, icons kept intact.

That of course would be to deny reality and deny the possibility of considering those involved as rounded human beings, faults, flaws, warts and all. More than anything, perhaps, it is fascinating to reflect on why there was so much extramural sexual activity and what that tells us about the chief characters and the world and the age they were living through.

It cannot be mere coincidence that this group of people—with moral values and political beliefs so important that they were prepared to risk their lives for them, or to face years in jail, or to endure torture and the breakdown of their mental and physical health—did not always apply the same probity to their personal lives.

It must have been so exciting to be at the center of these events that even the fear of discovery, arrest, jail, torture, or death must have had its own stimulus. These individuals were not conventional—many of us would have been too afraid, or too uninterested, to participate in the struggle. They were radicals in an ultra-conservative time and place, bucking and challenging the system, which must have been a thrill in itself, bringing the boldest, brightest personalities to the fore.

There is no easy walk to sainthood, and perhaps it was difficult to be so scrupulous about race and politics while continuing to treat your loved ones with respect as well. They were only human, after all. Then, too, there were so many opportunities as these men and women led uncertain and unstable lives, often forced to be apart from their families or partners, and pressed into close or intimate comradeship with others, often in brief but intense circumstances. Sometimes, in their oral histories or written memoirs, whether reaching us direct or via their offspring, the sexual charge in those memories is still palpable, even decades later.

Unfortunately, the pain and the disruption that these events, both political and personal, left in their wake has damaged many who were touched by them.

Arthur Goldreich has lived in Israel for the last forty-five years and was unavailable for interview during the research for this book, as he pleaded ill-health and being too busy, preparing the latest exhibition of his art.

He had made his way to Israel following a dramatic prison escape in

1963. Hazel had also escaped, too, from South Africa, after two months' detention without charge, and traveled with her sons to Israel to be reunited with her husband, only to discover him already in a new relationship. She had returned to London and set up home there instead. Her sons also live in the UK. Hazel said they had not seen much of their father over the years.

Ironically, perhaps, when Hazel first met Arthur in the early 1950s, it was shortly after he had returned from Israel where he had gone as a teenager, leaving South Africa to fight as a Zionist against the British, and helping to create the independent state where he would one day live. He had fought with the Palmuch, the origins of the Israeli army, and had been immersed in kibbutz culture, which may have influenced his move to communism on his return. He had studied design in London and shown talent as an artist, becoming politically committed but never so active that he was arrested or known to the police.

For the MK revolutionaries, the birth of the Israeli state, plus the fact that Goldreich had been there and played a part, however modest, was inspiring. As Mac Maharaj put it, "Arthur has gone over and joined the Israeli army. It has a romantic allure for MK because they have rubbed the noses of the British into the ground and forced the British to accept the Israeli state. They have created kibbutzes and used them as camps to train an army to defend itself."

In South Africa, Goldreich worked as a designer for the department store chain, Greatermans, and also designed and created the settings for the late-1950s theater production of *King Kong* whose opening night Mandela and Winnie had attended in February 1959.

Mandela described Goldreich as a flamboyant personality who brought a buoyant atmosphere to Liliesleaf. Arthur's cousin, Hazel Rochman, knew him as "this big, flashy, gorgeous guy." AnnMarie Wolpe said he was like Mandela, being blessed with a winning personality, and was the life and soul of the party. He was a showman, she said, who loved the limelight and the approbation, though she was surprised once when she said to one of his sons—she couldn't remember which—"Oh your father's so talented, he paints, plays piano, plays the guitar," and he replied, "He plays one tune on the piano, one tune on the guitar."

In 1957, Joe Slovo had visited Goldreich and asked him to become part of the underground movement, which meant Goldreich calling a halt to all his visible political activities. By chance, he had won a prestigious art award that year too and was widely celebrated. He felt his political friends, seeing all the newspaper articles and interviews about it, believed he had sold them out for his own glorification when he appeared to withdraw from politics, not realizing he was now leading a double life.

In his book *Rivonia's Children*, the author Glenn Frankel recounts the story told to him by a woman, Selma Browde, who watched Arthur one night at Franco's restaurant while he danced, drank champagne, flirted with women and "talked cynically of politics." Finally, Selma, a liberal, could take no more and challenged him: "How can you go on living like this in a country like South Africa? Why don't you do something?"

He laughed. "I enjoy the good life," he said.

"I was greatly relieved, I must say, when it all eventually emerged," Arthur said during a visit to Liliesleaf in 2004, "and they hugged me and welcomed me back to the fold... Everything around me was a façade and was immodest," he added, in a tone approaching sadness.

Joe came to him again, in 1961, and asked him to become involved in the armed struggle. Goldreich discussed it with Hazel and they didn't hesitate. They would move to Liliesleaf. Hazel told the police she never knew that Nelson Mandela was living in her house at Parktown, but of course that was nonsense: she knew all too well that "David" the painter and decorator/houseboy was in fact the commander-in-chief of MK. He was always special, something very special, she said, commanding respect long before he became a leader. He used to stay in the cottage at the back of the garden where Arthur had his studio and kept his printing press.

They would have meetings there; Mandela and others would come and go. Hazel later heard that a young neighbor had once asked her father, why can't we have black people visiting us, like the Goldreichs do? Even having black visitors was notable, and problematic, in the white suburbs of the racist city at the heart of the most racist country on earth.

Builders were brought into Liliesleaf ahead of the Goldreichs to make some refurbishments and amendments to the property. Mandela moved there in October 1961. At first he was often alone there at night, as the builders would leave at sunset, and he sometimes felt uneasy being on his own in such a remote and unfamiliar setting. He once had to go and look around in the darkness after he thought he heard someone moving in the bushes, but found nothing. He remembers weeks passing, before the Goldreichs arrived, but the time period must have been much shorter, as it appears they moved in later the same month as Mandela, in October 1961. Confusingly, Arthur Goldreich has dated the move to December 1961.

Mandela says he was invited to stay at Liliesleaf by Goldreich and was first taken to Rivonia by Michael Harmel—when he initially acted as cook and servant to the caretaker, Jelliman. The Goldreichs' domestic, Enith Kgopane, who moved with them, remembered that "David" occupied the room next to the servants' toilet, at first—a bare-brick, cell-like room—and later moved into the end room of the outbuilding that still had a thatched roof, after it was vacated by Jelliman.

Mandela not only cooked for Jelliman but also served breakfast and tea to the builders, who were African, from Alexandra. He liked Jelliman, finding him amiable, courteous and appreciative, unlike the Africans who, never troubling to ask his name, would send him on errands, or order him with a summons of "Waiter!" or "Boy!" to sweep the floor and clear their rubbish. He told the specific story of being made to stand and wait once, while serving tea, as one of the builders finished telling an anecdote before helping himself to sugar from the tray Mandela was holding. Mandela felt "mild exasperation," as he put it, and went to walk away. "Waiter, come back here, I didn't tell you to go."

There was a lot of traffic in and out of the property, not just of builders and routine deliveries but members of MK and communists coming for meetings. It seems remarkable that the police didn't cotton on to Liliesleaf sooner. A schoolboy, George Mellis, who lived nearby, soon became fascinated by the constant tide of visitors and must have been suspicious too. He befriended the Goldreich boys, Paul and Nicholas, after their arrival and used to play with them at the main house, often staying for lunch. He noticed white men and Bantu men together in the outbuilding and thought it strange. Sometimes there were a lot of cars parked in the yard. He once asked Nicholas about all the people who were there and Nicholas said he wasn't allowed to say anything. On one occasion George took down all the registration numbers of the cars at Liliesleaf and handed in the list to the police.

MK had set up an early channel, out of the country, for a select few to receive military training in China—Walter Sisulu had made contacts during a trip there some years earlier—and one of the first recruits was Raymond Mhlaba from Port Elizabeth in the eastern Cape, who would later become a key figure for MK. Mhlaba, a communist, a regional ANC official and a trade unionist, had been one of the earliest to be arrested during the Defiance Campaign of 1952. While he was at Rivonia, Mhlaba took part in the discussions that helped to shape MK, as a draft constitution was evolved, along with Joe Slovo and Rusty Bernstein, who was often used as a speech or policy writer.

When Mhlaba left for China, Mandela was joined at Liliesleaf by Michael Harmel who was supposed to be writing a policy document for the Communist Party. They would keep a distance from each other during the day, while Mandela played the houseboy, but often sat and talked in the evenings. Harmel's grasp of political theory was important to Mandela but his casual attitude to security was not so helpful.

Mandela came back from a meeting one night to find the front door of the house open, the lights on and the radio turned up loud. Mandela always kept the place in darkness so it was disconcerting to see it lit up like Christmas. Inside, he found Michael Harmel fast asleep and woke him up to complain. "Man, how can you leave the lights on and the radio playing?"

Harmel, said Mandela, was groggy but angry. "Nel, must you disturb my sleep? Can't this wait until tomorrow?"

"No," said Mandela."I reprimanded him for his lax conduct." Lax conduct was the story of Harmel's life.

In the absence of any proof that he was ever a member of the Communist Party, and in the face of his consistent denials that he joined, perhaps the greatest evidence that Mandela could have been a communist was found among papers in his handwriting when the police raided Liliesleaf. Those papers should have been destroyed, but instead, and contrary to Mandela's own instructions, they were kept on the site and poorly hidden.

Among them were what appeared to be the beginnings of a book, three chapters with the overall title, *How to Be a Good Communist*, amounting to nearly 100 pages of Mandela's meticulous, curling longhand. "The life of a communist revolutionary is no bed of roses," he had written in the opening chapter.

> It consists of serious studies in Marxist literature, of hard work and of constant participation in numerous and endless mass struggles. He has no time for worldly pleasures and his whole life is devoted to one thing and one thing only, the destruction of capitalist society, the removal of all forms of exploitation and the liberation of mankind...The cause of communism is the greatest and most arduous cause in the history of mankind...Under a CP government South Africa will become a land of milk and honey...There will be no unemployment, starvation and disease.

Chapter Two was a consideration of dialectical materialism; Chapter Three addressed political economy.

Naturally, Mandela had never written these pages for consumption by the police or to assist in his prosecution. It was amateur night at Liliesleaf when two of his ANC colleagues decided not to destroy them.

Is Liliesleaf clean? Is it clean? Mandela had repeatedly asked.

It turned out they were in part a reworking of a pamphlet that Rusty Bernstein had given Mandela, which was in turn a translation of a famous Chinese text, *How to Be a Good Communist*, first written and presented in lectures in 1939 by the revolutionary theorist Liu Shaoqi. Mandela tried to explain away the document during his famous—and famously long—speech at the Rivonia Trial in Pretoria in April 1964, when he said he had merely been trying to demonstrate to an unnamed "old friend" how you could simplify the seemingly impenetrable language of communist theory.

Those pages must have been written during these weeks at Liliesleaf, and the "old friend" he referred to in his speech was Moses Kotane.

Mandela said in his speech that the old friend had been trying for years to get Mandela to join the Communist Party and the two men had many debates about the role the party could play in the struggle. The friend would give him Marxist literature sometimes, which Mandela would not always find the time to read. The friend, he said, was someone who worked closely with him on ANC matters and occupied senior positions both in the ANC and in the Communist Party. They always stuck to their guns in argument. Mandela would tell him, as he said at the Rivonia Trial, that he accepted a role for communists and people of all races in the struggle to end race discrimination and establish democratic rights for black people in South Africa. But he did not share the communist view of Western governments as reactionary and undemocratic. Mandela believed in the Magna Carta, the Bill of Rights, the U.K. parliament, the U.S. Congress; he was a democrat, and a socialist.

His friend always said that only trained Marxists would be capable of tackling the problems of poverty and inequality, once freedom had been achieved, so a communist state would be needed. Mandela argued that ideology could wait until freedom had been won.

They saw each other several times at Liliesleaf and on one of the last occasions Kotane was busy writing with books around him. Mandela related in his speech what followed. "When I asked him what he was doing he told me that he was busy writing lectures for use in the Communist Party and suggested that I should read them . . . I told him that they seemed far too complicated for the ordinary reader in that the language was obtuse and they were full of the usual Communist clichés and jargon . . . he asked me if I would redraft the lectures in the simplified form suggested by me. I agreed to help him and set to work... but I never finished the task."

Quite how the redrafting of lectures explains away Mandela's reworking of a Chinese revolutionary pamphlet remains as unclear as any dialectic. The document that Mandela had written under the heading *How to Be a Good Communist* looks more like an attempt to adapt and modernize the original for a South African revolutionary readership—an MK handbook perhaps. Mandela later told Richard Stengel that had indeed been its purpose—to show Kotane how communism could be made suitable to South Africa.

However, it is an evocative image from that time: of Mandela and his friend—Kotane, probably—arguing into the night at Liliesleaf about the relative merits of revolution and social democracy.

Another is Mandela, sitting writing in a notepad at a small table in that bare-brick room, just as Arthur Goldreich remembered him:

> It was exactly like a cell, I mean it was like a Buddhist monk's cell when you have this notion of someone who has given up the vestiges of a [normal] life and that was prior to devotion and faith and trust and service. This room was an epitome of that kind of service, unenhanced and monklike, absolutely pure in that sense also, of course, which certainly impressed me. You know, I wasn't that young, I was in my thirties and I had a family, and I thought that we were treating Mandela badly but obviously correctly.
>
> I had this kind of thing, this conflict in my mind, about the image and what we were doing and it's still with me... Yes, look, it had a bare floor, bare walls, no decoration whatsoever. A table, a modest small table, a hard chair and a bed. That was it and a place for some books, I remember, because he read all the time. And he really was very diligent... there were very many books in the house... but I can't remember Madiba coming out of this place and going to the house to go through the books. We would be talking and I would say there's this and this and this, and that's about

the things we talked about, so I would bring him books but he never intruded, in that sense, in that world.

The Goldreichs, who paid an implausibly low rent of 100 rand a month, established some form and order at Liliesleaf as they set about joining the country set. People who knew them—but did not know of their secret life—were surprised at how rapidly they had risen in the world and wondered where the money came from. Hazel's cousins, the Rochmans, were not alone in feeling they had been dropped, or were no longer good enough for them, as they were not invited to the new address. The real reason, no doubt, was that they were being shielded from the potential fallout.

All the Goldreichs started horse-riding, though Hazel soon gave it up as it was not her thing—"I thought to myself, why should I suffer"—while Arthur kept a horse at Liliesleaf and would stride around in jodhpurs and riding boots, accessorized with yellow gloves. Hazel thought of the people around them in Rivonia as "more English than the English" hunting, shooting and fishing types, which was exactly the rôle Arthur slipped into. "The idea was to give the impression that one didn't really care about anything very much and just enjoyed oneself. We had a good time, we entertained." Hazel was happy to be involved and to play the role. She felt it was necessary and, besides, she liked being at Liliesleaf. Arthur set up his studio there and continued to paint. That, too, the bohemian, was part of his persona.

Len Lazarus, who lived nearby and was related to Hazel by marriage, used to visit the Goldreichs with his wife and guessed something was going on when he recognized the gardener as Nelson Mandela. Lazarus, in thrall to Arthur and his larger-than-life character, was quite envious when Arthur let his guard slip once or twice—you can imagine how he must have been bursting to tell—and would say, you know, I'm doing dangerous work. Lazarus wished he could be doing something exciting, too, though not too dangerous.

What a contrast, between the two worlds of Rivonia, between the superficial carry-on of the dressy dinners, cocktail parties and idle, flippant conversations, and the subterranean plotting for an armed struggle. Such role-playing and subterfuge must have been hard to sustain.

Hazel Goldreich remembers her mother coming round and seeing Michael Harmel at the house.

"What's he doing here?" she asked.

"Oh, he's just come to measure for the curtains."

Hazel's mother was not fooled. "Don't give me that, he doesn't do curtains."

The Goldreichs had comrades for dinner and drinks as well as the posh locals, but tried not to mix the two groups. There were occasional parties where they all rubbed shoulders. Amina Cachalia could recall going to the housewarming with her husband, Yusuf, a big buffet lunch with lots of people standing around drinking and chatting.

Mandela liked being at Rivonia and afterwards always spoke affectionately about the experience. At the trial in 1964, he referred to it as the ideal place for a man who lived the life of an outlaw. "Up to that time I had been compelled to live indoors during the daytime and could only venture out under cover of darkness. But at Liliesleaf I could live differently and work far more efficiently."

Hazel Goldreich recalled that Mandela would have meetings or sit writing during the day and then emerge in the late afternoon or early evening to roam the grounds, often in the company of her small sons, Paul and Nicholas, and the Goldreichs' dogs and geese.

In a letter from Robben Island, twenty-five years later, he said the whole place reminded him of the happiest days of his life: his childhood. Of course, the vast rural landscape of his earliest years must have been when he felt the greatest freedom—a place to escape to from his cell. As he wrote in another letter to the same correspondent, "The country boy in me refuses to die, despite so many years of exposure to urban life. The open veld, a bush, blade of grass and animal life make it a joy to be alive."

In late 1961 his days of freedom were already numbered, but he must have known he could not stay ahead of the police forever.

* * *

It would not be surprising if today Mandela in some way feels possessive of his time at Liliesleaf and, indeed, has an understandable attachment to his past experiences in general, as well as some concern when he fears they are being exploited.

Liliesleaf is now part of what might broadly be called the Mandela heritage trail and has been re-created as a museum site commemorating the events that took place there over twenty months in the early 1960s. The original look and feel have been elegantly re-created with considerable attention to detail, under the stewardship of Nicholas Wolpe, the son of Mandela's former friends and comrades, Harold and AnnMarie Wolpe.

Much of the Mandela heritage trail is in the hands of Mandela himself, or has been created in partnership with his Nelson Mandela Foundation. The latter has become a key resource while successfully positioning itself as what it calls "a Centre of Memory," maintaining its own substantial archive while also attempting to become a hub for the many other archives and historical collections attached to universities, libraries and various other state institutions around the country.

The new South Africa will probably never stop coming to terms with the old South Africa, certainly not so long as its painful past of cruel subjugation continues to intrude upon the present. History is always important, obviously, but somehow it seems even more important to this young country, which was born of so much blood and turmoil. Behind the broad sweep of events lie the individual stories of suffering and tragedy, sometimes triumph and heroism. In the great African tradition of oral storytelling there seems to be a limitless capacity for the country to record its past.

If the key is truth and reconciliation, then the latter is both a gesture of humanity and a matter of political will, while the truth is in the detail—a matter of fact; a question of perspective.

Not everyone around Mandela is happy about the idea of his Foundation—not least those members of his family who feel sidelined, once again, by its existence. Yet the people who surround him there seem mostly genuine and well-meaning in their intent and sense of purpose, whilst liking to have some influence and a role in events concerning their namesake. Nic Wolpe struck a defiant note of independence during his development of Liliesleaf, which set in motion a certain tension between the two camps—Liliesleaf on the one hand, Mandela on the other—and aroused suspicions that Wolpe was somehow exploiting history to feather his own nest.

It perhaps did not help that he built himself an enormous office—not much in the spirit of a monk's cell.

As has already been said, Mandela does not lose his temper often but in 2003 he came on an official visit to see the progress of the site at Liliesleaf. As they walked along side by side, Mandela asked Wolpe about the Liliesleaf book he had heard that Wolpe was planning.

Wolpe already knew Mandela thought he had a book planned as one of Mandela's aides had mentioned it. There was no book. Wolpe had told the aide this and now he told Mandela the same thing. Mandela roared, "Are you calling me a LIAR!" Wolpe is no stranger to the occasional outburst of ill-temper himself but later described how terrifying it was, being the focus of this brief explosion of Mandela's anger. He could only answer, humbly, that he was telling the truth.

Mandela did not go to the opening of Liliesleaf, possibly because of either his health or his schedule. Some rapprochement has since occurred, however. In 2008, Mandela's two glamorous and charming daughters, Zindzi and Zenani, came to Liliesleaf, bringing with them their mother, Winnie, and a considerable family entourage.

Zindzi, who was still under a year old in late 1961, has no memory whatsoever of Liliesleaf and, as already stated, has no memory at all of her father before the mid-1970s when she was able to visit him for the first time on Robben Island. Zenani, who was at the time a walking, talking toddler of two and a half, has floating memories of geese and fields and walks with her father by the river. She spoke of Liliesleaf at the time as her father's home.

They both made several trips to see him there with Winnie in 1961. There was a spontaneous moment when they went into the cell-like room in 2008 and Winnie said, "My God, I remember this, there was a bed over there and a table over there." She said that they had all slept together in that confined space: in fact, not just Mandela and Winnie and the two girls, but also Makgatho, Mandela's son from his first marriage. "On the floor?" exclaimed Zindzi and Zenani. It must have been a long time since either of these daughters of South Africa's first family had slept on a floor. Winnie admonished them straight away. It had been important, she pointed out, for them all to visit with their father and be together.

Makgatho, who in 1961 was around eleven years old, faced many difficulties in later life, becoming an alcoholic and eventually contracting HIV-AIDS before his early death in 2005. This perhaps lends a poignant edge here to his recollection of his father, whom he called Tata, at Liliesleaf.

> We knew Tata was in hiding. I can't say how I felt about it. It made me afraid. I couldn't say then why, but now [he was recalling these feelings for Fatima Meer in the mid-1980s] I know I was afraid because I thought we could lose him. I was excited and happy when I saw him. We saw him at different places. Mum Winnie took us to see him. One time I went to stay with him at Lillies farm [sic]. There was a big house which was the main house and there were outbuildings. Tata was staying in one of the outbuildings. The white people were staying in the big house.
>
> Mum Winnie stayed one night and left. I stayed for a week, or it may have been two weeks. Tata and I swam in the pool and we went for long walks. He taught me to shoot with a rifle and bought me a pellet gun. He used to cook for me. Thembi [Makgatho's older brother] was not with us. I didn't know why he was not there. I didn't think about it at the time. I saw a lot of Tata because I was close to mum Winnie then.
>
> I was very sad to leave Tata, but he told me I shouldn't worry, that we should go to school in Swaziland and we would have no problems.

As in other secret rendezvous with her husband, Winnie's trips to Liliesleaf, frequently arranged by Wolfie Kodesh, would involve circuitous routes and changes of cars midway. She would often go via the Josephs' home in Fordsburg, perhaps collecting one of Adelaide's curries on the way, to take to Madiba, or stopping on the way back with some vegetables from the farm.

They would not discuss where Mandela was hiding, but Paul would note that the car was covered in mud and had clearly just been on or near a farm. He knew too that his own house was under surveillance and feared Mandela would be found and caught. "They were all terribly careless but it was the early days of the underground movement, with a certain amount of romanticism."

When Winnie did not take food from the Josephs, she might cook for her husband at Liliesleaf, or Mandela would surprise her and prepare a meal himself. When that first happened she was suspicious that someone else must have cooked it for him and wondered whether he'd had another woman there. She at first refused to eat and only relented when he went into a detailed description of how he had cooked the rice, the chicken, the vegetables.

Arthur Goldreich has recalled that there was an airgun at Liliesleaf and that he taught Mandela to shoot with it. Mandela, he said, soon became quite proficient. According to Mandela, the airgun had been his back in Orlando and Winnie had brought it to the farm for him. He and Goldreich would use it for target practice and for shooting doves. One day he was on the lawn in front of the house and took aim at a sparrow in a tree. Hazel Goldreich joked that he would never hit it, but he shot the sparrow and it fell dead onto the lawn. Her youngest boy Paul, aged around five, was there and said through tears, "David, why did you kill that bird? Its mother will be sad." Mandela had been pleased with himself for hitting the bird the first time, but now felt ashamed.

He has described the visits of Winnie and the children as giving him the illusion that his family life was still intact. Winnie tended to see them as the opposite: as a reminder of how fragile their family existence was and what they were missing.

A reminder of that fragility came when Makgatho was leafing through a copy of *Drum*, together with the older Goldreich son, Nicholas, and came across an old photograph of his father. He knew not to disclose his father's name, but that was a heavy burden for a child to carry and now he blurted it out. "That's my father." When Nicholas didn't believe him, Makgatho explained that his real name was Nelson. According to Mandela, Nicholas asked his mother whether Mandela's name was David and she said it was. Nicholas then said that Makgatho had told him his father's name was Nelson. Hazel was alarmed and told Mandela about the incident.

Arthur Goldreich gives a different account in which his curious son, Nicholas, appeared in Mandela's room hiding something behind his back.

Your wife is Winnie?

Yes.

And these are your children's names?

Yes.

So you are Nelson Mandela, said Nicholas, producing *Drum* from behind his back.

Mandela took the young Nicholas into the grounds for a walk. Goldreich did not know what he said to him, but Nicholas must have learned something very important in his life that day as he became very responsible after that talk.

Fifteen

MANDELA REMEMBERS SITTING in the kitchen at Liliesleaf on "a warm December afternoon," listening to the radio broadcast, from Oslo, Norway, of the Address by that year's winner of the Nobel Peace Prize, the president-general of the ANC, Chief Albert Luthuli.

It was a Monday. Just five days later, on Saturday, December 16, 1961, the bombs of the ANC's (then unacknowledged) military wing MK would explode across the country for the first time. The armed struggle was about to begin.

As Mandela said, the juxtaposition of violence with a Peace Prize was awkward.

The listener, alone in his kitchen, Mandela was already familiar with the content of the speech, as he had discussed it with Luthuli before the chief's trip to Europe. Luthuli had in fact asked Rusty Bernstein to draft the speech for him, apparently because he had been impressed by Bernstein's call to the people in the early stages of the Freedom Charter Campaign. Bernstein's role in the Congress of the People had been tricky for the ANC, and his contribution to Luthuli's speech was not made public. There were many in the struggle, not just within South Africa but elsewhere among the African independence movements, who already thought

Luthuli was too close to whites and was selling out to the imperial powers in accepting the Nobel Peace Prize. They would have been even further displeased if they had known he had turned to a white man to write his speech for him (though in fact Bernstein says that little of his draft appeared in the final version).

The historians Karis, Carter and Gerhart quote an unnamed African academic as telling them in 1963 that Luthuli's acceptance of the prize had severely damaged his reputation among Africans.

Still, it was a rousing oration delivered by an ANC leader standing proud on a Western rostrum, and that was definitely a poke in the eye of the Nationalist government. The announcement of the prize had been made, with commendable timing, back in October, just five days after the Nats had been re-elected for a fourth term of office. It was clear that the Nobel award had hurt the government as they conceded to international pressure and gave Luthuli permission to travel to receive it, while commenting that it had done so "notwithstanding the fact that the government realizes the award was not made on merit."

Luthuli had been denied permission to attend celebrations near his home, where the ANC activist and singer, M. B. Yengwa, had praised him in song as the great bull who had broken the fence and wandered far—as far as Oslo. He paid tribute to Luthuli saying, *Nkosi yase Groutville! Nkosi yase Afrika! Nkosi yase world!*—"Chief of Groutville! Chief of Africa! Chief of the World!"

Many were proud of Luthuli's prize and felt they had a share in it, seeing the award as not just for Luthuli but for the movement. An old MK soldier in Durban, Sonny Singh, recalled being among the vast crowd that ran behind and alongside the open Cadillac convertible that took Luthuli and his wife on a hero's parade across Durban to the airport at the start of his trip to Europe.

"Through all this cruel treatment in the name of the law and order," Mandela heard Luthuli say over the radio,

> our people with a few exceptions have remained non-violent. If today this peace Award is given to South Africa through a black

man, it is not because we in South Africa have won our fight for peace and human brotherhood. Far from it. Perhaps we stand further from victory than any other people in Africa. But nothing which we have suffered at the hands of the government has turned us from our chosen path of disciplined resistance. It is for this, I believe, that this award has been given.

If Mandela could have seen him, he would surely have been pleased to note that Luthuli wore a traditional, leopard-skin Zulu cap and a necklace of lion's teeth as he presented his speech, which he completed by singing the African anthem. Luthuli arrived home the following Friday, just before the bombs went off.

If only it were possible to outline the role that Mandela, as commander-in-chief, had assigned for himself on the night the armed struggle began. But that story has never been told and now, it seems, it never will. Two or three people were requested to ask him during the research for this book and he claims he can no longer remember. It would appear he has never spoken about it. That could mean there is something to hide—or equally that there is nothing to tell.

Those who are still alive and were out that night, on active service in their cell units, do not recall him being there with them. No one else recalls him planting a bomb himself. They could all be protecting his secret. Or perhaps he really did keep away from the action, as the general on the hill, watching over operations, back at Liliesleaf beside the radio, maybe, waiting for news of the explosions to be reported.

MK was very clearly Mandela's creation, structured along the lines of the old M-Plan, in typical guerrilla pattern, as a series of cells, groups of four cells in a platoon, the platoon answering to a regional command, which answered to a national high command, presided over by Mandela himself. He was in charge but, after his participation in the test run at the brickworks, seems to have been removed from the action. Not, then, leading from the front.

Wolfie Kodesh was in the thick of things, of course, going back and forth from Jack Hodgson's flat in the weeks leading up to the opening night. Jack's wife, Rica, and their son Spencer were in on it all, and there were African comrades turning up "from all over the show"—as Wolfie put it—which was easy because they could just pretend to be workers coming to the apartment. Wolfie was busy with his own cell as they chose and prepared their targets. His unit eventually selected three government buildings, all in the Indian location of Fordsburg: a post office, a magistrates' court and a pass office.

They were soft targets, all of them, office premises that were closed by night when the bombs would go off, to minimize the risk of injury. No one was supposed to get hurt. Wolfie led a cell comprising three Indian comrades: Paul Joseph, Reggie Vandayar, and Laloo Chiba, a young married man with a couple of small children who combined being in MK with his day job at a dairy. Chiba, who had become politically active in the late 1950s, first formed a cell for the Communist Party in mid-1961, but was then told to disband that cell and merge with MK. He was a quiet, unassuming character who—almost unnoticed—possessed great reserves of courage.

Other than Joseph's instruction from Wolfie on how to throw a Molotov cocktail against a wall, there was no physical training or preparation. Joseph tried to do some reading and, as he had been told to do, would look out for recruits and potential targets for bombs while also trying to stockpile weapons. Chiba recalled they kept a stash of Molotov cocktails and dynamite at a doctor's storeroom. The doctor even came out with them one night, later, on a sabotage run.

Wolfie's own planning was meticulous. For the post office they needed to get onto the roof of some adjacent phone booths, so he and Chiba practiced running and jumping, using their comrade's cupped hands to gain the necessary elevation. They got so expert, he said, that they could have thrown each other over their shoulders.

The magistrates' court was straightforward but the pass office required entry through a window that needed to be broken, so here too they practiced, in Chiba's backyard, taping windows and then tapping them so they fell out of the frame without shattering.

The date of December 16 was not idly chosen for the start of the armed struggle. The Afrikaners celebrated it as the Day of the Covenant in commemoration of the Voortrekker commandos' victory over the Zulu *impi* of King Dingane at the Battle of Blood River in 1838. Fearing defeat, supposedly, the Boers had made a pact with God—a covenant—before the battle. It was sometimes known as Dingaan's Day, after a variation on the name of the Zulu king, and was mourned by Africans as a tragic massacre. No doubt, when he chose that date, Mandela considered that his MK warriors were avenging the memory of the 3,000 Zulus who were said to have died.

That night Wolfie's unit waited for the two large cinemas in Fordsburg to empty, following their Saturday-night shows, before they set off, being driven by Chiba in his white Volkswagen Beetle. They did not collect the bombs from the Hodgson "factory" in Hillbrow but were handed them at a rendezvous. As they went on, they passed Mosie Moolla, who also appeared to be carrying a bomb. Wolfie guessed he was part of another unit.

They placed bombs on top of the two phone booths at the post office, both the whites-only and the Africans-only booths. They handled the bombs gingerly as they seemed fragile and unstable. The timer was a plastic capsule being eaten away by sulphuric acid. When the acid reached the nitroglycerine it would trigger the explosion.

Jack Hodgson had been in a car once with his son Spencer when a bomb in the boot started smoking and they had rushed to a relative's home to hose it down and wash out the car. According to Wolfie, Hodgson had set out with a white comrade, Ben Turok, on the night before the 16th, to set a bomb with a long fuse at the main library in the city. That bomb too had started smoking. They had to stop and dismantle the bomb, then reassemble it before it could be planted at the library. Turok left fingerprints that would be found later and would lead to his conviction.

Wolfie's unit had a problem that night with the bomb at the law courts, which they had to move again after first putting it into position. The task fell to Paul Joseph who found the bomb lying on its side oozing explosive.

He set it upright and went back to the car, only afterwards thinking that he had danced with death.

When they reached the pass office, a place that Wolfie had checked night after night and found it always deserted, they came across an African guard sitting at a brazier by the gate. They improvised, pretending the car had broken down, one gunning the engine, another looking under the bonnet, while the other two used the cover of the car to knock the window out, as they had practiced, and place the bomb.

As they headed back to Joseph's home to clean out the car they heard the two bangs of the post office bombs, detonating a little earlier than planned but satisfyingly loud. They turned down a nearby street to see the impact and saw crowds gathering and police everywhere, which was just the effect they had hoped for.

Paul Joseph went home and got into bed. His wife, Adelaide, was already asleep, oblivious to his MK debut. He lay awake listening and suddenly there was a rush of sirens, which seemed to stop right outside. They had come for him already! He leaped out of bed. Adelaide woke up. Where are you going? Only for a glass of water, he lied. He looked out and saw that, happily, the car had only stopped to turn the corner of their street. He was safe for the time being.

Jack Hodgson had been present when Ahmed Kathrada's cell was selecting its target and considered the Portuguese Labour Office, where migrant African workers from Mozambique were being taken on at exploitatively low wages to toil in the mines. It was a legitimate target, but it was just next door to Kathrada's apartment at Kholvad House and he knew that children often played there by the building until late at night. When he raised an objection, Hodgson responded that this was a war and in war children got hurt, people died. The MK oath made it clear that deaths were to be avoided at all costs and Kathrada did not much like Hodgson's attitude.

The problem, for Kathrada, was that Hodgson had fought in a war and the belief within MK was that people with experience of real fighting were the ones best suited for guerrilla campaigns. In Kathrada's opinion, that was not necessarily the case. Kathrada said he let his feelings be known to Hodgson in reply to his crass remark but he was a disciplined young cadre and knew he had to be careful with his seniors, so he made sure they remained friends and there was never any tension between them. "I treated Hodgson with the respect he deserved, although I had made up my mind that his abilities in certain respects had been exaggerated."

On the night, Kathrada and his fellow cadres kept careful watch, going back and forth from the flat until the street was clear of all adults and children. They used a weak incendiary bomb, which they dropped through the building's letter box where it created a modest fire. Kathrada was glad when it was over. He did not feel he was cut out to be an urban guerrilla.

There were numerous minor mishaps, no doubt due to the amateurishness of both the equipment and the operatives. AnnMarie Wolpe remembered standing on the balcony of an apartment in Hillbrow where there was a party raging, as her husband, Harold, quietly told her he had planted a bomb but it had failed to go off.

Joe Slovo, the MK chief of staff, Mandela's number two, had wanted to play his part and had a bomb constructed from a tin tennis-ball tube, which he took in a carrier bag to the Drill Hall, an army building that the government had used in the early hearings of the Treason Trial. Slovo had been thorough in his preparation and knew there was a wooden floor, which he hoped to set alight, along with dozens of wooden chairs stored in the room. When he arrived the hall was being cleaned and there was an army of domestics at work, so he set off to find an office in the building instead. He had primed the timer, by turning the acid capsule upside down, and was just about to place the carrier bag and its contents in a cupboard when he was interrupted—"Can I help you, sir?"—by an army officer.

He had a story ready—that he was hoping to get a temporary military exemption for his brother, who had received call-up papers. The officer helpfully led him through the building, still holding the carrier bag, to find someone who could deal with his inquiry. Slovo was sweating, not knowing quite how long the acid would take to eat through its cover.

Luckily, the person he was being taken to speak to had already left, and the officer advised him to come back the following morning. Slovo quickly went out and, as soon as he could, snatched the bottle from the tin tube. He described it as the longest four minutes of his life.

Later that evening, Slovo, Bernstein, and Hodgson embarked on another mission. They went out to sever the telephone cables that intersected on the main road between Johannesburg and Pretoria. They pulled up by a manhole and used a pretend breakdown of the car, Bernstein standing by a raised bonnet, to shield Hodgson and Slovo as they lifted the manhole and clambered down to tape the dynamite to the cables. They lit the fuse and drove off in a hurry, waiting for the subterranean boom. Slovo thought he heard a distant rumble, but Bernstein never did. He was proved right later, during the Rivonia Trial, where every act of sabotage was listed and there was their manhole, where a routine inspection had found an unexploded cache of dynamite taped to the cables.

Bernstein believed that the leafleting campaign that accompanied the first explosions was a failure too. As usual, he had been involved in the drafting of the document, which came to be known as the MK manifesto. His was just a small contribution, he would say. Bernstein disputed Mandela's claims in *Long Walk to Freedom* that he had actually been recruited into MK and had helped Mandela and Slovo to write the MK constitution. Bernstein sees the constitution and the manifesto as separate documents, but they may be one and the same. Certainly, it would seem that only the manifesto has survived and most of it is Mandela's own work:

"The time comes in the life of any nation where there remain only two choices: submit or fight. That time has now come to South Africa. We shall not submit and we have no choice but to hit back by all means within our power in defense of our people, our future and our freedom."

MK—Umkhonto we Sizwe, Spear of the Nation—announced itself as a new, independent body formed by Africans but including in its ranks South Africans of all races. It was independent but its members were placing themselves "under the overall political guidance of that movement." It was striking out along a new road for the liberation of the people.

"The government policy of force, repression and violence will no longer be met with non-violent resistance only!"

The flyers were pasted up on walls and telegraph poles across Johannesburg and throughout the country. There were fifty-seven explosions that night—in Port Elizabeth, Durban and Johannesburg—but there were many hundreds of leaflets distributed and, in the absence of any other claim of responsibility or press statement, the leaflet was the only way in which the acts of terrorism could be identified.

Bernstein believes the police went around tearing them all down so that there was confusion as to exactly who had been behind the bombs and, from the start, some bewilderment about who or what MK was. Perhaps, to a degree, the uncertainty and anonymity created among white South Africans a greater sense of menace from an unknown enemy.

The great tragedy of the night was the death of one cadre and the serious injury of another when their bomb apparently detonated while they were placing it, in Johannesburg. Ben Ramotse lost an arm and Petrus Molefe was killed. Ruth Mompati remembered attending his funeral, expecting the police to arrive and arrest the priest at any moment. Mandela told Ahmed Kathrada, in 1990, that the MK leaders had felt some responsibility for the loss of Molefe as he was their soldier. The incident was additionally disturbing as it suggested a lack of training. But, he said, they took it in their stride. Casualties could not be avoided when starting a "new method of political activity."

The young woman who had typed for him at Wolfie's flat, Amy Reitstein, was driving with a friend on the road to Johannesburg from Cape Town when news of the explosions came on the radio. She remembered how excited they were and how she expected the government to fall within the week. "We were very naive," she said.

The next morning, Paul Joseph went out and walked among the crowds, examining the debris of the previous night's actions. He saw the damaged symbols of apartheid—the *nie blankes* sign dangling—and saw how the spectacle excited the crowd. It was then that he realized the power of those actions and what could be achieved by them.

There was another round of explosions over the New Year and they continued sporadically through 1962. A number of recruits were being sent for training, initially in China, then in Moscow and in some independent African states.

The recruits invariably came from the ranks of political activists. There were growing concerns that the tail was wagging the dog, that MK was dictating events to the ANC and the Congress Alliance. Sisulu was forced to defend the independence of MK at a review meeting where, according to his biographer, Elinor Sisulu, Chief Luthuli was unhappy with the timing, so soon after his peace award, and troubled at the reckless action that had led to casualties. Another leader—not named—was said to have severely criticized Sisulu as a wild character, not up to the responsibilities of his leading role.

When Mandela set off at the beginning of 1962, in search of support throughout independent Africa, he left behind a flimsy, barely competent structure that now faced an increasingly efficient Special Branch with developing powers of detention without trial. Arrests were just beginning to lead to prolonged episodes of interrogation and torture. By 1963 it would be no holds barred.

Kodesh came to Chiba and told him that they were breaking up their cell unit and that each of them would form their own new unit, multiplying the number of people involved. Paul Joseph recalls that Reggie Vandayar was suspended after the police raided his home and found an old gun hidden there, in spite of the instruction they had been given to clear their homes of arms. Vandayar was reinstated and allowed to form a cell.

Chiba became a platoon leader and now discovered for the first time that Jack Hodgson was above him in the chain of command. Chiba occasionally visited the bomb-making flat at Hillbrow but never shared any of Kathrada's concerns about poor security.

After Mandela's arrest in August 1962, Hodgson ordered him to carry out a special one-off act of sabotage to remind the authorities that MK would fight on. Chiba said there was no unit ready to act at short notice but Hodgson insisted it must be done. So Chiba formed a special unit, which he led himself, and Elias Motsoaledi prepared a twenty-pound dynamite bomb, which they took to an electricity substation at Vrederdorp not far from the city center.

They used an electric timing device set for two hours, which was then supposed to ignite a spark and trigger a ten-second fuse. When it didn't go off they couldn't decide what to do but eventually went back and retrieved the timer. Chiba lit the fuse from a burning cigarette. He had seen all the films where people get blown up disconnecting bombs and was shit scared, he said, as he fiddled with the fuse to get it alight. When it started fizzing he had ten seconds and reached the car just before the "massive bloody explosion."

Hodgson was as pleased as punch that the mission had succeeded but, as Chiba put it, reprimanded him severely for the risk he had taken. Chiba was arrested for the first time a few months later, immediately after one of his units was captured in mid-mission by a railway line. The unit was led by Reggie Vandayar, and one of the cell members was a police informer—later assassinated, probably by MK in revenge. Another member, Indres Naidoo, was shot and wounded by police during the arrest.

The captured members of MK were kept together in a room at the headquarters of the railway police and then taken out one at a time to be questioned. Chiba was the last to be called. He was first assaulted for about thirty minutes, his eardrum was perforated, and then a wet hessian sack was placed over him. He was straitjacketed and electric wires were tied to his fingers and toes. They wanted the name of his contact and when he refused they sent electric currents through him. "All I could do was to scream out in pain. I could only scream and scream and plead ignorance." He felt good, he told the Truth and Reconciliation Committee (TRC) years later, that he had not given away a name but would always be haunted by the deep sense of shame he felt for pleading with the enemy to stop torturing him. "I don't think that a revolutionary should actually give the enemy the pleasure of listening to one's screams."

Chiba was eventually released and went on to serve on the so-called second national high command under Wilton Mkwayi, who took over as commander from Mandela. Chiba began carrying out more acts of terrorism and was arrested again a year later, in July 1964, when he was interrogated at the notorious Gray's Building, by the equally notorious Special Branch officer, Theunis "Rooi Rus" (Red Russian) Swanepoel. He was not physically harmed this time but—and this was a popular tactic employed by Special Branch at the time—he was made to stand on one spot, on a sheet of A4 paper that had been laid on the floor for the purpose, for around fifty hours. He was not allowed to move or sleep, but again did not give anything away. Chiba served eighteen years on Robben Island, alongside Mandela. He was freed in 1982.

Many others of course were severely tortured and some suffered more than Chiba. He was not dangled from a high window, as others were, with one leg being held by an officer, who would let go and then catch the other leg before the prisoner fell. Sometimes, it seems, they fell anyway.

Suliman "Babla" Saloojee, an MK comrade, was arrested at the same time as Chiba in July 1964. He smuggled a message to his wife, Rokaya: Pray for me.

On September 9, 1964, he fell to his death from a seventh-floor window at the Gray's Building during questioning by Swanepoel, who said Saloojee had jumped in an attempt to escape. By 1990 there had been seventy-three deaths during detention, five of them people who had fallen, jumped, been pushed or thrown from buildings.

Rokaya Saloojee was still on medication when she testified to the TRC thirty-one years later. Her husband's inquest had lasted five minutes, she said.

She still hated some whites, she was sorry to say.

Sixteen

NOT EVERYONE APPRECIATED Frene Ginwala's role as the ANC's "travel agent" in Dar es Salaam, the capital of newly independent Tanganyika. What was this Indian woman doing in the heart of black Africa, in a place that had become the liberation movement's gateway to the rest of the continent? Julius Nyerere had just become the country's first prime minister. In 1964 he would become president of Tanzania—the union of Tanganyika and Zanzibar. Nyerere was a committed socialist who lived modestly and drove around in a small Austin or Ford Prefect saloon car. He was a friend to the struggle in South Africa and much admired by Mandela. But he was also a keen nationalist.

Ginwala, who in 1961 was around thirty years old, had been sent to Dar es Salaam by Walter Sisulu, the day after Sharpeville. He had told her to prepare the way for somebody coming through and she had assumed it was Chief Luthuli, but it turned out to be Oliver Tambo. Ostensibly, she was running a magazine, a pan-African publication, *Spearhead*, but in practice she was arranging travel for exiles and recruits to training. They would send her a photo of whoever was on their way and she would file it in a box until they turned up.

One day, in late 1961, Tambo arrived unexpectedly and asked, "When is Nel coming?" Ginwala told him she had no information, though in truth she already had an inkling.

"What?" said Tambo. "Haven't you been told?" She pulled out her box and showed him one of the recent photos that had arrived. "Is this Mandela?" she asked. It was the Eli Weinberg image that would soon be famous around the world. In the photo Mandela looked to Ginwala as if he was already a prisoner. "He should be here by now," said Tambo. So the two of them went to the main bus station and sat waiting for a couple of days. Ginwala knew Mandela was living underground and speculated that he might have changed his appearance.

"How will I know him?" she asked Tambo. "Has he had plastic surgery?"

Tambo laughed. "Frene, I promise you, when Nel comes he'll be wearing a three-piece suit."

Ginwala was doing a good job, she knew, but she was quite aware that her presence as a woman of Indian origin was resented sometimes. Even some of the ANC people didn't like it. Paul Joseph said there was "disquiet" around Africa at the ANC's use of non-Africans. Ginwala's presence was not always appreciated. He knew of another occasion when African leaders were expecting a fellow African representative at a conference and Mary Turok, a white comrade, turned up instead, which did not go down well. According to Ginwala, having a non-racial nationalist organization in southern Africa was unheard of then. "People used to think, about me, what is she doing? And not only me—when whites came out and so forth. Oliver would not compromise on that and his biggest challenge often was to ensure African leadership and yet not ignore people who'd sacrificed so much. That balance caused confusion and at times people felt marginalized."

The original idea was for the ANC to work together with the PAC—the slogan was unity in action. There was an occasion when two PAC people were in Dar waiting for passports from Ghana, where Kwame Nkrumah was a particular friend of the PAC. Tambo asked Ginwala to help them and she laughed to herself, thinking: what, you want this Indian woman to put you in contact with Ghana? But when she spoke to Tambo about it, he told her she must never think in those terms.

Some days after their wait at the bus station, Ginwala took a call from the border town of Mbeya. It was the regional commissioner who said he had two men with him claiming to be South African leaders and was it OK to clear them. The commissioner passed the phone to one of the men. It was Joe Matthews, the son of the Prof. Ginwala told the commissioner they could be let through.

Later that afternoon her doorbell rang and there on her doorstep was "the most enormous man" in a conical Sotho hat, mosquito boots and a khaki safari suit. "Ha!" said Ginwala. "And I'm supposed to hide you?"

"That's a nice way to greet me," said Mandela.

He could not go to a hotel so Ginwala arranged for him to stay at a Tanganyikan minister's beach house. He soon met Nyerere and brought him up to date with recent events, the launch of MK the previous month, the need for funds and support for military training. The response was not what Mandela had hoped for. Nyerere said they should delay the armed struggle until Robert Sobukwe had been released and then joined forces with the PAC.

Suddenly, since Sharpeville, the whole world was aware of the PAC and, if he hadn't known before, Mandela certainly knew now what he would be up against when seeking help from other African nations. He told Nyerere that the PAC was weak and a delay in the military campaign would be disastrous.

Mandela had begun touring Africa in early 1962, after the ANC was invited to address the forthcoming conference of the Pan-African Freedom Movement for East and Central Africa (PAFMECA). The ANC was anxious to forge links across the region and hoped to be admitted to the organization. Mandela's wider task was to raise funds for the armed struggle and pave the way for MK recruits to receive training in friendly countries. Mandela also hoped to have some training of his own — he was a commander-in-chief with absolutely no military experience beyond the books he had read. The only weapon he had ever fired was the airgun at Liliesleaf.

He also needed to leave the country so that he could discuss the turn to armed struggle with Tambo, who remained in exile. There were hints in the messages going back and forth between Tambo and the South African–based leadership that Tambo was feeling marginalized or out of the loop.

On the eve of his departure, Mandela had been to see Chief Luthuli at a secret meeting in Groutville, Natal. In the sparing notes of these events that he kept in a diary, Mandela wrote, "Monday 8th January. At 11pm I see AJ [Albert John Luthuli]. He is in high spirits. Approve of trip. Suggests consultation on new op."

The "new op" was the launch of the armed struggle. In truth, Luthuli complained to Mandela that he had not been consulted about the formation of MK and knew nothing about it. This was bizarre as, of course, he had been present at the long meeting of the Congress Alliance in July 1961 where it was finally approved. There could be no doubt he had been there, but now, in a development that Mandela blamed on Luthuli's poor health and failing memory, some would cast doubt on his role in the decision, and on the legitimacy of the armed struggle itself. Perhaps, with the peace prize on his shelf, he had reimagined himself as a man of peace. There was no other obvious explanation for the paradox and, equally, no doubt he had been a party to the original decision.

Mandela returned to Johannesburg, where he called a meeting with Duma Nokwe (nicknamed Gowanini in his diary), Sisulu (Qamela) and Kathrada (K). K failed to turn up. Mandela noted this in his diary. Kathrada said it was really all Madiba's fault because he was in Johannesburg a day earlier than expected. The diary entry led later to a funny exchange at the Rivonia Trial when the prosecutor, Percy Yutar, had Kathrada on the stand and was trying to humiliate him by teasing out the truth behind the diary entry. Yutar asked Kathrada whether he was sometimes referred to as K.

He was not, he said. He didn't know anybody who referred to him as K.

Do you know anybody else, asked Yutar, who goes under the initial of K?

Yes, said Kathrada, Mr. Khrushchev. Even the judge laughed.

Mandela's diary for the following day records that he and K had a brief tiff and then patted each other and made up. Meanwhile, Kathrada's friend and underground comrade Amien Cajee (AM) was arrested. Mandela was censorious and complained of AM getting himself arrested as an act of amazing irresponsibility and betrayal. He was supposed to be driving Mandela out of South Africa. Mandela had never ever left his own country before and was nervous on a number of fronts about his forthcoming trip.

When he reached Lobatse in Bechuanaland (later Botswana), he discovered there would be a delay. He was forced to wait there for some days until Joe Matthews joined him and Mandela insisted they press on, after being warned of the threat of being kidnapped by the South Africa police if he remained. The British security services were already monitoring his movements and filing reports on his trip.

A plane was chartered and they eventually took off from the nearby town of Gaborone, aiming for the small northern airstrip at Kasane. During the flight there was a storm, which Mandela, a master of understatement, described to his friend Kathrada as "disturbing." They could not land at the usual place in Kasane because the strip was waterlogged and littered with grazing animals. They landed further along the road and by the time they were picked up—the driver told them he had been delayed by rogue elephants—it was dark. There was a sleeping lion on the road and others roaring outside the rooms where they slept. Mandela was unused to these aspects of African life and admitted he was scared of the animals.

The journey did not get any easier the following day when they took off again for Tanganyika. This time the pilot got lost and Mandela called out in panic when he feared they were heading straight into a mountain. Instead they hit some mist. As the pilot didn't know where he was, he dropped down and followed the road, while trying to call the airport.

"Mbeya? Mbeya!" the pilot exclaimed, becoming annoyed by the silence on the other end of the radio. When Mbeya finally answered, he said, "Shut up! I'm landing!" Mandela told Kathrada the controller at Mbeya airport had been playing draughts, but that may just have been one of his little jokes. "I am sometimes adept at appearing brave and pretended that I was unconcerned."

They went to a Mbeya hotel where whites and blacks were mingling on the terrace. A black guest was telling off a white receptionist. This was all new to Mandela and he felt the burden of oppression—a burden he must have known from childhood—begin to lift.

An aide of Nyerere's assisted with onward travel documents—Mandela had no passport at this stage, only a letter of authentication from the Tanganyikan government. He set off for the PAFMECA conference in Addis Ababa, the capital of Ethiopia, flying first into Nairobi, Kenya, and then going on to a smaller conference in Lagos, Nigeria, where he met a minister from the Congo who appeared "extremely arrogant and not altogether sober." He met the Liberian president, Tubman, who invited him to visit his country during this trip. Mandela kept a low profile in Lagos, not wanting to alert the South African authorities to his whereabouts before he went public at PAFMECA.

On the plane out of Lagos he met his old friend and early political influence, Gaur Radebe, who was no longer in ANC or a communist but had joined the PAC. Although disappointed by his choice of affiliation, Mandela did not want to let it affect their friendship. He continued to hold the door open to all PAC activists in spite of the difficulties they had created for Mandela and the ANC.

The last leg took him via Khartoum in the Sudan where he was in the queue next to another old legal colleague, the white Jewish attorney Hymie Basner, who was going into exile. Basner had the same Tanganyikan papers as Mandela but he was stopped and was being questioned. Mandela went back and stood by him, bowing silently to the Sudanese official, who realized Mandela was endorsing Basner and let him through.

On January 30, 1962, Mandela finally arrived in Addis Ababa and was reunited with Tambo at the airport. Both men had changed and barely recognized each other to begin with. Tambo was bearded and had adopted military-style dress. Mandela was bearded too and, as he told Kathrada, "I used to pay attention to new clothing and so on. Now I was wearing a windbreaker, corduroy trousers and sandals and I had long hair which was not properly combed."

The reunion must have evoked some sadness and nostalgia in Mandela as he reflected on their lives together at college, then in the Youth League, which they had started together, and in their legal practice. He thought too of the sacrifices Tambo had made: "A man of ability, a musician, a well-groomed speaker, an individual; a man who had now thrown all these wonderful opportunities away and committed himself to the struggle."

Mandela had to apply for the ANC to be accepted into PAFMECA. There were objections from delegates, the Ugandans complaining that the ANC was a tribal organization, which was an echo of a grievance sometimes aired in South Africa: that the ANC was dominated by Xhosa, though Chief Luthuli was actually a Zulu.

Other countries were seeking affiliation too and there were moves to deny them as well, which Mandela argued against, running the risk of being dismissed himself for interfering. One objection was that some of the other new delegates were too long-winded, making speeches of several hours' length. It was agreed that they should be warned to be more brief.

Mandela was accepted and PAFMECA took South Africa into its name, becoming PAFMECSA. His success was mainly due to his impressive opening words, rousing the conference with his warning to the South African authorities that the recent explosions were only a small beginning "with much bigger explosions to come." His speech was reported in *The Times* of London. Another speaker was Kenneth Kaunda who was leading the way for Northern Rhodesia to become independent as Zambia. He was famous for crying during speeches; here too he was overcome and had to pause. The delegates sang the African anthem until he was able to continue.

Kaunda's party had already aligned itself with the PAC. Mandela hoped to change Kaunda's mind, but when he approached him, he was told he would be preaching to the converted. Although Kaunda already believed in the ANC, it was the rest of his party, especially his deputy, who needed to be convinced. Mandela spent the day with the deputy and discovered the black arts of the PAC propaganda machine. They were going around telling African leaders that MK had been formed in Swaziland by the communists and the Liberal Party, and that they planned to use Africans as cannon fodder.

Mandela demolished this tall tale and won over Kaunda's deputy, who said that actually he had admired the ANC from the moment their delegation arrived at the conference, and they had carried themselves more like leaders. He went back and persuaded his party to support the ANC.

Mandela was also playing politics with the PAC over a white Christian activist, the Reverend Michael Scott, who had been involved in the squatter camps around Orlando and had been to jail for passive resistance. He had gone over to the PAC because he was anti-communist. The PAC had accepted his support and he had raised funds for them, but in public at PAFMECSA they disowned him, not wanting to be seen with a white supporter. Mandela took Scott under his wing and had dinner with him, which was a risk, as many of the Africans at the conference were uneasy at the ANC being too close to whites. Scott said he was disgusted with the way the PAC had behaved.

The conference had been opened by the Emperor Hailie Selassie. Mandela was fascinated by his tiny, uniformed, overdecorated frame—"a small man but an African giant"—and the way he bowed without moving his body, with just a slight inclination of his head. At the end of the conference the Emperor received all the delegations in turn and Tambo invited Mandela to address him on behalf of the ANC. The Lion of Judah sat in a chair listening impassively, never once even nodding or moving. The ANC group watched the Emperor at a military parade later, giving medals to a group of white Americans who stepped forward to receive them. White soldiers bowing before a black monarch! Mandela liked that.

He continued his journey with Tambo, Joe Matthews and Robert Resha, flying via Tripoli in Libya into Cairo, Egypt. That must have seemed very exotic? Mandela was asked by his ghost-writer, Richard Stengel. "Gee whizz, it was," said Mandela. He and Tambo haggled over the price of a boat-ride on the Nile. They saw the pyramids and the Sphinx, and went to the museum where Mandela was fascinated by the preserved mummies. He told Fatima Meer he was dazzled by the beauty of an unbandaged, partially restored mummy of a young woman with black African features, thousands of years old, looking "lovely in death." There was another, more earthly beauty working at the ANC offices in Cairo, an Egyptian girl who could have been a beauty queen, but who was also "well-behaved."

While he was there he went to the home of an old comrade, Vusumzi Make, now a PAC representative in exile. Make was living with a young African-American woman, Maya Angelou, then working as a desk editor at a weekly newspaper, the *Arab Observer*. Mandela spent some hours talking with the couple and planned to keep in touch with them but that was ended by his arrest. As the years passed, he became aware of Angelou's rise as a writer of prose and poetry. They have never met, but spoke on the phone when he visited Washington, DC, after his release in 1990.

Traveling onwards to Tunisia with Resha, Mandela agreed they would present their case openly, in each country, and Mandela said he would not shy away from speaking of the success of the PAC. He started telling a senior Tunisian official of the impact the PAC had made, and about their humble, talented leader Sobukwe, who was now in prison, when the Tunisian stopped him and said, well, if that is the case, what are you doing here, because when that fellow comes out he will smash you, he will finish you.

This made Resha very uncomfortable as he had not supported the idea of singing the PAC's praises. Mandela had wanted to be honest and open but he could see Resha thinking, I told you so. Resha told him, "No, man, you are putting the PAC case better than they would put it, you see?" Fortunately, the official agreed to give them an audience with the president and promised them they would receive the £5,000 funds they wanted. Resha relaxed.

Mandela had by now begun wearing military-style khakis, donning a suit only for meetings with heads of state. Resha wore a suit most of the time. He was looking after the money and needed to appear more businesslike.

In Morocco, Mandela met leaders of the Algerian revolution and was much inspired by their achievements. There were other guerrilla leaders present, from Mozambique and Angola, but it was the Algerian Dr. Mostefi who moved them, with his description of how a small guerrilla force had risen in numbers and stood up to the far bigger French army. The struggle was hard and long, he warned his guests, but they should never despair.

Mandela visited a military camp near the Algerian border and had his first real experience with weapons: "After lunch we have a spree with G [German] Mauser and an automatic Mach. I am warmly complimented on accuracy." He talked with the Algerian leader, Ahmed Ben Bella, and found him a brilliant and pleasant man.

Back in the Moroccan capital, Rabat, they met an aide to the Moroccan king who gave them a further £5,000, telling them he wanted no record of the gift and also promising facilities for military training, even offering to fly in recruits from Dar es Salaam.

"Where do you want us to send the weapons?" he asked.

Dar es Salaam, said Mandela.

Resha flew to London to deposit the funds, while Mandela went on to Mali where he patiently explained the MK story to a government official who warned him not to tell anyone else as people would think he was mad for trying to challenge the mighty South African state. He still gave Mandela some funds though. Mandela was traveling on limited resources and relying on the hospitality of his hosts. In Mali they initially refused to pay his hotel bill, but after some embarrassment the problem was resolved.

Unable to see Sekou Toure in Guinea, as he was busy with an American official, Mandela flew on to Sierra Leone where a mix-up caused him to be introduced to the country's prime minister as Chief Luthuli, winner of the

Nobel Peace Prize. He went from there to Liberia, to take up the invitation from the president who expressed keen support for the ANC's struggle.

On April 27, Mandela flew to Accra in Ghana, where he met up with a widowed white woman activist from home, Hilary Flegg, who was there as a sociologist. Her husband, Norman, a communist, had helped finance the *Guardian* newspaper—the voice of the struggle in South Africa—before his death. Mandela's diary records that Flegg took him out and about sightseeing and that they had dinner together one night. The following night they went to a nightclub at the Ambassador hotel where a Ghanaian man came up to Mandela and asked him whether he was a white man.

Mandela said, what do you think?

The man peered at him and at Flegg and said, "I think you are a white man."

"But I look like you," said Mandela, "and you are not a white man."

The Ghanaian said, "You whites spoil everything," but he bought Mandela a beer, which, as a non–beer drinker, Mandela gave away.

Mandela had hoped to see Ghana's leader, Kwame Nkrumah, but the PAC were well established there and Mandela believed they blocked his way. As Mandela told Meer later, he had always been fascinated by Nkrumah's vision of a united states of Africa but now, as he traveled around the continent for the first time, he began to realize that dream was unlikely ever to be realized. The countries and the people were too diverse.

Tambo arrived back from Europe to join him but even he could not get to see Nkrumah. So, after some further difficulty over paying for the hotel, they flew via Lagos, Nigeria, back to Guinea, where they were finally able to meet Sekou Toure.

Toure, who wore a threadbare suit at their meeting, listened carefully to the South African story. When they had finished, he told them that Guinea had their interests at heart and had raised their plight with the United Nations. He went out of the room and they must have hoped he would return with some money but instead he brought them two copies of a book he had written, which he signed for them. "Gee whiz!" Mandela said, recounting the incident years later. They had gone all that way back, for a book. He and Tambo were so annoyed that they couldn't eat any lunch but at about four o'clock that afternoon a man came carrying a suitcase "bulging with money." Unfortunately it was the local currency and useless outside Guinea so they had to exchange it at the Czech embassy.

They flew now to Senegal and arranged an appointment with the country's scholarly president, Leopold Senghor. As they approached the presidential palace in Dakar, Tambo had an asthma attack, apparently brought on by the heat and humidity of the city. He refused to abandon the meeting but was in such a bad way that Mandela had to carry him on his back up the stairs. The president called a physician but Tambo still needed to spend a few days in bed, looked after by Mandela as best he could in their cheap hotel.

Mandela's diary for June 7, 1962: We fly by BOAC to L.

Tambo was living in London with his wife, Adelaide, Winnie's former roommate at the Helping Hand hostel. Some people within the movement felt that Adelaide became grand as her husband rose in status, and that she embraced Western ways. It was said she refused to live in Africa and favored London, where for a long time they had an apartment in Fulham. Eyebrows were raised in Johannesburg later, when their daughter was taken to be married in an ostentatious, horse-pulled carriage.

Mandela always said he went to London to make contact with politicians and the press, as well as to collect some revolutionary literature. According to Mac Maharaj, it was at Tambo's urging that he went. He and Adelaide were Christian and anti-communist, and Tambo needed Mandela to persuade Adelaide of the need for an armed struggle. Mandela had told Tambo he was beginning to grasp that African support would be piecemeal and that the real help was likely to come from the Eastern bloc. "Nel, you better come and explain that to Adelaide." Mandela told Kathrada he had been given a hard time by the British immigration officials when he arrived, claiming he was coming to do research for a book.

He had a wonderful time in London, by his own account, visiting the likes of Denis Healey and Hugh Gaitskell, Labour Party members. If

Mandela had not spent so much time with journalists, he said, he could also have met the incumbent prime minister, Harold Macmillan. He stayed with Tambo and enjoyed visiting bookshops. David Astor, the editor of the *Observer*, was then pro-PAC, which Mandela told him was a mistake; he ought to be promoting unity between the two organizations. Michael Scott was there at that meeting too and said he was surprised Astor had anything good to say about the PAC.

The journalist Mary Benson, who was by now also living in London, kept her own diary in which she noted, "cooked. 7pm. Tambo" on Thursday, June 14, 1962. There was a knock at the door and when she opened it, there beside Tambo was Mandela. "N. gorgeous," she wrote in her diary, "talked til 1.30." She elaborated later on how superb he looked in his immaculate suit as he paced across the floor, giving a thrilling account of slipping across the border into the rest of Africa. Benson arranged meetings for him and took him sightseeing around the Houses of Parliament and Westminster, then along the Thames to dinner with friends in Chelsea. Benson took a famous photograph of Mandela in front of the Houses of Parliament. They saw the statue of Jan Smuts outside Westminster Abbey and Mandela joked that perhaps one day there might be a statue of them there too.

Todd and Esme Matshikiza had also left Johannesburg to settle in London and were living modestly in a one-bedroom flat in North London. They were in bed when the doorbell rang. It was after midnight, possibly around 1 a.m., but they put on their dressing gowns and Todd went to the door. There were Tambo and Mandela. The two men were ushered into the small room, messy with bundles of bedding. Esme could see that Tambo was edgy, tense, she thought, with the responsibility of looking after Mandela. So much had changed, for all of them, since Todd and Esme had stood chatting with the Mandelas at the opening night of *King Kong*, just three years earlier. Esme noted how Mandela seemed oblivious to the surroundings as he described his flight from South Africa. He said that if he went back he was likely to be sent to jail. Esme asked him, innocently, "Why, then, would he go back?"

"Look," he said—and these were his exact words, Esme would never forget them—"I'm the leader of the people and the leader of the people must be with his people."

He was not the same person anymore, not the person she had known back home. Esme had the feeling that he was up there, way above them all somewhere, a visionary, with the aura of someone special. She just sat awestruck and watched and listened as he spoke.

It seems possible that the tension Esme sensed in Tambo was also connected with the political fallout from the Africa trip, as well as the difficulties that he and Mandela quickly encountered when they tried to explain how the ANC was going to counter the impact of the PAC to Alliance comrades such as Dr. Yusuf Dadoo and Vella Pillay. Dadoo, especially, feared the ANC was having a change of heart over its links with the Congress Alliance and there was evidently conflict between him and Tambo on the matter. Mandela suspected that Dadoo, now based in London, was out of touch with events back home. But here was the first evidence that he would be caught between a rock and a hard place as he tried to maneuver the ANC into a position of credibility with the African states, while retaining the confidence of his Alliance partners.

Mandela did want to stop using the Alliance as a mouthpiece for the ANC. He also wanted the ANC to be able to speak for itself and to give at least the appearance of separation from the Alliance. Like others back in South Africa, later, Dadoo thought Mandela was abandoning his core belief in non-racial co-operation.

Mandela described how Dadoo took exception to the ANC's apparent shift and thought they were turning nationalistic. "He kept asking, 'What about policy?' We tried to reassure him that we were not suggesting any changes in policy: we were concerned about the image we projected. We felt at the time that Dadoo was falling short in appreciating the problem from our perspective."

Towards the end of June, Mandela left London and returned to Africa for his appointment with the Ethiopian military. He flew first to Khartoum and then on to Addis Ababa where he was driven out to the headquarters of the Ethiopian Riot Battalion. He was immediately set to work—on the first day he had lessons in demolition with explosives, and then the following day some practice. He was expecting to be there for six months, and in the early weeks was often training alongside the elite presidential guard, becoming friendly with his trainers, Lieutenant Befikadu and Colonel Tadesse. They went out to dinner together and to the cinema.

He fell into a daily routine, training from eight till one, with an hour's break for lunch, and continuing from two until four, after which there would be lectures in military science at which Mandela would take notes. Incriminating notes that would later be found at Liliesleaf.

He had demonstrations in mortar fire and spent hours on two shooting ranges. He learned to make small bombs and mines and also how to avoid them. He felt he was being molded into a soldier, a guerrilla leader, and believed he was starting to think like a soldier. He learned to shoot at moving targets while he himself was running. There were fatigue marches on which he would be weighed down with a supply of bullets on an ammunition belt, a gun, a knapsack of provisions and a full water bottle.

His diary entry for July 13: "Lt Befikadu and I cover 26 kilometers in fatigue marches. We do it in 3 hours."

He was physically fit, he told Kathrada years later, as physical training had always been a part of his life, but he valued the weekly fatigue marches.

> When you are going to be a leader of a guerrilla army you must know what guerrilla warfare means, how it is brought about and you must know how to use a gun and you must know the whole military science.
>
> The idea was to fight a war and change the system by fighting and the death of human beings was unavoidable. It was a question of necessity not a path that we chose. We chose peace and negotiations but we were dealing with a regime that was impervious to any form of negotiations.

Mandela was taught by Colonel Tadesse that he would be leading a liberation army, not a capitalist army, and that he must lead with authority while always remaining equal even to the most junior of men. "Even when you get your food you must not eat your food in your office, or in a room; go out and chew with the men, for your food, they must see what you get, what you eat. And once they do that they will be happy with you."

Mandela recalled an occasion when Tadesse was talking to him in the officers' mess (not a particularly egalitarian venue to start with), when they were interrupted by a sergeant. "Yes, what do you want?" Tadesse barked, unequally, at the sergeant. The sergeant said he was looking for somebody. "Get away from here. He's not here. Get away." Tadesse turned back to Mandela and continued telling him how to treat his soldiers fairly. Mandela felt embarrassed, but still admired Tadesse, even if the colonel did not practice everything he preached.

In late July, Mandela received a telegram from colleagues in Johannesburg, saying he was needed back home. It was as if he was being summoned to his mission... He had been trained and was ready to answer the call. The ANC needed him at the head of the escalating armed struggle. It also appears that, after the tensions with Dadoo in London, rumors had begun flying around the Congress Alliance that Mandela had become a nationalist once again, reverting to the position he had held in the late 1940s within the Youth League. The PAC, cheekily, were even claiming he had joined them, so it seems highly likely that this was another urgent reason for his return.

As he said goodbye to Colonel Tadesse, the Ethiopian officer presented Mandela with a handgun and 200 rounds of ammunition. Today, of course, it would be difficult to travel around with such items, but evidently in July 1962 you could get on and off planes and cross borders with ease, while armed to the teeth. The gifts were cumbersome, heavy even for a man who had been trained to peak condition. Mandela put the ammunition on a belt around his waist and kept the gun hidden in a holster. Back in Khartoum he had hoped to stay discreetly at a cheap inn but the airline arranged a first-class hotel on the banks of the Nile. When Mandela went onto the terrace many white people there began staring at him and he imagined they knew he was armed. He returned to his room and stayed there, taking his meals alone, not wanting to leave the gun and bullets, or go out with them. He was also carrying several thousand pounds sterling in cash.

He flew to Dar es Salaam the next morning and immediately reported what he was carrying to the police chief. Meanwhile he crossed paths with twenty-one recruits, the first batch, on their way out of South Africa and heading for training in Ethiopia. The recruits slaughtered a goat and honored Mandela with a dinner, then left him with a salute, which was the first time he had ever been saluted by his own men as a military leader.

Julius Nyerere made a plane available to take Mandela into Bechuanaland (now Botswana). He was met by two local white officials. Fearing they had come to arrest him, he told them he was David Motsamayi, but when they said they had come to meet a Mandela it became apparent they were not hostile after all. He was driven into Lobatse where he was reunited with Joe Modise. His colleague warned him that the South African police knew he was coming and that he should not wait around too long.

Seventeen

THE ANC HAD expected Mandela sooner. Kathrada and Sisulu had traveled to Bechuanaland two weeks earlier to prepare the way for his return. They had sent armed MK recruits to provide a safe escort but, when Mandela did not appear as planned, the recruits were called home.

In the end he was collected, not by armed guards, but by Cecil Williams, the middle-aged, gay, white communist. Like many others, Williams was leading a double life, but his was really a multi-layered existence, living discreetly with his male partner at his elegant high-rise flat in the Anstey's Building at Hillbrow, sometimes going looking for casual sex in public parks and toilets. He had been beaten up on at least one occasion, working in the theater, being overtly involved in politics with the Congress of Democrats while covertly involved through the Communist Party.

He kept most of this almost entirely to himself, never speaking of his secret political activities to his partner or anyone else. Only once, in later life, did he talk to an oral historian about what it had meant to be gay in South Africa in the first half of the last century. He did so on the condition of anonymity and on a promise that the tapes of the interview would be destroyed afterwards.

Thus, the role of one of the more extraordinary figures in the history of the struggle passed unrecognized for many years, until in 1998, two decades after his death, he was made the subject of a drama documentary, *The Man Who Drove With Mandela*, which some old comrades (such as Kathrada) criticized for being too focused on Williams' identity as a gay man, and not enough on the other areas of his life.

Mandela and Winnie had been to dinner at Williams' flat—traveling up twenty-one floors in the service lift for the use of natives—at which Mandela had left a vivid impression of greatness on Williams' then partner, John Calderwood: "A few times in my life I have met someone and thought immediately or within half an hour you are someone very special. That was my reaction to Nelson Mandela. I thought, you are somebody." He had the same thought later, when he met the British politician Chris Patten.

The Anstey's Building was then one of the landmarks of the city. Ann-Marie Wolpe remembered that there used to be tearooms on the first floor, where it was all "cream puffs and teapots."

Calderwood said Williams could not tolerate intolerance in any form and though he gave the impression of being a strong person with a tremendous driving force, behind the scenes there were tears and frustrations as he sometimes struggled to cope with the complexities of life.

His wealthy guardian angel, Mrs. Sharp, had bought Williams his elegant Austin Westminster car, a black six-cylinder automatic with a sumptuous brown-leather interior. It looked the part, as Calderwood said. But Williams had never given Calderwood any indication of what he was about to do when he set off in the car in late July 1962 to collect Mandela from Lobatse. Indeed, the couple never, ever spoke about it, before or afterwards. Williams was really remarkably secretive.

Once he had reached Mandela, they drove back through the middle of the night, with Williams at the wheel, and went straight to Liliesleaf, rolling into the farm at around dawn. Mandela recalled that he was still wearing his beat-up khakis and drank in the South African air after they had crossed the border.

It seems likely they arrived on the morning of Monday, July 30, six days before his arrest. (The journalist Anthony Sampson believes the date to be Tuesday, July 24, but that seems too early for the sequence of Mandela's remaining days of freedom and, anyway, Mandela says he arrived at Liliesleaf on a Monday). That evening, Mandela was reunited with colleagues at a Working Committee meeting, comprising Sisulu, Duma Nokwe, Govan Mbeki, J. B. Marks and Dan Tloome. He briefed them on his trip and emphasized the need to reshape the Congress Alliance, making the ANC the clear leader.

He had written a report on his trip and the impact of the PAC, which he probably presented to this meeting. Describing the PAFMECSA allies, he said it was clear there were "great reservations about our policy and there is a widespread feeling that the ANC is a communist dominated organization." He wrote that it was tactics, not policy, that were the problem and that the ANC must regard itself as the vanguard of the movement.

He itemized the funds he had obtained during his trip: £10,000 from Nigeria, £5,000 from Tunisia, £3,000 from Morocco (with a further £7,000 to come), £2,000 from Liberia to be repeated annually and £5,000 from Ethiopia. Perhaps thinking of the days he had spent reading in hotel rooms or waiting aimlessly for meetings, Mandela noted that "money collection is a job which requires a lot of time. You must be prepared to wait." He said the position of their people was pretty grim, possibly a reference to the financial hardship faced by many colleagues, including, it appears, Tambo himself.

There was an oblique reference in the report to information not being shared with Tambo in London, followed by the statement that the "impression [is] being given that ANC is a cover organization, leaders [are] repeatedly ignored." There was Luthuli's claim that he had not been consulted about the armed struggle; there was Tambo out of touch in London; and no doubt there had been complaints fed back to the Alliance in South Africa by Dr. Dadoo in London that policy was being changed without discussion.

Mandela's notes on the PAC must have made depressing reading for his ANC colleagues. He stated that the PAC had started off with tremendous advantages ideologically and had skillfully exploited their opposition to whites and partnerships. Sharpeville had "boosted them up and the stand of their leaders during the trial, imprisonment of Sobukwe fostered the impression that they were more militant than the ANC." In the PAFMECSA area, the Nobel Peace award to Chief Luthuli had created the impression that Luthuli had been bought by the West. In addition, Luthuli's book (his memoir) and some of his statements had been extremely unfortunate in creating the impression of a man who was the stooge of whites. Finally, the Congress Alliance itself did not allay that impression; on the contrary it perpetuated it. The mere allegation of being a stooge, wrote Mandela, "is of itself so damaging that it must automatically discredit the ANC."

"These things have made it appear that the PAC is the only hope for the African people. There were many who would say that the PAC might be naive but they were the only organization in South Africa that was in step with the rest of Africa."

Personal spats and squabbles, as well as the recent inactivity within the ANC, had not helped, he observed, and the ANC had a lot of work to do before it could say it had nailed the PAC. But, he added in a handwritten attachment to the typed notes, "no cause for pessimism, my morale is high."

Kathrada recalled how critical Mandela had been of the PAC when they met after his return, blaming them for fomenting the idea that he'd become an Africanist and joined them. But the PAC would have been delighted if they had read Mandela's notes about them, which disclosed just how far they had been propelled into the forefront by the tragedy at Sharpeville, while exposing the extent to which the ANC was unloved by the rest of Africa, with a white stooge at its head, and communists dictating events behind the scenes.

According to Anthony Sampson and evidence presented at the Rivonia Trial, at the meeting, Sisulu had urged his comrades to bear in mind the sensitivity of other minority groups, while Nokwe had been more militant, saying they were the prisoners of their own sins, having allowed themselves to drift and carrying co-operation too far.

Mandela said, "What we lack is initiative. We should change our attitudes and exert ourselves. Our friends must understand that it is the ANC that is to pilot the struggle."

Kathrada relates that Mandela was impatient to return to Natal to talk to Luthuli and to the Indian Congress leaders in Durban. The committee that had looked after Mandela's security before he left for his tour of Africa now met again. Kathrada recalled they might have met and talked while driving around Johannesburg. He could not remember exactly who—Joe Modise probably; maybe Jack Hodgson—had suggested a covert meeting in a moving car. Kathrada wanted to make special arrangements for Mandela's journey. After all, the police knew Mandela was back, which made him very vulnerable, but he was anxious to get under way without delay.

Wolfie Kodesh likely was not part of the driving committee meeting, as he recalled that Hodgson had said to him, "Somebody wants to see you up in Cyrildene [one of the Johannesburg suburbs]." When he got there it was Mandela, back from Africa, wearing a lovely, thick jersey that he had bought in Europe. He grabbed Wolfie in a huge, smothering bear-hug, then proceeded to tell him about the problems with the PAC and how black Africans needed to come to the fore of the Alliance. Wolfie remembered, too, how keen Mandela was to talk to Chief Luthuli.

News of Mandela's alleged return had been in the newspapers a month before he actually arrived at Liliesleaf. "The Return of the Black Pimpernel" had been reported in June 1962.

Winnie told a reporter on June 24 that the police had been making visits to number 8115 every night for the past three weeks. Whenever she and the children were about to go to sleep, Security Branch officers would arrive, asking her where her husband was and sometimes conducting searches of the house. "Sometimes they joke and at other times they are aggressive which frightens the children." Winnie maintained that, despite the rumors, she hadn't seen Mandela.

Meer described how the police had arrived at Winnie's home at ten o'clock one night and become vicious when finding Winnie was not there. Her sister had tried to bar their way, demanding a warrant, but they had pushed her aside and barged into the small property. Neighbors had gathered outside, angry with the police, and some youths had set light to a police motorbike, which exploded just as Winnie returned, prompting the police to rush outside with guns drawn. The crowd instantly vanished. When the police tried to find out from Winnie who had torched the bike, she told them, "Don't ask me to do your dirty work."

Winnie said later that, in addition to turning up at her home, the police had also followed her, arrested her in the street and carted her off to police headquarters.

When she was at last told that Mandela was back in the country, it had been Wolfie Kodesh who took her to Liliesleaf for the reunion. She took the usual circuitous route to rendezvous with Wolfie and avoid leading the police to her husband. When he left number 8115 at the end of March 1961, he had never actually told her he was going on a trip around Africa but while he was away she had received some messages from him, through the offices of the newspaper *New Age*. When she arrived at the farm and saw him again, after a gap of sixteen months, he promptly told her they did not have long together as he had a meeting to attend and would be going away again soon.

Mandela had briefed Winnie on the politics of his trip, putting it in perhaps plainer terms than he had used in conversation with his comrades. He told Winnie that the ANC had lost their dignity and that the leaders in Africa despised them because they couldn't understand why the black people of South Africa had not risen up in revolt against such a small minority of whites. Why had it taken them so long to realize they could never defeat the state by peaceful means? Mandela told Winnie how difficult it had been to communicate the ANC's message to Nkrumah and many other African leaders who just could not understand how a majority could continue to be oppressed by such a minority.

Winnie had detected something different in her husband—as others too had noticed: he seemed more militant and determined after his training. There was a look about him that she could not define, linked with an ominous feeling that they would never again have a normal life.

It had been the most emotional meeting Winnie could remember between them. Mandela had been desperate to see his children and she could not recall ever having seen him as demonstrative as he had been that day.

Winnie must also have seen the effect on him of her changed appearance. He later described the meeting in a letter to Zindzi and Zenani, telling them that he had been terribly shaken when he saw their mother again at Liliesleaf in July 1962. "I had left her in good health with a lot of flesh and color but she suddenly lost weight and was now a shadow of her former self. I realized at once the strain my absence had caused her." He had looked forward, he said, to a time when he would be able to tell her about his journey, the countries he had visited and the people he had met, but his arrest had put an end to that dream.

Mandela told Fatima Meer that Winnie's eyes brimmed with tears at their parting and that was how he remembered them.

Perhaps, too, Mandela might have noticed the loss of innocence in Winnie. The country girl, aged just twenty-four, who had broken a sandal strap on the veld was already becoming hardened by the harassment that would increasingly twist her life out of shape in the years ahead. Without Mandela to guide her, she was making bad judgments, becoming too close to a local married man, Brian Somana, who had helped take her to and from Liliesleaf. He was eventually suspected of being a police informer. When Somana's wife sued him for divorce, she would name Winnie as the co-respondent. That particular allegation was never proven, but it offered an early warning of the greater troubles ahead.

In 1962, Mandela had a reunion with his son Thembi, then a lusty lad of seventeen. He had worn a pair of Mandela's trousers to the meeting, a shade too big and too long, which Mandela had taken to be significant and was deeply touched by. "For days thereafter my mind & feelings were agitated to realize the psychological strains and stresses my absence from home had imposed on my children."

At the time Thembi had been on his way back to boarding school.

They had discussed Shakespeare's *Julius Caesar* and Mandela had been reminded that he was talking to a child but "to one who was beginning to have a settled attitude in life." Mandela was sad when they parted, unable to accompany his son to a bus stop or see him off at a station, "for an outlaw, such as I was at the time, must be ready to give up important parental duties." So he had left his son—no! his friend—to step out alone and fend for himself in the world.

"I knew you had brought him clothing and given him some cash," Mandela wrote to Winnie, "but nevertheless I emptied my pockets and transferred to him all the copper and silver that a wretched fugitive could afford."

Knowing the financial friction between Winnie and the first-family children, it is hard to resist the notion that Thembi may have been making a different point altogether when he wore his father's ill-fitting trousers to their meeting. Mandela must have thought he was doing it to connect to his father, but Thembi may have been wearing them to show he could afford nothing better.

From the confines of Robben Island, Mandela seems to have begun to romanticize his "wretched fugitive" or "outlaw" existence, whereas, in reality, it had ended in prison, and caused his wife and his children untold harm.

The Goldreichs were still living at Liliesleaf in July 1962. Hazel remembered being afraid for Mandela as he set off for Natal with Cecil Williams. "You shouldn't be going," she told him but he said the arrangements had been made. He was always single-minded, said Hazel.

Mandela had either overruled, or simply ignored, the request of Kathrada and Co. that he wait until a more secure trip could be planned. He had won over the working committee, all except Govan Mbeki, who had been strongly opposed to him traveling with Cecil Williams. If the police had been alerted to his trip from Bechuanaland with Williams, they would know exactly what to look for in Williams' flashy, conspicuous Austin Westminster car. In fact, Mbeki had not wanted Mandela to come back to

South Africa at all and thought he ought to have stayed outside the border in Lobatse. But Mandela was in a hurry. It was almost as if he was courting arrest.

The drive down to Natal was uneventful. Mandela went first to a meeting with his Indian colleagues the Meers and Monty Naicker and his wife. "I want to tell the chief that I have briefed you and I want to know your reaction," he told them. While they were clearly not happy, opposing anything that would affect the Alliance, Mandela said the ANC must move to the forefront. Fatima Meer recalled him telling her how one African head of state said he had torn a copy of the Freedom Charter from his wall when he found out it had been written by whites.

Mandela sat with Fatima Meer in her kitchen and recounted stories of his trip that she would later use as the raw material of her biography of Mandela. They had gone out driving in her Volkswagen. She said he was very aware that he was a sacrificial lamb and bound to end up in jail. He was just trying to live day by day.

It was the ANC praise-singer activist, M. B. Yengwa, who drove Mandela out to meet Luthuli. He would have gone to Groutville but Luthuli warned him that the police might be looking for him there, so Mandela went to Tongaat instead and met Luthuli at the safe house of a trusted Indian woman, Mrs. Singh, a teacher, where Mandela stayed that night.

The chief did not like the idea of outsiders — other African states — telling the ANC what to do. But Mandela said, no, you're wrong, they're not telling us, but these are the views they hold. They believe the leadership of South Africa is with the ANC, but the PAC represents aspirations they understand, while the ANC is speaking for an amorphous group, failing to concentrate on African aspirations and grievances. For Mandela, that was precisely what they needed to focus on. He told the chief, "I am recommending that we should take their views into account because we have to operate from these neighboring territories and if they decided to give their support to the PAC, the PAC being a small organization can suddenly become big." The chief eventually said he understood, but Mandela could tell that he had doubts about the approach.

His other task in Natal was to revive the spirits of the MK regional command who were so disheartened by the conditions in which they were operating, especially the lack of funds, that they had more or less given up on acts of sabotage.

MK's commander-in-chief had gone AWOL in Africa, but now he was back and newly militarized. He wore his khakis for the meeting with the regional command, which was held at the home of an Indian in Reservoir Hills. Salaam! Mandela greeted his comrades when he entered the room in which they were gathered.

The meeting would form a controversial part of the Rivonia Trial, as one person who was present would betray MK and become the prosecution's star witness, known as Witness X. This was Bruno Mtolo, a long-standing member of the Communist Party and a trade union activist who had been in the ANC since 1957.

In the months before his own arrest in August 1963, a year after that of Mandela, Mtolo would be sent on MK business to Johannesburg, staying at Liliesleaf. Hazel Goldreich, who gave him a lift to the bus station when he was going back to Durban, passed on her suspicions at the way he kept asking her questions. His persuasive evidence at the trial certainly helped to put Mandela in line for a death sentence. He told the court that Mandela had warned the Natal regional command to keep their communist views to themselves when they went abroad for training because the African states were not prepared to help communists. Mandela denied the deception in court, but it certainly sounded at least a plausible paraphrasing of his position.

Alongside Mtolo at the meeting were Billy Nair, who was then the head of the regional command, Ronnie Kasrils and Sonny Singh. Singh recalled that there had been about ten people in the room and that tea was served with Indian snacks. He remembered it as being a Saturday afternoon, August 4, the day before Mandela's arrest. The meeting had been inspired as Mandela told them of his meetings with African leaders and his experiences in London. There was joy and excitement, said Singh, and they were like children in his presence, hugging and embracing him as if he was Father Christmas.

Singh was so exhilarated that he rushed to the ANC offices in Durban on the Monday morning after reading of Mandela's arrest, and blurted out that he had just met Mandela. Word went round and he was called to Room 316, the office of MK, and interrogated in case it had been he who had given Mandela away. All Singh was guilty of was overenthusiasm.

Mtolo had extraordinary recall of the meeting, recollecting during the Rivonia Trial that Mandela had asked them to outline their grievances to him and had promised to take them to the national high command in Johannesburg. They were not getting enough money, they told him, and did not trust the comrade who was supposed to be their treasurer. Mandela had asked for the private address of the regional command. Billy Nair had given him the details, which he had written into the notebook he was carrying with him.

He was still wearing his khakis when he went to a gathering at the home of the *Drum* photojournalist G. R. Naidoo. In some accounts, this took place in the late afternoon following the MK meeting on Saturday. In others, it was the following lunchtime and Mandela left straight after the event, to be arrested on the road back to Johannesburg. In his memoir, Mandela says the Naidoos' party was a pleasant evening—not, then, a lunch—and his first relaxation for a long while. Fatima Meer recalled how they hugged and remembered the feel of the thickened cloth in Mandela's khaki embrace. It was a purely social occasion, like a going-away party—with perhaps the idea of smoothing over the transition that Mandela hoped to make in the way the Alliance operated. There were various prominent local Indians there, and no other Africans that Meer could remember, only Cecil Williams, "a gentle person, somewhat effeminate."

In retrospect, perhaps, it was the sort of event that Mandela ought to have avoided. Anthony Sampson describes it as a larger function with many unfamiliar faces, but that was not how it seemed to Fatima Meer. There was no ceremony at Mandela's departure. He and Williams merely left, leaving Meer with the memory of a towering, broad-shouldered, robust man, who had shriveled by the time she next saw him, in prison.

You've grown thin, she told him. "He turned round and ungraciously said to me, 'You've grown fat!' "

Once again, Williams was driving, with Mandela next to him in his chauffeur's coat and cap. Some people, such as Rica Hodgson, thought this a stupid mistake as Williams was supposed to be in the back as the white *baas*, with Mandela masquerading as his driver, but it probably wouldn't have made any difference. The police clearly knew he was coming and were waiting for him.

How and why they knew has never been explained, though many people have been suspected: G. R. Naidoo, Bruno Mtolo, the British security service. Kathrada thinks the British could very easily have picked up Mandela's trail from the two white officials who met him when his plane landed in Bechuanaland and who may have either followed him back or passed on the information to their South African colleagues. If it was the British, it must have been a very secret operation, as the British embassy in Pretoria reported to the Foreign Office in London that the most widely held theory was that Mandela had been betrayed by the "communist wing" of the ANC as part of their fiendish plan to take over the ANC completely. "In view however of the known co-operation between Mandela and communist sympathizers this theory does not seem altogether likely. On the contrary there seems some reason to believe that the feud between the PAC and the ANC may have more to do with it. If we can find out more in due course about this we shall let you know." The PAC may well have been keen to get Mandela out of the way, but no evidence of their involvement has ever emerged.

There have been suggestions over the years that the CIA had forewarned the South African Security Branch. This theory has been given some credence by an *Atlanta Constitution* article that ran at the time of Mandela's release, which claimed the CIA's "Durban office" had warned South African authorities, telling them exactly where Mandela would be the next day. The tip-off had been disclosed at the state department in Washington at the time, it was reported. This *Constitution* story may in turn have had its origins in a 1986 newspaper report from *The Star* in

South Africa, which claimed that an American diplomat who got drunk at a dinner had blurted out that he was actually a CIA agent and had betrayed Mandela. A later story in the *Washington Post* named Donald Rickard as the drunken diplomat and described him as a colleague of another CIA diplomat, Millard Shirley, who had moved among members of the liberation movement in Johannesburg. Rickard supposedly had been the consul in Durban with a "high-ranking" Deep Throat, a local Indian.

Rickard, who retired back to the States, never spoke publicly of these matters but they received some corroboration from a Security Branch officer, Gerhard Ludi. Ludi had penetrated the Communist Party in Johannesburg, having a brief relationship with Rusty Bernstein's daughter Toni during a trip to the Soviet Union. Ludi gave evidence against Bram Fischer after Mandela's arrest and claimed to know the CIA had an agent within the Natal ANC.

In any case, it seems likely there was some kind of betrayal and, equally, that it emanated from Natal, since that was where the arrest took place. But that is informed speculation. Mandela was probably right not to care who had given him away. It didn't matter and would only have been one more score to settle.

Howick is just about an hour beyond Durban, on the road that heads northwest to Johannesburg and only a few minutes outside Pietermaritzburg.

Mandela was captivated by the lush green landscape of the Natal highlands in the afternoon light of that clear, cool day. He noted how the railway line followed the course of the road they were driving along and thought it would be a good spot for some sabotage. He took out his notebook and made a note about it.

He and Williams were discussing sabotage as they passed through Howick and were just at Cedara when a Ford V-8 full of white men went past them on the right. Mandela turned round and saw behind them two more cars both filled with men. In front of them, the V-8 was slowing and signaling to them to stop.

They pulled up just before a bend in the road with a steep bank to the side. As he slowed, Williams asked, "Who are these men?" It was a rhetorical question; they both knew what was happening and who the men were. The police had chosen the spot well as there was nowhere for them to go and they could have forced the Austin off the road into the bank if Williams had tried to use his high-performance car to outpace them.

In his memoir Mandela said he considered jumping out and making a run for it, trying to escape into the woods, but realized it was ridiculous, as he would have been shot in seconds. He told his ghost-writer, Richard Stengel, that he was very fit in those days and could climb virtually any wall. To Ahmed Kathrada, he said he could see the mountains, the Lesotho mountains, but decided it would be a risky thing and opted to remain where he was. He had no fear of being shot once he had decided to stay put.

A tall, slender man with a stern expression came over to the window on Mandela's side of the car. He looked as if he had not shaved or slept in a while, leading Mandela to assume they had been waiting for him for several days. He said he was Sergeant Vorster from Pietermaritzburg, and produced an arrest warrant. He asked Mandela who he was.

Mandela said he was David Motsamayi, but the officer knew better.

"No, but aren't you Nelson Mandela?"

Mandela again insisted he was Motsamayi.

The officer again said, "Oh, you are Nelson Mandela and this is Cecil Williams. I am arresting you and we will have to turn back to Pietermaritzburg."

In his memoir Mandela says the officer asked him a few questions about where he had been and where he was going, seeming irritated when Mandela parried and did not give much away. "Agh, you're Nelson Mandela and this is Cecil Williams and you are under arrest!"

"Very well," said Mandela.

Vorster said a major would sit in the back with them for the journey. There was no examination of the car or frisking of the arrested men. Mandela turned to distract the major with conversation and, as he did so, he surreptitiously pulled out his gun and his notebook. With the loaded gun still in his hand, Mandela had again considered escape. "At one time I thought I could open the door fast and roll down," he told his ghost-writer, "but I didn't know how long, you know, this bank was and what was there. I was not familiar with the landscape. No, I thought that would be a gamble and let me just go and think of a chance later." So he pushed the firearm and notebook into the gap between the front seats. The police, witless to the end, never bothered to search the car and those items were never found. They have never been recovered and no explanation for their disappearance has ever been given. That can only mean that they were one more secret that Cecil Williams took with him to his grave in 1978. He must have retrieved them when the car was returned to him after their arrest.

Williams was released on bail and escaped the country, making his way to Scotland where he set up home in Glasgow with John Calderwood. Ruth First later stayed with them for three weeks, to write her memoir of her detention and interrogation, *117 Days*.

Williams died a communist, said Calderwood. He never changed his mind. Never gave up his secrets.

In a 1991 newspaper interview, Mandela claimed he had buried a gun in the grounds of Rivonia, which has provoked the current owner, Nic Wolpe, to invest considerable effort in trying to locate it, so far without success. Have you found my gun? Mandela was supposed to have said on a visit to Liliesleaf in 2003. "I buried it somewhere over there," he said, pointing across the acres. The buried gun was a puzzling claim for Mandela to make as he only ever referred to one gun, the gift from the colonel in Ethiopia, and it was with him when he was arrested. That, too, is a mystery that cannot be solved.

At the police station in Pietermaritzburg, Mandela, still pretending to be David Motsamayi, a chauffeur, was led into an office. Among the several officers present was Warrant Officer Truter, who had won Mandela's respect at the Treason Trial for being an honest witness. They exchanged pleasantries before Truter said, "Why do you keep up this farce, because you know that I know you?"

"I have given you a name," said Mandela. "I have given you my name, and that is the end of the matter, I am not going to discuss the matter." But then they chatted about other things, including the Treason Trial, before Mandela was locked up alone in a cell for the night.

He described in his memoir how upset and agitated he felt. He must have been living all those months in denial, as he was clearly unprepared for his capture and confinement. He fretted for a while about how he might have been betrayed, then fell into a deep sleep.

In the morning he appeared before a magistrate and was ordered to be transferred to Johannesburg. News of his arrest had already become known in Durban. Fatima Meer had brought some food to the jail, which he took with him on the journey to Johannesburg. Everything seemed very casual and informal; he was sitting unrestrained on his own in the back of a car with two officers up front. At Standerton they let him get out and stretch his legs, and he offered them some of his food.

Then, as they neared Johannesburg, other police cars appeared as an escort. The car stopped so that Mandela could be handcuffed and placed in a locked van with reinforced windows. The convoy went by a roundabout route in case of ambush to Marshall Square, where Mandela was put in a cell. He began to think about how he was going to manage appearing in court the next day.

He heard a cough from the neighboring cell. A familiar sound.

"Walter?"

"Nelson, is that you?"

The mixture of relief, surprise, disappointment and happiness, Mandela said, was indescribable.

Eighteen

IS IT CLEAN?

Mandela's anxiety about Liliesleaf following his arrest was not misplaced. He had left all his recent papers there when he departed for Natal—his diary, his briefing on the PAC, notes of his successes with fund-raising, his own military training as well as plans for the military training of others, and, of course, his writings on *How to Be a Good Communist.* Everything, in fact, except the small notebook he had been carrying with him in the car.

It was a ready-made package of prosecution evidence for his complicity in sabotage and in plans for an armed revolution. So far he was facing five years for leaving the country without a passport. But those writings could get him hanged. No wonder he kept asking his lawyers for reassurance that the papers had been removed and destroyed. They said they had checked and were told he was safe. But as we have seen, the opposite was the case.

By his own admission, the culprit was Arthur Goldreich, together with Ruth First. Goldreich has never said he was specifically asked to destroy the papers but he does say he found them in Mandela's room at Liliesleaf after his arrest. He must have told the others about them, as he describes how he had a visit from Ruth First who said, "We have to take care of these papers. What shall we do?"

"What do you think we should do?" Goldreich answered.

"We have to hide them somewhere," said First. "They must be saved."

Goldreich initially wanted to send them out of the country but decided that would be too risky. Then he thought of giving them to friends, but feared implicating them. Finally he decided to bury them instead, in the primary coal bunker just outside the kitchen of the main house at Liliesleaf. He did at least go to some trouble to hide the papers, putting them first in a wooden box with reinforced metal edges, then removing the coal from the bunker, digging a hole—he called it a "slick"—in the floor and putting the box into the hole, before replacing the coal to cover it.

Goldreich even discussed his idea with Rusty Bernstein, the pair of them, Goldreich the designer and Bernstein the architect—a cautious, security-conscious character—agreeing that it was a good plan and bound to work. But, on July 11, 1963, an officer named Dirker looked inside the bunker and saw bits of cardboard protruding from the coal. There is no doubt that the mishandling of Mandela's incriminating papers epitomizes the general level of amateurish incompetence with which the remaining plotters went about their business after Mandela had been removed from them.

Perhaps other revolutions have begun with the same careless, haphazard approach, but in South Africa in 1963 the would-be revolutionaries underestimated the enemy, while dramatically overestimating their own capabilities. It is easy to criticize, from the vantage point of history, but the truth is that they incited a fierce clamp-down by the state and set back their cause for a generation.

The blame is probably not entirely theirs, as the PAC's armed wing, Poqo, seems also to have been entirely unregulated, committing a number of atrocities in and around the eastern Cape. Poqo distributed leaflets with the slogan, "Freedom comes after bloodshed." They were blamed for a mob attack on a police station at Paarl in November 1962 and the ensuing rampage through the town when two white people were killed. They were also alleged to be behind one of the most notorious incidents of the period, when five white people, including a woman and two young girls, were attacked and killed while camping at the roadside by the bridge over the Mbashe River in early 1963. A few weeks later Poqo were thwarted in their plans for a mass rural uprising, drawn up in Maseru, the capital of what was then Basutoland.

Continuing acts of sabotage from MK, albeit disciplined to prevent injury or death, added to the general air of insurrection that provoked the state's new hardline justice minister, John Vorster, to bring in the General Law Amendment Act of May 1963, which allowed the police to arrest suspects without warrants and detain them without charges for up to ninety days, after which they could immediately rearrest them. The law even denied courts the power to order release. Vorster had told Prime Minister Verwoerd that one could not fight communism by following the Queensberry Rules (for boxing like gentlemen).

Special banning orders for the house arrest of named activists, such as Rusty Bernstein, were also being granted. At one stage, Jack Hodgson was under twenty-four-hour house arrest.

Vorster had appointed a new head of Special Branch, Hendrik van den Bergh, who used his headquarters in the Gray's Building to, as he must have seen it, meet terror with terror, in the shape of torture and interrogation with the use of violence, electric shock and techniques for inducing psychological breakdown. As Ruth First later put it, "Men holding key positions in the political movement, who had years of hard political experiences and sacrifice behind them, cracked like eggshells." First herself would be taken to the edge of reason, making a vain attempt at suicide and becoming embroiled in a game of seduction with her interrogator, J. J. Viktor, during her arrest and rearrest under the ninety-day law, an experience she would describe in *117 Days*.

Ruth could be talking about the frailty of any number of her colleagues, but she formed a close bond with the young advocate Bob Hepple in the weeks before he was caught up in the Rivonia arrests and was subjected to the vicious interrogation that unhinged him. First and Hepple engaged in agonized discussions about the next phase of the armed struggle as they shuttled back and forth between the city and Liliesleaf, deep in the northern suburbs.

Though still in his twenties, Hepple had been politically active since his teens and was used to living with secrecy, moving around from one illegal meeting to another without a qualm. "Youth!" as he said, from the high hill of his seventies in 2008, "You just thought you were immortal." After Mandela's arrest he had been invited to join the Secretariat of the Communist Party by Bram Fischer and Joe Slovo. Rather than making policy on the secretariat, he was involved in organizing and supporting the leaders. He quickly concluded that the whole setup was blurred, that at the top, the party and the ANC—the central committee of the former and the national executive of the latter—were virtually one and the same, indivisible from MK. The activists were not just the nice, white, middle classes sitting in their nice, white, middle-class homes, however. Black comrades were very much involved too, said Hepple.

One new presence in Johannesburg was Govan Mbeki, who had come to the city from Port Elizabeth on the cape in late 1962 when he was served with a five-year banning order. He had been active in the ANC since the mid-1950s, but had earlier been a storekeeper and a member of the precursor of the Bantustans, the Transkei *bunga*. Mbeki (the father of Thabo, the country's future president) was eight years older than Mandela but a baby in politics by comparison. Some doubted, were even suspicious of his credentials (how come he had never been arrested before 1960?) while others did not warm to his abrasive style. It is said he was not much admired by Mandela, and Mac Maharaj thought Mbeki was ruthless and unprincipled.

By late 1962, Mbeki had run a sabotage cell in Port Elizabeth before going underground to evade his banning order. He was staying at Liliesleaf after being co-opted onto the national high command of MK and showed some impatience to move on from sabotage and begin the armed struggle in earnest. He found support from Joe Slovo, and they, along with Arthur Goldreich, wrote a document called "Operation Mayibuye." "The time for small thinking is over," began the document. It was a brief but high-reaching blueprint for a revolution. "It can now be truly said that very little, if any, scope exists for the smashing of white supremacy other than by means of mass revolutionary action."

The plan required "hundreds of activists" who would leave the country for training and return equipped to spark the revolt, at the head of several thousand men in four main areas who would join them in the initial onslaught. The plan envisaged an army of 7,000 in total.

"We are convinced that this plan is capable of fulfillment. But only if the whole apparatus of the movement both here and abroad is mobilized for its implementation and if every member now prepares to make unlimited sacrifice for the achievement of our goal."

Arms would have to be manufactured in substantial volume to supply the guerrillas. Fantastic, pie-in-the-sky figures were proposed as "production requirements": 48,000 landmines, 210,000 hand grenades, 1,500 timer devices for bombs. Medical care required 1 million aspirin. All this was way beyond the scope of the living room of Jack Hodgson's Hillbrow flat. In any event, Hodgson fled the country a few weeks after Mayibuye was completed and first presented to the high command in April 1963. A pity, or perhaps it was just as well, as the plan would have been right up his street.

Along came Denis Goldberg, a white Jewish comrade from Cape Town known as "Mr. Technico." He too was going into exile abroad, but when he arrived in Johannesburg in May 1963 he was asked to stay and take charge of "logistics." He began sleeping on a camp bed on the floor of the dining room at Liliesleaf, with the wind blowing up through the parquet floor. It was romantic, he thought. The Long March begins with the first step. The Long March of Mao had come to South Africa.

Slovo attended endless meetings at Liliesleaf during and after the writing of "Operation Mayibuye," which meant having to leave his Innes Chambers offices downtown as often as three times a day to go to Rivonia. He wanted to present the document to the leadership abroad, he said, and asked for permission to take it out of South Africa (getting in a visit to his homeland in Lithuania at the same time). He spoke of sending back parachutists. Some comrades, such as Kathrada, suspected he really just wanted to leave to put Operation Mayibuye into action.

The great controversy among them all later was why they began to make plans based on the document before it had ever been approved. Slovo and Mbeki claimed it had been given the green light but the evidence of this was non-existent.

A new property, Trevallyan, was purchased by Goldberg for use in preparing his arsenal. He started going around iron foundries, concealing his identity with an overcoat, hat and glasses, and using an assumed name, one of several, to get quotes for the manufacture of the parts he wanted. The hand grenade was based on a design Goldreich had brought back from China. He hoped he had disguised that too but one foundryman asked, "How many of these do you want?" And when Goldberg said that he needed 210,000 in six weeks, the man replied, "Ah, during the war we made 15,000 hand grenades a day."

As others have noted, in spite of his false names and his overcoat, Goldberg left an all too obvious trail of his preparations for terror.

As Trevallyan was a farm location, the plan was to make it look like a smallholding for free-range chickens and storing arms in the sheds that would normally hold the animals. The men who stayed there—Mbeki, Raymond Mhlaba, Wilton Mkwayi and sometimes Sisulu—would pose as chicken laborers.

Kathrada had nearly left the country, but he had gone underground instead—first at Liliesleaf, and then at a new underground home he rented in the suburb of Mountain View. Before Kathrada could live in his new home, he was transformed, with the help of the theatrical Arthur Goldreich, into Pedro Pereira, a Portuguese man, with dyed hair, a beard, glasses and a false shoe to create a limp. For thirty-four years he'd been an Indian; now suddenly he was not. Kathrada was not very comfortable with his disguise and thought it looked unnatural, but Goldreich had even greater plans to create a plaster cast of Kathrada's face and make a latex mask that someone else could wear to leave the country. The idea was that if the police thought he had gone, they would stop looking for him.

The ranks of the underground were swelling. A steady trickle of recruits or comrades passed through Liliesleaf from Cape Town and the eastern Cape, including Bruno Mtolo, who was remembered for wetting the bed while he was there. Security seemed lax and Kathrada was not the only one who was getting nervous.

Bob Hepple had offices near Slovo in Innes Chambers. Sometimes the Liliesleaf foreman, Thomas Mashifane, would come to his office with messages, blatantly connecting Hepple to the farm. Thomas himself was concerned at the number of cars going in and out of Liliesleaf, declaring that if it carried on they would all be in jail.

One day, Hepple went out to Rivonia and found Kathrada enraged after finding a gun under a bed. It belonged to Govan Mbeki, who said he was not going back to prison without a fight, and if the police came he would shoot it out with them. He was a hothead, said Kathrada, and a tyrant, to boot, who would not let his comrades eat decent food or drink alcohol as they had to learn to live like revolutionaries. They were not even allowed to kill and cook the roaming fowl. Still, Kathrada and Wilton Mkway, a once-illiterate former shepherd—made sure to obtain the occasional bottle of brandy, revolution or no revolution.

The revolutionaries would often all sleep there in the thatched cottage after meetings. Although it was cramped and cold, Mbeki would try to deny them a warming fire. Kathrada laughed at the preposterous idea of Operation Mayibuye but in truth, he didn't mind admitting, he was scared of its consequences and feared ending up on the gallows. He was called a coward, later on Robben Island, by another comrade, Elias Motsoaledi, but he wasn't stung because it was true. Kathrada discovered, too, that his friend Wilton Mkwayi had sharpened a stick to beat him with, because Mkwayi was impatient for the revolution and Kathrada's reservations about Operation Mayibuye were getting in the way.

Bob Hepple remembered being told by Bram Fischer at the end of

May 1963 that Joe Slovo and the ANC communist J. B. Marks were going to Dar es Salaam to present Operation Mayibuye to the external leadership. Hepple said that at that stage neither the Communist Party nor the ANC had seen the document, let alone approved it.

Would Mandela have supported Operation Mayibuye? In many ways it appeared to fit neatly into his own preparations for the greater struggle ahead. He had read the theory, listened to the guerrilla heroes of Africa, such as Algeria's Ahmed Ben Bella, and had training himself, while organizing the training of others. Training for what? He never really spelled it out, but some kind of revolutionary war must have been in his thinking. "Much bigger explosions to come," he had promised PAFMECSA.

According to Mac Maharaj, the armed struggle was only ever a means to an end for Mandela, and the end was political negotiation. Let's bomb them to the negotiating table. He might have trained for war but he was thinking like a political leader. That was not the Cuban model.

According to Mac, Mandela read Operation Mayibuye during the Rivonia Trial and was shocked. What is this, chaps? But they closed ranks and never discussed it until they reached Robben Island, when he began to punch holes in its loose thinking and theory, gaining himself a reputation as an uncompromising debater, showing no mercy to Mbeki or Joe Gqabi, who also tried to take him on. In the end, unable to cope with having his baby torn apart, Mbeki asked for, and was granted, a ban on all talk about Operation Mayibuye. That was the end of it.

After Mandela's arrest, there had been political discussions about the best way forward, which Hepple had engaged with. Did you subscribe to the Che Guevara theory that a small group could ignite a revolution or did you accept the long struggle, organizing resistance internally? Hepple preferred the latter and thought Operation Mayibuye was crazy. A plan for the military invasion of South Africa? Absolute lunacy.

Being junior and carrying little weight himself, he discussed his concerns with Ruth First—as, indeed, did Kathrada—but she was glad something was finally happening and hoped it might be the spark that started the prairie fire. Ruth liked the MK men, whose efficiency and resolve she contrasted with the tiresome meetings of the political committees. Hepple was torn between her infectious urgency and his own unease.

How much longer could they go on without being caught? Hepple wondered. On one occasion some friends of Goldreich visiting the main house had burst in on them during a meeting at the thatched cottage. The whole set-up seemed insecure. Hepple thought Mbeki must be in a disturbed state of mind if he imagined he could shoot it out with the police.

There was further alarm in the third week of June when the police made a number of arrests including a couple of comrades, Bartholomew Hlapane and Patrick Mthembu, who knew all about Rivonia. Hlapane would later claim that Mandela really had been a communist. Mthembu had been abroad for training and used to boast he would "make the Boers shit bricks," but he quickly broke in interrogation and gave evidence for the state at the Rivonia Trial. He was later assassinated in revenge.

Two days after those arrests, on June 26, 1963—Freedom Day for the ANC—they pulled off a brilliant propaganda coup, broadcasting an address by Walter Sisulu over the airwaves of so-called Radio Freedom. It was Goldberg's handiwork, using aluminum tubes for the mast, which he spray-painted black to make them invisible in the dark. They had the speech on tape, written and recorded at Liliesleaf, and transmitted it over a home-made radio. Sisulu had wanted forty-five minutes but Goldberg said he would be a sitting duck out there and to keep it to a quarter of an hour instead.

They did not dare broadcast from Liliesleaf but used the back garden of a friendly family in Parktown. Goldberg had two white comrades standing sentry, with a torch and a walkie-talkie. When it was over he dropped the aerial and rushed to the cinema to buy a ticket and watch the film—he had forgotten the title; it was about the Gestapo—as an alibi. He went back and collected the materials of the broadcast later.

The transmission reached the media and was reported in *The Times* of London on June 28. "Freedom radio broadcast in South Africa." "Message from ANC leader in hiding." The story said that the broadcast had been made by Mr. Walter Sisulu, who could not be quoted in South Africa because he was a banned person. He had disappeared from his home a month ago while under twenty-four-hour house arrest and on £3,000 bail. Expert opinion said it could have come from anywhere within 250 miles of Johannesburg.

A week later, on July 6, there was a meeting at Liliesleaf to discuss Operation Mayibuye, which Bob Hepple and Ruth First traveled out together to attend. Rusty Bernstein was there too and made plain his opposition to the plan. He had prepared a paper of his own, which proposed a more gradual move to armed incursion, involving quick attacks on border outposts and hasty retreats back across the frontiers. Bernstein's belief was that this would set off an international incident that could precipitate a political crisis and the downfall of the state. The alternative, he said, would be a serious mistake, a long, protracted guerrilla war that was unlikely to succeed. Mbeki, unsurprisingly, disagreed. He believed an armed invasion was the only way to win. Bram Fischer, who was also present, said it was not a good time to start a guerrilla war.

Hepple, listening, felt that the leaders were becoming isolated and divorced from reality. The discussion was heated and tense. It looked as if a major rift was developing between them. Bernstein was under house arrest and had to get home, so the meeting was cut short. They agreed to meet again five days later, on Thursday, July 11. Kathrada asked whether Bernstein could leave his paper behind so he could read it in the meantime. Bernstein refused. Very sensible, thought Kathrada.

By now they were winding down life at Liliesleaf and the meeting on July 6 was supposed to have been the final one at the farm—but no one could suggest a safe alternative that would not further compromise security. So, in the end, they opted to go there one more time. They were breaking the rules of the underground, said Kathrada. Don't go back. You should never go back. Kathrada and Bernstein both later claimed it was Hepple's idea to meet once more at Liliesleaf, but he doesn't think it was his decision.

Ruth First, who was not going to that day's meeting, left messages at

Hepple's home, early on the morning of July 11, for him to pass on to Sisulu and Mbeki. Hepple went to his office and was getting ready to leave around lunchtime when an Indian man he didn't know appeared, saying he had a message from Natalie for Cedric—meaning from Natal for the Centre/Liliesleaf. Hepple asked him to come back tomorrow as he was about to go out. He wanted to check the contact first with Kathrada. There were suspicions even then, within the movement, of a leak in Natal that could have lead to Mandela's arrest.

Kathrada, who had arrived at Liliesleaf the night before, slept in the thatched room after a small glass of brandy. He would always say he had his last drink on July 10, 1963. "How do you know?" he would be asked.

"Because it was the night before I was arrested."

After finishing the beverage, he had a black coffee and went to bed. There was no one else there, just him and the Goldreichs and the staff.

Hepple was nervous that day and took a roundabout route, not only to thwart anyone who might be following him but also to avoid the usual journey past the Rivonia police station. He got to Liliesleaf about 3 p.m. and parked his Vauxhall at the back of the house beside Bernstein's car and near Denis Goldberg's VW Kombi.

Goldberg had bought the VW to transport comrades and had just that morning collected it from the garage after having it fitted with blue curtains, so that others would not see a white man driving black people. It was such an unusual sight that it would have aroused suspicion.

Goldberg had earlier driven to town in a little Austin A40, taking with him Wilton Mkwayi who was going into Soweto for the day to organize MK recruits. He was always going into the townships and coming back with reports of hundreds of volunteers. So far, it was mostly hearsay. He was lucky to be out of Liliesleaf on that particular occasion. He had been saved again by *muti*, he would later claim. Goldberg put the A40 into the garage at Mountain View, took a cab to retrieve the VW and then collected Sisulu, Mbeki and Raymond Mhlaba.

As they drove into Liliesleaf, they were chatting and someone asked what they were going to call Trevallyan.

"Shufisa!" cried Goldberg.

"That sounds African," said Mbeki, "but it isn't. What does it mean?"

"Well," said Goldberg, "Eisenhower had his Supreme Headquarters Allied Expeditionary Force Europe, that's Shaefe, and we've got Shufisa, Supreme Headquarters United Front in South Africa."

They all roared with laughter but Sisulu cautioned, I'm not sure that's right, we don't have a united front yet, you know.

Goldreich's cousin, a dentist, arrived to work on Sisulu, as Goldreich had plans to disguise his face by using a mold to reshape his gums. The dentist seemed twitchy and said he was due to play golf. As he arrived, Hepple passed the dentist leaving and wondered who it was. Kathrada said he was embarrassed as he was sure the dentist had seen through his disguise and recognized him. They were all a little on edge as they gathered in the room to begin the meeting. Hepple was wondering whether he could carry on. If Operation Mayibuye was adopted he didn't know what he would do. He was not cut out to be a revolutionary soldier.

Goldberg, who was not part of the meeting, sat in the lounge of the main house reading Robert Jungk's account of the development of the atomic bomb, *Brighter Than a Thousand Suns*. Even those who were in the meeting seem unsure what body had been convened. Was it MK high command? Neither Bernstein, Hepple nor Kathrada was on the high command and they were there. Wilton Mkwayi was part of the body and he wasn't there. Mbeki, Sisulu and Mhlaba were there. Andrew Mlangeni was on the high command and probably would have been there—if he had not already been arrested on June 24. All six of those present were communists. What else was it, if not a meeting of the high command? What authority did it have to approve Operation Mayibuye? No one could say for sure. The underground was well and truly muddled.

Bernstein had left home with his alternative-to-Mayibuye document under the mat of his car but had got cold feet and turned back, hiding it in his garage before continuing his journey, and stopping on the way to sign in at Marshall Square police headquarters. As the meeting started he had on his lap the copy of "Operation Mayibuye" that Mbeki had brought.

There was another copy that had been loaned to Dave Kitson, a member of the logistics committee, by Arthur Goldreich, which he had gone to collect so that it could be referred to during the meeting. When he got to the house, Kitson was ill in bed with his family around him, and the document was under his bed. Goldreich wanted it and was in a hurry to get back. Soon, soon, Kitson was saying, not wanting his family to know. Finally the document was handed over. Goldreich hid it inside the hubcap of his Citroën DS and set off for Liliesleaf. His wife, Hazel, was out teaching and the children were at school.

It was about 3:15 when Hepple and the others head a vehicle coming down the drive. Mbeki got up and went to the window. "It's a dry cleaning van, I've never seen it before."

Bernstein got up and looked too. "My God, I saw that van outside the police station on the way here."

Hepple got up and went to the door. The side panel of the van read, as he remembered, Trade Steam Pressers. There was a man in a white coat, hat and glasses in the front seat.

At that moment, Thomas, the farm manager, was coming towards the cottage with a parcel. "Go and see what that van wants!" someone yelled. Hepple closed the front door.

The rear door of the van opened and policemen got out. Dogs began barking.

"It's the cops," yelled Bernstein. "They're heading here."

Mbeki grabbed the copy of "Operation Mayibuye" and some other papers and thrust them into the chimney of the stove. If the stove had been alight they would have burned. But it wasn't.

The back window was open. Hepple helped Sisulu and Kathrada as they scrambled out of it to escape. The front door flew open and a Special Branch officer named Kennedy entered. Hepple had cross-examined him in a trial earlier that year.

"Stay where you are! You're all under arrest!" Hepple remembered that Kennedy came up to him with an excited sneer. "You're Advocate Hepple, aren't you?"

Kathrada and Sisulu began running but were soon stopped by officers with guns.

Another officer Hepple knew, whom they all knew, was there too. Warrant Officer Dirker was an unpleasant character. "Oh Heppie ! Now we have you all," he said. He searched Sisulu. They were gradually handcuffed and put into the dry cleaning van. The officers did not at first recognize Kathrada.

Other officers had gone to the main house, interrupting Goldberg's reading. He grabbed his jacket, which had incriminating notes about landmine manufacturing in the pocket, shot out of his seat and tried to reach the loo to flush away the evidence. He was stopped and asked his name. He gave a pseudonym, Charles Barnard, but was not believed. They initially thought he was Arthur Goldreich but eventually an officer from Cape Town recognized him.

They could hear the officers' excitement as they realized what they had stumbled into.

"Look at this!"

"Jesus! Look what's here!"

Outside, an officer said to Hepple, "I'm surprised to find you mixed up with these dangerous communists."

The officer in charge, Willie van Wyk, phoned his bosses and told them, "We've hit the jackpot."

Goldreich saw the police before they saw him, as he drove into Liliesleaf, but there was no chance to turn around. Before he could stop, they jumped forward and put a pistol to his head. He turned off the engine and got out with his hands in the air. He could see the police were everywhere and knew his wife and children would soon be coming home to Liliesleaf at the close of the school day. It was the end of everything.

Goldreich was not the only one to experience some relief. The pressure of the existence was immense. One simply could not keep up the subterfuge, and mistakes were bound to be made. Goldberg had meant to go out and buy a forge that day, but was so tired he hadn't bothered. Tired? "Shit, the tension of living underground." His theory was that revolutionaries often almost wanted to get caught, because the stress became too great. He had only been in Johannesburg six weeks but, Christ, had he worked.

According to Goldreich, the head of Special Branch, Van Den Bergh, came out later that day, after Hazel and the children had returned. Hazel had with her a friend's child who was coming for a sleepover. The police were everywhere but she did her best to ignore them as she made supper and put the children to bed. She told Nicholas, aged nine, the men had come for a meeting.

"Well, they look like police to me," he said.

She gave him all the money she could find and told him to hide it under his pillow.

Both Arthur and Hazel recalled Van Den Bergh telling them their children were going to end up in an orphanage or an asylum. The officer claimed he had lost a child too, a daughter who had died, so knew how it felt. He seemed sad, Goldreich recalled. There was a silence. Some officers had entered and were searching a cupboard. Then he said, "See these okies, here? They are professionals, they do this every day. Not like you," he pointed at Goldreich. "The trouble with you, Goldreich, the trouble with all of you is you are amateurs. You always have and you always will underestimate your enemy and that's why you're in the shit."

If he didn't already know it, Goldreich quickly came to believe that there were nasty racists and anti-Semitic assumptions behind the cockiness of Special Branch.

As long days of interrogation began, he was warned that he would pray to talk and was constantly abused as *jou fokken jood.* All the whites were *fokken jude.* Goldreich was convinced that the police never believed that black people could do anything for themselves and that behind a black person there had to be a white person pushing them forward.

Nonetheless, was it not true that the ANC had struggled to achieve a degree of separation from its white communist colleagues?

Hazel Goldreich spent eighty-seven days in prison, a term that was extended after her husband, Arthur, made a spectacular escape from Marshall Square, exactly a month after the Rivonia arrests, on August 11,

1963. With him went the white lawyer, Harold Wolpe, the husband of AnnMarie, and the Indian activists Mosie Moolla and Abdullah Jassat. They had bribed a young warder, Johannes Greef, who left doors open for them in return for payment. He went to prison himself while the escapees got clean away.

Wolpe's legal partner was his wife's brother, James Kantor, a wealthy, carefree character who was almost entirely apolitical. He was arrested after the escape and became a defendant at the Rivonia Trial. Special Branch suspected he was deeply involved, or claimed they did, but they were mistaken. He suffered a breakdown during detention and never fully recovered, remaining resentful of his sister, AnnMarie, and her husband, and eventually dying of a heart attack at the age of forty-seven.

It was the escape of his brother-in-law, Harold Wolpe, that made Kantor's own arrest inevitable. The prison break was approved by Bram Fischer who took a central role in trying to control the chaos that ensued after the Rivonia arrests. He attempted to restore the high command of MK, organized a committee to get people out of the country and tried to support those who were arrested. Ruth First was soon picked up. Bram feared arrest himself. Much of his calm, urbane surface was stripped away as he was affected by insomnia, becoming short-tempered and impatient with legal juniors and other around him, and often flushed red in the face with anger. When he was asked to join the defense legal team for the forthcoming trial, he at first refused, but later changed his mind and accepted.

Part of the difficulty was that, as with the arrest of Mandela, no one knew who had betrayed Liliesleaf. They would never know. Kathrada and others speculated that it might have been the anxious dentist, the cousin of Goldreich, who had visited that morning. It could have been the bed-wetting Mtolo, though supposedly he turned state witness only after the Rivonia arrests. Patrick Mthembu was a possibility. So too was George Mellis, the small boy who had once written down the registration numbers of all the cars he could find and handed in the list at the Rivonia police station.

Wolfie Kodesh was in the UK when Oliver Tambo told him that he had been identified as a possible traitor. Some people accused Winnie Mandela, mainly because of her association with Brian Somana who was suspected of being an informer. A wide net was cast, which was just what the police must have hoped for. Spreading fear, suspicion and paranoia was part of the game that the police were now winning.

The men who had been arrested at Rivonia were held in solitary confinement for most of the next three months. They were brought out in early October to be fingerprinted and charged. They were now "awaiting trial prisoners" and no longer confined. They could talk again with visitors as well as with one another.

The state had let it be known that the trial was being moved from Johannesburg to the Palace of Justice in Pretoria, which meant they intended it to be a show trial, for the world to watch. Bram called together George Bizos and a younger advocate, Arthur Chaskalson. The attorney was Joel Joffe, who had been about to emigrate to Australia. Vernon Berrange would join them too, when he returned from abroad. Just as he had been reluctant to take part in the trial at all—he was lucky not to be in it as a defendant—so Bram was equally resistant to the idea of leading the defense. The other lawyers did not then know of his primary role in the underground movement and insisted he was the best man to take on the state.

Although they were not yet sure exactly whom they would be defending, they were told the day before that there was to be a hearing on October 8, 1963. With Bram busy on another case, Bizos, Joffe and Chaskalson were sent on a merry dance around the courts, prisons and law offices of the state, trying to find out whom they would be representing and to have a consultation with their clients. There was no hearing and at first they were told they could not have both black and white clients in a consulting room together.

Finally, that day, they were shown into a prison room and the defendants were brought in: Sisulu, Mbeki, Mhlaba, Kathrada, Goldberg, Bernstein, Hepple and three others who had not been arrested at Rivonia—James Kantor and two ANC members, Elias Motsoaledi and Andrew Mlangeni.

They had all half expected Ruth First to be among them, but she was in fact never put on trial. The best guess of the defense was that the state would be seeking to execute the accused and that would be harder if there was a woman among them.

There was an unexpected final guest. In came Mandela, in short pants, sandals and a prison-issue khaki shirt. His appearance was both surprising and shocking. Joffe had met him in the past but he looked different now, withered by his fourteen months in prison, looking thin and "miserably underweight" with pale skin, hollow cheeks and bags under his eyes. His manner, however, was unchanged and he still seemed confident and easygoing.

Soon after his conviction and five-year sentence in November 1962, Mandela had begun studying for his unfinished LLB law exams in a correspondence course with the University of London. At the end of May 1963, only three weeks before his first exams, he had been transferred suddenly out of Pretoria prison to Robben Island. He had written to the commander of Robben Island, complaining of the interruption to his studies. Two weeks later, on June 13, again without warning or explanation, he had been transferred back again to Pretoria.

It seemed at first like an excited reunion, said Joffe, but Hepple soon put a dampener on that with his announcement that he had been "asked" to give evidence against the others and was still considering what to do.

I sensed Hepple's discomfort, forty-five years later, as we discussed these events at his rooms in Clare College, Cambridge, where he is an emeritus master and emeritus professor of law. He has threatened to sue over the years when the subject has been discussed and I think he is sensitive to being judged, especially by his comrades.

George Bizos later said that he thought of Hepple as a tragic figure and, especially, a disappointment to Bram Fischer for whom, to some extent, he had been a protégé. Goldberg remembered asking Hepple why he was going to give evidence and he replied, according to Goldberg, because they are going to hang me. Goldberg said, you mean it's OK to hang the rest of us? Hepple himself said he did not recall this exchange with Goldberg.

Others were more considerate of his position. Who could say how they might fare under torture and interrogation? And who would want to sit in judgment of those who broke "like eggshells"? Hepple was made to stand on the spot over three days and nights. He was also subjected to a game of Russian roulette by the infamously cruel Swanepoel, who spun the cylinder of his gun, pointed it at Hepple and asked, "What's it going to be, the rope or the bullet?"

Hepple could not cope with the pressure and made an eight-page statement. Although it did not make any significant admissions about the role of others, it enabled the prosecutor, Percy Yutar, to rise up triumphantly one day and proclaim that Hepple would be his first witness. Hepple felt badly about that, and about the fact that, when granted bail, he had then escaped, with the help of Bram Fischer. Perhaps he ought to have stayed, faced down Yutar and refused to testify, but he hadn't and that was a regret.

He remembered talking to Mandela about it at the trial.

They stood by a window to avoid being bugged as Mandela expressed his sympathy for Hepple's predicament but said if he testified it might be used politically against the ANC. Mandela told him, "You realize that if you give evidence you're finished?" There was also a chance that Hepple could have been assassinated, like Patrick Mthembu.

"So if you get the opportunity to escape that would be good, but it's got to be your decision. I'm not going to tell you what to do."

Hepple actually wanted someone to tell him what to do after three months in solitary.

But Mandela didn't tell him. None of them did.

Hepple hoped he could still persuade Percy Yutar to release him unconditionally, and asked Mandela how he would feel if that happened.

"That would be excellent," said Mandela.

They shook hands and parted.

Nineteen

THE PEOPLE WHO assembled in the public gallery for the opening hearings of the Rivonia Trial were shocked to see Mandela emerge wearing shorts. When she first saw him, Hilda Bernstein, Rusty's wife, wondered, have they so easily reduced this proud and sophisticated man to the dress and status of a boy? But then he smiled and raised his clenched fist. He called, *Amandla!* The crowd's response was, *Ngawethu!*

There was a false start when the initial indictment was challenged by the defense and quashed by the judge. By December 1963, the trial proper was ready to begin again, with four charges constructed around the broad allegations that the accused had carried out some 200 acts of sabotage and had adopted a plan to embark on guerrilla warfare. Perhaps mindful of the debacle of the five-year Treason Trial, the state never charged the Rivonia accused with treason.

In his own memoir of the trial, Joel Joffe has great fun, characterizing Percy Yutar—Percy-Cutor, as he was known—as a malicious, incompetent buffoon who relied on sarcasm and accusation as substitutes for hard evidence and cogent oratory. His greatest gift, you might think from reading Joffe's book, was his presentation of his case in elegant, bound volumes of papers.

Yutar was a right-wing Jewish state lawyer who appeared to hate the Jewish communists on trial. Bob Hepple had not been raised a Jew but his mother was Jewish. Before Hepple's flight, Yutar had appealed to him to give evidence against his fellow accused and "save the Jews of South Africa." That, apparently, was Yutar's mission. He was convinced of his case and believed they all deserved to hang.

Operation Mayibuye—had it been adopted? Was it being acted on by the accused?—was central to the case. While he kept his own feelings to himself at the time, Bram Fischer later called it "an entirely unrealistic brainchild of some youthful and adventurous imagination."

Bram was living on a knife-edge during the trial. Yutar once handed him a prosecution exhibit, supposedly a document written by Harold Wolpe, which Bram recognized as in his own handwriting. He cross-examined Patrick Mthembu, both of them knowing Bram had been at some of the same meetings Mthembu had attended at Liliesleaf. Mthembu never gave him away and only once, in an apparent fit of pique over a minor grievance, did Yutar try to expose his other life as the leader of the underground. Fischer believed the state had, for some reason, allowed him indemnity for the duration of the trial.

Undeterred, Bram took prosecution papers from the court—maps, plans for sabotage targets—and showed them to members of the re-formed MK, which he himself had helped to shape, with Wilton Mkwayi, Dave Kitson and others. The new MK, already keen to punish Mthembu and all traitors, had formed a hit squad to make an example of them. Bram was sure the accused's fate would be sealed if a state witness was killed in revenge in the middle of the trial, so implored the hit squad to hold their fire.

Although all the accused, including Mandela, had pleaded not guilty—"the government should be in the dock, not me"—Mandela had no intention of dissembling to save his neck. He said he could not believe his eyes when Bruno Mtolo appeared as the mysterious Witness X, but conceded the truth of much of Mtolo's detailed evidence.

Mandela insisted, however, on having his defense team challenge Mtolo over his claim that Mandela was a communist and that he had told his recruits to deny they were communists when they went abroad. That was simply not true and if he had to admit he was involved in MK to nail the lie, that would not stop him. In any event, if the notes he had left at Rivonia made it likely he would be convicted, then Mtolo's evidence made it a certainty.

In discussions with the legal team, he said he wanted to explain "to the country and the world where Umkhonto we Sizwe stood, and why; to clarify its aims and policy, to reveal the true facts from the half-truths and distortions of the state case." He was prepared to put his life at stake to do it.

It seemed to Joel Joffe, after Mtolo's evidence, that Accused No. 1, Mandela, would bear the main burden of the charges. The entirely innocent James Kantor, whose wife was pregnant, was granted bail over Christmas 1963 and went home with an affectionate message for his wife. "Tell Barbara I apologize," said Mandela.

"What for?" Kantor asked.

"Because you are here."

That January, Kantor—Accused No. 10—passed a note all the way down the row to Accused No. 1, asking him whether he would be a godfather to his unborn child, and saying it would be an honor to the child.

Mandela's note of reply went back down the line just before the afternoon break. "I would be more than delighted, and the honor is mine, not the baby's." Mandela hung back at the break and spoke briefly to Kantor. "Now they dare not hang me," he said, with a smile.

Kantor was discharged and acquitted on all charges at half-time in the trial, after the prosecution had concluded its case. Kantor went back to his old life, but it was not the same life he had known.

There was now an adjournment of five weeks during which the accused and their lawyers finalized plans for the defense case. There were many hundreds of documents to read, and a clear position on so many points to be established.. The defendants were keen to go into the witness box and declare themselves for the world to hear. All of them, including Mandela, wanted to be questioned and cross-examined. That strategy, their lawyers knew, could be dangerous, leading them to make damaging admissions at Yutar's hands. He would keep relentlessly to the facts, surely, and not try to argue politics with them.

Joffe believed that Yutar had established only a weak case against Kathrada, Mhlaba and, notably, Bernstein. There was the real possibility of three acquittals so they needed to proceed with caution in terms of how much they decided to reveal in their testimony.

Bizos was a lone voice of dissent, feeling certain that Yutar's vanity would get the better of him and that he would try to meet the accused on their home ground. He turned out to be right. Yutar made some extraordinary blunders during his questioning of Sisulu and his fellow accused, neglecting to press them on their association with Operation Mayibuye and other crucial matters. Furthermore he tried too hard to catch them off guard and expended a lot of effort smearing others, such as Chief Luthuli, who were not even in the trial. Too often, Yutar was too busy sneering about the "so-called grievances" of the ANC. "Never bet against a Greek," said Bizos.

According to him it had been decided at an early stage that Mandela would not give evidence and part of the reason was that he would be forced to answer questions on all the documents that he had left lying around at Liliesleaf. Mandela was also reluctant to participate in the rituals of the trial and make it seem as if he had given in since his trial the previous November, when he had complained of feeling like a black man in a white man's court and argued that he could not be fairly tried by the state that did not give him the vote.

Now Mandela was torn. Although he wanted to be cross-examined, he did not want to relinquish any of his moral authority. He was the same everywhere, in court as in prison, arousing, as Joffe noted, not so much deference as respect in almost all, though not quite all, who encountered him. Even those who did not respect him would be cowed by his commanding manner. He had got into an argument with an officer during his brief stay on Robben Island, in which the officer had advanced towards him, raising his arm as if to strike him. Although scared, Mandela held his ground. "If you so much as lay a hand on me, I will take you to the highest court in the land. And when I finish with you, you will be as poor as a church mouse." Mandela saw the man was shaking and stood firm. Eventually the officer backed down.

During the trial the accused got into a dispute one day in the Pretoria prison yard. They were complaining about something, perhaps about being handcuffed on the journey to court, with Mandela leading the protests. The warder said to him, "When your time comes you will do the same to us." When, not if, Rusty Bernstein thought, as he observed the white warders going to Mandela for help writing their applications for promotion.

Joel Joffe also noted that Mandela's personality and stature impressed themselves on everyone around him, not just the accused but on the prison and the prison staff. It seemed to Joffe when he first met Mandela that he was an attractive and interesting character. By the end of the trial he had come to regard him as a "really great man."

One day the lawyers went to consult with their clients at the prison, only to find strange new arrangements in place around a raised table dotted with bar stools. Mandela was behind the bar, lined up with the others. He stood up and smiled as the lawyers entered. "What will it be today, gentlemen, chocolate or ice-cream soda?"

They all finally agreed that Mandela would read a statement, rather than give evidence, speaking, in a sense, not just for himself but for all the accused and, indeed, for the entire liberation movement. He would take the chance of this platform, with the whole world listening, to make a thorough statement of their aims and their beliefs. There is an original typed copy of the speech, from Joel Joffe's own trial papers, in the archive at Wits in Johannesburg—forty-four pages of foolscap, with some longhand markings and Mandela's own signature at the end. If it is not the greatest political speech of the last 100 years, it is certainly among the most significant and is surely the best speech of Mandela's political career.

The state had intended the Rivonia Trial to be a show trial, exposing Mandela and his co-defendants to all who were watching as mere rabble-rousers and communists, intent, as Percy Yutar put it, on "savage slaughter." The apartheid state had wanted everyone to know it was firm and right in its values, and would not be bowed by a few agitators.

But in five hours, on April 20, 1964, Mandela stole all that from them, ensuring that Rivonia would be remembered above all for the dignity and courage of Mandela and his fellow accused, and for the eloquent phrasing with which he articulated his readiness to be a martyr for his cause. The court was packed. A cliché, but true. Mandela's mother, who had never been to school, was there alongside her daughter-in-law, Winnie. As the correspondent Mary Benson noted, Nosekeni Fanny was strong and dignified, proud of her son. Winnie, who had initially been refused permission to attend her husband's trial, made a special appeal to the prime minister. He had conceded with a warning that permission would be revoked if "at any time your presence or action at the court, by the manner in which you dress or in any other respect, leads to an incident or incidents caused by you or others present." Winnie was demure in Western dress. Rusty Bernstein's daughter Toni attended much of the trial and recalled it as desperately boring. "But Winnie always caused a sensation, she was so beautiful."

Mandela's speech had been the big secret of the defense. Yutar had expected Mandela to go into the witness box to give evidence and had prepared for a cross-examination. He was thrown when Bram Fischer announced that Mandela would be making a statement from the dock instead. Yutar jumped up.

"My Lord!" Yutar squeaked. "My Lord, I think you should warn the accused that what he says from the dock has far less weight than if he submitted himself to cross-examination."

In a normal jury trial, this might have been a tactic to alert the jury to the suggestion that Mandela was trying to avoid giving evidence. But this was South Africa, 1964, and there was no jury. Mandela was not being tried by his peers but by Judge Quartus De Wet. Neither he nor Mandela and his lawyers needed reminding, by Yutar, of the implications of Mandela's decision.

"I think, Mr. Yutar, that counsel for the defense have sufficient experience to be able to advise their clients without your assistance." In his response, Fischer said he appreciated his learned friend's advice. Mandela stood up and began reading, slowly.

"My Lord, I am the first accused. I hold a bachelor's degree in arts and practiced as an attorney in Johannesburg for a number of years in partnership with Oliver Tambo. I am a convicted prisoner..."

Like all the best speeches it had a narrative, shaped around the story of Mandela's political life up to that moment. Mandela admitted his role in MK but, truthfully, denied many of the acts of sabotage attributed to it. He talked of the early history of the ANC and the events that had led to the armed struggle. He described his trip round Africa and the people he had met, adding that he had undergone military training himself and stating his reason for doing so: "If there was to be guerrilla warfare, I wanted to be able to stand and fight with my people and to share the hazards of war with them."

MK had remained a "small organization," he said, recruiting its members from different races and organizations, and trying to achieve its own particular object. Mandela was keen to stress the separation of the ANC from MK. He said the overlap in membership that sometimes occurred between the two organizations did not change the nature of the ANC or give it a policy of violence.

He denied that the ANC was communist-led or -inspired. "The ideological creed of the ANC is, and always has been, the creed of African nationalism. It is not the concept of African nationalism expressed in the cry, 'Drive the white man into the sea.' The African nationalism for which the ANC stands is the concept of freedom and fulfillment for the African people in their own land. The most important political document ever adopted by the ANC is the Freedom Charter. It is by no means a blueprint for a socialist state."

He stressed the differences between the ANC and the communists, the latter seeking to emphasize class distinctions while the ANC tried to harmonize them. It was true there had been close co-operation between them but that was only because of the common ground they shared—"in this case the removal of white supremacy."

It might be difficult for white South Africans, he said, with their ingrained prejudice against communism to understand why experienced African politicians so readily accepted communists as their friends. "But to us the reason is obvious. Theoretical differences amongst those fighting against oppression is a luxury we cannot afford at this stage."

For decades, communists had been the only people prepared to treat Africans as human beings, as equals. The only people "who were prepared to eat with us, talk with us, live with us and work with us."

Mandela described himself as an African patriot. "After all, I was born in Umtata forty-six years ago..."

He invoked the Magna Carta and the Bill of Rights. He spoke of the poverty and inadequate education faced by black South Africans, the lack of dignity they felt, and their hatred of the pass system for the way it criminalized them all and kept husband and wife apart, causing the breakdown of family life. People wanted jobs and fair wages; they wanted their families with them, and the freedom to come and go without fear of pass restrictions or a curfew.

Above all, they wanted equal political rights. He knew this sounded revolutionary to whites and that whites feared democracy because it must lead to black majority rule. "But this fear cannot be allowed to stand in the way of the only solution which will guarantee racial harmony and freedom for all."

It was not true, he said in the last moments of his speech—perhaps unconvincingly—that votes for all would lead to racial domination. Political domination based on color was artificial and when that disappeared so would the domination of one color group by another.

The ANC had been fighting racism for fifty years and would not stop when it came to power. "It is a struggle for the right to live," he said.

It was said that Mandela paused at this moment, and his voice had dropped and began to waver as he continued.

"During my lifetime I have dedicated myself to this struggle of the African people. I have fought against white domination, I have fought against black domination. I have cherished the idea of a democratic and free society in which all persons live together in harmony and with equal opportunities. It is an ideal which I hope to live for and to achieve. But if needs be, it is an ideal for which I am prepared to die."

Mandela sat back down in the dock. The silence, said Joffe, was profound, like the silence in a theater before the applause thunders out. Only here there could be no applause.

Sighs were audible as people stopped holding their breath. Some women in the public gallery were in tears.

Goldberg, sitting near Mandela in the dock, remembered the strain and the hoarseness that inflected Mandela's voice, and how he had seemed very conscious of what he was saying, which, so far as Goldberg remembered, was "Hang me, hang Sisulu, hang Kathrada, hang Goldberg..." and so on. Personally, Goldberg felt a sense of elation at sharing that moment: at being associated with the intense meaning of Mandela's words. If you took on the state, you expected the worst; you expected to die. Mandela had shown his comrades and lawyers the speech in draft and there had been grave misgivings among the lawyers about the last lines. It was an invitation to a death sentence.

Mandela later recalled hearing that Bram Fischer had shown the draft to another lawyer, Harold Hanson, who had handed it back. "Is this what they are going to read? Is this what they are going to say in court?"

"Yes," Bram had said.

"Then take them straight out and hang them."

Bram had not told the accused about that at the time but returned to them depressed and had tried to polish the speech, improving what Mandela modestly referred to as his original, "rather crude" remarks. According to George Bizos, the ending of the speech was initially much plainer, merely saying that Mandela was ready to die. It was he, Bizos, who had suggested inserting the words "if needs be," to soften the point.

In fact there is a draft of the paragraph in Mandela's hand, which shows he planned to say, "It is an ideal for which I have lived, it is an ideal for which I still hope to live and see realized. But if it should be so I am prepared to die for it." Then these words have been crossed out: "should" and "so I am prepared to die for it" and others added, so that it would now read, in second draft, "but if it needs be it is an ideal for which I am prepared to die," which is almost (minus the first "it") the finished version.

This might be imagined as the climax to the case—it was certainly the high point—but in fact the trial still had two months to run. After Mandela came the questioning and cross-examining of his fellow accused, all except Elias Motsoaledi and Andrew Mlangeni, who had not been senior members of the leadership and might do themselves more harm than good if they testified. Like Mandela, they too read statements, which, unlike Mandela's, were brief.

It seemed at times as if the courtroom was a bubble, apart from the outside world, but the outside world was watching and clearly forming a view. Mandela was surprised at the support from the old colonizer, Britain, and would have been even more surprised had he known of some of the Foreign Office traffic of sympathetic dispatches and approving noises being made by officials about Mandela, with equal weight for the disapproval of the state's conduct of its trial.

Bizos had been briefing British diplomats on the case, at their request. Later on, after a few whiskies, the British consul general, Leslie Minford, clapped his arm around George Bizos' shoulders and said, George, there won't be a death sentence. Bizos could not ask him how he knew, and could hardly rely on it, so never told anyone else.

The United Nations had voted for the release of the accused, the World Peace Council had awarded them a medal and, in a shade of things to come, Mandela had been elected president of the Students' Union at London University. The support was heartening but did little to ameliorate the accused's fears of the death sentence. Raymond Mhlaba alone seemed untroubled by it. "What does it matter?" he told Mbeki one day during the trial. "You go there, they put a rope around your neck, pull a lever, and it's all over. What is there to be frightened or bothered about?"

People like to think of lawyers as being cool and dispassionate but that was far from the case in the Fischer household. Bram's wife, Molly, told Joel Joffe that he was crying out in his sleep, "We must save them!" Joffe too admitted to Mary Benson that he had dreamed of the accused stepping onto the scaffold, and would wake in a cold sweat.

Fischer advised the defendants that they had to be sure they had proved that MK had never intended to kill. "I must be frank," he said, "that even if we succeed, the judge may yet impose the death sentence."

A warder asked Mandela what sentence he was anticipating. "Well, I am sure they are going to hang us," said Mandela, expecting a comforting reassurance. The warder said he thought so too. Harold Hanson, who would handle the mitigation, went to see the judge and asked him whether he was going to impose the death sentence. The judge said, no. But no one could be sure what would happen and they all continued to fear the worst.

The accused resolved that, if they were convicted and sentenced to death, they would not appeal.

As Mandela said, many years later in conversation with Ahmed Kathrada, they wanted to leave a good impression, to their people, that these were heroes and that even when they were facing death they stood by their principles.

If that was so, their courage must have reached deep into the hearts and minds of their lawyers. No wonder Joffe and Fischer were personally affected, though in the case of Fischer it is tempting to think that his crying out in his sleep was not merely a reflection of the strain he was under or the responsibility he felt towards his clients, but also, at some subconscious level of magical thinking—we must save *her*—prefigured the personal tragedy that would soon befall him.

The day after the end of the trial he would set off on the long drive to

Cape Town with his wife, Molly, and a friend, Liz Lewin. The Fischers were on their way to join their daughter Ilse who was studying in Cape Town, for her twenty-first birthday, three days later.

Bram was at the wheel of his Mercedes, which he habitually drove too fast. As they reached Koolspruit, south of Ventersburg, and were crossing a bridge over the river, a motorbike came past them in the opposite direction, startling a cow lingering on the bridge. Bram braked and turned the wheel. The car came off the road, it slipped down a gentle gradient into the river. Bram and Liz got out but Bram could not free Molly. She was trapped in the back seat of the Mercedes and drowned.

Some days afterwards he traveled to Robben Island to meet his clients. He never mentioned the death of his wife but when Mandela asked after Molly, he hid his face and walked away without answering. After the visit a warder told Mandela what had happened and he quickly wrote a letter of condolence, which the prison never posted.

Fischer was finally arrested in 1965 and was still in prison when he was diagnosed with cancer in 1975. He was granted compassionate release shortly before his death that same year.

George Bizos prepared Fischer's defense after his 1965 arrest and could not help asking him, had it all been worth it, sacrificing his career and his family to the cause?

Fischer rounded on him.

Had he asked Mandela that question? Didn't he have a legal practice and a family too?

Bizos had not asked Mandela.

"Well, then, don't ask me," snapped Fischer.

The Rivonia verdicts were delivered on June 11, 1964. Each of the accused was found guilty on all four counts, except Kathrada, who was found guilty on only one charge, and Bernstein, who was acquitted and discharged, only to be immediately rearrested. Sentencing would come the following morning. It was agreed that Mandela would speak for the accused if the death sentence was passed down.

He made notes that night, five small points on a slip of paper that has been preserved, but are so unusually scrawled that they can no longer be fully deciphered, not even by Mandela himself, no doubt betraying the stress of their author as he contemplated how he could meet his fate. The fourth point is illegible and may well have been something else altogether. However, it seems like a forewarning of the bloodshed to come. The fifth point was also wrongly numbered the same as the previous point but was presumably meant to be separate.

1. Statement from the dock.
2. I meant everything I said.
3. The blood of many patriots in this country has been shed for demanding treatment in conformity with civilized standards.
4. That army is beginning to grow.
4. If I must die, let me declare for all to know that I will meet my fate like a man.

The writer and liberal activist Alan Paton had agreed to give evidence in mitigation (many other people had apparently refused). Mandela had insisted that neither Paton nor the lawyer, Hanson, should say anything that might imply the accused had regrets or were pleading for mercy. So Paton spoke of the sincerity of the accused and their deep devotion to their cause. He knew of Mandela as the likely successor to the Nobel Peace Prize winner, Chief Luthuli, as the leader of the ANC. He had come to testify, he said, because he loved his country and it seemed to him that the exercise of clemency in the case was important to the country's future.

None of the lawyers could ever recall a judge changing his mind after mitigation. This judge interrupted Paton when he tried to remind the court of the violence used by the Afrikaner people to defend their rights from the British. The judge said that many had not only used violence but had been convicted of high treason and executed for it. In the light of history they might have had legitimate grievances but that did not entitle them to break the law by force.

That sounded very much like a judge who had decided to pass the death sentence. They waited while Yutar tried to have his way with Paton, taking the unusual step of cross-examining a witness called in mitigation, trying to humiliate or smear him.

After a few words from Hanson, the judge called the accused to their feet. Mandela recalled the moment with Kathrada thirty years later.

> Well, it's easy to say now I didn't care. But we did expect a death sentence and in fact the moment before the judge delivered his judgment, the sentence, because he had already found us guilty, but before he delivered his sentence, you remember he was breathing... he seemed to have himself been nervous and we said, well, it's clear he's going to pass the death sentence... we were expecting the death sentence, resigned ourselves to that, but of course it's a very serious experience where you feel that somebody is going to turn to you and tell you now this is the end of your life and that was a matter of concern but nevertheless we tried, you know, to steel ourselves for this eventuality, tragic as it was. My colleagues seemed braver than myself. I would like to put that on record.

The judge quickly, briefly, told them that he had decided not to impose the supreme penalty. "The sentence of all the accused will be one of life imprisonment." With those words, he got up and left.

Many of those involved in the case could not understand why Mandela extended the hand of reconciliation to Percy Yutar after his release, three decades later. He "whitewashed" him, in the expression that was current at the time, with invitations to his presidential inauguration and once to lunch at the president's home. Mandela shook Yutar's hand for the cameras.

Mandela told Joel Joffe that he was trying to rebuild South Africa and he could not afford the luxury of revenge.

The prisoners went back to Pretoria, changed out of their suits and back into their prison clothes. They had some supper and were in bed by around nine. At about midnight they were woken and assembled at the reception area. The colonel came along and said, "Mandela, we are now taking you to a place where you can be free."

Kathrada asked, "Is this only Mandela who is going to be free?"

The colonel said, "No, all of you."

Sisulu was upset with Kathrada for asking that question and, speaking quietly, so the colonel and the warders would not hear, he said, "No, that was not proper. When they are talking about Madiba they are talking about all of us. It was not proper of you to ask that question."

Thirty years later, Mandela and Kathrada talked together about the night they went to Robben Island, struggling through failing memory to recall precisely what had happened, arguing over which of them was correct.

They were taken to the military base and put on a military plane. They were handcuffed and put in leg-irons. At least, that was how Kathrada remembered it. Not Mandela. He was insistent that they had not been handcuffed. But Kathrada had it right there in his notes, he insisted, they were handcuffed and in leg-irons.

"No," said Mandela.

"Hey," said Kathrada.

"No," said Mandela.

"Handcuffs certainly," said Kathrada.

"No," said Mandela.

"Yes," said Kathrada, because he remembered that he had been tied to someone who wanted to vomit on the plane and he had to walk with him.

"Oh, I see," said Mandela. But finally he remembered how they used to handcuff the others going to court, but never him. He had not been handcuffed going to the airport and had not noticed that the others were handcuffed.

Kathrada said, "Maybe not leg-irons."

"I don't think so at all," said Mandela. "Because they were being very friendly, they gave us sandwiches and so on?"

"Ja," said Kathrada. "Biltong they gave us."

"Yes, quite," said Mandela. "We were heavily escorted by the warders and I think by the military. It was a long escort."

They remembered that Van Wyk, the Special Branch officer, had said, "Well, you chaps won't be in prison very long, the demand for your release is too strong. In a year or two you'll get out and you'll return as national heroes. Crowds will cheer you. Everyone will want to be your friend, women will want to know you. You chaps have made it." However, Van Wyk had also added that they would be released, not because of any victory on their part, but because the Nationalist government would change its attitude and they would release them.

Mandela and Kathrada then fell to arguing about the journey from the prison. Mandela thought it was an oddly quiet journey without the usual escort of police vehicles and screaming sirens. They were departing quietly, secretly in the middle of the night in a single van.

"Now, I'm saying here you are wrong," said Kathrada. "We were heavily escorted, in fact by police and warders. In fact, the police, the security police, Dirker and the rest of them had gone right to the island with them."

"Yes, quite," agreed Mandela. "And in less than half an hour we found ourselves at a small military airport outside the city. We were hustled into the belly of the plane. There were no seats, we crouched on the floor."

"That's not so," said Kathrada.

"There were seats, said Mandela.

There were seats, said Kathrada, we sat on the seats.

They disputed the engines of the plane. Was it two, was it four? They agreed it was a Dakota. A large plane. Hard seats. Wooden seats and no heating.

"We were very cold, if you remember, on the plane," said Kathrada. "These chaps were sitting with their big overcoats, the warders, in jerseys and overcoats. We just had our prison clothes."

It was very cold on the plane.

At Robben Island, Kathrada, because he was Indian, was issued with long trousers while Mandela and the other black South Africans were handed shorts. Mandela complained. A few days later some long trousers were left in his cell.

No pin-striped, three-piece suit had ever pleased him as much.

His African comrades, however, still had shorts, so he complained again and his long trousers were taken away.

It took him three years to achieve long trousers for all.

Three years to win long trousers.

Twenty-six more years to be free.

Acknowledgments

In February 2009 I was ushered, nervously, into a vast office in the Johannesburg suburb of Houghton. There was only one person in the room as I entered, sitting formally behind a substantial desk, and he did not stand up but apologized instead, for his impoliteness at remaining seated. "My knees will not allow it," he said by way of explanation, extending a hand for me to shake. The knees were 90 years old and belonged to Nelson Mandela. I was not there to interview him — age and natural decline had put him beyond interviews — but he had agreed to meet me, the very welcome outcome of my many months of research into Mandela's early life.

The meeting was arranged by the Nelson Mandela Foundation and I want to emphasize my gratitude to the people there, not just for that "audience" with Madiba, but for their support and enthusiasm for this project and their kindness and hospitality to me. This is not in any way an "authorized" biography, but it certainly reflects the open attitude of the Foundation and its staff. No doubt this, in turn, reflects the open attitude of their namesake.

The Foundation knew from the outset that my plan was to rescue the sainted Madiba from the dry pages of history, to strip away the myth and create a fresh portrait of a rounded human being, setting his political achievements in the context of his natural character, while also considering the impact of his involvement in the struggle on his personal and family life. For a variety of reasons, perhaps, much of this aspect of Madiba's story had not been subjected to much scrutiny in the past.

Verne Harris and Sahm Venter at the Foundation especially made me feel welcome and opened so many doors, generously sharing resources, patiently offering advice and guidance. Their friendship means as much—if not more—to me as their help with this book. Others at the Foundation, such as Ruth Muller, Zanele Riba and Razia Saleh were also unselfish, sharing contacts and information.

I think some people at the Foundation were feeling sorry for me that February. I had returned to South Africa for one last interview, with Winnie Madikizela-Mandela. No sooner had we met briefly for the first time than Winnie was hospitalized following a minor accident. As days turned to weeks, her daughters Zindzi and Zenani were sympathetic and friendly and assured me it would be all right in the end, and so in the end it was, as I finally sat and talked with their mother at Zenani's home one Sunday afternoon towards the end of the month. Both Winnie and her daughters and some of their grown children showed me warmth and kindness, accepting me briefly into their lives. I am indebted to them all.

Equally, the family of Mandela's first wife, Evelyn, were open and generous, their grandson Mandla showing me a regal welcome in Mvezo, and their granddaughter Ndileka speaking eloquently and sensitively about difficult personal issues. I hope they will feel I have respected the trust they gave me. Researching this book was sometimes a poignant exercise, the pain of the past still very much alive in the present.

Any writer is lucky to find someone who not only shares their passion for the subject but is prepared also to share their own knowledge and research. I met Sarah Haines, a heritage consultant for Haley Sharpe, while she was developing the site at Liliesleaf Farm. She later went on to play a leading role in transforming Mandela's old home in Soweto, number 8115, Orlando West, into a thriving museum. Her wisdom and expertise on Mandela's early life were an unexpected gift, as too were the resources of Liliesleaf which Nic Wolpe was kind enough to put at my disposal.

Special thanks are due to all those people—see the Notes—who gave up their time to be interviewed. Many were old. Not quite as old as Madiba, perhaps, but even so, interviews are a tiring business and I was especially grateful for their willingness to talk. Ruth Mompati in Vryburg/Naledi, the late Fatima Meer in Durban, AnnMarie Wolpe in Cape Town, and in Johannesburg, Ahmed Kathrada, George Bizos, Nat Bregman, Mosie Moolla, Amina Cachalia, Peter Magubane, Esme Matshikiza...all of them alert and sometimes brilliant with their thoughts, stories and analysis. Mac Maharaj, a mere stripling by comparison, spent many hours sharing ideas and illustrative anecdotes. I was glad to have the benefit of his keen intelligence. In London, Paul and Adelaide Joseph cooked curry and talked, just as they used to sometimes with Madiba. So many people were so hospitable and I am very thankful to them all.

Others were generous with research, information, recommendations and advice, such as Albie Sachs, Richard Stengel, Mark Gevisser, Nandha Naidoo, historians Tim Couzens and Phil Bonner, the writer Anna Trapido, filmmaker Joe Menell, Stanley Sello—sound archivist—and the staff at the Mayibuye Archive, University of the Western Cape, Diana Madden who steered me through the Percy Yutar papers while they were still held at the Brenthurst Library, Michele Pickover, curator at the Historical Papers Library, Wits University, Mike O'Brien at Haley Sharpe, the staff at GALA, the Gay And Lesbian Archive at Wits, the staff at the various branches of the Nelson Mandela Museum in Mthatha and elsewhere in the eastern Cape, the staff of the National Archives of South Africa and the National Archives of the UK, the staff of the Standard Bank Archives.

High Life, the BA in-flight magazine, were kind enough to support my first research trip, when David Crookes was a good traveling companion and William Ross of Wild Coast Holidays a knowledgeable guide and driver. Further thanks to Corlien and the staff of Ginnegaap, the Melville guest house where I lodged and worked. Back in the UK the Mount Pleasant Writers' Retreat in Reigate was a welcome bolt hole in which to work uninterrupted. Edith Stokes, the former housekeeper, now retired, will be much missed.

I thank Alan Samson at Weidenfeld & Nicolson for the opportunity to write this book, his colleague Lucinda McNeile for her work on the text and my agent Georgina Capel for her representation. As in the past, the *Sunday Times Magazine* showed admirable patience at my absence. Heather Wood, my transcriber, was reliable and consistent as ever.

A nonfiction book can be a massive undertaking requiring full attention, and inevitably places strain on the home life you temporarily opt out of, or leave behind. Thanks to all those who supported, encouraged and helped where they could: Jamie Bruce, Tim Lott, Steve Mason, Anthea Barbary, Ashok Prasad, Allan Nazareth, Chris Williams, Ted Nixon, Sarah Hinks, Jo Nixon, Andy Saunders, Simon Yates, Sarah Jackson, Mark Robertson, Jo Charlton, Pete Luetchford, Helen Chappell, Geraint Roberts, Mamta Patel, Mark Birbeck, Sara Clifford, Sheila and Paul Cullen, Charlotte Blant, Julie Parsons, Dominic Lloyd, Kamella and Ryan Emmanuel, my parents Pat and George Smith and many other friends and colleagues too numerous to name, in Lewes and beyond.

Of course it's the family who suffer most, especially when you are away for months at a time. They know I hope that their love and support matters more than anything, and I hope feel loved and supported in return: Sitira, Kitty, Orealla and Mackenzie Felix-Smith, and their mother, the incomparably wonderful Petal Felix.

Timeline

July 18, 1918	NM born
1927 or 1930	NM's father dies
1930	Bloemfontein conference
1933	NM goes to Clarkebury, aged 15
1943	NM completes BA at beginning of year and graduates from Fort Hare
April 19, 1944	formation of ANC Youth League
July 17, 1944	Sisulus marry
October 5, 1944	NM and Evelyn marry
February 23, 1946	Thembi born
December 1946	NM leaves Witkins to become full-time student
1949	mixed marriages outlawed

1949	Slovos get married
December 1949	NM has been studying for LLB for 7 years
August 1950	Makgatho born
June 26, 1950	national strike called
June 26, 1952	Freedom Day (start of Defiance of Unjust Laws campaign)
September 1953	NM gives "no easy walk" speech
1954	second Makaziwe born
June 26, 1955	Freedom Charter drawn up at Congress of the People
July 1955	Evelyn alleges assault by NM
August 1955	ditto
October 1955	ditto
late 1955	NM leaves for trip home to eastern Cape
February 1956	NM gives Evelyn a week in which to leave 8115
March 25, 1956	Evelyn leaves 8115 permanently
May 1956	Evelyn lodges petition for divorce
November 5, 1956	Evelyn withdraws from divorce case
December 5, 1956	Treason Trial begins/mass arrests
March 19, 1958	divorce from Evelyn finalized
June 14, 1958	Winnie and NM married
June 1958	Winnie moves into 8115

Timeline

February 2, 1959	*King Kong*
March 21, 1960	Sharpeville
March 30, 1960	NM arrested
April 1960	PAC inaugurated
December 1960	secret meeting of Communist Party to discuss armed struggle; NM present
March 29, 1961	Treason Trial ends; everyone discharged
March 1961	NM writes "arrogant" letter to Verwoerd
end March 1961	NM becomes a fugitive
May 1961	NM hiding in Kodesh's flat
May 1961	South Africa becomes republic
June 26, 1961	NM releases statement on Freedom Day; historic talks soon follow
July 1961	historic talks re founding of MK
September 22, 1961	Liliesleaf Farm bought by Communist Party; used by MK
October 1961	NM moves to Liliesleaf
December 11, 1961	Luthuli receives Nobel Peace Prize
December 16, 1961	first MK bombs go off
January 8, 1962	NM goes to see Luthuli
January 9, 1962	NM leaves South Africa for tour
April 27, 1962	NM in Accra in Ghana
June 7, 1962	NM in London to see Tambo

June 14, 1962	NM still in London
end June	NM leaves London and returns to Ethiopia for military training
July 13, 1962	NM in Ethiopia on military training
late July	NM is summoned home by ANC
July 30, 1962	NM driven to Liliesleaf by Williams
August 5, 1962	NM arrested at Howick with Cecil Williams and will not be free again for more than 27 years
October 15, 1962	first day's hearing of Rivonia Trial, Joburg
October 22, 1962	trial restarts in Pretoria
November 1962	NM sentenced to 5 years
[May 2] 1963	General Law Amendment Act passed (90-day law)
June 26, 1963	Freedom Day: Sisulu's broadcast
June 26, 1963	some arrests connected to Rivonia
July 10, 1963	night before Rivonia arrests
July 11, 1963	last meeting at Liliesleaf at which everyone arrested
July 11, 1963	NM's papers found at Liliesleaf
August 11, 1963	Arthur Goldreich escapes
October 8, 1963	defendants in Rivonia arrests reunited with NM
December 1963	Rivonia Trial begins

Timeline

April 20, 1964	NM gives long speech at Rivonia Trial
June 11, 1964	Rivonia verdicts given
1967	Luthuli killed by train
1968	mother, Nosekeni Fanny, dies at 75
1978	Cecil Williams dies
1969	Thembi killed in car crash, aged 23
1990	NM released from prison
2004	Makgatho dies

Notes

ONE

3 "Wolfie Kodesh, was assigned the unenviable duty..." Oral history interviews with Wolfie Kodesh conducted by John Pampallis, 1989. Held at the Mayibuye archive, University of the Western Cape.

4 "—but Winnie herself says that Kodesh had come, not to her place of work..." Author interview with Winnie Madikezela-Mandela, 2009.

4 "Winnie had given a long series of interviews a quarter of a century ago..." Winnie Mandela, *Part of My Soul Went with Him* (interviews conducted by Annie Benjamin).

5 "Kodesh was at the Johannesburg magistrates' court..." Pampallis interviews, ibid.

6 "Mandela favored Khan's..." Author interviews with George Bizos and Ahmed Kathrada, 2008; Bizos, *Odyssey to Freedom.*

7 "Kodesh had never seen anything like it..." Pampallis interviews, ibid.

7 "According to Winnie, his costume had been her idea..." Author interview with Winnie Madikizela-Mandela, 2009.

8 "Kathrada remembered, when going with Slovo to see Mandela in jail..." Author interview with Ahmed Kathrada, 2008.

9 "Slovo and his colleagues wondered whether they could get a mask made..." Joe Slovo, *Slovo: The Unfinished Biography.*

10 "'If I hadn't seen it with my own eyes,' said Mandela..." Nelson Mandela, *Long Walk to Freedom.*

11 "Hepple was happy to be Mandela's adviser..." Author interview with Bob Hepple, 2008.

11–12 Description of court hearings from the digital archive of *The Times*, London.

12 "An observer from the British embassy..." Viscount Dunrossil's dispatches are contained in Dominions' Office records, DO 119/1478 in the UK National Archives.

13 "They clearly regarded the tribal costume as inflammatory..." Mandela, ibid.

15 "Louis Blom-Cooper, then a young lawyer for Amnesty..." Author interview with Bob Hepple, 2008.

17 "As they talked there was a knock on the cell door..." Author interview with Bob Hepple, 2008.

17 "In fact, as Mandela later described it..." Mandela, ibid.

TWO

Mandela's early family history is told by him in his autobiography, *Long Walk to Freedom*. I am grateful to Richard Stengel, Mandela's ghost-writer, and to the Nelson Mandela Foundation for allowing me access to a selection of some of the many hours of interviews Stengel conducted with Mandela. They contain a few nuggets of useful unpublished material which appears in this chapter and elsewhere in the book. The paper archive in Mthatha on the Eastern Cape was, so far as I know, first spotted by Anna Trapido, while researching her own book *A Hunger for Freedom*. She alerted the Foundation who asked the historian Phil Bonner to examine the papers. I am grateful to Bonner and the Foundation for access to Bonner's discoveries. Fatima Meer's marvelous first biography of Mandela contains valuable, neglected material from many people who were no longer around to ask by the time I came along. The second biography of Mandela, by Mary Benson, is also an important source of early material.

THREE

Mandela's schooldays were only briefly dealt with in the biographies of Fatima Meer and Mary Benson. I have relied mainly on *Long Walk* and on the interviews that Mandela gave to Stengel, where I think you can hear Mandela's voice, which is not always apparent in the sometimes westernized prose of *Long Walk*. I was lucky to find Nozolile Mtirara in Mqhekezweni in 2008. She had known Mandela and had her own version of the events surrounding his 1941 flight from his homeland to the big city.

FOUR

The early days, following his arrival, in Johannesburg are detailed in *Long Walk* and, in some instances, in even greater detail in the interviews Mandela gave to Richard Stengel. He described the knobkerrie and whistle he used as a night watchman to Mary Benson, as she recorded in her memoir *A Far Cry*. Walter Sisulu's life was meticulously recorded by his daughter-in-law, Elinor Sisulu, for her biography of Walter and his wife Albertina, Walter and Albertina Sisulu: *In Our Lifetime*. The first meeting between Mandela and Sisulu was described by Mandela to Fatima Meer.

55 "Alexandra! That is a remarkable place..." Nelson Mandela letter to Mrs. Onica Madshigo, November 1970.

56 "Gladys was only six or seven..." Author interview with Gladys Xhoma, 2008.

60 "Bregman did not even remember this moment; to him it meant nothing. He was not a racialist..." Author interview with Nat Bregman, 2008.

61–64 History of the ANC taken from various sources, most notably the Karis and Carter volumes, *From Protest to Challenge.*

65–68 Formation of the Youth League from Karis and Carter, Fatima Meer, Elinor Sisulu, *Long Walk*, Walter Sisulu interview conducted by Wolfie Kodesh in 1995.

68–69 Historical description of the Bantu Men's Social Centre from the Centre's archive held at Wits University, Johannesburg.

FIVE

72 "As one of his granddaughters said, 'I feel that men like him...'" Author interview with Ndileka Mandela, 2008.

74 Elinor Sisulu's biography of Walter and Albertina Sisulu describes the links with the family of Mandela's first wife, Evelyn Mase. Fatima Meer knew Evelyn and interviewed her for *Higher than Hope*. Evelyn gave one newspaper interview at the time of Mandela's release to reporter Fred Bridgland. It appeared in the *Sunday Telegraph*, London, on February 25, 1990. These sources may be weighed against Mandela's own account in *Long Walk.*

75 "One possible clue is a surviving file of correspondence..." Mandela's revealing exchange of letters with the Bantu Welfare Trust, regarding his loans, are kept at the Historical Papers Library of Wits University in Johannesburg.

79 "After the sudden death of Thembi in a car crash..." Mandela described his memories of an earlier loss in a letter to Mrs. Irene Buthelezi, the wife of Chief Mangosuthu Buthelezi on August 8, 1969.

82 "We were just courting at the time..." Author interview with Fatima Meer, 2008.

82 "When Ruth First wrote to invite the Youth League..." Correspondence in Karis and Carter, *From Protest to Challenge*, Volume 2.

83 "...his loss creating a 'gaping wound in one's soul for a lifetime...'" Comment on Anton Lembede's death in a letter written by Jordan Ngubane, quoted in Sisulu, *Walter and Albertina Sisulu: In Our Lifetime.*

83 "Mandela later reflected that he hardly ever went out with his wife..." Mandela interview with Ahmed Kathrada, during research for *Long Walk.*

83 "However, when he was at home he changed nappies..." Fatima Meer, *Higher than Hope.*

83–84 "Apparently she once answered the door to one of his Indian colleagues..." Letter Nelson Mandela to Amina Cachalia, April 8, 1969.

84 "Ruth Mompati...remembered Evelyn in the ANC Women's League..." Author interview with Ruth Mompati, 2008.

84 As Evelyn herself told the reporter..." *Sunday Telegraph*, London, February 25, 1990.

84 "Evelyn told Fatima Meer..." Fatima Meer, *Higher than Hope.*

85 "When he wrote to the Dean of the Law Faculty..." Mandela's original letter from December 1949 is retained at the Wits' Law Library, together with the minutes of the meeting at which his fate was decided.

87 "George Bizos had first met Mandela..." Author interview with George Bizos, 2008.

88 "Nelson had not spoken about politics when he courted me..." Evelyn Mandela quoted in the *Sunday Telegraph*, London, February 25, 1990.

92 "Paul Joseph, then a young Indian communist..." Author interview with Paul Joseph, 2008.

92 "Ahmed Kathrada became incensed by the Youth League's opposition..." Kathrada, *Memoirs;* author interview with Ahmed Kathrada, 2008.

93 "Like Paul Joseph and Kathrada, Mosie Moolla had been active..." Author interview with Mosie Moolla, 2008.

SIX

96 "Joe Matthews, the Professor's son..." Joe Matthews' oral history interview 2001, archived at SADET (South African Democracy Education Trust).

97 "In Mandela's version of events, he was asked to take the letter..." Nelson Mandela, *Long Walk to Freedom.*

98 "That evening, after the council meeting, there was a farewell dinner..." Joe Matthews' oral history interview, ibid.

100 "Mary Benson, a future Mandela biographer, recalled seeing him for the first time..." Benson, *A Far Cry.*

101 "But perhaps too, as some members of his own family have articulated,..." Makaziwe Mandela, the daughter of Nelson and Evelyn, has expressed her feelings on the theme of her father's ambition. See *Femina* magazine, May 1990.

102 "Years later, Mandela recalled the incident in a letter to Amina Cachalia..." Letter Nelson Mandela to Amina Cachalia, April 8, 1969.

110 "Mandela would visit him there during the lunch hour..." Callinicos, *Oliver Tambo: Beyond the Engeli Mountains.*

111 "When the office opened..." Author interview with Ruth Mompati, 2008.

111 "Winnie recalled that, when she visited, she would sit reading quietly..." Author interview with Winnie Madikizela-Mandela, 2009.

113 "Ruth Mompati joined the firm later in 1953..." Author interview with Ruth Mompati, 2008.

118 "Evelyn was, she would say, happy in her love for her husband..." Fatima Meer, *Higher than Hope.*

118 "Fatima Meer also remembered those weekends..." Author interview with Fatima Meer, 2008.

118 "When she questioned him about it...he said, 'No policeman asks questions like you.'" *Sunday Telegraph,* London, February 25, 1990.

SEVEN

119 "Mandela's autobiography...owes its origins to events on Robben Island twenty years earlier..." Kathrada, *Memoirs;* O'Malley, *Shades of Difference: Mac Maharaj and the Struggle for South Africa;* author interviews with Ahmed Kathrada and Mac Maharaj, 2008.

121 "I could not put my finger on it at first..." Fatima Meer, *Higher than Hope.*

124 "Meer has said she believed the neighbors had once had to intervene..." Author interview with Fatima Meer, 2008.

124 "In fact, it was Evelyn who first began divorce proceedings against Mandela..." Native Divorce Court Case no. 342, 1956, and the Supreme Court of South Africa, Witwatersrand Division Case No. 1579, 1958. Files held at the National Archives of South Africa.

129 "Winnie has said she was too shy to ask Mandela about his marital status..." Author interview with Winnie Madikizela-Mandela, 2009.

132 "At an ANC conference around 1953/54 a beautiful activist, Mrs. Malopo..." Joe Matthews' oral history interview 2001, archived at SADET (South African Democracy Education Trust).

132–33 "Amina Cachalia describes Mandela as very tight-lipped about these matters..." Author interview with Amina Cachlia, 2008.

133 "Ngoyi, according to Fatima Meer, was not among those beautiful women..." Author interview with Fatima Meer, 2008.

134 "Evelyn's granddaughter, Ndileka, noted that her grandmother never remarried..."Author interview with Ndileka Mandela, 2008.

135 "Ruth Mompati took exception to Mandela being described as old-fashioned..." Author interview with Ruth Mompati, 2008.

135 "As he rose steadily in the world, Mandela was still getting letters from the Bantu Welfare Trust..." Bantu Welfare Trust's Mandela file held at the Historical Papers Library, Wits University.

136 "Adelaide Joseph and her husband, who would ride in that car too..." Author interview with Adelaide Joseph, 2008.

137 "He must be wearing a suit from Alfred Khan..." Author interview with Ahmed Kathrada, 2008.

137 "No, nothing is going to deprive Mandela of his evaluation of himself..." Author interview with George Bizos, 2008.

137 "There is a story Winnie once related to Paul Joseph..." Author interview with Paul Joseph, 2008.

137 "Then one night in the early 1950s he was out in a car with Sisulu..." Author interview with Amina Cachalia, 2008.

138 "Some people won't hear a word against him..." Author interview with Ann-Marie Wolpe, 2008.

138 "One weekend Mandela called on Bizos for his advice..." Author interview with George Bizos, 2008; George Bizos, *Odyssey to Freedom.*

139 "Ruth Mompati remembered another occasion, closer to home, when an African bellboy..." Author interview with Ruth Mompati, 2008.

140 "A future comrade, Denis Goldberg would listen to Mandela recounting tales from the bench too..." Author interview with Denis Goldberg, 2008.

141 "Bizos remembered Tambo expressing his concerns..." Author interview with George Bizos, 2008.

EIGHT

144 "No easy walk was Nehru's phrase, not Mandela's..." Sampson, *Mandela.*

144 "Meanwhile, some eight years ahead of the formation of Umkhonto we Sizwe (MK), Mandela was already anticipating the necessity for armed conflict..." Sisulu, *Walter & Albertina Sisulu: In Our Lifetime.*

145 "A quiet, studious young academic from Fort Hare..." Pogrund, *How Can Man Die Better: The Life of Robert Sobukwe.*

147 "Professor Matthews brought the idea to the organizers of the regional ANC..." Z. K. Matthews, *Freedom for My People.*

147 "But first the raw material of the charter had to be collected..." Rusty Bernstein, *Memory Against Forgetting.*

149 "Abigail Kubeka, who sang with Makeba in the Skylarks..." Author interview with Abigail Kubeka, 2008.

149 "Makeba also sang with the jazz vocal group, the Manhattan Brothers,..." Author interview with Joe Mogotsi, 2008.

151 "Forty years later Mandela was giving a round of additional interviews..." Material held at the Nelson Mandela Foundation.

153 Sisulu remembered a meeting of senior figures..." Sisulu, *Walter & Albertina Sisulu: In Our Lifetime,* ibid.

153 "As Anthony Sampson said, that did not deter..." Sampson, *Mandela*, ibid.

156 "Perhaps because he had never been consulted, Chief Luthuli did not mind acknowledging..." Luthuli, *Let My People Go.*

157 "At some point, late in the proceedings, the records tell us that the organizers announced..." Karis, Carter, Gerhart, *From Protest to Challenge*, Volume 3.

160 "Some city friends gathered at number 8115 to mark the occasion..." Nelson Mandela, *Long Walk to Freedom.*

160 "But Mandla, the son of Makgatho..." Author interview with Mandla Mandela, 2008.

160 "According to Evelyn..." Fatima Meer, *Higher than Hope,* ibid.

161 "The idea was also expressed in simple, traditional terms..." Author interview with Sitsheketshe Mandela, 2008.

161 "During the additional interviews he conducted with Ahmed Kathrada..." Material held at the Nelson Mandela Foundation.

163 "The young woman claimed not to know she was beautiful..." Author interview with Winnie Madikizela-Mandela, 2009.

NINE

164 "According to Winnie Madikizela-Mandela, she was a country girl from Pondoland..." Author interview with Winnie Madikizela-Mandela, 2009.

166 "Esme Matshikiza, whose husband Todd..." Author interview with Esme Matshikiza, 2008.

170 "Z. K. Matthews wrote regularly to his wife, Frieda,..." Frieda Matthews, *Remembrances* (Mayibuye, 1995).

170 "Further confirmation is to be found in the 1970 letter from Robben Island..." Nelson Mandela letter to Winnie Mandela, August 1, 1970. Held at the Nelson Mandela Foundation.

171 "Fatima Meer has written how Winnie's boyfriend, Barney Sampson, took it badly..." Fatima Meer, *Higher than Hope.*

172 "Mandela sent Winnie to meet the Meers in Durban..." Author interview with Fatima Meer, 2008.

173 "Ruth Mompati has said that she did not detect any shyness in Winnie..." Author interview with Ruth Mompati, 2008.

173 "The journalist and activist Joyce Sikhakhane..." Author interview with Joyce Sikhakhane, 2008.

173 "In spite of everything that happened later, everything Winnie might have done or been involved in..." Author interview with Adelaide Joseph, 2008.

173 "Amina Cachalia suspected that it took Winnie a while to get used to Mandela's interracial world..." Author interview with Amina Cachalia, 2008.

174 "Mandela began taking her to Sunday lunch at the home of Michael (Mick) Harmel..." Author interview with Barbara Harmel, 2008.

175 "Ruth was at the wedding in Bizana..." Author interview with Ruth Mompati, 2008.

177 "'I have married trouble,'" "Mandela told his advocate friend George..." Author interview with George Bizos, 2008.

177 "Your birth was a great relief to us..." Nelson Mandela letter to his daughter Zenani, March 1, 1970. Held at the Nelson Mandela Foundation.

179 "Even before her father was freed, she was refereeing arguments..." Author interview with Zindzi Mandela, 2008.

181 "The Sisulu children knew that things changed after Evelyn and Mandela divorced..." Author interviews with Lungi Sisulu and Beryl Simelane, 2008.

183 "In 1958 Thembi was home from school..." Makghatho Mandela quoted in Fatima Meer, *Higher than Hope,* ibid.

184 "According to Ndileka, her father, Thembi..." Author interview with Ndileka Mandela, 2008.

186 "Now Mandela wrote to Evelyn, a letter composed in formal terms, in stark contrast to the letter he wrote on the same day to Winnie..." Nelson Mandela letters to Evelyn Mandela and Winnie Mandela, July 16, 1969. Held at the Nelson Mandela Foundation.

186 "Ndileka's mother, Thoko, never recovered..." Author interview with Ndileka Mandela, 2008.

187 "If Makgatho had, as he said, sided with his father in childhood, that did not last through the years..." Fatima Meer, *Higher than Hope*, ibid.

TEN

196 "You just can't tear Nelson from the people..." Winnie Mandela, *Part of My Soul Went with Him.*

197 "He was mad about her, Rica remembered..." Author interview with Rica Hodgson, 2008.

197 "There were 144 arrests on the first day, among them Mandela himself..." Fatima Meer, *Higher than Hope*; Sampson, *Mandela;* Nelson Mandela, *Long Walk to Freedom.*

198 Mosie Moolla relates that Oliver Tambo, who was also a renowned singer..." Author interview with Mosie Moolla, 2008.

198 "Joe Slovo, who was among the white accused..." Joe Slovo, *Slovo: The Unfinished Autobiography.*

201 "Like all children, the children of the white middle class communists did not want to stand out from their peers..." Author interviews with Toni Strasburg and Barbara Harmel, 2008.

202 "AnnMarie Wolpe says that, even though 'crossing the color line' was difficult..." Author interview with AnnMarie Wolpe, 2008.

203 "Ilse Fischer, the daughter of Bram and Molly Fischer, could not remember..." Author interview with Ilse Fisher, 2008.

203 "Paul Joseph, an Indian communist who was as alert as anyone to the casual racism of the times..." Author interview with Paul Joseph, 2008.

204 "Latent resentments sometimes spilled over during drink-fueled moments..." Author interview with Mac Maharaj, 2008.

205 "Esme said that Mandela was not then the world celebrity he later became..." Author interview with Esme Matshikiza, 2008.

206 "The Africanists had chosen the Transvaal ANC..." Nelson Mandela's *Long Walk to Freedom* skirts around the tensions with the Africanists. The story emerges with more clarity from Fatima Meer, *Higher than Hope;* Pogrund, *How Can Man Die Better: The Life of Robert Sobukwe;* Karis, Carter, and Gerhart, *From Protest to Challenge*, Volume 3.

211 "The reporting of Sharpeville came from *Drum* journalist Humphrey Tyler..." *Contact*, April 2, 1960 cited in Pogrund, *How Can Man Die Better: The Life of Robert Sobukwe.*

211 Slovo recalled that he and Mandela waited alone together for the others to arrive..." Joe Slovo, *Slovo: The Unfinished Autobiography.*

212 "He had known what was coming from a tip-off the previous day..." Author interview with Ahmed Kathrada, 2008.

212 "Most of the other key figures were among the 2,000 arrested, everyone, that is, except Wilton Mkwayi..." Author interview with Ahmed Kathrada, 2008.

216 "Mandela wrote about that night in a letter to Amina Cachalia..." Nelson Mandela letter to Amina Cachalia, April 8, 1969, held at the Nelson Mandela Foundation

216 "Amina had retained a vivid picture of the end of the trial..." Author interview with Amina Cachalia, 2008.

ELEVEN

217 "It has been written elsewhere that Mandela made some financial provision..." Mary Benson, *Nelson Mandela.*

217 "Winnie says there was no such provision..." Author interview with Winnie Madikizela-Mandela, 2009.

217 A verbatim account of Harold Macmillan's Wind of Change speech appeared in *The Times*, London, February 4, 1960.

219 Among those at the committee meeting was Mandela's closest colleague, Walter Sisulu, who said later..." Anthony Sampson, *Mandela.*

219 "'This would be a hazardous life...'" Nelson Mandela, *Long Walk to Freedom.*

220 "As *Drum* magazine reported..." cited in Fatima Meer, *Higher than Hope.*

223 "Fatima Meer remembered Mandela arriving at her home..." Author interview with Fatima Meer, 2008.

225 "Kathrada got lost on the way..." Author interview with Ahmed Kathrada, 2008.

225 "Amina Cachalia remembered Mandela being with her husband..." Author interview with Amina Cachalia, 2008.

226 "Bob Hepple, the young white advocate..." Author interview with Bob Hepple, 2008.

226 "The journalist Mary Benson..." Mary Benson, *A Far Cry.*

TWELVE

228 "Like most of the young white Jewish people..." Oral history interviews with Wolfie Kodesh conducted by John Pampallis, 1989. Held at the Mayibuye archive, University of the Western Cape.

231 "As he told Richard Stengel..." Nelson Mandela interview with Richard Stengel. Held at the Nelson Mandela Foundation.

232 "As Mandela's reading tastes broadened..." Author interview with Mac Maharaj, 2008.

233 "They were, in fact, Adelaide and Paul Joseph..." Author interviews with Adelaide and Paul Joseph, 2008.

234 "One driver was Rica Hodgson..." Author interview with Rica Hodgson.

235 "Sometimes Winnie would bring their daughters..." Nelson Mandela letter to Zeni Mandela, March 1, 1970.

237 "Sometimes Wolfie tried to come up with diversions for Mandela..." Author interview with Amy Thornton, 2008.

242 "Mary Benson describes meeting Mandela..." Mary Benson, *A Far Cry*.

THIRTEEN

The story of the ANC's decision to move to armed struggle is one of those episodes in history that continues to elude the most meticulous historian. At the time, secrecy was so paramount that almost no one involved can have known the full picture. The confusion became part of the story itself. There were no minutes of meetings to fall back on and most of the participants had their own perspectives and agendas and their own reasons for not disclosing everything they knew. Even now, there are those who say that the ANC President, Chief Albert Luthuli—who ignores these events completely in his memoir—was bitterly opposed to armed struggle. I do not think that was the case but the full facts will surely never be known. I have done my best to piece together a reliable account, from the following sources: Nelson Mandela, *Long Walk to Freedom;* Anthony Sampson, *Mandela;* Fatima Meer, *Higher than Hope;* Elinor Sisulu, *Walter and Albertina: In Our Lifetime;* Ismail Meer, *A Fortunate Man;* Joe Slovo, *Slovo: The Unfinished Autobiography;* interviews with Wolfie Kodesh conducted by John Pampallis, 1989, held at the Mayibuye Archive, University of the Western Cape; Joe Matthews' oral history interview 2001, archived at SADET (South African Democracy Education Trust; author interviews with Mac Maharaj, Ahmed Kathrada, Sonny Singh, Paul Joseph, Fatima Meer, Hazel Goldreich, Bob Hepple, Laloo Chiba, Mosie Moolla, Rica Hodgson, Spencer Hodgson and Winnie Mandela.

FOURTEEN

259 "Though Wolfie Kodesh had lived in the slums of Cape Town..." Oral history interviews with Wolfie Kodesh conducted by John Pampallis, 1989. Held at the Mayibuye Archive, University of the Western Cape.

261 "According to Mandela in his memoir..." Nelson Mandela, *Long Walk to Freedom.*

261 "...but Wolfie says that it was in fact..." Oral history interviews with Wolfie Kodesh, ibid. Also accounts given in ANC pamphlets, held in the personal papers of Wolfie Kodesh, held at Mayibuye Archive, University of the Western Cape.

263 "The party was keen to find an isolated safe house..." Author interview with Ahmed Kathrada, 2008.

264 "Fyffe had been at the farm since 1954..." D. R. Fyffe's letter is among the papers of Percy Yutar, prosecutor at the Rivonia Trial. When I saw them, they were held at Oppenheimer's private Brenthurst Library but they have since been handed over to The National Archives of South Africa.

264 "Valeloo Percival Jelliman, then in his sixties..." Police statement of Jelliman among the papers of Percy Yutar, ibid.

265 "Nearly fifty years later, Ahmed Kathrada could still become agitated..." Author interview with Ahmed Kathrada, 2008.

266 "'Arthur was a womanizer and Hazel knew and tolerated it...'" Author interview with Denis Goldberg, 2008.

268 "Ironically, perhaps, when Hazel first met Arthur in the early 1950s..." Author interview with Hazel Goldreich, 2008.

268 "'Arthur has gone over and joined the Israeli army...'" Author interview with Mac Maharaj, 2008.

268 "'...this big, flashy, gorgeous guy...'" Author interview with Hazel Rochman, 2009.

268 "AnnMarie Wolpe said he was like Mandela..." Author interview with AnnMarie Wolpe, 2008.

269 "In 1957, Joe Slovo had visited Goldreich...." Arthur Goldreich, oral history interview, 2004. Held at Liliesleaf Farm.

269 "In his book *Rivonia's Children*..." Glenn Frankel, *Rivonia's Children.*

269 "'I was greatly relieved, I must say, when it all eventually emerged...'" Arthur Goldreich, oral history interview, ibid.

269 "Hazel told the police she never knew..." Hazel Goldreich's police statement among the papers of Percy Yutar, ibid.

270 "The Goldreichs' domestic, Enith Kgopane..." Enith Kgopane's police statement among the papers of Percy Yutar, ibid.

270 "Mandela not only cooked for Jelliman..." Nelson Mandela, *Long Walk to Freedom*

270 "A schoolboy, George Mellis, who lived nearby..." George Mellis' police statement is among the papers of Percy Yutar, ibid.

272 "Among them were what appeared to be the beginnings of a book..." Nelson Mandela's papers found at Liliesleaf are among the papers of Percy Yutar, ibid.

272 "Is Liliesleaf clean? Is it clean? Mandela had..." Author interviews, Ahmed Kathrada and Bob Hepple, 2008.

273 "Mandela tried to explain away the document during his famous—famously long speech—at the Rivonia Trial..." An original typescript of this speech is held at the Historical Papers Library, Wits University.

274 "'It was exactly like a cell...'" Arthur Goldreich, oral history interview, ibid.

275 "All the Goldreichs started horse-riding..." Author interview with Hazel Goldreich, 2008.

275 "Len Lazarus, who lived nearby..." Author interview with Len Lazarus, 2008.

279 "'We knew Tata was in hiding...'" Fatima Meer, *Higher than Hope.*

281 "Arthur Goldreich gives a different account..." Arthur Goldreich, oral history interview, ibid.

FIFTEEN

282 "Mandela remembers sitting in the kitchen at Liliesleaf..." Nelson Mandela, *Long Walk to Freedom.*

283 "Luthuli had in fact asked Rusty Bernstein to draft the speech..." Rusty Bernstein, *Memory Against Forgetting.*

283 "Karis, Carter and Gerhart quote an unnamed African academic..." Karis, Carter, Gail Gerhart, *From Protest to Challenge,* Volume 3.

283 "Many were proud of Luthuli's prize..." Author interview with Sonny Singh, 2008.

284 "Wolfie Kodesh was in the thick of things, of course, . . ." Oral history interviews with Wolfie Kodesh conducted by John Pampallis, 1989. Held at the Mayibuye Archive, University of the Western Cape.

285 "Chiba, who had become politically active in the late 1950s . . ." Author interview with Laloo Chiba, 2008.

285 "Other than Joseph's instruction from Wolfie . . ." Author interview with Paul Joseph, 2008.

286 "Jack Hodgson had been in a car once with his son Spencer . . ." Author interview with Spencer Hodgson.

287 "Jack Hodgson had been present when Ahmed Kathrada's cell . . ." Author interview with Ahmed Kathrada, 2008.

288 "AnnMarie Wolpe remembered standing on the balcony of an apartment . . ." Author interview with AnnMarie Wolpe, 2008.

288 "Joe Slovo, the MK chief of staff, Mandela's number two . . ." Joe Slovo, *Slovo: The Unfinished Autobiography.*

289 "Bernstein believed that the leafleting campaign . . ." Rusty Bernstein, *Memory Against Forgetting.*

290 "Mandela told Ahmed Kathrada, in 1990, . . ." Ahmed Kathrada interview with Nelson Mandela. Held at the Nelson Mandela Foundation.

290 "The young woman who had typed for him at Wolfie's flat . . ." Author interview with Amy Thornton, 2008.

291 "Sisulu was forced to defend the independence of MK . . ." Sisulu, *Walter and Albertina: In Our Lifetime.*

291 "Kodesh came to Chiba and told him that they were breaking up their cell unit . . ." Author interview with Laloo Chiba, 2008.

291 "Paul Joseph recalls that Reggie Vandayar was suspended . . ." Author interview with Paul Joseph, 2008.

SIXTEEN

294 "Not everyone appreciated Frene Ginwala's role . . ." Author interview with Frene Ginwala, 2008.

297 "On the eve of his departure, Mandela had been to see Chief Luthuli . . ." Nelson Mandela's original 1962 diary held at the Nelson Mandela Foundation.

297 "In truth, Luthuli complained to Mandela that he had not been consulted . . ." Nelson Mandela, *Long Walk to Freedom.*

298–310 The bare detail of Mandela's African tour is contained in his 1962 diary. There are accounts in Meer's *Higher than Hope* and in *Long Walk to Freedom.* I have been able to extract some additional detail from the original interviews, now held at the Nelson Mandela Foundation, which Mandela gave to his ghost-writer, Richard Stengel. Mac Maharaj was also able to provide some fresh detail and perspective. Esme Matshikiza gave me a vivid account of the "visionary" who appeared late one night in her London flat.

SEVENTEEN

311 "Like many others, Williams was leading a double life . . ." Porter and Weeks, eds., *Between the Acts: Lives of Homosexual Men 1885–1967.*

312 "Mandela and Winnie had been to dinner at Williams' flat..." John Calderwood interview for the drama documentary *The Man Who Drove with Mandela*, archived at GALA, Gay And Lesbian Archive, Wits University.

313 "He had written a report on his trip and the impact of the PAC..." The report is among the papers of Percy Yutar, prosecutor at the Rivonia Trial, previously held at Oppenheimer's private Brenthurst Library but now at The National Archives of South Africa

314 "Kathrada recalled how critical Mandela had been of the PAC..." Author interview with Ahmed Kathrada, 2008.

314 "According to Anthony Sampson and evidence presented from the Rivonia Trial..." Sampson, Anthony, *Mandela*.

315 "Wolfie Kodesh likely was not part of the driving committee..." Interviews with Wolfie Kodesh conducted by John Pampallis, 1989. Held at the Mayibuye Archive, University of the Western Cape.

315 "Winnie told a reporter on June 24..." *Sunday Times*, South Africa, June 24, 1962, cited in Fatima Meer, *Higher than Hope*.

316 "Mandela had briefed Winnie on the politics of his trip..." Author interview with Winnie Madikizela-Mandela, 2008.

317 "He later described the meeting in a letter to Zindzi and Zenani..." Nelson Mandela letter to Zindzi and Zenani Mandela, June 23, 1969, held at the Nelson Mandela Foundation.

317 "Mandela told Fatima Meer that Winnie's eyes brimmed with tears..." Fatima Meer, *Higher than Hope*.

318 "The Goldreichs were still living at Liliesleaf in July 1962..." Author interview with Hazel Goldreich, 2008

319 "She said he was very aware that he was a sacrificial lamb..." Author interview with Fatima Meer, 2008.

320 "Alongside Mtolo at the meeting were Billy Nair..." Author interview with Sonny Singh, 2008.

321 "Fatima Meer recalled how they hugged..." Author interview with Fatima Meer, 2008.

EIGHTEEN

327 "By his own admission, the culprit was Arthur Goldreich..." Arthur Goldreich oral history interview, 2004. Held at Liliesleaf Farm.

328 "The blame is probably not entirely theirs,..." Karis, Carter, and Gerhart, *From Protest to Challenge*, Volume 3.

329 "Ruth could be talking about the frailty of any number of her colleagues,..." Author interview with Bob Hepple, 2008.

331 "Along came Denis Goldberg..." Author interview with Denis Goldberg, 2008.

331 "Slovo attended endless meetings at Liliesleaf..." Joe Slovo, *Slovo: The Unfinished Autobiography*.

332 "Kathrada had nearly left the country,..." Author interview with Ahmed Kathrada, 2008.

333 "One day, Hepple went out to Rivonia..." Author interview with Bob Hepple, 2008.

333 "He was a hothead,..." Author interview with Ahmed Kathrada, 2008.

334 "According to Mac Maharaj, the armed struggle was only ever a means to an end for Mandela, . . ." Author interview with Mac Maharaj, 2008.

334 "Being junior and carrying little weight himself, . . ." Author interview with Bob Hepple, 2008; Bob Hepple, "Rivonia: The Story of Accused No. 11," *Social Dynamics*, Volume 30, Issue 1, Summer 2004, pages 193–217.

335 "They did not dare broadcast from Liliesleaf . . ." Author interview with Denis Goldberg, 2008.

337 "He would always say he had his last drink on July 10, 1963 . . ." Author interview with Ahmed Kathrada, 2008.

337–43 Description of the Rivonia arrests and aftermath from Author interviews with Ahmed Kathrada, Bob Hepple, Denis Goldberg and Hazel Goldreich; Arthur Goldreich, oral history interview, 2004, held at Liliesleaf Farm; Bernstein, *Memory Against Forgetting;* Sisulu, *Walter and Albertina: In Our Lifetime;* Hepple, "Rivonia: The Story of Accused No. 11," ibid.

343–45 Description of the trial preparations from Author interviews with Denis Goldberg, Bob Hepple, Joel Joffe and George Bizos; Joffe, *The State vs Nelson Mandela* (Oneworld, 2007); Clingman, *Bram Fischer* (David Philip, 1998); Bizos, *Odyssey to Freedom;* Bob Hepple, "Rivonia: The Story of Accused No. 11," ibid.

NINETEEN

Description of the trial from Author interviews with Ahmed Kathrada, Denis Goldberg, Bob Hepple, Joel Joffe and George Bizos; Joffe, *The State vs Nelson Mandela* (Oneworld, 2007); Clingman, *Bram Fischer* (David Philip, 1998); Bizos, *Odyssey to Freedom;* Bob Hepple, "Rivonia: The Story of Accused No. 11," ibid; Bernstein, *Memory Against Forgetting;* Sampson, *Mandela;* Meer, *Higher than Hope;* Nelson Mandela, *Long Walk to Freedom;* Joel Joffe papers at the Historical Papers Library, Wits University: Benson, *A Far Cry;* Benson, *Nelson Mandela;* Nelson Mandela interviews with Richard Stengel and Ahmed Kathrada, held at the Nelson Mandela Foundation.

Selected Bibliography

Bailey, Jim, and Adam Seftel. *Shebeens Take a Bow!!* (Baileys African History Archives, 1994)

Benson, Mary. *A Far Cry* (Ravan Press, 1996)

———. *Nelson Mandela: The Man and the Movement* (W. W. Norton, 1994)

Bernstein, Hilda. *The Rift* (Random House, 1994)

———. *The World That Was Ours* (SAWriters, 1989)

Bernstein, Rusty. *Memory Against Forgetting* (Penguin, 1999)

Bizos, George. *Odyssey to Freedom* (Random House, 2007)

Blaxall, Arthur. *Suspended Sentence* (Hodder & Stoughton, 1965)

Bunting, Brian. *Moses Kotane, South African Revolutionary* (Inkululeko, 1975)

Callinicos, Luli. *Oliver Tambo: Beyond the Engeli Mountains* (David Philip, 2004)

Clingman, Stephen. *Bram Fischer* (David Philip, 1998)

Crwys-Williams, Jennifer, ed. *South African Despatches* (Ashanti, 1989)

De Villiers, H. H. W. *Rivonia: Operation Mayibuye* (Afrikaanse Pers-Boekhandel, 1964)

Finnegan, William. *Dateline Soweto* (Harper & Row, 1998)

First, Ruth, ed. *No Easy Walk to Freedom* (Heinemann, 1965)

———. *117 Days* (Penguin, 1980)

Frankel, Glenn. *Rivonia's Children* (Weidenfeld & Nicolson, 1999)

Gilbey, Emma. *The Lady* (Vintage, 1994)

Glasser, Mona. *King Kong* (Norman Howell, 1960)

Guiloineau, Jean. *Nelson Mandela: The Early Life of Rolihlahla Madiba* (North Atlantic Books, 2002)

Harrison, Nancy. *Winnie Mandela: Mother of a Nation* (Victor Gollancz, 1985)

Joffe, Joel. *The State vs Nelson Mandela* (Oneworld, 2007)

Johns, Sheridan, and Hunt Davis, eds. *Mandela, Tambo and the African National Congress* (Oxford University Press, 1991)

Joseph, Helen. *Side by Side* (Zed Books, 1986)

Karis, Thomas, and Gwendoline Carter. *From Protest to Challenge,* Volume 2 (Hoover, 1973)

Karis, Thomas, Gwendoline Carter, and Gail Gerhart. *From Protest to Challenge,* Volume 3 (Hoover, 1977)

Karis, Thomas, Gwendoline Carter, and Sheridan Johns. *From Protest to Challenge,* Volume 1 (Hoover, 1972)

Kathrada, Ahmed. *Letters from Robben Island* (Zebra Press, 2000)

———. *Memoirs* (Zebra Press, 2004)

———. *A Simple Freedom* (Wild Dog Press, 2008)

Kumalo, Alf, and Es'kia Mphahlele. *Mandela: Echoes of an Era* (Penguin, 1990)

Kuzwayo, Ellen. *Call Me Woman* (The Women's Press, 1985)

Luthuli, Albert. *Let My People Go* (Tafelberg & Mafube, 2006)

Maharaj, Mac, and Ahmed Kathrada. *Mandela* (Andrews McMeel, 2006)

Mandela, Nelson. *Long Walk to Freedom* (Little, Brown, 1994)

Mandela, Winnie. *Part of My Soul Went with Him* (W. W. Norton, 1985)

Matshikiza, John, and Todd Matshikiza. *With the Lid Off* (M&G Books, 2000)

Matthews, Freida. *Remembrances* (Mayibuye Books, 1995)

Matthews, Z. K. *Freedom for My People* (Collings & Philip, 1981)

Meer, Fatima. *Higher than Hope* (Skotaville, 1988; Penguin, 1990)

Meer, Ismail. *A Fortunate Man* (Zebra Press, 2002)

Meredith, Martin. *Nelson Mandela* (Penguin, 1997)

Modisane, Bloke. *Blame Me on History* (Thames & Hudson, 1963)

Mtolo, Bruno. *The Road to the Left* (Drakensberg, 1966)

Nicol, Mike. *A Good-Looking Corpse* (Secker & Warburg, 1991)

O'Malley, Padraig. *Shades of Difference: Mac Maharaj and the Struggle for South Africa* (Penguin, 2008)

Pogrund, Benjamin. *How Can Man Die Better: The Life of Robert Sobukwe* (Peter Halban, 1990)

Porter, Kevin, and Jeffrey Weeks, eds. *Between the Acts* (Routledge, 1991)

Rose, Martial. *Forever Juliet* (Larks Press, 2003)

SADET (South African Democracy Education Trust). *The Road to Democracy, Volume 1, 1950–1970* (SADET/Mutloatse, 2008).

Sampson, Anthony. *Mandela* (HarperCollins, 1999)

———. *The Treason Cage* (Heinemann, 1958)

Schadeberg, Jurgen. *The Fifties People* (Bailey's African Photo Archives, 1987)

Shope, Gertrude. *Malibongwe, Volume 1* (Shope, 2002)

———. *Malibongwe, Volume 2* (Shope, 2006)

Shubin, Vladimir. *ANC: A View from Moscow* (Jacana Media, 2008)

Sisulu, Elinor. *Walter and Albertina Sisulu: In Our Lifetime* (David Philip, 2002)

Slovo, Gillian. *Every Secret Thing* (Little, Brown, 1997)

Slovo, Joe. *Slovo: The Unfinished Autobiography* (Ravan Press, 1995)

Stapleton, Chris, and Chris May. *African All Stars* (Paladin, 1989)

Winter, Gordon. *Inside Boss: South Africa's Secret Police* (Penguin, 1981)

Wolpe, AnnMarie. *The Long Way Home* (David Philip, 1994)

Zug, James. *The Guardian* (Unisa, 2007)

MUSEUMS AND ARCHIVES

The National Archives of South Africa

Mayibuye Archive, University of the Western Cape

Historical Papers Library and GALA (Gay And Lesbian Archive), Wits University

The Nelson Mandela Foundation

Liliesleaf Farm

The Apartheid Museum

Sophiatown Community Museum

Brenthurst Library

The National Archives, London

The Standard Bank Archives

AUTHOR INTERVIEWS

George Bizos, Nat Bregman, Donald Bruce, Amina Cachalia, Luli Callinicos, Donald Card, Laloo Chiba, Frene Ginwalla, Denis Goldberg, Hazel Goldreich, Derek Gowlett, Barbara Harmel, Bob Hepple, Rica Hodgson, Spencer Hodgson, Adelaide Joseph, Paul Joseph, Ahmed Kathrada, Alf Khumalo, Abigail Kubeka, Len Lazarus, Winnie Madikizela-Mandela, Peter Magubane, Mac Maharaj, Mandla Mandela, Ndileka Mandela, Sitsheketshe Mandela, Zindzi Mandela, Esme Matshikiza, Fatima Meer, Joe Mogotsi, Ruth Mompati, Mosie Moolla, Nozolile Mtirara, Shanti Naidoo and family, Hymie and Hazel Rochman, Gertrude Shope, Joyce Sikhakhane, Beryl Simelane, Sonny Singh, Lungi Sisulu, Toni Strasburg (Bernstein), Amy Thornton (Reitstein), Ilse Wilson (Fischer), AnnMarie Wolpe, Nic Wolpe, Gladys Xhoma.

Index

Note: The abbreviation NM in subheadings refers to Nelson Mandela.

About the Author

David James Smith has been a journalist all his working life. He now writes for the *Sunday Times Magazine* and lives in Lewes, East Sussex, with his partner and their four children. He is the author of *The Sleep of Reason: The James Bulger Case, All About Jill, Supper with the Crippens,* and *One Morning in Sarajevo: 28 June 1914.*